Constitutional Law in Spain

Constitutional Law in Spain

Third Edition

Agustín Ruiz Robledo

This book was originally published as a monograph in the International Encyclopaedia of Laws/Constitutional Law.

Founding Editor: Roger Blanpain
General Editor: Frank Hendrickx
Volume Editors: André Alen & David Haljan

Wolters Kluwer

Published by:
Kluwer Law International B.V.
PO Box 316
2400 AH Alphen aan den Rijn
The Netherlands
E-mail: lrs-sales@wolterskluwer.com
Website: www.wolterskluwer.com/en/solutions/kluwerlawinternational

Sold and distributed by:
Wolters Kluwer Legal & Regulatory U.S.
920 Links Avenue
Landisville, PA 17538
United States of America
E-mail: customer.service@wolterskluwer.com

ISBN 978-94-035-3366-7

e-Book: ISBN 978-94-035-3686-6
web-PDF: ISBN 978-94-035-3696-5

The Author

Agustín Ruiz Robledo is a professor of constitutional law at the University of Granada, where he obtained his doctorate for his thesis on the Autonomous Community of Andalusia, which received the Extraordinary Prize for Doctoral Theses in the Law Faculty. He has combined his teaching work with other legal activities; he was a supplementary magistrate in the Provincial High Court of Granada (1988–1991), a consultant to UNO (Chile, December 1989), and has been director of the Analysis Advisory Council of the Presidency of the Andalusian Parliament (1996–2004). He has also taken courses in Business Studies and has a Diploma in Business Planning from the Polytechnic University of Madrid. He has widened his studies and research in several centres outside Spain (the Universities of Montreal, London, Florence and Bayreuth, amongst others). He was Visiting Academic Professor at University College Dublin in 2011–2012 and 2018. In 2022, he was a Visiting Professor at Jindal Global Law School in India. He has published more than 200 works on his speciality in Spain, Chile, Colombia, Italy, Ireland, Germany, the Netherlands and the United Kingdom. Amongst the most important of his books are *El Estado autonómico, El ordenamiento jurídico andaluz, El derecho fundamental a la legalidad punitiva, Constitutional Law of Spain, Subnational Constitutional Law in Spain* and *La mirada de Argos: Pequeño tratado constitucional de política española*. He has participated in many national and international conferences, speaking on his special topics, especially in the Constituent Assemblies of Bolivia and Nepal. In addition, he is a regular contributor to the radio and the newspaper *El País*, the most widely read and influential newspaper in Spain.

The Author

Table of Contents

List of Abbreviations

Table of International Instruments

ECFR	European Charter on Fundamental Rights of 7 December 2000, Adopted at Strasbourg on 12 December 2007
ECHR	European Convention on Human Rights (Treaty of Rome, 1950, Ratified by Spain on 26 September 1979)
TEU	Treaty on European Union (Version Consolidated by the Treaty of Lisbon, Signed on 13 December 2007)
ICCPR	International Covenant on Civil and Political Rights 1966
ICESCR	International Covenant on Economic, Social and Cultural Rights 1966
TFEU	Treaty on the Functioning of the European Union (Version Consolidated by the Treaty of Lisbon, signed on 13 December 2007)
UDHR	Universal Declaration of Human Rights 1948
VCLT	Vienna Convention on Law of Treaties 1969

Table of Spanish Statutes

CC	Código Civil de 24 julio 1889 – Civil Code
EAA	Ley Orgánica 2/2007, de 19 de marzo, de reforma del Estatuto de Autonomía para Andalucía – Autonomy Statute, Andalucía
EAC	Ley Orgánica 6/2006, de 19 de julio, de reforma del Estatuto de Autonomía de Cataluña – Autonomy Statute, Catalonia
EAG	Ley Orgánica 1/1981, de 6 de abril, de Estatuto de Autonomía para Galicia – Autonomy Statute, Galicia
EAPV	Ley Orgánica 1/1981, de 6 de abril, de Estatuto de Autonomía para el País Vasco – Autonomy Statute, Basque Country
LECrim	Ley de Enjuiciamiento Criminal, de 14 de septiembre de 1882 – Criminal Procedure Code
LG	Ley 50/1997, de 27 de noviembre, del Gobierno – Law on Government

List of Abbreviations

LJCA	Ley 29/1998, de 13 de julio, reguladora de la Jurisdicción Contencioso-Administrativa – Law Regulating Contentious-Administrative Jurisdiction
LOCE	Ley Orgánica 3/1980, de 22 de abril del Consejo de Estado – Organic Law on Council of State
LODA	Ley Orgánica 1/2002, de 22 de marzo, reguladora del Derecho de Asociación – Organic Law Regulator of the Right of Associations
LODP	Ley Orgánica 4/2001, de 12 de noviembre, reguladora del Derecho de Petición – Organic Law Regulator of the Right of Petition
LOEAES	Ley Orgánica 4/1981, de 16 de junio, de los estados de alarma, excepción y sitio – Organic Law on States of Alarm, Exception and Siege
LOFCA	Ley Orgánica 8/1980 de 22 de septiembre, de financiación de las Comunidades Autónomas – Organic Law on Financing Autonomous Communities
LOPD	Ley Orgánica 3/2018, de 5 de diciembre, de Protección de Datos Personales y Garantía de los Derechos Digitales – Organic Law on Protection of Personal Data and Guarantee of Digital Rights
LOPJ	Ley Orgánica 6/1985, de 1 de julio, del Poder Judicial – Organic Law on Judicial Power
LOPSC	Ley Orgánica 4/2015, de 30 de marzo, de Protección de la Seguridad Ciudadana – Organic Law Regarding Protection of Citizen Security
LOREG	Ley Orgánica 5/1985, de 19 junio, del Régimen Electoral General – Organic Law on General Electoral Regime
LORMR	Ley Orgánica 2/1980, de 18 de enero, de regulación de las distintas modalidades de referéndum – Organic Law on Regulating Different Forms of Referéndum
LOTC	Ley Orgánica 2/1979, de 3 de octubre, del Tribunal Constitucional – Organic Law on the Constitutional Court
LPA	Ley 12/1983, de 14 de octubre, del Proceso autonómico – Law on Autonomous Process
LPCAP	Ley 39/2015, de 1 de octubre, del Procedimiento Administrativo Común de las Administraciones Públicas – Law on Common Administrative Procedure of Public Administrations
LRBRL	Ley 7/1985, de 2 de abril, reguladora de las Bases del Régimen Local – Law on Regulation of Bases of Local Regime
LRJSP	Ley 40/2015, de 1 de octubre de Régimen Jurídico del Sector Público – Law on Legal Regime of Public Sector

LTAI	Ley 25/2014, de 27 de noviembre, de tratados y otros Acuerdos Internacionales – Law on Treaties and other International Agreements
LTBG	Ley 19/2013, de 9 de diciembre, de transparencia, acceso a la información pública y buen Gobierno – Law on Transparency, Access to Public Information and Good Governance
RCD	Reglamento del Congreso de los Diputados, de 10 de febrero de 1982 – Parliamentary Standing Orders for Congress, 10 February 1982
RDL	Real Decreto-ley – Royal Decree-Law
RS	Reglamento del Senado de 3 de mayo de 1994 – Parliamentary Standing Orders for Senate, 3 May 1994
SC	Spanish Constitution of 27 December 1978

General Abbreviations

CDS	Centro Democrático y Social
CiU	Convergencia i Unión
CJEU	Court of Justice of the European Union
ECtHR	European Court of Human Rights
EU	European Union
FJ	Fundamento Juridico (Legal Ground)
GCJP	General Council of Judicial Power
JCJEU	Judgment of the Court of Justice of European Union
JECtHR	Judgment of the European Court of Human Rights
PSOE	Partido Socialista Obrero Español
PNV	Partido Nacionalista Vasco
PP	Partido Popular
STC	Sentencia del Tribunal Constitucional – Judgment of Constitutional Court
STS	Sentencia del Tribunal Supremo – Judgment of the Supreme Court
UCD	Unión de Centro Democrático

Note on Case Law

Judgments of the Spanish Constitutional Court are available on its website: www.tribunalconstitucional.es.
Judgments of the Spanish Supreme Court may be found at the judicial power's website: www.poderjudicial.es.

List of Abbreviations

Acknowledgements

I must thank Professor André Alen for his trust in commissioning me to write this book and Wouter Pas, a member of the Institute for Constitutional Law of the Katholieke Universiteit Leuven and a Council Magistrate in the Legislative Division of the Belgian Council of State, for his generosity in putting my name forward for this task. I would also like to express my gratitude to the Kluwer Editorial and Mr David Haljan for their stoic patience in putting up with my continuous delays in finishing a work that, at times, seemed overwhelming. That I have finally succeeded in finishing it, it has been thanks to the support of a great group of people, beginning with Ms Bridgit McQue, who has turned my text into elegant, legal English; to professor Ramón Orza Linares and to Cristobal del Moral Peralta, two good friends who revised the original and drew up the index; to Professor Thomas Würtenberger, who gave me academic shelter in his admirable Institut für Offentliches Recht of the University of Freiburg im Breisgau for two summers; and to Inmaculada Ramos Tapia, who has always been willing to shoulder the greater part of the logistics of our family. A heartfelt thanks to everyone.

Granada, November 2011

Acknowledgements

General Introduction

§1. An Outline of Spanish Constitutional History

1. In the Spanish collective imagination, the conquest of Granada in 1492 by the Catholic monarchs marked the end of the Middle Ages and the achievement of the unity of Spain. However, this unity was produced only through the person of the monarch because the ancient kingdoms and medieval territories (Castile, the three Basque provinces, the four kingdoms of the Crown of Aragon and Navarre, incorporated in 1512) maintained their own institutions, with no other common link than that of the Head of State. Under the House of Austria, this 'personal union' was slowly developing towards a closer political union until after the War of the Spanish Succession (1701–1715) when Felipe V, the first Bourbon king, established a much more centralist regime by the suppression of the political and administrative institutions of the four Aragonese kingdoms (Aragon, Catalonia, Valencia and the Balearics). This decision was taken, in part, due to the centralist mentality of the new king (and of not few Spaniards) and, in part, as a reprisal against the support given by the Aragonese territories to the other aspirant to the Spanish throne, Archduke Carlos. This wave of uniformity did not affect the Navarre and Basque institutions that had supported the triumphant French pretender.

2. The War of Independence (1808–1814), against the invasion by Napoleon's army, strengthened national consciousness and brought about the first attempt to put an end to the absolute monarchy. Throughout the country, 'provincial councils', who grouped together in a 'Central Council', rose up against the king imposed by the French, José I – the Emperor's brother. In 1810, this Council summoned a parliament to confront the serious political situation; this was held in Cadiz since Madrid was already under the power of the French, as was the majority of the Peninsula territory. In these conditions, the electoral process was no model of democratic participation; in spite of that, on the very day of its formation, 24 September 1810, parliament proclaimed three revolutionary principles: national sovereignty; the separation of powers; and the annulment of the rights granted to Napoleon by Ferdinand VII. The latter was based not only on the concessions being 'unjust and illegal acts but principally because of the lack of the nation's consent'.

3. Based on these principles, and after long and passionate debates, parliament drew up a liberal Constitution, which has passed into the collective memory as the 'Pepa', having been finally approved on 19 March 1812, the day of St. Joseph, which is popularly known in Spain as 'Pepe'.

The Cadiz Constitution was a liberal creation in a mainly conservative Spain. Aware of this, its authors grounded its legitimacy on the appeal to certain, supposedly liberal, traditions of the Middle Ages, reflected in the 'ancient fundamental laws of this monarchy' crushed by absolutism. They also tried to gain its acceptance by the conservatives and the Catholic Church by avoiding any express declaration of rights (although scattering all civil rights, except freedom of worship, throughout the text) and establishing the Catholic religion as the 'only true faith'.

The progressives did not succeed in integrating the absolutists into the constitutional family, but the Constitution itself did indeed become an object of veneration by European liberalism until the 1848 revolutions. Without doubt, this was because behind its 384 articles lay a great moral inspiration, such as a complete reform plan for the Spanish State and society: national sovereignty, suppression of the nobles' privileges, equality for all Spaniards 'of both hemispheres', a guarantee of rights, separation of powers, reform of the administration and the courts, unification of the codes, encouragement of education, etc.

From what we could call a technical point of view, the Cadiz Constitution was characterized by its length (the longest fundamental law of our history, due to the detail with which it regulated the electoral system), its inflexibility against its reform, its lack of express dogma, and an organic section ruled by the strict separation of powers. That said, it must be added that the separation of powers offered various formulas for the collaboration and resolution of conflicts between the legislative and the executive, such as the legislative initiative of the king, his speech at the opening of parliament, and his capacity to delay the coming into force of the laws.

4. There was no opportunity to see if these collaborative techniques were sufficient or not for the good functioning of the organs of State, for when Fernando VII, 'the desired', returned from his exile in France, he dissolved parliament and declared 'that Constitution and such rights are null and void, now or at any time, as if such acts had never been passed, and they are eliminated for all time'. In spite of this emphatic phraseology, Ferdinand VII took the opportunity to renovate absolutism, and he did not re-establish certain institutions of the *Ancien Régime,* such as torture, the jurisdictional rights of the nobility, and commercial monopolies.

5. Lieutenant colonel Rafael del Riego, in command of the troops about to embark to fight against the American independents, pronounced himself in 1820 in favour of the re-establishment of the Cadiz Constitution; Fernando VII abided by it until a French army – 'the hundred thousand sons of St. Louis' – restored absolute power to him in 1823, and he ruled with an iron fist until his death in 1833. Then the Queen-Regent, María Cristina, brought the liberal Francisco Martínez de la Rosa into the government with the aim of reforming the system and so gaining political support for the heir, her daughter Isabel, against whom Prince Carlos, with the assistance of the traditionalists, was disputing the throne. He argued that the Salic Law (imposed in 1713 and repealed by Fernando VII) prevented the accession of women to the throne.

Martínez de la Rosa drafted the Royal Statute of 1834, conceived as a Charter granted by the Queen, with the intention of being equidistant, both from the absolutism of the 'despicable decade' as from the liberalism of 1812. The declared objective of the Statute was simply to convoke a parliament, so justifying its brevity and the absence of any declaration of rights; it also avoided references to sovereignty, separation of powers, and other liberal principles. The underlying ideology was what came to be called the 'moderate principle', aiming at reconciling tradition and change, freedom and order by establishing the joint sovereignty of parliament and the king and collaboration of powers (with the absolute veto of the monarch).

Historians have emphasized the importance of this text, in appearance so modest in its brevity, both in length (fifty articles) and in duration (two years). Its importance in the first instance was because it entailed the final abandonment of absolutism by the monarchy and, furthermore, because it brought together (or so it was shaped by political practice) the fundamental political decisions of most of the nineteenth-century Constitutions:

> bicameralism; a restricted suffrage; the King's power to dissolve parliament; the figure of the President of the Council of Ministers; and motions of censure and confidence.

6. The majority of liberals did not accept a text that did not even call itself a 'Constitution' and demanded the return to the venerable Cadiz Constitution. In the summer of 1836, a series of insurrections culminating in the 'rebellion of La Granja' (the King's summer residence) led to the proclamation of the 1812 Constitution and to the calling of parliamentary elections. The new parliament prepared to reform the Constitution – considered by the majority to be too radical, too extreme – and ended by drafting a completely new *Lex legum*. In today's words, we would call it transactional or consensual between the two branches of liberalism (moderates and radicals). Perhaps the best example of this pact is the solution adopted for the thorny subject of sovereignty: neither the silence of the Statute nor the proclamation set out in the articles of the Cadiz Constitution, but rather a brief reference in the Preamble, where 'the Nation's will to revive, in the question of its Sovereignty, the 1812 Constitution' was declared.

Improving on the 1812 technique, the 1837 Constitution did not itself regulate the electoral system but remitted it to the ordinary legislation, elevated the courts to the category of 'Judicial Power', and in Title I, systematically regulated rights and duties where the references to the Catholic religion were maintained, though not as ardently as in 1812. The most relevant changes were produced in the organic section and focused on reinforcing the position of the king and the most powerful sectors of society. Thus, a two-chamber system was established, with a Senate of conservative composition; the king was given the power to summon and dissolve parliament with an absolute veto over the laws; the government needed to gain the confidence of both the king and the parliament, etc.

7. The 1837 Constitution required regulations to complete its framework laws on the controversial questions of the era (such as the electoral system, municipal government, and the national militia) to be designed in a different way according to the party in power. So, it could be said that in the hands of a moderate politician, such as Martínez de la Rosa, the political system would resemble the Statute, while in the hands of a progressive, like Agustín de Argüelles, it was more like the Cadiz Constitution. Such a flexible fundamental law could have lasted for many years and have given rise to a liberal regime that developed peacefully in the British manner. That it did not happen was not because the absolutist rebellion triumphed but, on the contrary, because the so-called embrace of Vergara (a reconciliation pact finalized in the town of Vergara which was celebrated by a famous embrace between the rival generals), in August 1839, ended in the Carlist War (so-called after Prince Carlos), thanks to the agreement to maintain the charters of the Basque provinces. If the 1837 Constitution was not able to ensure a long period of peace and prosperity, it was due to the very politicians who should have been its champions but who did not respect it. Thus, the following years were marked by rebellions, military uprisings, and more than irregular accessions to power, always regardless of what was established in the constitutional text.

Of course, if any party could have been expected to change the 1837 Constitution, logically, it should have been the progressive party, which had made the most concessions in the constituent pact; more so bearing in mind that, at the legislative level, other disputed matters (such as the abolition of ancient manorial rights) had also been decided in a less radical way than in the Cadiz Constitution. Yet, it was the moderates who brought about change: when in May 1844, General Ramón María Narváez became President of the Council of Ministers, he dissolved the parliament and summoned a new one with the express mission of reforming the Constitution, it being implicit that it would incorporate moderate ideas into the Constitution.

8. It is difficult today to understand the conduct of certain nineteenth-century politicians who – like the ancient Greeks with their gods – at the same time, both believed and did not believe in the Constitution. If they believed in it, why did they fail to comply with it with such facility? And if they did not, why were they so anxious to include their ideological concepts in it? To explain the desire to draft 'partisan' constitutions, many authors have referred to the 'myth' of the Constitution as the idea that by the simple fact of including a proposition in the fundamental norm, the problem would be resolved. Personally, I do not, finally, think that Narváez and other seasoned politicians were so ingenuous as to have a miracle-working vision of the Constitution. I am more inclined to think that what they did was to use it as yet another weapon in the struggle for power. Thus, by carving in stone in the text any option whatever, they were applying the modern theory of obstacles: they knew that including specific provisions in the Constitution would not definitively prevent the adversary from taking power, but it would be yet another obstacle in his way.

9. Be that as it may, the truth is that in 1845 a new moderate Constitution was drawn up against the express opposition of the progressives that inaugurated a dynamic that, in some way, was maintained until 1978: the plans of constitutional policy and ordinary policy were mixed, drafting sectarian (or better, partisan) constitutions that made political alteration within the constitutional framework unviable.

Following the 1837 technique, the 1845 Constitution was presented as a simple reform of the previous Constitution to the extent that it kept many of its articles and all its general structure. However, the modifications made were rejected by both the progressives and a minority of the moderates, defenders of constitutional consensus, since all the modifications were designed to eliminate the Constitution's progressive principles and to establish a moderate regime. Thus, the new Preamble omitted the reference to national sovereignty, substituting for it joint sovereignty between the king and parliament; trial by jury in crimes of the press was deleted from the declaration of rights and a categorical assertion of the Catholic faith was included. The powers of the king and the conservative strata in society (only property owners could be deputies, and senators were appointed by the king from amongst the social elites), etc., were reinforced in the organic section of the law. At the height of its passion for erasing all progressive principles, the authors of the 1845 Constitution changed the name of Title X from 'On Judicial Power' to 'On the Administration of Justice' but maintained all its articles intact without altering a single comma.

10. In 1854 a military uprising against the moderate government took place. It succeeded. A new government under General Baldomero Espartero was set up, and a one-chamber constituent parliament was summoned. The progressives won the election and embarked on lengthy debates that lasted throughout 1855. These debates ended in January 1856, and it only remained for parliament to formally decree the validity of the new Constitution, but it preferred to draw up seven accompanying organic laws. That delay was fatal for the validity of the new progressive text, which has passed into history as 'the unborn Constitution of 1856': General Leopoldo O'Donnell took power, and without thinking twice, he dissolved the constituent parliament and returned to the 1845 Constitution.

11. Although there was no shortage of reform projects, the subsequent moderate governments did not know how to adapt the 1845 Constitution to the new times, and the system became increasingly oligarchic. This policy of exclusion had the foreseeable effect of uniting the progressive party and the anti-system sectors, which then formed the Democratic Party. In 1866 Progressives and Democrats signed the Ostend Pact to put an end to the moderate regime, including Queen Isobel. In September 1868, General Juan Prim rebelled in Cadiz against the government and his action was immediately followed in other parts of the country, giving rise to the 'Glorious Revolution' because, this time, it was neither a question of changing a government nor even of changing the Constitution but rather of creating a new regime: the expulsion of the Queen, universal suffrage, social demands, etc.

The first elections in Spain with universal male suffrage were held in 1869. The new constituent parliament rapidly drew up a new Constitution that not only brought together the traditional progressive proposals (national sovereignty, separation of powers, inflexibility of the constitutional text) but went far beyond them by confirming universal male suffrage, freedom of worship, rights of assembly and association, an open clause for new rights, the irremovability of judges, etc. In the organic section, the Constitution tried to construct a democratic state: the predominance of the bicameral parliament over the government, the limitation of the King's powers, democratic elections for Municipal Councils and Provincial Councils, etc.

12. The parliament sought a king for Spain from outside the House of Bourbon and found him in Amadeo de Saboya (of Savoy), who was chosen as king in 1870, but he abdicated in February 1873, as disillusioned by the insurrection of the pro-independence Cubans as by the Carlists, the Republican uprisings, and, especially, by the lack of support of the very politicians who had summoned him. On the same day as the abdication, parliament proclaimed the Republic (thus ignoring the reform procedures in the Constitution that they themselves had approved), but this did not bring about political stability. Quite the contrary, for in little less than a year, there were four Presidents of the Republic, while the Carlist War continued and proclamations of 'Independent Cantons' proliferated throughout a good part of the national territory. In January 1874, General Manuel Pavía dissolved the new constituent parliament chosen in May, and so the project of a federal Constitution that had started to be discussed in Congress could not be approved and, regrettably, the word 'federal' passed into the collective memory as little more than a synonym for disorder and lack of government. General Francisco Serrano was appointed President of the executive power with the aim of restoring public order, which he managed to do in good measure outside the 1869 Constitution, declared valid but suspended for a year.

In spite of political instability and public disorder, the six-year revolutionary term succeeded in modernizing Spain considerably: it established free trade, with duty-free tariffs and laws enabling the free creation of stock exchanges and banks; justice was modernized, with a provisional law on the organization of judicial power (that remained in force for more than a century, until 1985) and the law of criminal procedure, etc.

13. In December 1875, a military revolt in favour of Alfonso XII triumphed without much resistance, thus restoring the Bourbon dynasty. The new President of the Council of Ministers, Antonio Cánovas del Castillo, sought popular legitimation of the regime through the drawing up of a new Constitution, for which he convoked general elections with universal male suffrage in accordance with the Republican electoral system. He won them without a great problem thanks to a selective repression of the forces of the left and astute electoral manipulation.

If it was indicated earlier that the return of Fernando VII meant the return to a renovated absolutism, since all the institutions of the *Ancien Régime* abolished by the Cadiz parliament could not be restored, now it can be said that this restoration, too, was no simple return to the past but rather a renewed and updated moderate regime. Thus, the new Constitution proclaimed a sovereignty shared between the king and the parliament, endowed the king with the capacity to dissolve parliament and to veto its laws, and included other points from the moderate ideology; at the same time, it kept many of the provisions of the 1869 Constitution, such as the rights of assembly and association, and the maximum period of twenty-four hours for governmental detention. To some extent, it can be said that the 1876 Constitution was halfway between that revolutionary Constitution and that of 1845, as illustrated by the regulation of the religious problem: a state religion, but with the establishment of religious tolerance.

The 1876 Constitution left expressly to subsequent laws: the concrete expression of all the rights of the Spanish people, the determination of the electoral system, and the establishment of municipal government. In light of this technique of remitting matters to later legislation and given the lack of any special procedure for the reform of the fundamental Law, Cánovas intended to favour a slow change of the political system, consonant with his theory of an 'internal Constitution' of the nation based on the historical development of parliamentary monarchy. On a purely political level, Cánovas sought stability through the peaceful alteration in the government of the two main parties, Conservative and Liberal. Clearly, for that to happen, it was necessary to manipulate electoral results, which was done through the system of the local ruling elite with a network of 'clients' to enable the political elite to control the electoral districts.

14. For a couple of decades, the regime functioned just as its creator had designed it, giving the country stability, facilitating a period of economic growth, and adapting itself to the new times. Thus, laws of assembly (1880), of association (1887), of universal suffrage (1890), industrial accidents (1900), etc., were passed. But in the early years of the twentieth century, the development of this fictitious parliamentary system stagnated, and a long crisis began that discredited the forces of the regime, ever more divided and unable to resolve the country's problems. Amongst the most important of these were serious social conflicts, regional (nationalist) demands, and the unpopular war with Morocco. All this ended in 1923 with the *coup d'état* of General Miguel Primo de Rivera, who at first counted on wide support from King Alfonso XIII to the socialists and Catalonian regionalists.

The first years of Primo de Rivera's dictatorship were years of economic prosperity, stimulated by intelligent government policies (promotion of public works, creation of a petrol monopoly, etc.) and various political successes, such as the ending of the Moroccan War, but little by little, the dictator lost support, particularly because of his project to institutionalize himself through a corporative type of Constitution. So, when the world economic crash of 1929 occurred, and it was urgent, a devaluation of the Peseta, Primo de Rivera found that he had lost the confidence even of his own comrades in arms and presented his resignation at the beginning of 1930. His successor, General Dámaso Berenguer, tried to return to the 1876 Constitution, but it was already too late to win the support of the main democratic forces, which preferred the Republic. Thus, it was that the local elections in April 1931 were understood as something much more decisive than the simple composition of some administrative bodies; it was considered to be a consultation on the dilemma of monarchy or republic. As the Republicans won the elections in the cities (not so in the country, where the local elite again proved its efficiency), everyone thought that the hour of the Republic had come, including the king, who abdicated and fled Spain.

15. The Second Republic was proclaimed on 14 April 1931 and its provisional government, in June of that year, called all men over 23 years of age to choose the constituent parliament made up of only one chamber, the Congress; curiously, women, who could not vote, enjoyed the right of passive suffrage since they could be elected deputies. The new parliament – where the forces of the left occupied the majority of its 469 seats – rapidly and rather controversially drafted a constitutional text that was promulgated in December of that same year. The old dilemmas of liberal constitutionalism were excluded in 1931; this did not mean the end of constitutional disputes but rather their substitution by new questions (religious, social, and regional) that divided the political class and society with a bitterness unknown in the previous century.

In its drafting, the Constitution's authors were inspired by everyone's latest constitutional fashions. So, it incorporated new social rights, certain mechanisms of what was then beginning to be called rationalized parliamentarianism, a Court of Constitutional Guarantees was set up, renounced 'war as an instrument of national policy', etc. The most original contribution was the 'integral State', a formula for political decentralization that aimed at being equidistant from the federal and the unitary State, intended to grant self-government only to those regions that manifested a true desire for autonomy. Although this formula displeased the conservative sectors, as did the possibility of expropriation without compensation (under a law passed by an absolute majority) and other articles of socialist stamp, the provisions that really caused the Constitution to be rejected by many citizens were its proposed solutions to the religious question. These were not limited to proclaiming freedom of worship and forbidding subsidies from public funds for religious institutions – just as the draft Constitution of the First Republic had envisaged – but developed a broad policy against the Catholic Church, considered by most of the members of the constituent body to be an adversary of the new regime: public demonstrations of worship required previous governmental authorization; the Order of the Jesuits was dissolved, and their assets nationalized; other Orders were subjected to a special law that banned 'industry, trade and teaching' and could determine the dissolution of those considered to be a danger to the State, etc.

The lack of harmony between the various social and political sectors was the predominant note of the Second Republic, whose political life was passed almost entirely outside the provisions of the constitutional norm, itself partially suspended due to the Law of the Defence of the Republic, approved by the constituent parliament itself. However, whatever its failures, the truth is that it enabled the democratic alternation of power, for, in the first ordinary elections (1933), the parties of the right won, while in the second (1936), those of the left did. It was precisely against this victory that various Generals (Franco, Mola, Queipo de Llano, etc.) took up arms, but unlike what had happened when Martínez Campos rebelled against the First Republic, there was a government in 1936, and a sector of the army itself and many citizens prepared to confront them. As a result, the *coup d'état* of 18 July 1936 failed and became a bloody civil war that lasted three years and ended in the dictatorship of General Francisco Franco, which lasted until his death in 1975.

16. Franco's regime, which began by being a pro-fascist dictatorship, developed into an institutionalized authoritarianism under certain 'Fundamental Laws', which created a strange 'organic democracy' without political parties, without freedom of expression and without the other rights typical of true democracies. With these cosmetic changes, some skilful decisions (substitution of the economic policy of self-sufficiency by a more liberal one, the Concordat with the Holy See, the granting of military bases to the USA, etc.), and a selective and efficient repression, he maintained himself in power for almost forty years. When he died in November 1975, under 'the succession provisions' of the Fundamental Laws, Juan Carlos de Borbón was proclaimed king as Juan Carlos I. He prepared to dismantle all the pseudo-democratic structure of the Franco regime while still respecting the channels established by those Fundamental Laws. To achieve this, he appointed Adolfo Suárez as President of the Government, who had been secretary general of the Movement (the only party) and who, therefore, knew well the mysteries of that Francoist structure. Suárez persuaded the organic parliament to pass – in what the press called his 'harikari' policy – a Law for Political Reform that, endorsed by the citizens in December 1976, allowed the calling of free elections to a two-chamber parliament and the peaceful transition from dictatorship to democracy.

§2. The Drafting of the 1978 Constitution

17. The elections of 15 June 1977 were for a constituent parliament, although formally they were not convoked with this character, and so, unusually in Spanish history, the new democratic regime did not entail a formal, express rupture with the previous one. As it was realized that the majority electoral system of plurality voting used in the Second Republic had not consolidated the party system; the government and the democratic opposition agreed on the proportional system, unprecedented in Spain. The Unión de Centro Democrático (UCD), the coalition formed around Suárez, won the elections but without an absolute majority, followed by Partido Socialista Obrero Español (PSOE); far behind were Franco's heirs (Alianza Popular) and the Communist party; the same was true of the Catalonian nationalists (CiU) and the Basques Partido Nacionalista Vasco (PNV), although their representation was significant in their own territories (Table 1).

Table 1 General Elections of 15 June 1977 Distribution of Votes and Seats in the Congress of Deputies

Party	*Votes*		*Seats*	
	Number	*%*	*Number*	*%*
Unión de Centro Democrático (UCD)	6,309,517	34.52	165	47.14
Partido Socialista Obrero Español (PSOE)	4,467,745	24.44	103	29.43
Alianza Popular (AP)	1,471,527	8.05	16	4.57
Partido Comunista de España (PCE)	1,150,774	6.3	12	3.43

Party	*Votes*		*Seats*	
	Number	*%*	*Number*	*%*
Socialistes de Catalunya (PSC_PSOE)	870,362	4.76	15	4.29
Partido Socialista Popular_U. Socialista (PSP_US)	816,754	4.47	6	1.71
Partit Socialista Unificat de Catalunya (PSUC)	561,132	3.07	8	2.29
Pacte Democrátic per Catalunya (PDC)	514,647	2.82	11	3.14
Partido Nacionalista Vasco (PNV)	296,193	1.62	8	2.29
Coalición Electoral Unió del Centro i la				
Democracia Cristiana de Cataluña (UDC_CD)	172,791	0.95	2	0.57
Esquerra de Catalunya (EC)	143,954	0.79	1	0.29
Candidatura Independiente del Centro	67,017	0.37	2	0.57
Euskadiko Ezquerra_Izquierda de Euskadi				
(EE_IE)	61,417	0.34	1	0.29
Total	16,903,830	92.5	350	
Candidates who did not obtain seats	1,374,255	7.5		
Total votes for all Candidates	18,278,085	100		

Source: Central Electoral Council and author.

18. The parliament resulting from these democratic elections decided to draw up a new constitutional text following the most classical and orthodox model; it would not be a government initiative but rather Congress itself that would choose, from amongst its members, a committee to carry out the project; what was not so classical – at least for Spain – was both the manner of selecting the members (it was arranged that there would be a balanced representation of all the political forces) and the spirit in which they worked (seeking agreement amongst everybody). Without a doubt, the new parliament had learnt from history the uselessness of drafting a partisan Constitution and strove to achieve a Constitution of 'consensus', to use the word that became fashionable at that time. The common aim was not so much to find a text situated in a hypothetical midpoint between all the political options as to get an integrating text, a text under which everyone could govern later on.

19. To win this basic accord, it was necessary, evidently, for the parties to surrender their most radical approaches (e.g., PSOE and PCE did not make a *casus belli* of their Republican ideology and gave up their demand for responsibility against those who had collaborated with the dictatorship), to devote a lot of time (the committee alone took nearly seven months to present the project, against the twenty days needed in 1931), and to show much goodwill. Inevitably, this method of drafting the Constitution left its mark on its contents, giving it certain characteristics that are not always desirable from the technical point of view and that can be summed up in two words: ambiguity and lengthiness. The ambiguous formulations abounded in polemical topics and especially in the delicate matter of the territorial distribution of political power rather than a pact about the model of the State; what was achieved was an agreement on two or three models that could be adopted in the future. At other times, the consensus was won by including various counter-posed positions (as in the right to education) or by bringing together initiatives on the most varied subjects so that everyone saw their own proposals reflected. The sum of these two characteristics of ambiguity and length has had the paradoxical effect that the 1978 Constitution is the longest in our history (with the exception of 1812, but that was because it included within it the electoral system) and, at the same time, the most open, that needed most parliamentary regulations, and that is most susceptible to different interpretations. Fortunately, the constituent assembly took the precaution of creating a Constitutional Court that, as the ultimate interpreter of the Constitution, clarifies its meaning and watches over its normative powers.

20. Thanks to this spirit of harmony, the Constitution Bill was passed with all the major parties voting in favour, although it is to be regretted that, after some hesitation, the Basque nationalists abstained. The final result in Congress was 325 votes in favour, fourteen abstentions, and six against. In the Senate, the voting was 225 in favour, eight abstentions, and five against. On 6 December 1978, the bill was submitted to a referendum, winning a vote in favour of 15,706,873 Spaniards, 88% of the voters and 59% of the electorate. Of no legal significance but political relevance, it should be added that abstention – recommended by the PNV – exceeded 50% in the three pro-Basque provinces. In Galicia, the turnout was also well below average, as seen in Table 2. The king solemnly sanctioned the Constitution before parliament on 27 December 1978, and it entered into force on the very day of its publication in the Official State Gazette (BOE) on 29 December 1978.

Table 2 Results of the Referendum on the Draft Constitution

	Electorate	*Voters*		*Yes*		*No*		*Blank*		*Invalid*
		%	*Number*	*%*	*Number*	*%*	*Number*	*%*	*Number*	*%*
Andalucía	4,347,542	69.5	2,775,521	91.9	165,882	5.5	62,817	2,.1	17,574	0.6
Aragón	894,403	73.6	579,734	88.1	44,287	6.7	30,624	4.7	3,430	0.5
Asturias	864,796	61.8	473,348	88.6	44,874	8.4	11,395	2.1	4,726	0.9
Baleares	450,115	70.2	282,598	89.5	15,251	4.8	15,394	4.9	2,648	0.8
Canarias	879,963	62.9	508,668	91.9	24,174	4.4	17,580	3.2	3,088	0.6
Cantabria	374,559	71.2	222,559	83.5	33,232	12.5	9,150	3.4	1,573	0.6
Castilla-la Mancha	1,207,525	73.8	751,614	84.3	105,034	11.8	27,801	3.1	6,933	0.8
Castilla-León	1,950.813	71.4	1,184,361	85.1	127,545	9.2	69,245	5.0	11,175	0.8
Cataluña	4,398,173	67.9	2,701,870	90.5	137,845	4.6	126,462	4.2	20,549	0.7
Extremadura	765,235	70.5	481,808	89.3	39,637	7.3	14,801	2.7	3,296	0.6
Galicia	2,107,613	50.2	942,097	89.0	61,892	5.8	42,092	4.0	11,961	1.1
Madrid	3,047,226	72.2	1,896,205	86.1	222,638	10.1	66,575	3.0	15,684	0.7
Murcia	630,268	71.4	408,722	90.8	27,975	6.2	10,975	2.4	2,570	0.6
Navarra	361,243	66.6	182,207	75.7	40,804	17.0	15,415	6.4	2,269	0.9
País Vasco	1,552,737	44.7	479,205	69.1	163,191	23.5	39,816	5.7	11,098	1.6
Rioja	192,597	72.5	120,847	86.6	10,940	7.8	6,569	4.7	1,205	0.9
Valencia	2,545,481	74.1	1,676,680	88.8	131,664	7.0	65,010	3.4	13,789	0.7
Ceuta	32,488	72.8	20,849	88.2	1,997	8.4	670	2.8	134	0.6

	Electorate	Voters		Yes		No		Blank		Invalid
		%	Number	%	Number	%	Number	%	Number	%
Melilla	29,403	66.1	17,185	88.5	1,643	8.5	511	2.6	84	0.4
Total	**26,632,180**	**67.1**	**15,706,078**	**87.9**	**1,400,505**	**7.8**	**632,902**	**3.5**	**133,786**	**0.7**

Source: Central Electoral Council and author.

§3. Form of Government

I. The Social and Democratic State of Law

A. The State of Law

21. As the Preamble of the Spanish Constitution states, the rule of law is characterized, throughout the world, by the empire of law 'as the expression of the popular will', which means the obligation of all citizens and all public powers to comply with the laws, which can only be modified by a special procedure attributed to the representatives of the citizens. The aim of the Rule of Law is nothing but the implementation of a series of legal techniques (starting with the separation of powers and the guarantee of individual rights) that prevent the monarch from having absolute power over lives and goods according to the principle *regis voluntas suprema lex est*. For this reason, the Rule of Law is a state that, first, is subject to a legal system that it itself has created (the objective or normative aspect of the Rule of Law) and second, its actions – including the creation of law itself – are limited by the previous existence of certain rights of the citizens enshrined in the Constitution. Moreover, the State is not only limited by these rights but has the obligation to guarantee and defend them; they are public subjective rights, rights whose protection the citizen can demand of the State (the subjective aspect).

The Preamble of the Spanish Constitution proclaims the creation of a State governed by the Rule of Law, a State that, according to Article 1.1, is configured as 'social and democratic'. Its articles broadly develop these two aspects, which we have called 'objective and subjective'. As we shall study it more thoroughly later, I shall now point out only its two most relevant provisions: Article 9 brings together, more comprehensively than is usual in comparative law, the fundamental elements of the normative aspect; thus, it sets out that the Constitution guarantees the principle of legality, the hierarchy of norms, the non-retroactive nature of penal sanctions that are not favourable to or restrictive of individual rights, legal certainty, the responsibility, and the prohibition of public powers. The subjective aspect that is concerned with the citizen has its maximum expression in Article 10, which establishes that the dignity of the person, her/his inviolable rights, the free development of personality, respect for the law and for others 'are the foundation of political order and social peace'.

B. Superior Values of the Legal Order

22. But the 1978 Constitution does not limit itself to establishing the Rule of Law in the classic liberal style, in which the Constitution is conceived of as an instrument to protect the citizens from the public powers but asserts in Article 1 that Spain is 'a social and democratic State of Law that advocates liberty, justice, equality and political pluralism as the superior values of its legal order'. In this way, the 1978 Constitution asserts in its very articles the objectives of the political community and the foundations of the legal system with unprecedented care (with hardly any references in the Preambles to the 1812 and 1869 Constitutions and in Article

1 of that of 1931). At the normative level, Article 1 requires that the whole legal system shall be interpreted in accordance with these superior values, an interpretation known as a finalist or teleological interpretation (*see* paragraph 45); in the institutional scheme, it not only determines that the State of Law is founded on popular sovereignty but also that the State is obliged to play an active role in society, which goes far beyond the simple police State of the nineteenth century in which there is a clear divide between State and society, as the Constitution itself takes care to specify in subsequent articles (especially those dealing with the governing principles of social and economic policy, Chapter III of Title I). To put it in the words of the Constitutional Court itself:

> The shape of the State as a society of Law thus concludes the development in which the attainment of the aims of general interest are not absorbed by the State, but is harmonised in a mutual action between State and Society, which blurs the dichotomy of public and private Law (STC 18/1984, 7 February, case *Caja de Ahorros de Asturias*).

II. The Parliamentary Monarchy

23. In this short review of Spanish constitutional history, we have seen how, at the two historic moments in which a republic was proclaimed in Spain (in 1873 and 1931), the reason was not so much the overwhelming desire for a republic as the overwhelming desire for democracy, made more difficult by the existence of the monarchy itself. However, in the years following General Franco's death, the king was not an obstacle to democracy but rather became the 'engine' of change. Thus, it was relatively easy for the constituent assembly to reach an agreement to accept the monarchy despite the fact that its holder had been appointed by the dictator and that almost half the political representatives were convinced Republicans. Another factor that facilitated the agreement was the fact that all the parties held that the only sovereign were the people, thereby rendering anachronistic the theory of the co-sovereignty of nation and king or any other formula – such as national sovereignty, understood as an alibi to establish a restricted suffrage – that would result in the political preponderance of one social group.

24. In all current democratic monarchical States, organization is based on the separation of powers: in the case of the parliamentary system, there is a clear separation between the executive power, exercised by the government emanating from parliament, and the position of the Head of State, reserved for the monarch. Historical development has put an end to the idea of attributing to the monarch the exercise of executive power, as had been customary in the 'constitutional monarchy' of the nineteenth century. It is this same history that has made the power of appointing the executive the bone of contention between monarchy and parliament since it does not reside directly in the electoral body, as occurs in presidential systems, which, until that date, had only existed in republics.

Evidently, this historical development was not present in Spain in the 1970s, so the members of the Spanish Constituent Assembly could regulate, as they wanted, the articulation of State organs, including a presidential system. But, with good reason, they fled from innovations in this matter and limited themselves to put in writing, to codifying, many of the political practices of parliamentary monarchies (not always followed by the Spanish kings under the Constitution of 1876), taking as their own the famous expression 'The King reigns, but does not rule' (le Roi règne mais ne gouverne pas), popularized by Adolphe Thiers in 1830 against Charles X and first uttered by the Polish Chancellor Jan Zamoyski at the end of the sixteenth century to ask parliament to limit the powers of King Sigismund III. The technique that followed was not so much a strict enumeration of his functions and the disappearance of certain institutions incompatible with the hereditary character of the head of a democratic State (such as the royal veto on laws) as the endorsement of the King's acts, a technique by which the decision formally adopted by the king (let us give the example of the appointment of the members of government) is, in fact, carried out by other State organs so that political and legal responsibility is shifted to them. In this way, the king performs the role of *auctoritas*, an ability to influence, but not of *potestas*, the day-to-day exercise of real and effective powers.

25. Unlike the presidential system, the parliamentary one implies, in theory, the subordination of the executive to the legislative since the latter appoints and controls the former. However, the fact that the Members of Parliament belong to political parties with an internal discipline means that, in modern practice, the confrontation is not between parliament and government but between the majority in the Chamber, who support the government, and the minority, who form the opposition. Moreover, as the political leaders of the majority are normally part of the government, it is usual for the will of parliament to be subordinate to that of the government, if only for the purely technical reason that the social state involves the continuous taking of decisions for which the executive power is much better adapted than the legislative. In this new scenario, parliament is not so much the place where the representatives of the citizens freely discuss common affairs as the place in which the government and the opposition make their differences public – 'the ring', to use a very usual metaphor – in which their programmes clash daily.

The Spanish political system has similarities with the parliamentary system. The Constitution itself establishes certain institutions that favour the greater power of the executive, such as its responsibility to direct domestic and foreign policy (Article 97); the constructive censure motion, which requires the presentation of an alternative candidate for the removal of the President of the Government (Article 113); the monopoly to prepare the General Budget and its power of veto on the proposals; and amendments that involve an increase in expenditure or a decrease in revenue (Article 134). In short, an accumulation of rules that have given rise to what everyone – the Constitutional Court included – calls the rationalized parliament.

26. But the Spanish Constitution not only has mechanisms designed to achieve the parliamentary stability of the government but has also adopted decisions that facilitate the establishment of the leadership of the President of the Government: only he is chosen by the Congress of Deputies (Article 99), only he can present a question of confidence and dissolve parliament (Articles 112 and 115), etc. Political practice has reinforced this leadership to extremes not envisaged in 1978 due to various factors, amongst which the most important are the formation of one-party governments (with an absolute majority in five of the fourteen elections held since the approval of the Spanish Constitution), iron party discipline, the accommodation of ideological differences amongst the parties, the role of television – primarily pictorial – as the transmitter of political activity, the personalization of the presidential candidates in the electoral campaigns, etc. In short, Law 50/1997 on Government indicated 'presidential direction' as one of the principles of the functioning of the government. Because of this leadership of the President of the Government and the predominance of the government over parliament, just as has occurred in other parliamentary systems (the cases of the United Kingdom and Germany are good examples), it is no exaggeration to state that as a general rule, the de facto power of the President of the Government within the Spanish political system falls little short of that of a President of a republic within a presidential system, however much greater that may seem.

III. The Autonomous State

27. When in 1812 the liberals had the opportunity to design the form of the Spanish Constitutional State to their liking, they were very clear as to their model: the French Unitarian State, to such an extent that the Cadiz Constitution introduced the principles of this type of State, beginning with the proclamation of one legislative power and the 'unity of codes', which entailed the disappearance of the self-governing institutions of Álava, Guipúzcoa, Navarre, and Vizcaya and the suppression of their particular legal systems as well as the disappearance of the territorial legal norms of the Crown of Aragon that had been maintained in spite of the loss of their institutions, as the civil rights of Aragon and Catalonia. At first, the only ones to oppose the unitary State were the sympathizers of the *Ancien Régime*, as their war cry shows: 'God, country, king and regional laws'. But as the nineteenth century passed, various liberal sectors were considering the possibility of organizing the State in a different way, although without abandoning the principles of national sovereignty, equality of all citizens, and the unity of the market, the basic ideological foundation for the unitary State. We have already seen how they tried out several formulas in this direction, from the restoration of the Basque regional government, agreed in the 'embrace of Vergara' of 1839, to the integral federal States of the Second Republic, and how this contrasted with the rigid centralism of Franco's dictatorship.

28. Without wishing to be more precise – given the chronological distance – it could be said that the constituent assemblies of 1977–1978 brought about a change in the roles, in relation to those of 1812, amongst the supporters of the old and new regimes: all the progressive forces showed themselves to be against the unitary State while the heirs of Franco, Alianza Popular, defended its validity, although even this group favoured a great measure of decentralization. But apart from rejecting the unitary State, the various political groups had little in common, thus resulting in the constitutional design of an Autonomous State, an original Spanish creation intended both to satisfy the aspirations of those regions which most desired self-government and to grant a certain measure of decentralization of political power in the rest of the country. So, the Constitution did not establish a territorial map but remitted the matter to a later date through the creation, basically, of two processes to achieve autonomy, with two different levels of autonomy: a political one of the first degree for the 'nationalities' and an administrative one of the second degree, for the 'regions'.

29. Forty years later, the Autonomous State is completely established in Spain and has meant a radical transformation in political power that is now shared between the State and seventeen Autonomous Communities. Although the Constitution permits (and almost encourages) it, there has not arisen a division into two groups of Communities with major differences between them; all are substantially equal, although some have certain autonomous features (such as their own police forces and the ability to collect taxes) that others lack. As we shall analyse in Part III, this gradual development of the Autonomous State has meant that there are no great differences in content between this type of State and the federal, although, in legal form, there are some that are relevant. Moreover, the subject of the form of the State is politically far from a closed question because, since 2003, a generalized process of reforming the Autonomous Statutes has occurred, whose driving forces are once again the Basque Country and, especially, Catalonia. Here, somehow, the dichotomy between a certain asymmetric federalism (based on some 'differential facts') and equality amongst all Communities is once more being planned. However, unlike what happened in the first manifestation of the Autonomous State, the new Catalan Autonomous Statute was passed in 2006 without the support of the opposition party, the PP, which appealed more than one hundred articles of this legal text to the Constitutional Court. After several procedural vicissitudes, the Court pronounced one of its most long-awaited decisions, 31/2010, 28 June, which were hotly contested by the Catalan political forces that defend the Statute. Fortunately, the reform of the other Statutes (Valencia, Andalusia, the Balearic Islands, Castile-León, Navarra, Extremadura and Murcia) passed with the votes of both major parties. Unfortunately, this consensus was broken yet again in 2014 when the Statute of Castilla-La Mancha was reformed with the sole objective of modifying the number of deputies per province, although this limited reform was considered constitutional by the Constitutional Court (STC 197/2014, 4 December). The political consensus on the Andalusian Statute and the other statutory reforms has brought about a legal paradox: those Statues contain some clauses similar in content to those declared unconstitutional in Catalan. However, as they have not been appealed, a technical problem has been created for Spain's legal system to which there has been no express response, although the rules of interpretation oblige us to think that those articles cannot be applied in future.

IV. The Integration into Europe

30. In the years of the Transition (1975–1978), all the major political parties, as well as almost all intellectuals and society in general, fully identified with the phrase 'Spain is the problem, Europe the solution', written by the philosopher José Ortega y Gasset in 1910. That is why, when on 26 July 1977, the government of Adolfo Suárez submitted its application to join the European Economic Community, all parties supported the application, which would allow Spain to join the European democratic family, something unthinkable under the Franco dictatorship. As this decision had great repercussions for society as a whole, it seems to me that it should be considered a fundamental political decision like the State of Law, the Parliamentary Monarchy and the Autonomous State. However, as the consensus on it was very broad (unlike NATO membership), the only thing that the constituent members debated was how to include a mechanism in the Constitution that would allow it to be implemented. To this end, they drew inspiration from the constitutions of other states, which, without mentioning Europe, provided for 'limitations of sovereignty to create a grouping to ensure peace' (Italian Constitution of 1947), transfer of 'sovereign rights by law to international institutions' (Grundgesetz of 1949), and so on. In the Preliminary Draft Constitution, this clause on the transfer of state competences was included in Article 6, thus underlining its great importance. However, for reasons of systematics, in the Draft, the fathers of the Constitution moved it to Chapter Three of Title III, where they grouped all the rules relating to international treaties.

31. Moreover, and given this consensus, they did so by establishing a procedure that was relatively easy to achieve: employing an organic law. We will see later on how this opening clause of the Constitution has brought about a substantial change in the day-to-day functioning of Spanish institutions (*see* paragraph 47) and in those legal norms (*see* paragraph 61). We will now limit ourselves to commenting that if it was understandable that in 1978 a modest technical formula was used to carry out the transcendental decision to join the then so-called European Economic Community, today it is deplorable that we still lack a solemn reference to the process of European construction, as almost all the Constitutions of the Member States of the Union already have. The French Constitution, to give a nearby example, has an entire title devoted to Europe, which begins by stating that 'The Republic shall participate in the European Communities and in the European Union constituted by States which have freely chosen by virtue of the treaties which established them to exercise some of their powers in common.'

§4. State Territory

32. Spain occupies the greater part of the Iberian Peninsula as well as the Balearic Islands in the Mediterranean, the Canary Islands in the Atlantic, and the Cities of Ceuta and Melilla in North Africa; in total, 504,750 km^2, the second largest State in terms of territory in the European Union (EU). It is bounded on the north by France and Andorra and on the west by Portugal; Ceuta and Melilla mark the southern frontier. There is no continuous geographical border between Spain and Portugal, though, between France and Spain, the Pyrenees form a natural barrier, 435 km long, making communication with the Continent difficult, since although at the extremes its width is minimal, at the centre it reaches 150 km.

The coastline is 3,904 km long, to which must be added the 852 km of the Baleárics and 1,064 of the Canaries: in total, 1,820 km of coast. Law 10/1977, 4 January 1977, fixed the Spanish territorial limit at 12 nautical miles. Beyond this, Law 15/1978 established an Exclusive Economic Zone (EEZ) of 200 nautical miles in the 'coasts of the Atlantic Ocean, including the Cantabrian Sea'. A similar decision has not been adopted for the Mediterranean because of the difficulty of delimiting the jurisdiction with other riparian owners who have also not marked out EEZs. In the Atlantic, Spain has not reached an agreement to delimit its EEZ with either France or Portugal in spite of numerous conversations.

33. As with all European countries, Spain's borders have undergone frequent changes. At present, it is claiming the re-integration, within its territory, of the Rock of Gibraltar, under British sovereignty, and it does not accept Morocco's claim over Ceuta and Melilla, alleging that these cities have been part of Spain since 1580 and 1497, respectively.

Amongst the most important territorial changes in the Spanish State made since 1492, the following can be mentioned:

- 1494: Treaty of Tordesillas, under which Spain and Portugal divided America.
- 1496: Peace of Los Realejos, recognizing the conquest of the Canary Islands.
- 1504: Incorporation of the Kingdom of Naples.
- 1512: Incorporation of the Kingdom of Navarre.
- 1519: Carlos I was named Emperor, thus controlling the destinies of the governments of Spain and the German empire.
- 1580: Incorporation of Portugal.
- 1640: By the Peace of Westphalia, Spain recognized the independence of Holland.
- 1659: The Peace of the Pyrenees fixed the French-Spanish frontier. Spain ceded Roussillon and Sardinia to France.
- 1713: The Treaty of Utrecht marked the end of the Spanish Empire in Europe in exchange for the recognition of Felipe de Bourbon as the king of Spain, Flanders, Milan, Naples, Sicily, Gibraltar and Minorca (recovered by the Treaty of Versailles of 1783) were surrendered.
- 1801: By the Treaty of Badajoz, Spain incorporated Olivenza, previously conquered in the War of the Oranges.
- 1824: Defeat of Spain in the Battle of Ayacucho, signalling the independence of all the American colonies, except the islands of Cuba and Costa Rica.
- 1898: By the Treaty of Paris, Spain lost Cuba, Puerto Rico and the Philippines.
- 1912: Spain and France divided Morocco. Spain exercised its 'Protectorate' over the poorer, more mountainous north.
- 1955: Independence of the Moroccan Protectorate.
- 1968: Independence of Guinea.
- 1975: Decolonization of Sahara.

34. Although all the peninsular territory lies in temperate latitudes (between 43.47 in Cape Estaca de Bares and 36.0 in Tarifa), its climate is not uniform, given its varied orography. Above all, the existence of many mountains and particularly the large central plateau, the Meseta, more than 200,000 km^2 in extension, results in Spain being the second highest European country, only exceeded by Switzerland. The plains are small, and only 11% of the territory (53,897 km^2) is below 200 metres, almost all in the valleys of the Ebro (in the northeast) and the Guadalquivir (in the southwest).

From the point of view of climate, the national territory can be divided into three large areas: (a) the northern coastline, known as the 'Cantabrian Cornice' or 'Green Spain' due to the high rainfall, with a temperate climate thanks to the influence of the Atlantic Ocean; (b) the central zone, with the Meseta, and the Depression of the Ebro, with a continental climate, with great variations of temperature – very cold winters, hot summers and moderate or scant rainfall; and (c) the Mediterranean and south Atlantic coastline with mild winters, hot summers and very irregular, often stormy, rainfall.

35. Historically, the Meseta and the great mountain ranges have isolated some territories from others as there are no natural means of communication. Many historians have considered that a good part of the centrifugal tendencies seen in Spanish history has their origin in the Peninsula's geographical structure, which has given rise to two distinct, opposed types of human beings: the austere and warlike Castilians and the open and vital people of the coast. Without a doubt, such a scheme is too simplistic, as proved by the fact that most of maritime Spain have never been involved in any serious conflicts with the centre. However, it cannot be denied that the orography does have an influence on the characters of the people. So, for example, the flat and fertile lands of the Guadalquivir were a magnet for all the invaders (which explains its profound Romanization and subsequent Arabization), while the mountainous Basque Country was never especially attractive to conquerors. The result is that while in one part racial mixing has been a historical constant, in the other part, people from outside were only received with the advent of industrialization at the end of the nineteenth century.

36. The national territory is divided into fifty provinces, grouped into seventeen Autonomous Communities plus the Autonomous Cities of Ceuta and Melilla. As can be seen in Figure 1 and Table 3, the Communities are far from homogeneous both in size and population. Such heterogeneity is not precisely a rationalizing factor in helping the better functioning of the public powers.

Figure 1 Spain Political Map

Source: Ontheworldmap.com.

§5. Population and Demographics

37. The official municipal census of 1 January 2022 gave the Spanish population as 47,435,597. The population density is 94 persons per km^2, in the middle to low range of the twenty-seven EU countries (average of 109 inhabitants per km^2, the highest being Malta with 1,595 inhabitants per km^2 and the lowest Finland with 18 inhabitants per km^2). In absolute numbers, Spain is the fourth most populated country in the Union, only behind Germany, France, and Italy. Historically, the Spanish population has grown continuously in the decades after the Second World War, although in the 1980s, there was a spectacular fall in the birth rate. In spite of that, the population did not stop increasing due to the incorporation of foreigners, such that that the census of 2005 showed the greatest growth in population in one year in all the history of Spain (910,846 persons, 2.10% of the total) due to the incorporation of 696,284 foreigners. However, the world economic crisis of 2008 not only slowed the arrival of foreigners but caused many of them to return to their country of origin such that in 2009 the number of foreigners resident in Spain began to drop. As this decrease has not been compensated for by an increase in births, Spain lost its population from 2012 until 2015, but this tendency was reversed in 2016 because the economic improvement attracted new emigrants. Internally, these population movements have not been uniformly shared throughout the territory, with the result that all of the Mediterranean arc is augmenting its population, while the interior (apart from Madrid) and some territories on the Cantabrian Corniche have experienced substantial declines; thus some provinces such as Soria, with only 9.2 inhabitants per km^2, have become semi-depopulated (Table 3).

Table 3 Size and Population of the Autonomous Territories (In Order of Territorial Size) in 2022

Official Name	*Size*		*Population*		*Inhabitants/km²*
	km²	*%*	*Absolute*	*%*	
Castilla y León	94,223	18.62	2,370,064	5.21	25
Andalucía	87,597	17.31	8,494,155	17.99	97
Castilla-La Mancha	79,463	15.70	2,052,192	4.36	26
Aragón	47,720	9.43	1,325,342	2.81	28
Extremadura	41,634	8.23	1,054,245	2.32	25
Cataluña	32,114	6.35	7,783,302	16.23	242
Galicia	29,574	5.84	2,689,152	5.82	91
Valencia	23,255	4.60	5,090,839	10.60	219
Murcia	11,313	2.24	1,531,439	3.16	135
Asturias	10,604	2.10	1,004,499	2.22	95
Navarra	10,391	2.05	663,612	1.38	64
Madrid	8,028	1.59	6,744,456	13.98	840
Canarias	7,447	1.47	2,176,412	4.53	292
País Vasco	7,234	1.43	2,207,201	4.71	305
Cantabria	5,321	1.05	585,222	1.25	110
La Rioja	5,045	1.00	319,485	0.68	63
Baleares	4,992	0.99	1,176,254	2.40	236
Ceuta	19	0.004	82,566	0.18	4,346
Melilla	13	0.003	85,159	0.18	6,551
Other territories	34	0.007	0		
Total	**505,988**	**100**	**47,435,597**	**100**	**94**

38. The inflow of immigrants received by Spain at the end of the twentieth and beginning of the twenty-first centuries has meant that in scarcely ten years, the proportion of foreigners in the resident population passed from 2.3% in 2000 to 12.2% in 2010, being 5,708,940 in absolute figures. On 1 January 2022, the total number of foreigners in the census was 5,512,558, 11.6% of the total Spanish population. Of this number, 1,605,384 persons are European citizens, and 2,791,357 are from outside the EU. Spain has become the eleventh country in the world with the greatest number of immigrants, according to the UN Department of Economic and Social Affairs. The bulk of the foreigners is in the Communities of Catalonia (1,263,135), Madrid (945,933), and Valencia (778,655), although the Communities with the highest proportion of foreigners are the Balearic Islands (18.8%), Catalonia (16.1%) and Murcia (14.6%). At the opposite extreme are Extremadura with only 3.3%, Galicia with 4.4% and Asturias with 4.5%.

39. Spain has traditionally been a country of emigration, which has its roots in the repopulation of the Middle Ages that, in some ways, continued after the arrival of Europeans in the Americas. In addition to economic migration, based on individual reasons of self-improvement, there has been no lack of political emigration, as with the expulsion of Jews in 1492 (about 165,000) by the Catholic Monarchs and of the Moors in 1602 ordered by Philip III (approximately 300,000). The nineteenth century brought about turbulent waves of political exiles, beginning with about 10,000 Francophiles in 1811 and followed the next year by a similar number of Liberals. The victory of General Franco in the 1936–1939 Civil War led to the departure from Spain of approximately half a million Republicans. The deplorable economic situation following the war fuelled purely personal migration in the 1950s that may have involved more than 1.5 million people who went mostly to America and especially to Venezuela, which was experiencing rapid growth thanks to oil production. In the 1960s, with Spain developing, migration did not cease, although in this case, it was mainly to Europe, with France and Germany in the first place. The 1973 oil crisis put a major brake on emigration, but as democracy and accession to the European Economic Community in 1986 eventually turned around the situation, Spain went from being a producer of migrants to becoming a receiver.

In the Register of Spanish Persons Abroad (PERE), as of 1 January 2022, there were recorded 2,742,605 persons of Spanish nationality, as a percentage of the sexes (51.1% women and 48.9% males) similar to that of the total Spanish population. By continent, 59% of those registered in the PERE have a fixed residence in America, 37.4% in Europe, and only 3.8% in the rest of the world. The countries where most Spanish nationals are living are Argentina (480,159), France (290,033), and the USA (183,003). Perhaps the most interesting statistic is the birthplace of these people: only 31% of Spanish nationals living abroad were born in Spain, which not only shows that mass emigration has disappeared in recent years but also suggests that the vast majority of these Spaniards abroad are deeply rooted in their locality, with little prospect of going back to live in Spain. If this is so, it is not surprising that at the beginning of the century, there was a debate about whether it makes sense that Spanish people living abroad not only vote in general but also in regional and local elections. The debate, backed by a favourable Report of the Council of State on the electoral system in February 2009, resulted in Organic Law 2/2011, 28 January, which amended Organic Law 5/1985, 19 June, on the General Electoral System. This excluded absent residents from voting in local elections, a law that is totally consistent with the literal tenor of the Constitution that states that councillors 'shall be elected by the residents of the municipality'.

Part I. Sources of Constitutional Law

Chapter 1. The Constitution

§1. General Characteristics

I. A Consensual Normative Constitution

40. Historically, Constitutions have been conceived as norms produced by the will of the people to control the public powers and guarantee the rights of the citizen, as was established canonically by the famous Article 16 in the Declaration of the Rights of Man and the Citizen of 1789: 'Any society in which no provision is made for guaranteeing rights or for the separation of powers, has no Constitution.' As in Europe, the possessor of political power was the king; the Constitution laid special emphasis on reducing his power to the benefit of the parliaments. The self-confidence of the newly emerging class, the Bourgeoisie, resulted in Constitutions attributing to the State a laissez-faire role (responsible only for peace and order) and establishing the principle of the primacy of law in the system of sources, reducing the role of the Constitution to that of a programmatic norm, a text addressed to the legislator, who could develop it without legal controls, only the political control of the elections, in which restricted suffrage ensured that only men from the most favoured social sectors took part.

41. From the end of the nineteenth century, the struggle to widen suffrage and to bring the workers into the political system led to a transformation of the liberal State, first into a democratic one and then into a social State, an active agent able to become the engine in the fight for freedom and equality. Logically, this change has had its effects on how the Constitution is conceived, to such an extent that after the Second World War, many democratic political groups changed their idea about the Constitution as the political norm in which to embody their particular ideology (partisan Constitutions) for that of a pact between the most important political and social forces in society (consensus Constitutions). For this reason, in the majority of countries with a Constitution granted in recent decades, provisions have been incorporated in their texts that affect the social structure, and the need to guarantee this pact through its application in the daily life of the State has become important. As a result, it is no longer considered sufficient to proclaim the superiority of the Constitution and establish a special procedure for its reform but rather to ensure that the rest of the legal system is adapted to it; it has passed from being a programmatic

Constitution, with little binding force, to a normative one that is imposed on all public powers. To make this imposition effective various legal techniques are used, such as the immediate efficacy of the constitutional text, so that the courts can apply it directly in certain circumstances, above all, the creation of Constitutional Courts, which control the adaptation of the laws to the Constitution.

42. If we remember what was said in the earlier chapter on the drafting and contents of the 1978 Spanish Constitution, it will not be difficult to accept that our Constitution corresponds faithfully to the *ideal type* of modern Constitution just set out: it is conceived as a technical instrument at the service of certain ethical values; it establishes a social and democratic State of Law; it was drawn up through a great pact between the main political and social forces and received massive endorsement from the people. It has two basic functions: on the one hand, to create and order the State institutions and the production of legal norms, and on the other, to lay down the limits of the exercise of power and the scope of fundamental rights as well as the aims and services that the public powers must carry out for the benefit of society. To guarantee its normative character and its hierarchical position above all other norms, various provisions are set out in the articles to this effect (such as the statement in Article 9 that the citizens and public powers are subject to the Constitution and the legal order as well as the repealing provision derogating the fundamental laws of the Franco regime and those 'provisions that are opposed to what is established in this Constitution'); it is endowed with strictness and the Constitutional Court, the 'supreme interpreter' of the Constitution (Article 1 of LOTC), was created.

II. A Final Constitution with a Complex Structure

43. Seen as a homogeneous whole, the Constitution is the founding norm of the system. However, when its content is broken down, one realizes that within it, there are a number of very heterogeneous norms (from the form of the national flag to consumers' rights, from the order of succession to the throne to the municipal quorum needed to exercise the right of autonomy, etc.), and its structure is diverse (proclamation of legal principles, orders to the legislator, citizens' rights), not to mention those that are drafted in vague and generic terms. Thus, its legal effect is not homogeneous and depends on many criteria, starting from the addressees of the constitutional mandates, while some norms have a specific addressee, not directly linked to citizens in general (Article 62: functions of the king; Article 134: the government's monopoly over the Budget, etc.) others are directed to all public powers and to all legal and physical persons who, for one reason or another, are subject to our legal system, whether or not they are Spanish (right to life, inviolability of residence, etc.). The most relevant effect of this difference in the constitutional norms according to whom they are addressed is that the application of the Constitution in the relationships between private persons is usually indirect, in accordance with what the law establishes, giving some leeway to those individuals who are not in public powers. For example, while a businessperson, by virtue of the freedom of contract, does not have to adopt a system that ensures equality of opportunity and the application of the principles of merit and capability in the selection of staff, public administrations do have to comply with these constitutional requirements (Articles 23 and 103 SC). But because certain constitutional articles do not apply to the relationship between individuals, this does not mean all others are excluded, particularly fundamental rights. So, following the same example of the businessperson and referring to real cases that the Constitutional Court has had to resolve, contractual freedom does not permit different salaries to be paid to men and women for the same work (it would violate Articles 14 and 35 SC on equality), trade union freedoms to be curtailed (Article 28 SC), liberty of expression to be limited (Article 20 SC), etc. (*see* paragraph 345).

44. The structure of the constitutional norms itself determines their legal efficacy. Within the Constitution, one can distinguish between 'closed' norms, which are precise orders (Article 3: Castilian is the official language of the State) and 'open' norms, incomplete norms that require subsequent specific development (Article 13: foreigners may enjoy public rights in the terms established by treaties and laws). Although designating a particular norm as one or the other is clearly a political decision taken by the constituent assembly when drawing up the Constitution, there are matters that, by the very nature of their content (such as economic regulations), cannot be frozen in the constitutional text if one wants to achieve a text able to respond to future social situations that the State will have to confront. A scale of openness can be established in which at one extreme are the norms of procedure and organization (the most closed) and at the opposite end, the empowering clauses and policy declarations, such as those that incorporate values (Article 1.1) and principles (Articles 9.3, 27.2, 103, 117.5, etc.) on which the legal system and the actions of public powers must be founded.

45. The inevitable generality of the open norms makes it difficult for them to be applied immediately and directly, leaving their specific normative effect to the legislator. This does not totally exclude the possibility of their being declared unconstitutional even for the breach of one of the four superior values of the legal system, liberty, justice, equality, and legal pluralism, as the Constitutional Court itself declared (STC 132/1989, 18 July, case *Cámaras Agrarias* and 16 June, case *Cámaras de Comercio-I*). However, the most relevant function of the values and principles is to ensure the Court gives a teleological interpretation of the Constitution since (in the Court's words) the Constitution establishes 'a system of values whose observance requires a final interpretation of the fundamental norm' (STC 18/1981, 8 June, case *Blanco v. Gobierno civil de Barcelona*).

46. However, although the specific effect of a given constitutional article depends on its development by the legislative power, its inactivity does not make the constitutional order disappear, especially in the case of fundamental rights, which always have a 'minimum content' that the public powers have to respect (*see* paragraph 350). Thus, the lack of a law for local television more than ten years after the approval of the Constitution cannot be used as an argument to close down such a transmitter because the legislator cannot defer *sine die* the regulation of these television stations beyond a reasonable period of time, since to do so would violate Article 20.1 that establishes the freedom of communication (STC 31/1994, 31 January, case *TV por cable*).

III. An Open Text: The Real Constitution

47. The text of the Spanish Constitution consists of 169 articles, 4 additional and 9 transitional clauses, and a repealing and a final provision: a total of 17,380 words. But in spite of this unusual length, anyone who wants to have an idea of the effectively valid Constitution in Spain must consider other texts that, thanks to their role in completing what is set out in the *Lex legum*, are often referred to as secondary constitutional norms. So, in the first place, the judgments of the Constitutional Court, where the interpretation of the constitutional articles binding on all public powers is settled (Article 5.1 LOPJ), must be borne in mind. Nor can we omit what are traditionally known in Spain as the political laws, the norms regulating public powers and fundamental rights, particularly those that make up the 'block of constitutionality', a concept used to refer to the totality of the norms consisting of the Constitution, the Autonomy Statutes, and other laws delimiting competences employed by the Constitutional Court to enable it to determine the compatibility of the rest of the laws with the Constitution (*see* paragraph 237). Equally, international treaties cannot be ignored, many of which nuance the scope of the mandates of the *Lex legum* and, above all, those referring to fundamental rights and public liberties, which are to be interpreted 'in conformity with the Universal Declaration of Human Rights (UDHR) and the international treaties and agreements on those matters ratified by Spain' (Article 10.2 SC). Finally, attention must be paid to the conduct itself of the political agents who, through their uses and customs, determine the meaning of not a few constitutional norms.

As we shall see in different parts of this book, Spain's adhesion to the EU has substantially affected many constitutional articles that have had to be reinterpreted in light of the Union's fundamental treaties, particularly in two of the characteristics which, since Bodino, are considered the essential features of a State: the legislative power and the capacity to issue money which against the literal tenor of Constitution the Spanish State no longer fully retains since it shares it with European institutions; however, neither Law originating in the Union nor derived from it has a place within these secondary constitutional norms, they are not – in the words of the Constitutional Court – a 'canon of constitutionality' of Spanish legislation, to the extent that the eventual breach of European norms by subsequent Spanish laws 'does not transform into constitutional litigation what is only a conflict of infra-constitutional norms that must be resolved in the ambit of ordinary jurisdiction' (STC 28/1991, 14 February, case *Elecciones al Parlamento Europeo*). However, the Constitutional Court itself has considered that it is up to it to 'ensure respect for the principle of the primacy of Union law' when a judge does not apply a European rule and prefers the Spanish rule because that judge makes an unreasonable and arbitrary selection of a rule applicable to the process, 'which gives rise to a violation of the right to effective judicial protection' (STC 31/2019, 28 February, case Ximena Gaiborquiroz).

§2. Amending the Constitution

I. General Questions

48. It does not seem necessary to give formal and substantial reasons to justify a special procedure, more complicated than that used for ordinary legislation, for the modification of the Constitution, the founding norm of the legal system. It is a way of guaranteeing both the superiority of the *Lex legum* as well as updating the social and political consensus by which it was created, so allowing the constitutional text to be adapted to new social realities. It is, however, advisable to stop for a moment to point out that when the Constitution is reformed, the new text incorporated in it has the same scope and legal force as the original text, but the author is not in the same position as the authors of the Constitution, while the original author is under no constraints, the reformer is. For this reason, while the first receives the name of the original constituent power, the second is called the constituted or derived constituent power.

49. Many Constitutions (German, Belgian, Italian, etc.) not only regulate the constituted constituent power by obliging it to follow a specific procedure but also prohibit the modification of some of the decisions taken by the original constituent power (federalism, the abolition of the death penalty, the Republic, etc.). The 1978 Spanish constituent power did not establish any clauses that could not be altered, perhaps influenced by the unhappy memory of Franco's Law of the Principles of the National Movement, which fixed those anti-democratic principles as 'permanent and unalterable'. However, two procedures for the reform of the Constitution were laid down, one ordinary and the other extraordinary, more strictly, for which a good number of articles have been reserved. The idea of distinguishing two parts, one relevant and the other secondary, each with its amendment procedure, is based on the distinction between fundamental political decisions (the social and democratic state under the rule of law, the parliamentary monarchy, the autonomous state) and the constitutional rules of development. Therefore, it is logical to give a concrete example that it is more complicated to abolish the right of nationalities to form an Autonomous Community (Article 2) than to modify the constitutional regulation of cooperation agreements (Article 145). However, the constituent power did not follow this logic, which would have led him to reserve a few articles (the preliminary title) for the extraordinary procedure but included quite a few more. Reading the constituent debates, one gets the impression that the extraordinary procedure, which did not exist in the preliminary draft, was created to reinforce the monarchy's protection. Be that as it may, what is certain is that it seems that the constituent power did not get it right either in the content reserved for the extraordinary procedure or in its regulation, which is excessively complicated and rigid.

50. Constitutional reform is regulated in the four articles that make up Title X of the Constitution and is basically a special form of legislative procedure, so anything not envisaged in the Constitution and the Parliamentary Regulations of Congress and Senate for the processing of reform proposals is governed by the ordinary legislative procedure. Our attention is called to the different bodies that can initiate a draft law; Article 166 only excludes citizens from initiating constitutional reform (it does it by the technique of remitting it to Subsections 1 and 2 of Article 87, omitting Subsection 3 that regulates popular legislative initiatives). This shows, rather clearly, a certain caution on the part of the constituent power (as we shall also have occasion to see with other articles) towards the direct participation of the citizens and a disproportionate preference for representative democracy and the political party State. Without a doubt, that caution was justified in 1978 by the concern that minority groups could demagogically use the techniques of direct participation against a democratic regime that was just taking its first steps. However, at the present time, the limitations on direct democracy established by the Constitution and the LORMR have little sense, and, possibly, this is one of the points of our constitutional system most in need of substantial reform.

51. The initiating of reform is the same for both procedures; the government, Congress, Senate, and the Assemblies of the Autonomous Communities all have the power to propose reform under either procedure. The government can exercise this initiative under the usual procedure for draft laws, which is to say the agreement of the Council of Ministers is needed, and the bill is then sent to Congress for its approval. In what seems to be a lacuna by the legislator, neither the Law on Government nor other applicable legislation establishes any additional requirement for the government to exercise the initiative of constitutional reform. Especially noteworthy is the silence of the Organic Law of the Council of State (LOCE) on this point since it requires the government to consult this body on a good number of draft bills on less important laws, although the government can always voluntarily submit any reform proposal to the Council for its opinion, given that Article 21.10 LOCE allows it to be consulted on 'affairs of State to which the government recognizes special transcendence or repercussion'. For many years (until 2019, to be precise; in 2021, it presented another draft again, but neither of the two was approved), the government did not exercise the initiative for the constitutional amendment. In 1992, when Article 13.2 was reformed, it was not opposed to the initiative from outside the parliamentary groups, which can be a good precedent for modifying Spain's Magna Carta; not in vain was the 1977 project drawn up by a committee made up of representatives of the main political forces, the government ceding its first proposal to present a bill. In my opinion, the custom of initiating any constitutional reform by common accord amongst the main parties would be a good way of increasing the symbolic value of the *Lex legum* as the norm of all parties and all citizens. Regrettably, the second reform of the Constitution carried out in the summer of 2011 was initiated by the proposal of PSOE and PP such that the other parties felt excluded and accused the two main parties of breaking the constitutional consensus.

52. For the Congress and the Senate (not individual members or groups) to exercise the initiative for reform that they possess, the Standing Orders of both Chambers demand, as in the case of the ordinary legislative initiative, that the proposal is put before each Chamber in a plenary session. However, the requirements to enable a reform proposal to go before the Chamber are more demanding than in the case of an ordinary legislative bill, while Congress's Standing Orders set out that draft bills can be adopted by the plenary on the initiative of one parliamentary group or fifteen deputies (Article 126), reform initiatives must be proposed by two groups or 'a fifth part of the deputies' (Article 146) which, with the present composition of 350 deputies, would require 75.[1] For its part, the Senate, for a reform proposal, demands the signatures of fifty senators who do not belong to the same parliamentary group (Article 152), when for an ordinary legislative initiative, twenty-five would be enough (Article 108). On the other hand, the Legislative Assemblies of the Autonomous Communities can request the government to adopt a bill for constitutional reform or present such a bill themselves before the Congress of Deputies, being able to send a delegation of up to three members to defend their initiative. Until the present, only four regional assemblies have used this initiative (Asturias, Navarre, the Balearic Islands and Valencia[2]). Both in the Assembly that takes the initiative and in Congress, the proposal is processed according to the regulatory rules of the ordinary legislative procedure.

53. Article 169 of the Constitution forbids the initiation of an amendment in a time of war or during the exceptional states of alarm, exception, and siege established by Article 116. A restriction of this type is more than reasonable because it is not desirable from any point of view to carry through reform in an abnormal moment as it could distort the conduct of the constitutional agents in the reform procedure. For this reason, most of the doctrine has considered, just as the draft Constitution provided, that it would have been necessary to also prohibit proceeding with and concluding the reform proposal should any of these exceptional situations arise. Personally, I cannot see the advantages of this total prohibition, not only because it would give an unscrupulous government a weapon – the proclamation of a state of emergency – to stop a reform that it did not like (an assumption of police fiction that could not happen in a State with parties) but because a mandate of this kind can have counter-productive effects, quite apart from the strict process of constitutional reform. Let us imagine, for example, that a constitutional amendment on

1. The present Standing Orders of Congress dates from 10 Feb. 1982. The previous Orders were provisional from 13 Oct. 1977, which, logically, did not establish anything about reform initiatives. This enabled a parliamentary group of only five deputies (of the Andalucista Group), in 1980, to present a reform initiative that was not considered (*see* BOCG, 11 Jul. 1980).
2. The Asturian initiative sought to improve the mechanisms of direct participation, so it proposed the amendment of Arts 87.3, 92 and 166 of the Constitution. The Parliament of Naverre presented two constitutional amendment proposals in the Thirteenth Legislature: one to guarantee the sustainability of pensions (Art. 50) and the other to establish secular education (suppression of Art. 27.3). The Balearic Islands proposal aimed to attribute a deputy to the island of Formentera (Art. 69.3), while the Valencian proposal was to reintegrate Valencian civil law (second additional provision). The Navarrese initiative expired in 2019 because the new parliament did not maintain it after its regional elections. The other three are still alive in the current Fourteenth Legislature, although they are pending inclusion on the agenda for consideration.

which all the parties are in agreement is initiated (as occurred in 1992 when the Constitution was modified to enable Spain to ratify the Union Treaty), and during its passage, a catastrophe or one of the reasons justifying a state of emergency happened in a particular province; would it be reasonable to delay unavoidably the passing of the proposed constitutional amendment even if it meant that Spain could not ratify the treaty in the stipulated period? As the Constitution does not peremptorily demand that a reform initiated in ordinary times shall continue in exceptional ones, it seems to me that the better solution to adopt is to leave it to the wisdom of the politicians to decide whether to paralyse or continue with the passing of the amendment, in the event that it was necessary to proclaim one of the exceptional states. Article 4.1 of the LORMR does indeed seem a prudent foresight: no referendum can be held, either constitutional or ordinary, in the territories where the state of emergency or siege had been declared, as well as in the ninety days after it has been lifted. Therefore, the referendums for reform will be held in the rest of the national territory, waiting to be held in those under the rights restrictions of those two states of exception.

II. The Ordinary Reform Procedure

54. The ordinary reform procedure is defined by exclusion, that is, all those articles not reserved for the extraordinary procedure. The most relevant feature of this procedure is that it demands a final vote on the whole constitutional reform bill that will only be passed if it receives the favourable votes of three-fifths of the members of each Chamber.[3] Very farsightedly, the Constitution foresaw the possibility that the text approved by the Senate was not the same as that passed by Congress, and in that eventuality, it orders a joint Commission, made up equally of deputies and senators, be set up to prepare only one text. Logically, if this common text cannot be drafted by the Commission, the reform proposal will be considered to have failed. If an agreement is reached, the resultant text will be presented for approval to the plenary sessions of each Chamber. If the new agreed text fails to get a quorum of three-fifths, the Constitution has envisaged yet a third possibility before declaring the amendment rejected: it can be passed, provided that it is approved by a simple majority in the Senate and by two-thirds in Congress. In light of how the parliament really works, with the members ruled by party discipline, it seems most unlikely that such a wide discrepancy between the Senate and Congress could occur, and even more so bearing in mind that the two major parties added together have always been enough to exceed the three-fifths quorum in both Chambers.

3. In the Fourteenth Legislature, which began in 2019, the Congress is composed of 350 deputies and the Senate of 265 senators, which means that 210 votes in favour are needed in the Congress and 159 in the Senate, respectively. As explained later in the text, these quorums are achieved by joint agreement between the PSOE (120 deputies and 114 senators) and the PP (90 and 100, respectively). Historically, the sum of these two parties also achieved a two-third quorum for the extraordinary procedure (233 for the lower chamber and 177 for the upper chamber), but this is no longer the case from the Twelfth Legislature onwards (in the Fourteenth, they are left with 208 deputies), while they do achieve it in the Senate (214 senators).

55. The ordinary reform procedure does not require the participation of the people to ratify the amendment approved by parliament, although if a tenth part of the members of Congress or the Senate demands a referendum within fifteen days, then the government is compelled to call it (Article 167.3 SC). Once the referendum has approved the amendment, or the fifteen-day period has expired, the king must give his assent. If a referendum has to be convoked, the government – the constitutional organ empowered to do it – must consider that it cannot be held during the existence of any of the states of emergency or siege or within ninety days after it has been lifted; if a referendum has been called and such a declaration is subsequently made, it will be suspended, and a new one must be convoked (Article 4.2 LORMR).

Until now, two constitutional reforms have been made, one to amend Article 13.2 SC (*see* paragraph 51) in 1992 and the other in 2011 to Article 135. While the first enjoyed wide support (it was passed unanimously by both Congress and the Senate), the second was much disputed by minority parties, by some for the manner – since they were excluded from the initiative – and by others for its contents, too.

They considered that limiting the debt ceiling constitutionally was a decision contrary to general interests and restricted the capacity for self-government of the Autonomous Communities.[4]

It is interesting to note that in March 2005, the government requested a report from the Council of State on the reform of four sections of the Constitution which the Council made in February 2006. The subsequent policy discarded this project of the PSOE, so much so that it abandoned it in its programme for the elections in March, and it has not tried to deal with it again in the parliament. However, I think it is necessary to record the four aspects that, according to the government, need to be reformed (some of which would have to be processed by the extraordinary reform procedure) because the majority of the doctrine agrees that these are aspects of the Constitution that have to be amended for improving our political system:

(1) The removal of male preference in succession to the throne.
(2) The incorporation of the European construction process into the Constitution.
(3) The inclusion of the denomination of the Autonomous Communities.
(4) The reform of the Senate.

III. The Extraordinary Reform Procedure

56. The extraordinary reform procedure is to be used when a total revision of the Constitution is proposed or is a partial revision affecting the Preliminary Title, Chapter II, Section IA of Title I (fundamental rights), or Title II (the Crown). This

4. In the Congress of the Deputies, 321 votes were cast of which 316 were in favour and 5 against (DSCD, No. 270, 2 Sep. 2011), while 236 senators voted of whom 233 were in favour and 3 against (DSS, No. 130, 7 Sep. 2011). It should be pointed out that only PSOE, PP, and UPN voted in favour; neither PNV nor CiU voted in either Chamber. IU demanded a referendum of ratification but failed to win a tenth of the signatures of the deputies, as required by the Constitution. For this reason, the king sanctioned and promulgated the Constitutional Reform on 27 Sep. 2011.

'topographical' way of defining the content of the extraordinary procedure has met with well-deserved criticism from the doctrine because while it may be logical to reserve this procedure for fundamental political decisions, such as the social and democratic State of Law (Article 1.1), parliamentary monarchy (Article 1.3), the same does not apply – to give but two examples of constitutional casuistry – to the setting-up of a register for associations (Article 52) or the incompatibilities of the king's tutors (Article 60.2). This is even more relevant when it is remembered that not included in this reserve are articles as important as Article 10, which founded the political order on the dignity of the person, and Article 168 itself, which establishes the extraordinary reform procedure. This lack of express mention is saved by a teleological interpretation of the constitutional text: without doubt, an intention to reform Article 10 or Article 168 'affects' the Preliminary Title, if not the entire Constitution, so that the extraordinary procedure would have to be used, above all, if what is intended is the simple revocation of the extraordinary procedure in order, in a second step, to reform the content it now protects.

57. The quorum demanded by the Constitution – in its rather confusing phrase, 'the principle shall be approved' – for reform is two-thirds in each Chamber. The Standing Orders of Congress and the Senate, quite logically, specify that this first decision shall be on a text with specific articles and not only on the decision to reform some of the articles protected by the extraordinary procedure. Once Congress and the Senate have approved the reform, the Constitution stipulates that both Chambers shall be automatically dissolved. The new parliament must ratify the reform decision for which, since both the Constitution and Standing Orders are silent on the matter, a simple majority must be assumed to suffice. Then the new text will be examined as an ordinary draft law (thereby giving a period of time for the presentation of amendments) with no other particular requirement than a final vote when again, a two-thirds majority is demanded. The text, so approved, has to be compulsorily submitted to a referendum; there is a reasonable restriction on when this can be held (not during a state of emergency or siege) that we saw for the optional referendum in the ordinary procedure. Once ratified, it only remains for the Royal assent and publication in the Official State Gazette (BOE) for it to be incorporated into the legal system.

58. The strictness and complexity of this extraordinary procedure do not facilitate constitutional reform and can even be a hindrance to the necessary adaptation of the 1978 Constitution to the changes in society. That said, I would like to clarify that perhaps we jurists have exaggerated the complication of this procedure, giving, at times, the sensation that it is almost insuperable. Nevertheless, its four essential elements (two decisions of two different parliaments by two-thirds majorities, the automatic dissolution of parliament and a referendum), while not easy, are not impossible to achieve. Until now, the two main parties have always easily gained the quorum of two-thirds, both in the Congress and the Senate, so that this requisite is no more difficult to get than in the ordinary procedure, above all, if it is borne in mind that, year after year, the ideological differences between the parties are diminishing. And given the basic agreement between the big parties, the referendum also is not an especially arduous obstacle as those held until the present demonstrate. The most complicated requirement of the extraordinary procedure, in my opinion, is the automatic dissolution of parliament because the fact of facing elections immediately after approving a constitutional reform could decisively condition the attitude of the parties and the individual deputies, who might even vote against it for fear of losing their seat. The solution to this problem could be to leave the reform process until the end of the legislature so that the automatic dissolution would coincide with that required at the end of the maximum term of four years for the life of a parliament.

59. Things being what they are, and looking at practical politics in Spain, the difficulty of reforming the Constitution lies not so much in the legal obstacles but rather in an aspect of our political culture, embodied in the revealing, if inelegant, phrase in common use in the political world: the fear of opening the constitutional 'melon', the fear that if a reform, however slight, is proposed, the consensus of 1978 will be lost. And that is not because it is thought that the main parties are no longer capable of reproducing that consensus but because it is feared that political groups with little representation in parliament but with considerable social support (especially the nationalists) want to introduce major changes in the constitutional text. Yet, if this fear leads to the indefinite postponement of any moderately important reform – like those referring to the Senate (*see* paragraph 116) that everyone thinks should be modified – in the end, it is doing little favour for the very Constitution it is intended to protect. Although it is true that the stability of the *Lex legum* is essential to foster the 'constitutional patriotism' of the citizens, avoiding the continuous changes that give the sensation of fragility to the basic foundations of the political community, it is also true that an excessive petrifaction of the text can lead to the slow decline of the capacity to develop in a similar direction to that of society. In particular, the Spanish Constitution is practically the only Constitution of the Member States of the EU that has no express declaration on membership of the Union (although since the 2011 amendment, Article 135 does mention it), which sometimes requires a certain amount of constitutional engineering to make both systems compatible.

Chapter 2. International Treaties

§1. Treaty-Making Power

60. According to the precise definition in the 1969 Vienna Convention on the Law of Treaties (VCLT), ratified by Spain in 1972, a treaty is an international agreement concluded between states in written form and governed by international law, whether embodied in a single instrument or in two or more related documents and whatever its particular designations are.[5] This feature of agreement, of a pact between two or more States, makes the treaty a source of law with a special nature that, to understand it, we can call it 'two-faced' since it is regulated both by international and internal law.

The conclusion of a treaty is a set of acts by which a State binds itself internationally and is usually divided into two phases: the negotiation or initial phase and the conclusion or final phase. International law does not expressly regulate the first phase, which is remitted to the internal law of each State, but the Spanish Constitution does not establish any specific regulation in this matter beyond prohibiting a popular initiative in international affairs (Article 87.3) and attributing the direction of foreign policy to the government (Article 97). With this constitutional cover, Article 5.1 of the Law on Government grants to the executive the monopoly over the negotiation of treaties, as has been the invariable custom in Spain. For its part, Article 11 of Law 25/2014, 27 November, *de Tratados y otros Acuerdos Internacionales* (International Treaties and Agreements, LTAI) specifies that the agreement will be made on a prior report of the Ministry of Foreign Affairs on 'the initiative of the ministers concerned'. However, there is nothing to prevent Congress and the Senate, by virtue of their power of initiative, from passing motions urging the government to open negotiations to make a treaty with a specific State or to adhere to an already-existent treaty.[6] In the same way, the government can inform the parliament about treaty negotiations before their conclusion, a practice that is becoming habitual in our parliament, especially in those treaties referring to the EU.

61. Article 149.1.3 of the Constitution declares that exterior relations are the exclusive competence of the State, and so the authority to conclude treaties (*ius*

5. The specialists in International Law have counted more than thirty terms used for these international agreements, which the Vienna Convention gathers together in one legal category of treaties: agreements, covenants, conventions, charters, declarations, Statutes, memorandum, protocols, etc. Our Constitution is more hesitant; in general, it appears to distinguish between 'treaties' and 'conventions', considering the former to have greater substantial content than the latter. Law 25/2014, 27 November, *de Tratados y otros Acuerdos Internacionales* (which execute treaties and are subject to International Law) and non-normative international agreements that neither constitute international obligations nor are governed by International Law.
6. If in the theoretical plane this possibility is perfectly logical, in the practical plane a motion of this type has never been approved because the parliamentary majority does not allow it. Therefore, the opposition prefers to use the questions to incite the Government to a certain external action. For example, in the Twelfth Legislature, the Government has been asked about the reasons why the ratification of Convention No. 188 of the International Labour Organization on work in fisheries in 2007, with a date scheduled for signature of the Convention of 13/1/2000 on International Protection of Adults, etc., has still not proceeded.

tractatum or 'treaty-making power') resides exclusively in the central government, and the Autonomous Communities can take no part in international affairs. However, all the Autonomy Statutes contain provisions relating both to the drafting phase of treaties as well as to their subsequent conclusion once they have been incorporated into the domestic system. Thus, the government has an obligation to inform the respective Executive Councils of the drawing up of international treaties and conventions that affect the sphere of autonomous competences (Article 20.5 EAPV, 196.1 EAC, etc.). Equally, most Statutes give their respective Executives the capacity to request the central government to conclude treaties or conventions with States with which the Community in question maintains particular cultural or historical links (Article 196.3 EAC, 35.3 EAG, 240.3.5 EAA, etc.). The LTAI has established similar laws that stipulate the government's obligation to inform the Autonomous Communities on the treaties which are included in any of these three types: (1) whose scope deals with autonomous matters, (2) or are of 'specific interest' of the Communities, or (3) especially affect its respective territorial ambit (Article 50). In these three cases, all the Communities have the right to request the government to open negotiations. It is not obliged to initiate the treaty requested but to resolve it 'with reasons' (Article 49).

The new Statutes passed in 2006 go one step further and permit their executive organs to request the central government to include autonomous representatives in the negotiating delegations (Article 196.2 EAC, Article 240.2 EAA, etc.); a possibility that the LTAI has extended to all the Communities with similar regulations that stop the opening of negotiations: The petition has to refer to one of the three types of treaties mentioned above, and the government will have to resolve its answer with reasons. Furthermore, these new Statutes authorize their communities to sign agreements with foreign public powers on matters within their competences but without being subject to the regime of international treaties (Article 195 EAC, Article 241 EAA, etc.). The LTAI calls them 'non-normative international agreements' and demands that Communities remit them to the Ministry of Foreign Affairs before signing them so that it can check that they are using the most appropriate legal source according to international law.

62. Once the representatives of the negotiating States have agreed to a text, through its signature '*ad referendum*' (Article 12 VCLT), the second phase of treaty-making begins the conclusion, which in turn has two stages: the manifestation of the will of each state (which is governed by the internal system) and the external conclusion, by means of one or other of the forms recognized by the Vienna Convention: exchange of instruments, ratification, accession, (Articles 13–15 VCLT), etc. Logically enough, in view of its negotiating capacity, the government is in charge of bringing about the culmination of this process, although the formal expression of the State's willingness to be bound internationally by treaties is made by the king (Article 63.2 CE). To reach this stage, the Constitution establishes three different procedures based on the position that parliament takes in each of them (that the LTAI details), the more important the pact, the bigger parliament's role:

(1) Article 93 sets out that 'by means of an organic law, authorization may be established for the conclusion of treaties which attribute to an international

organization or institution the exercise of competences derived from the Constitution'. This article, basically designed for Spain's integration into what was then the European Community (EC), is an 'open' clause of the Constitution in that it allows the attributions of Spanish institutions (whether central or autonomous) to be significantly altered without modifying the constitutional text. In this way, its effect is very similar to a constitutional reform, transferring the exercise of sovereignty to supranational organizations, as is, in fact, being done with the successive ratification of EU treaties.[7] For this reason, it would not have been too much to demand, instead of a simple majority vote in Congress (required for the approval of an organic law), if a quorum similar to that needed for constitutional reform had been established, as with the constitutional bill proposed and is usual in other European constitutions for similar precepts. Until now, however, the authorizations granted by Article 93 have been practically unanimous. Thus, Article 93 was used for the first time in 1985 to pass Organic Law 10/1985, 2 August, to authorize Spain's adhesion to the EC; subsequently, it has been used some dozen times to pass treaties on Community questions and once at the world level, the Statute creating the International Criminal Court (Organic Law 6/2000 and 5/2014). All these organic laws are limited to ratifying the treaty in question and are, therefore, laws for one case alone and only used once (*see* paragraph 66). The only law that does not follow this model is Organic Law 1/2008, 30 July, authorizing the ratification of the Lisbon Treaty, whose second article declares, 'according with the provisions of Paragraph 2 of Article 10 of the Spanish Constitution and in Section 8 of Article 1 of the Lisbon Treaty, norms relating to fundamental rights and freedoms set out in the Constitution shall be interpreted according to the provisions in the Charter of Fundamental Rights', whose integral text the Law reproduces. From a strictly technical point of view, the constitutionality of this article is very doubtful since it is a norm whose only purpose is to interpret the Constitution, a function that laws cannot perform, as the Constitutional Court declared in its famous judgment 76/1983.

(2) Article 94 demands parliament's previous authorization for a good number of treaties, either to control the government's foreign policy or to guarantee legislative competences:

7. Many examples can be given of how the union treaties have affected the substantial content of the Constitution, but as we are speaking of treaties it seems that the most appropriate should be about them. As the organs of the European Treaty have the capacity to negotiate treaties that bind its Member States directly (Art. 37 TEU and Arts 207 and 217 TFEU), both parliament and the government suffer a reduction in their ability to participate in the conclusion of international treaties, without a comma of the Constitution having been changed, simply because of Spain's accession to the Union's integration of treaties in the Spanish legal system. For example, the Agreement between the USA and the EU, on 2 Jun. 2016, on the protection of personal information relating to the prevention, investigation, detection, and prosecution of criminal offences. Moreover, mixed Agreements may be signed that need the backing of Member States (but not their direct participation in the negotiations) to include matters on which the EU does not have exclusive competence; examples of these new generation agreements are the Free Trade Agreement between the EU and its Member States, of the one part, and the Republic of Singapore, of the other part, on 20 Sep. 2013 and the Strategic Partnership Agreement (SPA) between the EU and its Member States of the one part, and Canada of the other part, on 30 Oct. 2016.

(a) Treaties of a political nature.
(b) Treaties or agreements of a military nature.
(c) Treaties or agreements that affect the territorial integrity of the state or the fundamental rights and duties laid down in Title I.
(d) Treaties or agreements that involve important financial obligations for the public treasury.
(e) Treaties or agreements that involve modification or repeal of any law or require legislative measures for their execution.

This authorization does not need, as with Article 93, to be embodied in a formal law but rather requires the express consent of the Chambers; moreover, the Constitutional Court has expressly rejected that this can be done by a Decree-law or even by a Law, but only by the express procedure established by Parliamentary Standing Orders (STC 155/2005, 9 June, case *Decreto-ley sobre FMI*). Congress's Standing Orders determine that the government's request to ratify a treaty must be answered in a period of sixty days and must comment both on the proposed treaty itself and on the formulation of reservations and declarations should the government propose any. The deputies cannot make any amendments to the text of the treaty, but they can do so with the reservations and declarations (Articles 155–156 RCD). The time limits and procedures are similar in the Senate (Articles 144–146 RS), envisaging that in the case of discrepancies between the two Chambers on the terms of the authorization – something that still has not happened even once – a mixed Commission will be set up that will present a text to the plenary sessions of Congress and the Senate; if it is not approved, Congress shall decide by an absolute majority (Articles 158 RCD and 145 RS). In practice, discrepancies between the Congress and the Senate have never occurred. Even the discrepancy between the major parties when ratifying a treaty has been minimal, such that the processing of the authorization has usually been without difficulties and with the support of almost all members of both Chambers. The only important exception was the ratification of the Treaty of adhesion to NATO that was proposed by the Government of Calvo Sotelo in 1981 and was opposed by the PSOE in favour of a prior referendum.

(3) Other treaties and agreements do not need particular authorization from the parliament, but the Constitution demands that they be informed immediately of their conclusion (Article 94.2 SC). Examples of treaties recently ratified by the government only are the Agreement on Air Transport between the Kingdom of Spain and the Dominican Republic, done in Madrid on 21 January 2022, and the Agreement between the Kingdom of Spain and the United Nations for the organization of the Meeting on Dark and Silent Skies, done in Vienna on 26 July 2021.

§2. The Integration of Treaties in the Spanish Legal System

63. According to the Vienna Convention, a treaty enters into force when and how the negotiating states decide and, in the absence of this provision, it does so as soon as consent to be bound by it has been established for all states (Article 24

VCLT). Therefore, give or take some obvious differences, it has the normal effect of contracts that bind parties from when consent is given. But to bind third parties, as here the citizens and other public powers of a specified State, an internal acceptance of this international agreement is needed, which, in Spain's case, is simply its official publication (Articles 96.1 SC and 23 LTAI). The nature of the agreed norm, similar to a contract, explains another characteristic of treaties: they cannot be unilaterally revoked or modified but only by common accord between the parties. Thus (and totally in compliance with Article 42 VCLT), the Constitution establishes that the provisions of treaties 'may only be abolished, modified or suspended in the form provided for in the treaties themselves or in accordance with the general norms of international law' (Article 96.1 SC, which literally repeats Article 28.1 LTAI). So, a treaty can repeal or modify a previous law but cannot be modified by a subsequent one; it has a 'formal passive force' resistant to law, not even if it has been authorized by parliament since there is no difference between treaties according to the internal procedure adopted to process the formation of the will of the State. It is a much-discussed question as to whether subsequent laws mean that the treaty is a hierarchically higher source of law. In my opinion, this force does not come from what may be called a source hierarchically superior to law and other State norms but from its nature as a convention and its belonging to the international legal system. Of course, the LTAI has avoided expressing that resistance alluding to the hierarchy: 'The legal norms contained in international treaties validly made and officially published shall prevail over any other norm of the internal legal system in case of conflict with them, except norms of constitutional effect' (Article 36).

64. Another contentious issue is determining who is responsible for controlling whether a subsequent Spanish law is contrary to an international treaty in force for Spain. The Constitutional Court has been stating forcefully that, in principle, it is not responsible for this control of conventionality: 'The possible contradiction between the internal regulation and the international conventions and treaties ratified by Spain does not in itself determine any constitutional violation; it is a judgement of applicability that belongs to the sphere of ordinary legality' (STC 118/2019, 6 October, case *Artículo 52d del Estatuto de los Trabajadores*). In other words, any antinomy between an international treaty and a national law must be resolved by the ordinary jurisdiction because it is a problem of selection of norms applicable to a specific case. However, as the right to effective judicial protection includes the right of citizens to be judged with valid norms (*see* paragraph 414), it cannot be ruled out that the Constitutional Court may end up analysing an antinomy between a treaty and a national law using an Amparo appeal, as it is up to the Constitutional Court – as guarantor of Article 24. 1 EC – to verify 'that the basis of the judicial decision is the non-arbitrary or unreasonable application of the norms considered appropriate to the case' (STC 140/2018, 20 *December*, case *Derogación de la jurisdicción universal*).

65. However, the Constitution does demonstrate its superior hierarchy since it demands that in order to conclude a treaty containing stipulations contrary to its provisions, it has first to be reformed (Article 95.1 SC). With this in mind, Article 95 itself establishes that the government or either Chamber may request the Constitutional Court to declare whether or not such a contradiction exists (*see* paragraph 200). So far, this has only been used twice, once to ratify the Maastricht Treaty (1992) and on the other occasion, the Rome-II Treaty (2004).[8] Moreover, the Spanish Constitution, unlike others (Article 60 of the Dutch Constitution, for example), does not exclude the subsequent control of treaties, a possibility expressly recognized in Article 27 LOTC. For this reason, the possibility cannot be ruled out that a treaty ratified by Spain and valid under international law is considered unconstitutional by the Constitutional Court, either because it contains some provision contrary to the constitutional mandate or it has been ratified without following the procedure laid down in the *Lex legum*. In this event, although no such case has yet occurred, the state would have an international responsibility as the Vienna Convention establishes that States cannot adduce the fact that its internal law prohibits the application of the treaties beyond asking that its ratification be nullified when the consent of a State to be bound internationally was made in manifest violation of and concerned a fundamentally important rule of its internal law (Article 46 VCLT). Precisely, in the case mentioned above, STC 155/2005, 9 June, case *Decreto-Ley sobre FMI* (*see* paragraph 62), which is the only case where the Constitutional Court has had to analyse the constitutionality of the authorization to ratify a treaty, the Court was careful to assert that declaring the unconstitutionality of the Decree-law and the Law was sufficient 'without needing to add a phrase repealing it that would result in the revision of an unassailable international commitment from the perspective of the Law of Treaties' (FJ 10).

8. In its Declaration 1/1 July 1992, the Constitutional Court determined that in order to ratify the Union Treaty it was necessary to previously modify Art. 13.2 of the Constitution, since this gave foreigners the right only to vote in municipal elections, while the treaty also gave them the right to be candidates in these elections (passive suffrage). As a result, Art. 13.2 was reformed in the summer of 1992. On the contrary, in Declaration 1/2004, 13 December, the Constitutional Court held, (with three dissenting votes) no change was necessary in the Spanish Constitution in order to ratify Treaty establishing a Constitution for Europe (TeCE).

Chapter 3. Legislation

§1. Types of Legislation

66. According to Rousseau, law is an expression of the general will in two senses, in that it is the common will of all the people and that its content is addressed to all citizens. Thus, law, as a legal category in the liberal European State, has three distinctive features: it is drawn up through a free debate of the nation's representatives; its content is general and abstract; and it binds all the powers of the state and its citizens. Law, manifestation of the popular will, occupied the place immediately below the Constitution and above the system of parliamentary regulations, the law made by the government, but with an important difference; while the courts could control the validity of regulations, checking their compatibility to superior norms, there existed no legal control over laws, since these came directly from the only institution with a direct legitimation from the national sovereign, parliament.

The growing political and social complexity of present-day society has brought about a profound transformation of this concept of law and its three essential characteristics, and this is precisely reflected in the Spanish constitutional system. Thus, parliament no longer monopolizes the production of laws, for the executive can, simply by satisfying a number of requirements, pass norms with the status of law (Decree-laws and Legislative Decrees). Furthermore, Spain has become a compound state, which means that its seventeen Autonomous Communities can pass norms with that same status (all their parliaments can approve laws and most of their Governing Councils Legislative Decrees). On the other hand, although the great majority of laws are still norms of general application, it is not rare to find 'single' laws or those for 'one case', which, instead of regulating typical and general situations, are adopted to deal with specific and singular situations; therefore, they have very specific addressees and are passed to be applied only once (granting an extraordinary pension, sale of a particular public asset, expropriation of private goods, etc.) (*see* paragraph 68). The last feature of law, its capacity to impose itself on all public powers, now has two important qualifications: there exists a mechanism to ensure its effective submission to the Constitution, namely the Constitutional Court, and public powers must interpret the laws in accordance with the *Lex legum.* This subordination of law to the Constitution does not imply that law is limited to developing the norms decided by the constituent assembly, as happens with regulations in relation to laws, but that the political decisions of the law are formally and materially limited by the constitutional norms. Thus, it can be said that in the social and democratic State of Law, the 'Rule of Law' has been substituted by the 'Rule of the Constitution and Law'. And moreover, we may add a third nuance to the force of law: as Spain belongs to the EU, the judges may fail to apply a Spanish law in force if they consider it contrary to the European legal system (principle of primacy of European law), either directly or after presenting a 'pretrial question' before the Court of Justice of European Union (Article 267 TFEU) to confirm or reject whether or not that incompatibility exists, a matter that technically is done 'through Court order, after previously hearing the parties' (Article 4*bis* of LOPJ, introduced by Organic Law 7/2015).[9]

67. The variety of norms with the status of law in the Spanish legal order does not end with the diversity of its centres of production – parliament, the Autonomous Parliaments, the national government, and the Governing Councils of the Autonomies – but extends to the law itself emanating from the national parliament, since the Constitution creates several classes of laws: organic law, harmonization law, basic law, etc. The democratic-liberal tradition of one legislative procedure for one type of law is substituted by a plurality of laws produced by various procedures and with varying content:

– Ordinary procedure: Law.
– Shortened procedure: Law of Commission, Law, approved in one reading, urgently processed Law.
– Special procedure: Autonomy Statute, organic law, the Budget, harmonization law, framework law, law transferring competences.

The difference between the abbreviated and the special procedures is that the former does not create a special type of law, as shown by the fact that when it is published, there is no indication in the title as to the form in which it was processed, while this does occur with laws processed by the special procedure, and even more so with organic laws, which have a different numbering system from the rest of the laws. While the decision to use the abbreviated procedure is one that parliament can take freely, it is obliged to use the special procedure when it intends to regulate certain matters. Thus, the organic law must be voted on entirely in a plenary session of the Congress of Deputies (Article 81), the Budgets are passed by a special procedure that limits the deputies' power to make amendments (Article 134), and the law harmonizing the norms of the Autonomous Communities requires parliament to evaluate that necessity previously (Article 150), etc.

I. Ordinary Law

68. The Preamble to the Spanish Constitution refers to law as the 'expression of the popular will', which is manifested in Article 66 in the grant of legislative power to parliament and in the possibility given by several articles of Title VIII for

9. To be precise, for the national court to stop applying the internal law and not have to present the question it is necessary that the theory of the clear act is applicable: 'when the correct application of Community law can be imposed with such evidence that it does not give rise to any reasonable doubt about the solution to the question raised' (JCJCE 6 Oct. 1982, case *CILFIT*). Possibly the most famous preliminary rulings in Spain are both related to evictions in which it has been ruled that certain articles of the Spanish laws were incompatible with the European standards of consumer protection: the JCJEU, 14 Mar. 2013, case *Mohamed Aziz* and the JCJEU, 17 Jul. 2014, case *Sánchez Morcillo*. A case in which the Supreme Court failed to apply a Spanish law as it is contrary to European law is the STS (3) 807/2015, 10 February, which declares inapplicable the subsection 'and there are modules in the centre that guarantee unity and family privacy "of Article 62 bis 1.i) of the Organic Law 4/2000" given its contradiction with Article 17.2 of the Return Directive'.

Autonomous Statutes to create Legislative Assemblies with identical power. The Constitution demands no material requisite to define law, nor does it exclude the regulation of any social ambit (as does the 1958 French Constitution), and so its definition is purely formal: the norm passed by parliament.

Therefore, parliament can regulate, by law, any matter and in detail it considers necessary, 'in such a way that within the framework of the Constitution and respecting its specific limitations, the law may have in the Spanish legal system any content and in no way is the regulation of matters previously attributed to the regulatory power forbidden' (STC 73/2000, 14 March, case *Ley Foral 9/1996, de Espacios Naturales Protegidos de Navarra*). Although in a compound State such as Spain, the matters reserved to the Autonomous Communities must be very much borne in mind, for if parliament finds no constitutional limit to the government's power to make regulations, it will find it in the normative capacity of the Communities. The legislative power has yet another limit in the case of single laws: the law can only contain provisions typical of the executive power – such as a specific expropriation or the approval of a town planning scheme – if they are not discriminatory, if the case to be regulated is so complex that it cannot be dealt with correctly by the executive power and 'if it does not condition or impede the exercise of fundamental rights that are matters reserved to the general laws' (STC 203/2013, 5 December, case *Ley de Castilla y León 6/2007, de aprobación del proyecto 'Ciudad del Medio Ambiente'*).

II. Organic Law

69. Historically in Spain, the term 'organic law' had been used to denominate laws that regulate public institutions, such as the 1882 Organic Law of Judicial Power, the 1940 Organic Law of Industrial Tribunals, etc. but with no essential difference from the other laws. Article 81 of the Constitution re-adopted this term, but it was inspired by the French Constitution to establish a type of law characterized by two requisites:

(1) Its material ambit is limited to the regulation of fundamental rights, the approval of Autonomy Statutes and of the general election system as well as those established in other constitutional articles. Most of these matters reserved to organic law relate to State institutions: bases of the military organization (Article 8), order of succession to the Crown (Article 57), Council of State (Article 107), etc.

(2) Its procedure requires a final vote in Congress where the quorum must exceed the absolute majority of its members (176 out of a total of 350 in the present Congress). There is no special procedure for this law in the Senate beyond the general limitations imposed by the Constitution itself, namely, laws that have to be passed in plenary sessions that cannot be delegated to Commissions (Article 75) or to the government (Article 82) and from whose initiation citizens are excluded (Article 87.3).

70. The constituent assembly's aim in establishing organic laws was to ensure that the consensus amongst the parties was maintained in the matters it considered of greatest importance. So, it was thought that an absolute majority in Congress would be enough since, in 1977, it was strongly believed that the system of proportional representation for the election of Congress (*see* paragraph 120) would avoid absolute majorities, which has not been borne out in subsequent elections. Moreover, the political dynamic itself has resulted in the final vote on the text of many organic laws serving not so much to show consensus as to highlight different political positions. From the legal perspective, a norm without historical roots and not always well defined in the Constitution cannot fail to provoke a broad controversy about its legal regime, which was finally determined by the decisions of the Constitutional Court. The most relevant aspect of this jurisprudence is what we can call a strict interpretation of the organic law based on the fact that the procedure for its approval is an exception to the general principle of the simple majority that habitually governs in any other collegiate organ. This strict vision of organic law is maintained in three important requirements:

- Its content has to be only that fixed by the Constitution, as parliament cannot regulate other matters by it except those 'links' that the legislator can include 'by reason of their thematic connection or for the systemization of good legislative policy' (STC 5/1981, 13 February, case *Estatuto de Centros*).
- Matters reserved to the organic law must be interpreted restrictively; in particular, it must be understood that the reference in Article 81 to the 'development of fundamental rights and public liberties' does not mean that all legislation relative to Title I of the Constitution ('Basic Rights and Duties', Articles 10–55) is reserved to the organic law but only those referring to the first section of its Chapter II ('Basic rights and Public Liberties', Articles 15–29). But as these matters introduced in an Organic Law are not, strictly speaking, matters reserved to an organic law, in practice, a final provision has been imposed in most cases. This provision is entitled 'character' or 'nature' of the law, which specifies which articles are organic (and therefore can only be modified by an organic law) and which are not; logically, these last can be modified in the future by the ordinary law.
- Equally, the concept of 'development' of fundamental rights has to be understood strictly as the express regulation of a fundamental right and not of any norm that may have some bearing on a fundamental right. These limitations of the organic law reserve mean, to mention two real cases, that the ordinary state legislator can regulate a fundamental right in a specific case in which it is regulating another matter, such as the request for asylum (STC 53/2002, 27 February, case Modificación de la Ley de Asilo) or that the autonomous legislator can approve a law on associations whose activity is restricted to the territory of the Autonomous Community (STC 173/1998, 23 July, case *Ley vasca de asociaciones*). It is necessary to point out the great importance of this in an Autonomous State where only parliament can pass organic laws since if it had been understood that any legal provision on a fundamental right would require an organic law, it would have virtually deprived the Autonomous Communities of legislative competence.

71. Article 81 of the Constitution indicates that the Autonomy Statutes shall be approved by an organic law. Subsequently, in Title VIII, certain matters are reserved (name, organization, competences, etc., Articles 147 and 152). Moreover, the first Statutes included other norms not expressly mentioned by the Constitution, such as establishing the aims of public authorities. In the *Neo-Autonomous State*, beginning after the 2006 reforms, the Statutes have broadened their content, even setting out a catalogue of rights, doctrinally a very arguable decision, but which has been endorsed by the Constitutional Court (STC 247/2007, 12 December, case *Reforma del Estatuto de Autonomía de la Comunidad Valenciana,* and STC 31/2010, 28 June, case *Reforma del Estatuto de Autonomía para Cataluña).* The Constitution establishes two procedures for their drafting in which the will of parliament does not have the same degree of autonomy as in other organic laws. This is true, above all, when it is a question of using the special procedure of Article 151; in this, the Statute proposes that an assembly, made up of all the deputies and senators from the territorial areas that are going to be integrated into the Community, shall send the draft Statute to the Constitutional Commission of Congress which, within a period of two months, shall approve it by common agreement with the assistance of a delegation of the assembly. Subsequently, the agreed text shall be submitted to a referendum of the electoral corps of the province concerned, which is also required for their reform. This rigidity is the main explanation of the paradox, that of the four Statutes drawn up under this special procedure (the Basque Country, Catalonia, Galicia, and Andalusia), none has ever been amended, while those of the other thirteen, and even the Constitution itself, have been (in order to increase the degree of self-government).

III. The Legislative Decree

72. Article 82 of the Constitution allows the parliament to delegate its legislative capacity to the government so that norms with the force of law, called Legislative Decrees, can be passed. The Constitution has hedged this delegation around with a great number of precautions: it must be an express form for a concrete matter and for a specified term, matters reserved to organic law cannot be delegated, parliament can establish formulas to control the use the government makes of that delegation, etc. This article refers to two forms of delegation: (a) for the formation of an articled text, in which case the delegation must be granted by means of a basic law that must delimit precisely the aims and principles that the government shall follow; (b) to consolidate legal texts, which can be authorized through an ordinary law and that permits the government to clarify and harmonize the texts that are going to be consolidated. The first form of delegation, by means of a law of bases, attributes sufficient legislative capacity to the government, which is why it is used very rarely, to the extent that its lack of use has become a custom that has implicitly repealed the subsection of Article 82.1 referred to in it.[10] On the contrary, the delegation to consolidate legal texts distorts parliamentary democracy less since, in that

10. In the first years of the democracy, several base laws were approved, possibly because of a technical inertia left over from the Franco regime and for the exceptional situation of Spain's incorporation in

case, the function of the government is not so much to create law as to clarify it, which finds a theoretical basis in legal certainty. Even so, it is still an intrusion into the legislative power, so its use should be constrained, as it is in British constitutionalism where these delegations are known as *Henry VIII clauses,* highlighting in this way that their historical origin is due to the will of a king to cut parliament's powers. On the other hand, the Constitutional Court has held that the task of consolidation carried out by the government innovates law in that the government can create 'norms that are complementary to those that are the subject of the consolidation with the aim of filling lacunae, and in any case, to make them fit to carry out a technical clarification of the legal texts to be consolidated, clarifying and harmonizing precepts and eliminating contradictions and antinomies detected in the earlier regulation, so achieving that the consolidated text is consistent and systematic' (STC 166/2007, 4 July, case *Texto refundido de la Ley de Propiedad Intelectual*). So, this delegation is normally employed to recast texts of a certain technical complexity that have been much modified over the years, for example, Royal Legislative Decree 1/2001 approving the consolidated text of the Law on Water; Royal Legislative Decree 1/2013 approving the consolidated text of the Law of Rights of Persons with Disabilities; Royal Legislative Decree 3/2015 approving the consolidated text of the Law of Work; etc. The paradox is that those Legislative Decrees are again amended by other laws, and so legislative stability for which these legal norms were used does not last too long, to the extent that in 2014 parliament again authorized the government to consolidate three of these frequently amended Legislative Decrees, namely the General law of Social Security, the Law of Work, and the Land Law.[11]

73. As the Legislative Decree is a norm with the force of law, the Constitutional Court has the responsibility of ensuring its compliance with the Constitution, both in its material aspect and its normative content, as in the formal, that it satisfies the terms of the delegation. In addition to this control, the Contentious-Administrative Jurisdiction Law of 29/1998 also allows ordinary courts to control Legislative Decrees 'when they exceed the limits of the delegation' (Article 1). This has rightly been criticized by the doctrine since it creates a dual system of Legislative Decrees that not only breaks the Constitutional Court's monopoly over norms with the force of law but can also give rise to contradictory solutions to problems for which the legal system provides no answer. So, for example, in the case where the government is thought to have exceeded its delegation in an ordinary process but in a constitutional process, the Constitutional Court considers that such excess has not occurred; it is not ultra vires. In any case, if a law modifies a Legislative Decree –

the European Community (Law 47/1985, 27 December, *de Bases de delegación al Gobierno para aplicación del Derecho de las Comunidades Europeas*) but since 1989 when *Ley de Bases de Tráfico, Circulación de Vehículos a Motor y Seguridad Vial* were approved no new laws have been passed.

11. The authorization granted by Law 20/2014, 29 October, which delegated to the government the power to issue several consolidated texts, under what was established in Art. 82 and following of the Spanish Constitution. This law is the first law whose only content is, as its name implies, an authorization to the government to issue no less than eight Legislative Decrees in a year.

in practice very common, given legislative inflation – in no instance will it be submitted to the limits of delegation since it is a law directly amended by parliament, although intended to change the content of a Legislative Decree. Therefore, the control of that new law is the sole responsibility of the Constitutional Court, as the Supreme Court itself had occasion to remark in its judgment STS (3) 2158/2012, 28 March.

IV. Decree-Law

74. The Decree-law is the government's most important weapon of legislative power since in order to pass this norm with the force of law, it needs no previous authorization from parliament but only that the government itself considers that a state of 'extraordinary and urgent necessity' exists (Article 86), a decision that the Constitutional has considered an act of political direction in which the government enjoys a wide margin of appreciation. For this reason, for many years, the Constitutional Court admitted with a certain facility the existence of an emergency, particularly in the economic field, if it was possible to consider that it was a question of acting in what it itself calls 'problematic economic times'. However, in STC 68/2007, 28 March, case *Real Decreto-law 5/2002, de* medidas *urgentes para la reforma del sistem de protección por desempleo,* the Constitutional Court made a detailed analysis of the arguments put forward by the government to justify the urgency, rejecting them as being theoretical and abstract, such that for the first in its history, it declared a Decree-law to be unconstitutional because it did not see 'the enabling condition' of urgency for its approval. This line of the Constitutional Court allowing it to have greater control over the government has led it to declare unconstitutional Decree-laws in which urgency could not be justified either directly or indirectly, such as Decree-law 4/2000 on economic liberalization (STC 137/2011, 14 September) and Decree-law 10/2014, granting extraordinary credits to various ministries (STC 126/2016, 7 July). Without renouncing that (kind of) control of the extraordinary and urgent necessity to avoid an 'abusive or arbitrary use', the Constitutional Court has considered that the government has fully justified that enabling presupposition in a good number of Decree-laws issued since 2008 to struggle against the great recession, which has validated doctrinal criticism, beginning with several dissenting votes of some of the judges.[12] Urgency justifies that the Decree-laws come into force immediately, although they are 'provisional legislative regulations' until the Congress of Deputies – not the Senate – validates or revokes them within a period of thirty days. Validation (which, until now, the present Congress has almost always conceded) does not transform the Decree-law into a formal law but simply removes the 'stigma' of provisional nature with which it was approved

12. For example, the judgments SSTC 170/2012, 4 October; 233/2012, 13 December; 12/2015, 5 February; and 48/2015, 5 March and its dissenting votes. It is considered that the lack of extraordinary and urgent necessity in STC 211/2015, 8 October, case *Artículo 124 del Real Decreto-ley 8/2014, de aprobación de medidas urgentes para el crecimiento, la competitividad y la eficiencia.* In the doctrine, cf. Manuel Aragón Reyes, *Uso y abuso del decreto-ley. Una propuesta de reforma constitucional* (Madrid: Iustel, 2016). My personal opinion is set out in Agustín Ruiz Robledo, 'Sin luz y sin taquígrafos', *Anuario Joly Andalucía 2013*, Sevilla, 2013, 45 and 46.

by the government and makes it permanent. For my part, I would add another symbolic test to the evident test that a norm not passed by the Senate cannot be law: that the agreements of validation are published in the BOE with the signature of the President of Congress, but not that of the king. The consequence of not transforming it into law means that material limits of Decree-laws affect those Decrees both before and after their validation. The Constitution also permits Decree-laws to be processed within a period of thirty days as draft laws by the emergency procedure. Although the wording of Article 86.3 seems to provide an alternative decision (Congress can either validate the Decree-law or process it as a draft), the truth is that Congress's Standing Orders have interpreted it as a decision subsequent to validation: after this, Congress decides whether, additionally, to process it as a draft law, which would give rise to a distinct text, since, then, it would be a formal law passed by parliament.

75. The Constitution prohibits the use of the Decree-law for a broad group of matters that 'may not affect' the system of the basic institutions of the State; the rights, duties, and liberties of the citizens regulated by Title I; the regime of the Autonomous Communities; or the general electoral law. As with the empowering assumption of extraordinary and urgent necessity, the Constitutional Court has interpreted these restrictions in favour of the government, thus avoiding the need to consider whether a Decree-law exercises any influence in a forbidden sphere (e.g., a constitutional right) that would result in unconstitutionality. By acting in this way – as the Court itself admits – it maintains a balanced position that avoids extreme conceptions, such that 'the restrictive clause of Article 86.1 of the Constitution must be understood in such a way as not to reduce the Decree-law to nothing, since it is a normative instrument envisaged by the Constitution, yet not to allow it to regulate the general regime of the rights, duties and liberties of Title I'. (STC 100/2012, 8 May, case *Prórroga de la Tarifa Especial del Arbitrio Insular Canario* por *el Decreto-ley 7/1993*). Amongst the most striking cases in which the Constitutional Court has considered that the government exceeded its powers and regulated a matter prohibited by Article 86 is the self-authorization by Decree-law to ratify a treaty, to which we have already referred (*see* paragraph 62) and the fiscal amnesty that established the First Additional Provision of Decree-law 12/2012, 30 March, which according to the Constitutional Court could affect the duty of contributing taxes because it altered two 'basic pieces of the tax system', the personal obligation to pay and that of businesses (STC 73/2017, 8 June, case *Amnistía fiscal*). This prohibition against regulating by decree-law the essential elements of taxes, reserved to formal law, has led the Constitutional Court to declare the unconstitutionality of increasing corporate tax instalments by decree-law, a decision taken by the popular government in 2016, but which was not appealed by any political party, but was the subject of a question of unconstitutionality (STC 78/2020, 1 July, case *Decreto-ley 2/2016 por el que se introducen medidas tributarias*).

V. Autonomous Law

76. The seventeen Spanish Autonomous Communities can pass general norms with the status of law, with identical legal validity to State Laws, and so autonomous laws can be defined as abstract, general legal orders binding on citizens, public administrations, and the courts that can only be removed from the legal system by a decision of the Constitutional Court and are as fit as State laws to meet the reserves of law established by the Constitution. The main difference between the two types of laws lies in the strong limitation imposed by the principle of territoriality on the autonomous legal systems preventing them from regulating matters situated outside their territory as such regulations would have extra-territorial effect. However, from its first judgments, the Constitutional Court has avoided declaring as contrary to the Constitution autonomous norms that can have effects outside their territory because that 'would necessarily be equivalent to depriving them, purely and simply, of all their capacity of action' (STC 37/1981, 16 November, case *Centros de Contratación de Cargas*). Of course, to go to the opposite extreme and consider that any autonomous regulation that enables an activity would allow anyone who obtains the authorization in that Community to carry it out throughout the national territory, regardless of what other Communities have legislated (as was intended by State Law 20/2013, Guarantee of Market Unity), is a kind of regulatory dumping by which the least interventionist autonomous regulations would end up being imposed by the most regulatory, and violates 'the general principle of territoriality of Autonomous competences by allowing the application in one part of the national territory of differentiated regulations for those economic operators that differ only by their origin' (STC 79/2017, 22 June, case *Ley 20/2013, de Garantía de la Unidad de Mercado*).

77. So far as the other norms with the force of law are concerned, the Autonomous Parliaments can delegate, to their Governing Councils, the making of Legislative Decrees. Until 2006 no Autonomous Statute envisaged the possibility that the Autonomous Parliament should pass Decree-laws but the Organic Law 1/2006, 10 April. Reforming the Organic Law 5/1982, 1 July, of the Autonomous Statute of the Community of Valencia has incorporated that source of law (Article 50.4) as has the new Catalan Autonomous Statute (Article 64) and those passed thereafter, such as those of Andalusia, Aragon, the Balearic Islands, and Castilla-León. In general, the requirements made by those Statutes are similar to those of the Constitution: the Decree-law can be issued in cases of extraordinary and urgent necessity without being able to affect the rights established by the Statute, nor the electoral system or institutions and has to be ratified within a period of thirty days, using the emergency procedure.

Personally, I fail to see the advantages of introducing Decree-laws in the autonomous system since, from the formal point of view, it can lead to more than one conflict when specifying whether the Executive has exceeded its limits when approving it and from the practical point of view, it reinforces some already powerful Governing Councils while devaluing the parliaments that lack such power. This is not to mention that it is hard to see how, in the field of autonomous competences, such extraordinary circumstances could arise that would require such an urgent modification of the autonomous legislation that could not be made in autonomous Assemblies (all unicameral) through the emergency procedure or that of the single reading. However, the Councils of the Communities have seen it differently and have used them extensively, to the point that some legislatures (such as the Andalucian of 2012–2015) have passed more Decree-laws than laws (35–19). Of course, the COVID-19 pandemic declared in March 2020 has led to the widespread use of this regulatory instrument, which has outnumbered regional laws in all Communities. The Constitutional Court, following its general doctrine, has admitted that the economic crisis could justify the urgency of these Autonomous Decree-laws (STC 93/2015, 14 May, case *Decreto*-ley *6/2013 de Andalucía, de medidas para asegurar el cumplimiento de la Función Social de la Vivienda*).

§2. The Inter-relationship Between Norms with the Force of Law

78. In a simple scheme of three types of norms, Constitution, Law, and Regulations, each originating from three different powers, the relationship between them is very easy: it is ruled by the principle of hierarchy and, when of equal status, by temporality. The need to regulate new social phenomena has caused the principle of specialization to arise in the liberal State, such that the special norm is applied in preference to the general. In practice, this principle is almost complementary to that of temporality since most of the special laws are subsequent to the general (e.g., the 1960 Law of Horizontal Property in relation to the 1889 Civil Code). The 1978 Constitution, with its multiplicity of norms – reflecting the complexity of the modern State – has created what Alberto Predieri has wittily called a 'wasp's nest' of sources,[13] whose management is rather complicated and in which a new principle plays an important role: the principle of competences. These are those that govern the relations between laws that belong to distinct legal subsystems. Thus, when there is a conflict between two norms, one of the State and the other of an Autonomous Community, the deciding criterion to know which to apply in a specific case depends on which of the Public powers is responsible for regulating the matter without considering either the rank or the date of the entry into force of the norms in conflict.

79. When studying treaties, we saw that they were incorporated into the legal system in a position inferior to the Constitution and could be repealed and modified as norms with the force of law. However, a subsequent law cannot modify a treaty because it can only be modified by the procedures that they themselves establish. Spanish laws have a similar relation to European directives and regulations: in virtue of their primacy, these norms modify Spanish norms but cannot be modified by them.

---

13. 'Sistema de las normas y avispero de las fuentes' (*El constitucionalismo actual cuarenta años después de la Constitución italiana*), interview with Professor Alberto PREDIEERI by Pablo Pérez Tremps, *ADCR*, no. 1, 1989, 27.

80. Organic and other special laws have a constitutionally delimited content, only certain matters being reserved to them, so that, in theory, organic and ordinary laws should never regulate the same material beyond the 'linked matters' that we saw earlier (*see* paragraph 71). For its part, the Budget law necessarily brings together the annual forecast of the total expenditure and revenue of the State public sector and its eventual content 'is strictly limited to those matters or questions that bear a direct relation to revenue forecasts and the financing of the expenditure of the Budget and with the criteria of general economic policy on which they are based' (STC 195 /1994, 28 June, case *Artículo III de la Ley General Tributaria*).

State and autonomous laws are, in a similar situation, governed by the principle of competences since their material spheres of operation are different. However, it is by no means rare that due to the different levels of competences between the Communities, the State can pass laws on questions also regulated by the legislation of some autonomous regions, in which case the State law is purely supplementary (Article 149.3 SC).

Finally, validly promulgated Decree-laws and Legislative Decrees have all the force of law so that the relation between them and other norms is governed by the principles of temporality and speciality.

Chapter 4. Case Law

81. From the 1812 Constitution, the Spanish State of Law has tried to model itself on France; for this reason, the role of the judges was to apply the law to the case in hand, but with no authority to create law, so much so that in the 1812 Constitution itself they were denied even the capacity to interpret laws, requiring the courts to present their 'doubts' about 'the meaning of any law' to the parliament. As in France and the other countries of the civil law tradition, daily practice shows that the state cannot function with that scheme of division of powers, and so it is obliged to grant the judges a margin of interpretation when applying the laws in legal controversies. The Civil Code recognized, in 1973, that jurisprudence was a 'complementary source of law' and defines it as the doctrine that 'the Supreme Court repeatedly establishes when interpreting and applying the law, custom and the general principles of law'. Moreover, the Supreme Court has ruled that such reiteration occurs when at least two rulings have identical results. In this way, the usual practice of the ordinary courts of applying the 'constant jurisprudence' or 'legal doctrine' of the Supreme Court was legalized. In several procedural laws, it has even been conceded that the decisions of the lower courts can be appealed before the higher courts for 'infringement of the applicable jurisprudence' and for the 'unification of doctrine', such that the differences in the role of jurisprudence in the Spanish legal system and those of the 'common law' countries have been notably reduced. However, the Constitutional Court has held that although these remedies exist, judicial independence – which each of the judges and courts has individually – allows the lower judicial organs to disagree, through a reasoning grounded on Law, on the criterion held by superior Courts and even the jurisprudence established by the Supreme Court, with the exception 'of the assumption of the legal doctrine established by the Supreme Court in resolving the appeal in the interest of law' (STC 37/2012, 19 March, then repeated in three similar constitutional cases on the constitutionality of Article 81 of the articulated text of the Law on Traffic, Movement of Motor Vehicles and Road Safety. Precisely, the Constitutional Court has reinforced the role of jurisprudential precedent by considering that the fundamental right to effective legal protection and the equality of citizens requires that all courts solve a case according to its own precedents, from which it can only depart by putting forward 'a sufficient argument for its change of criterion' (STC 57/2001, 26 February, case *Calderón Muñoz*).

82. The role as the supreme interpreter of the Constitution and the guarantee of its supremacy attributed to the Constitutional Court means that its decisions are binding on all the institutions of the state, such that it has power even to strike down laws contrary to the Constitution approved by the democratic legislator (Article 164 SC). In the specific sphere of ordinary jurisdiction, Article 5 of the LOPJ compels the Courts to interpret the laws and regulations according to constitutional precepts and principles, just as they have been interpreted by the resolutions of the Constitutional Court 'in every type of process'. And Article 4*bis* of the LOPJ itself (introduced in 2015) obliges them to apply the law of the EU 'in conformity with the jurisprudence of the Court of Justice of the European Union'.

Chapter 5. Unwritten Law

§1. Customary Law

83. Article 1 of the Civil Code determines that 'the sources of the Spanish legal system are law, custom and the general principles of Law' and specifies that custom shall only apply in the absence of applicable law. Neither the Code nor any other modern norm expressly defines the concept of custom, no doubt because, since the Siete Partidas of Alfonso X the Wise in 1265, it has always been clear that 'Custom is called the unwritten law or law of the land, which men have used for a long time, making use of it in the things and reasons for which they have used it.' Traditionally, customary law has played an important role in civil and mercantile law, a much smaller part in Administrative Law, and has been completely absent from Criminal Law. Now that the Spanish Constitution has been in force for more than forty years, the creation of certain constitutional customs can be seen, especially in the functioning of the institutions and the role of the monarchy in the State. So, the king performs the solemn opening of parliament and of the legal year, broadcasts a message to the nation at Christmas, etc. Other constitutional customs are the simultaneous dissolution of Congress and the Senate, the designation within each party of a candidate for the Presidency of the government before the holding of general elections (with the arguable practice of always presenting them for the electoral district of Madrid), etc.

84. Custom, as a source of constitutional law, cannot have the same binding force as the norms of the Constitution itself, playing only a complementary and supplementary role to the written text. However, the lack of legislative development of a constitutional article can lead to the establishment of a custom that no political power dares to contradict. In this way, and to quote three notorious examples, it seems very unlikely that the Spanish parliament would ever pass a law that regulated the functioning and structure of political parties in more detail than the existing law on the subject (Article 8 SC), the right to strike (Article 28 SC), or a law of harmonization of the autonomous normative provisions (Article 150 SC). Moreover, failing to use an article can be a custom which ends by considering it as binding, as could be the disuse of base laws that delegate to the government the approval of articulated texts (*see* paragraph 72).

§2. The General Principles of Law

85. Historically, general principles of law have been understood as those fundamental concepts that give coherence to a legal system. Accordingly, legal practitioners have used them to interpret legal norms whose application was in doubt. For this reason, they are not a closed catalogue but a set of propositions, often expressed in aphorisms. The reform of the Civil Code in 1973 entailed the legal recognition of the general principles as a source of law, which the Spanish courts have been using to fill in the lacunas of the system and to modify the meaning of certain Francoist provisions, although without ever putting in doubt their essential bases. The 1978

Constitution included many of these principles in its text, beginning with the consideration of the 'superior values of the legal system', liberty, justice, equality, and legal pluralism. Article 9 sets out the principles of legality, normative order, publication of norms, non-retroactivity of punitive provisions, legal certainty, responsibility of the public powers, and the interdiction of those who act arbitrarily. The Constitutional Court has recognized other principles in its decisions, such as the preservation of legal acts, presumption of the legitimacy of the decisions of public powers, etc.

86. The general principles of Law fulfil the function of providing unity to the legal system, requiring it to be interpreted in a conclusive sense to realize the constitutional values and principles. They can, however, be a direct source of law, applicable directly by the courts when the written norms do not deal with the case that must be resolved; that is to say, when there is a legal lacuna, Article 11.3 of the LOPJ stipulates that judges and courts 'should always decide on the intentions that are formulated' This mandate had already been set out in the Civil Code: 'The judges and courts have the absolute duty to resolve in every case the matter that they are hearing, in accordance with the established system of sources' (Article 1.7). Moreover, the principles set out in Article 9 of the Constitution have the full force of law, and thus the Constitutional Court uses it – albeit infrequently – as the criterion to analyse whether a norm has breached the Constitution, and the courts can raise questions to the Constitutional Court if they think that the law applicable to the case violates them.[14]

14. Until now, the greatest number of questions of unconstitutionality presented for a possible breach of some of these principles of the legal system has been against the decision to stop revaluing pensions in accordance with the Retail Price Index in 2012 and 2013, as set out in Real Decreto-Ley 28/2012. To many judges and courts, this seemed a violation of the principle of non-retroactivity of the norms restrictive of individual rights. Nevertheless, the Constitutional Court has continued to dismiss them all starting with the doctrine fixed in STC/49/2015, 5 March, in which it resolved an appeal of unconstitutionality on the same matter. The decision to stop making the extra payment of salaries for December 2014 adopted by Real Decreto-Ley 20/2012, 13 July, on measures to guarantee budgetary stability also gave rise to many questions of unconstitutionality that the Court has also dismissed, arguing equally based on Ley 36/2014, 26 December, on the general budget of the State for 2015. This law ordered budgetary recuperation which meant the disappearance of the object of the questions, a doctrine fixed in STC/ 83/2015, 30 April.

Chapter 6. Administrative Regulations

87. Historically, in Spanish law, the government has had the capacity to pass regulations or development laws to complete framework laws. For this reason, most State laws usually order the government to enact the regulatory norms needed for the effective application of that law, and the laws of the Autonomous Communities normally give the same power to their respective Governing Councils. In addition, the state and the regional executive powers can promulgate regulations without any express legal mandate since the Constitution, and the Autonomy Statutes expressly recognize regulatory power; however, in that case, it can only be exercised in matters that are not reserved to law; as a result, the normal scope of action of these 'independent regulations' is that of the organization of the administration itself, while they are almost never addressed directly to the citizens.

88. Article 97 of the Constitution recognizes the regulatory power of the government 'in accordance with the Constitution and the laws', which implies that regulations are legal norms subordinate to law; in Spain, unlike in France, the Constitution does not reserve to the regulatory system its own normative sphere from which law is excluded. Laws and regulations are inter-related through the principle of hierarchy within their own system, but when it is a question of two different systems (e.g., that of the state and an autonomous region), the principle of competences and not that of hierarchy governs, such that, at times, a state regulation can be imposed on a regional law by virtue of this principle. Thus, it has happened that the 'bases' and the 'basic legislation' that the Communities must develop in certain matters (e.g., in economic activity planning and the environment) are, in some cases, established by regulations.

89. Article 117.3 of the Constitution determines that judges and magistrates are 'subject only to the rule of the law'. Thus, Spanish judges who are not empowered by the Constitution to refuse to apply a law they consider unconstitutional (they must consult the Constitutional Court) do have that power when required to apply a regulation they consider unconstitutional or illegal. Moreover, judicial power can itself annul illegal regulations; for this reason, the LJCA establishes a system of appeals directly against the regulations by attending to the authorities that made them. So, the Supreme Court admits appeals against regulations approved by the government, the Court of First Instance, those against ministries, and the Supreme Courts of the Communities against those made by the regional Governing Councils. In addition, judges of inferior courts may refer to those courts any 'question of illegality' in order for certain articles to be declared contrary to law that previously the judge had refused to apply when giving judgment. This power to remit a 'question' was created for the first time by the LJCA in 1998 with the aim of guaranteeing legal certainty since the decisions of the judges *a quo* that refuse to apply a regulation only affect the parties to the litigation but not other citizens, while the new sentence given by the court *ad quem* has a general effect.

Chapter 7. Codification, Interpretation and Publication

§1. Codification

90. As a state belonging to the 'civil law' tradition, Spain has striven over the last two centuries to order the various laws systematically within the same sector of the legal system, a process known as 'codification'. For this reason, since the end of the nineteenth century, there have been a Civil Code, a Commercial Code (modified on innumerable occasions), and a Criminal Code, repealed and completely substituted several times, the last being in 1995. As a procedural complement to these Codes, we have also had, since the nineteenth century, one law of Civil Procedure and another of Criminal. In the sphere of Administrative Law, as in the other countries of this legal tradition, Spain has not achieved codification here, although the LRJSP and the LPACAP give a general norm to this sector of the system, one from the perspective of the organization of public bodies and the other from the proceedings from which it governs its relations with individuals.

But not even in the sectors in which a Code does exist can it be said that the codification has been so complete that it contains all the laws in that section such that it has been necessary to resort to special laws to regulate specific matters. Three examples will suffice: the law of Horizontal Property in Civil Law, the Law of Cheques in Commercial, and the Law of the Suppression of Contraband in Criminal Law. Furthermore, the codification of Spanish civil law has always been partial because, historically, certain territorial civil laws have continued to exist, such as those of Catalonia, Aragon, and Navarre.[15]

§2. Interpretation

91. All public powers and all citizens are not only bound by the Constitution, but we also interpret it in many of our political and legal activities, for as Peter Häberle has said, in modern democracies, there is an 'open society of constitutional interpreters'. However, the Constitutional Court is the 'supreme interpreter' of the *Lex legum*, and so its interpretation of a specific mandate is imposed above all others, even the legislator itself, as can be seen when its norms are overruled for violating a constitutional norm. It goes further: parliament cannot pass laws whose purpose is to only interpret specific constitutional articles, for then they would not so much be exercising their ordinary legislative function but rather playing the role of the constituent body without using the relevant reform procedure (STC 76/ 1983, 5 August, case *LOAPA*).

15. In 2006 the Statute of Autonomy of Valencia reformed its civil law because, as its Preamble stated, it had been 'for the promulgation of the Decree of 29 June 1707'. However, the Constitutional Court considered that Art. 149.1.8 SC only authorizes the updating of special civil laws that had been in effect at the time of the 1978 Constitution entering into force but not 'regional, local or customary civil norms who validity had expired before that date', the reason why the Court declared several Valencian civil law unconstitutional (STC 82/2016, 28 April, case *Ley de Régimen Económico Matrimonial Valenciano*).

92. We have already had the occasion to refer to the fact that the Constitution has a system of values that demands not only a systematic but also a teleological interpretation of its norms (*see* paragraph 44), and Article 10.2 of the Constitution requires it to interpret fundamental rights in accordance with the treaties on human rights ratified by Spain (*see* paragraph 44). We would now add that, from its first judgments, the Constitutional Court has pointed out the obligation of all public powers to interpret the legal system in 'conformity with the Constitution', which means that when 'two interpretations of a precept are possible, one compatible with the Constitution and the other not conforming to it, the former must prevail' (STC 122/1983, 16 December, case *Juramento Diputados del Parlamento Gallego*), a technique that it has used to save from unconstitutionality many laws that it has had to judge, whose literal sense was incompatible with the Constitution. The most substantial and controversial example of this type of judgment is that of 31/2010, 28 June, where the Constitutional Court interpreted more than fifty articles of the Autonomous Statute of Catalonia of 2006 as being in accord with the Constitution.

§3. Publication

93. There cannot exist a democratic state that does not publish its norms, so enabling its citizens to know the general nature of the rights and obligations that the law attributes to them. Thus, Article 9 of the Spanish Constitution guarantees 'legal certainty', and Articles 91 and 96 require the publication of laws and treaties. Until a norm, whatever it may be, even a reform of the Constitution is published, it is not incorporated into the legal system and cannot bind citizens. Correctly speaking, it does not have the status of a norm until it is officially published, although, in the case of a treaty validly concluded and ratified by Spain, its lack of publication could have international consequences in relation to the other signatory States as it is a legally enforceable commitment according to the Vienna Convention (*see* paragraph 63). Generally, and if the norm itself does not establish anything to the contrary, Article 2 of the Civil Code orders that norms are binding from twenty days after their publication.

94. The traditional instrument in Spain for publishing norms with the status of laws and general regulations is the Official State Gazette (Boletín Oficial del Estado-BOE) which, from 1 January 2009, has been exclusively published on the Internet (www.boe.es), which has caused it to adopt certain technical measures to guarantee its authenticity and prevent its manipulation. With the creation of autonomous regions, the Official Gazettes of each Community are ideal instruments to comply with the requirement of publication. These autonomous gazettes are published both in Spanish and any other official language of the region (according to the Statutes, they are: Basque, Catalan, Galician, and Valencian). For pure information, the general autonomous provisions are also published in Spanish in the Official State Gazette. Since 1997, and with the same informative function, state laws can be published in autonomous gazettes in the respective co-official language.

State norms with the status of law and Royal Decrees are published with the king's signature and the endorsement of the President of the Government. Without a doubt, the fact that the President of the Government endorses a law that parliament has drafted is a small formal error that accurately reflects the reality: in the Spanish parliamentary system, laws are clearly political decisions of the government. The Presidents of the autonomous regions publish autonomous laws 'in the name of the king', except in the Basque Country, where the publication formula used by the *Lehendakari* (the President) is limited to 'Let it be known to all the citizens of the Basque Country that Parliament has passed the following Law'. In two Communities, the signature of their President is endorsed by the Minister (Catalonia and the Balearic Islands).

Since Spain's accession to the EC in 1986, the Official Daily Bulletin of the European Community (today the Official Journal of European Union, OJEU), published in Spanish since that date, is also a source of publication sufficient to integrate the norms published there into the Spanish legal system. These European norms cannot even be published in the Official State Gazette by way of information only, for this would be a breach of Community Law which has as one of its principles the validity of exclusive publication in OJEU, according to the declared jurisprudence of the Court of Justice of the European Union (CJEU).

Part II. Form of Government

Chapter 1. A General Overview

§1. Introduction

95. In the traditional contest between progressives and conservatives that runs throughout Spanish constitutional history, there were two especially controversial concepts about sovereignty and the way of articulating the relationship between the powers of the State (*see* paragraphs 3 et seq.) that, by the end of the 1970s, they had lost all their capacity to cause confrontation because no important political or social force still doubted that Spain had to become a democratic state in which all adult inhabitants had the right to decide its destiny. No one then defended national sovereignty as a theoretical formula opposed to popular sovereignty, but they did so rather as an expression of the unity of the State. For this reason, Article 1.2 of the Constitution was drafted in terms that previously would have been considered contradictory: 'National sovereignty resides in the Spanish people from whom emanate all the powers of the state.' Equally, the position of the king in the institutional framework of the State posed no great problem for the constituent assembly, for now, no one argued that the king should effectively direct the government; on the contrary, everyone considered that the monarchy should become a symbolic institution with representative functions above the daily activities of the State powers (*see* paragraph 20). The formula used in Article 1.3 of the Constitution to express this is rather original: 'The political form of the Spanish state is parliamentary monarchy.'

96. The division of powers established by the Spanish Constitution is based on the classic triad of our historical constitutions. However, the 1978 Constituent Assembly took the decision to create a multiplicity of territorial political powers, the Autonomous State, in such a form that neither legislative nor executive powers were now the monopoly of one institution. Thus, after the formation of the seventeen Autonomous Communities, there were eighteen legislative and eighteen executive powers. Nevertheless, there is only one judicial power made up of judges and magistrates, 'independent, irremovable, responsible and subject only to the rule of law' (Article 117.1 SC). The Constitution wanted to show the distinct composition of the three powers (the first two plurals, the judicial not) even in the different designations of their Titles: while Titles III and IV are called 'On Parliament' (in Spanish, adding to the traditional word 'parliament' the qualifying word 'General' lest any of the Communities called their Legislative Assemblies 'parliament') and 'On Government and Administration', the VI is simply called 'On Judicial Power'.

§2. Political Parties and Interest Groups

97. After the Second World War, Germany and Italy put an end to the tradition of omitting any reference to political parties in their Constitutions, abandoning the liberal idea of not admitting intermediate bodies between the political power and the citizen since the terrible experience of Fascism confirmed that democracy without political parties was impossible. As Spain came out of forty years of dictatorship, where political parties were expressly forbidden, the Spanish Constituent Assembly had few doubts about including a reference to them in the Constitution, so much so that, to show their importance in the Preliminary Title political pluralism was declared to be one of the superior values of the legal system (Article 1.1) and subsequently devoted a complete article to political parties (Article 6) where it was set out that 'they express democratic pluralism, assist in the formation and manifestation of popular will and are a basic instrument for political participation'. However, this constitutional relevance does not make them organs of the State, but instead they maintain their legal nature as private legal persons, a manifestation, therefore, of the right of association of Article 22; as the Constitutional Court already had to specify in the early years of its existence: the parties are 'private associations' qualified by the constitutional relevance of their functions, which make them an 'element of integration between governors and governed' (STC 10/1983, 21 February, case *Ceses concejales de Madrid*). Precisely because they are associations, they must be regulated by an organic law, not an ordinary law. This also explains why the Organic Law on Political Parties is a special law concerning the Organic Law on Associations.

98. The same assembly that drew up the Constitution approved Law 54/1978 on Political Parties, a law of only six articles that established the minimum legal Statute for the parties, in general very much in accordance with the will of the founding members, both externally, the acquisition of legal personality, as internally, in their organization. So far as the former is concerned, the Law established that parties acquire legal personality by registering their Statutes in a 'Party Register' maintained by the Ministry of the Interior. Unlike other countries, Spanish law does not demand that a party must present itself at elections to maintain its status as such. It can only be suspended and dissolved by a legal judgment when it commits the offence of illicit assembly or when 'its organization or activities are contrary to democratic principles'. As to the aspect of the parties' internal organization, the Law repeats the constitutional mandate that the organization and operation must be democratic and then limits itself to requiring that the supreme organ be a general assembly of all members or delegates to the assembly and that all members have the right to elect officers and be eligible for all offices in the party.

99. This 1978 Law on Political Parties was far from meeting the demands for democratic organization in Article 6 of the Constitution, as shown by the simple comparison of its brevity with the lengthy German law on the subject. Thus, the requirement of a democratic structure and functioning depends, to a great degree, on what is laid down in each party's Statutes. In practice, Spanish parties have an iron structure, making them hierarchical and disciplined. The new Organic Law 6/2002 on Political Parties does not fill in this lacuna but limits itself to repeating this regulation, with scarcely any modifications, and only changing, substantially, the regime for suspending and dissolving political parties. The aim of the Act was to facilitate the criminalization of the political friends of terrorism who, even at the beginning of the twenty-first century, were maintained in Spain, an aim that was upheld, following the decisions of the European Convention on Human Rights (ECHR), by the Constitutional Court (STC 48/2003, 12 March, case *Ley Orgánica de Partidos Políticos*). Thus, in 2003 the Supreme Court criminalized Herri Batasuna, the political arm of the terrorist organization ETA, a decision subsequently upheld by the Constitutional Court (STC 6/2004, 16 January, case *Ilegalización HB*) as did the European Court of Human Rights (ECtHR). In the following years, various attempts of the *'izquierda abertzale'* (Basque independent socialists) to present itself at the elections have led to new judgments of the Supreme Court, subsequently appealed to the Constitutional Court, with varying results. Thus, while in STC 31/2009 it confirmed the dissolution of the party Acción Nacionalista Vasca, in that of 126/2009, 21 May, it annulled the prohibition against the coalition Initiative Internationalist from presenting itself at the European elections, although this coalition had won no seats in the elections of 7 June 2009. Similarly, in STC 62/2011, 5 May, the Court annulled the Supreme Court Judgment of 1 May 2011, which prohibited the submission of candidacies to the Bildu coalition, and in STC 138/2012, 20 June, the Court Order of Supreme Court, 30 March 2011, which banned the registration of Sortu in the register of political parties violated the right of association. Apart from the legal controversies, the fact that the terrorist group ETA definitively renounced violence in October 2011 and its self-dissolution in May 2018 created a new political and social climate that allowed the nationalist left to defend its ideals in the same way as the other parties, in the arena of political controversy, without the elongated shadow of the pistols of their ETA cousins.

100. The social demand for a higher quality democracy brought Law 19/2013, 9 December, on transparency, access to public information, and good governance to be also applicable to political parties and trade unions. In 2015 Congress passed an Organic Law that, just by reading its long title, is evidence of its concern to control the parties better: Organic Law 3/2015, 30 March, on control of the economic-financial activity of the Political Parties, by which the Organic Law 8/2007, 4 July, on financing of the Political Parties, Organic Law 6/2002, 27 June, on Political Parties, and Organic Law 2/1982, 12 May, on the Court of Auditors is modified. In what we are now interested in the internal organization of the parties, this law advances – it seems to me timider than its Preamble promises – to regulate the democratic functioning of the parties. Thus, it details the minimum content that the Statutes must set out and the legal status of its members. Parallel to this Law, Organic Law 1/2015 corrected a pair of truly scandalous legislative omissions: in 2010, the Criminal Code was amended to introduce criminal liability of legal persons without including political parties or trade unions; this Law was corrected by 1/2015, at the same time as introducing the crime of illegal financing of political parties, non-existent until that moment in the Criminal Code.

101. The passing of the years has shown the inadequacy of the Spanish legislation to guarantee the internal democracy of the parties, and the same occurred with the Organic Law of 1987 on financing the parties. The specialists and the Court of Auditors itself, the state institution in charge of controlling the parties' accounts annually, had long demanded reform to ensure that they were more transparent and controllable. To meet these demands and even to make the cases of corruption associated with the management of party funds more difficult, which had had a great impact on public opinion, Organic Law 8/2007, 4 July, was passed. It broadly modified the technical aspects of both Organic Law 5/2012, 22 October (that, for the first time in history, included a reduction in the funding of the parties, unlike what had happened in 2007) and the previously mentioned Organic Law of 3/2015. This Law, on financing the parties, established a strict system of supervision of the parties' accounts along with the possibility that the Court of Auditors could impose fines on the parties in breach of the rules. So far as funding was concerned, the law maintained the traditional mixed system, with funds from both public and private sources. The three public sources are: subsidies for electoral expenses (governed by electoral law) 'annual state subsidies for the running costs' and state subsidies for the parliamentary groups of Congress and the Senate; the respective autonomous Assemblies have allotted similar subsidies for the political groups in the Municipal Councils and Regional Councils. The criterion for sharing these subsidies is electoral, according to the number of seats and votes obtained. The law also regulates the private funding of the parties, beginning with the quotas of their members and permitting donations from private individuals and businesses, although subject to strict regulation: donations are forbidden from anonymous givers, public companies or contractors with the administration, etc.[16] In practice, according to the Reports of the Court of Auditors, the revenue from these private sources comprises one-fifth of the income of the largest parties (more in the case of the most voted, for nationalists), a low percentage, without comparison, in Europe, which reveals the scant holdings of the parties – with few members in relation to the population – in Spanish society.

102. From 1977 to 2011, eleven general elections were called, and a similar number of regional and local elections were held under the D'Hondt formula of proportional representation. The Spanish party system seemed substantially consolidated, dominated by two great forces, one of the centre-left (PSOE) and the other of

16. This stricter regulation of the private financing of political parties, with an express prohibition of corporate donations, follows the opposite direction of what has happened in the United States, where the Supreme Court considered in 2010 (*Citizens United v. Federal Electoral Commission*) that freedom of expression prevented placing limits on donations from individuals, companies and trade unions. Other states have also shown reluctance to public funding of parties. Thus, in Italy, they were banned entirely in December 2013; in Germany, its Constitutional Court only admits it as long as it is not the only source of funding and allows parties, as social organizations, to 'maintain their independence from the State' (Judgment of 9 Apr. 1992, BVerfGE 85, 264).

the centre-right (PP), who, between them, hold more than 75% of the vote. However, the general elections of 2015 resulted in a substantial change in this pattern because although PP (with 28.72% of the votes) and PSOE (22.01%) continued to be the most voted parties, two new political forces arose who took many votes away from them: Podemos, (We Can) an amalgamation of left-wing parties (20.66%) and Ciudadanos (Citizens)(13.66%), a liberal party with its origin in Catalonia, as a response to the nationalist forces of that territory. The new elections of 2016, held precisely because of the impossibility of achieving a pact for the government, confirmed the new scenario of four parties, although the increase in PP's vote (33.06%) enabled it to form a minority government with the external support of Ciudadanos (13.05%) and the abstention of PSOE (22.66%). In 2018 Rajoy's minority government was replaced, thanks to a motion of censure (*see* paragraph 149), by a minority government led by Pedro Sánchez (PSOE), who, after two general elections in 2019, managed to preside over a coalition government between PSOE and UP. From the view of electoral analysis, it can be affirmed that at the end of the second decade of the twenty-first century, the great right-left ideological division in Spain continues with an electoral weight similar to that of previous eras. However, unlike in the previous forty years, the two major parties that almost monopolized the vote on each side of the ideological spectrum now share the seats in Congress (and, to a lesser extent, also in the Senate) with other parties: in the general elections of November 2019, the right-wing bloc included PP (21% of the vote, 89 deputies); Vox (15.2%, 52) and Ciudadanos (6.9%, 10), while on the left were PSOE (28.3%, 120) and Unidas Podemos (13%, 35).

A characteristic feature of the Spanish political system is the existence of a good number of parties with a territorially limited scope: *Convergencia i Unió* (later transformed into *Pdecat), Partido Nacionalista Vasco, Esquerra Republicana de Catalunya, Coalición Canaria, Bloque Nacionalista Galego, Partido Andalucista, Partido Aragonesista,* etc. The first two are particularly important, as both are the political expression of century-old nationalist movements and have governed Catalonia and the Basque Country, almost without interruption, since the creation of their respective Communities in 1980. Due to their control of the autonomous institutions in the State parliament, they play a role superior to their strict numerical weight, which, at some moments, reached the point where they made pacts in the legislature with the most voted party, who, nevertheless, do not have sufficient seats to govern alone, as happened with PSOE in 1993 and 2004 and with PP in 1996. In 2018, they were decisive in the motion of censure against Rajoy and, after the 2019 elections, in the investiture of Pedro Sánchez as president.

Table 4 Results of the Constitutional Elections to Congress of Deputies

Party	*1979*		*1982*		*1986*		*1989*		*1993*		*1996*		*2000*	
	Votes	*Seats*	*Votes*	*Seats*	*Votes*	*Seats*	*Votes*	*Seats*	*Votes*	*Seats*	*Votes*	*Seats*	*Votes*	*Seats*
AP-PP[1]	1,067	9	5,548	107	5,247	105	5,117	101	8,089	138	9,716	156	10,321	183
PSOE	5,469	122	10,127	202	8,901	184	8,115	175	9,150	159	9,425	141	7,918	125
Podemos[2]														
Ciudadanos														
PCE-IU[3]	1,911	22	844	4	768	6	1,627	14	1,905	15	2,342	19	1,263	8
UCD	6,268	168	1,354	11										
CDS			600	2	1,838	19	1,617	14						
ERC	123	1	138	1		0		0	189	1	169	1	194	1
CiU-PDCAT	483	8	772	12	1,014	18	1,032	18	1,165	17	1,151	16	970	15
PNV	275	7	395	8	309	6	252	5	291	5	318	5	353	7
HB-Bildu	172	3	210	2	215	5	217	4	206	2	181	2		
Others	2,162	10	963	1	1,786	7	2,372	19	2,405	13	1,497	10	1,793	11
Total[4]	17,930	350	26,489	350	20,078	350	20,349	350	23,400	350	24,799	350	22,812	350

Party	*2004*		*2008*		*2011*		*2015*		*2016*		*2019 (A)*		*2019 (N)*	
	Votes	*Seats*	*Votes*	*Seats*	*Votes*	*Seats*	*Votes*	*Seats*	*Votes*	*Seats*	*Votes*	*Seats*	*Votes*	*Seats*
AP-PP[1]	9,762	148	10,278	154	10,830	186	7,125	123	7,906	137	7,513	123	6,792	120
PSOE	11,026	164	11,289	169	6,973	110	5,530	90	5,424	85	4,373	66	5,047	89
Podemos[2]							5,189	69	5,049	71	3,750	42	3,118	35
Ciudadanos							3,500	40	3,123	32	4,155	57	1,650	10
PCE-IU [3]	1,160	5	969	2	1,680	11	923	2						
UCD														
CDS														
ERC	652	8	296	3	256	3	599	9	629	9	1,020	15	874	13
CiU-PDCAT	835	10	779	10	1,014	16	560	8	481	8	500	7	530	8
PNV	420	7	306	6	323	5	301	6	286	5	395	6	379	6
HB-Bildu	–		–		333	7	218	2	184	2	259	4	277	5
Others	680	8	884	6	739	12	81	1	78	1	469	6	1,182	12
Total[4]	24,535	350	24,801	350	22,148	350	24,026	350	23,160	350	25,122	350	23,505	350

Source: Central Electoral Board and author.

1. Alianza Popular changed its name in 1989 to Popular Party (PP). Since 1996 it has presented itself in coalition with various nationalist parties. Thus in 2016, it campaigned with UPN in Navarra and with Foro Asturias in Asturias.
2. Podemos campaigned in 2016 in an electoral coalition with IU under the name of 'Unidos Podemos'.
3. This grouped the votes of PCE and of PSUC; the Catalan Communist party, in 1986th PCE, presented a united front as Izquierda Unida. From 2004 to 2015, in coalition with Izquierda de Cataluña (IC).
4. Total votes obtained by candidatures with representation in Congress. For this reason, ERC is shown without votes in 1986 (it obtained 84,000) and in 1989 (also 84,000).

103. The Spanish Constitution recognizes, in Title I, not only political parties but also includes in it other social groups relevant to the State: trade unions and employers' associations. As in the case of political parties, the Constitution establishes that their creation and the exercise of their activities are free within the terms of the Constitution and the law and requires their internal structure and functioning to be democratic. The Organic Law 11/1958 on Freedom of Trade Unions regulates the legal system of the unions; an interesting point here is that those unions that obtain more than 10% of the members of the works committees in the elections are considered 'more representative'. At the national level, only two unions exceed this percentage, the Unión General de Trabajadores (UGT) (the General Workers' Union) and Comisiones Obreras (CC.OO.); the first is a socialist union, now more than a hundred years old and the second, founded clandestinely in the 1960s, is close to the PCE – the Spanish Communist Party. Since the 1980s, the united action of both trade unions has been very general, mostly in major decisions, such as general strikes against government decisions (e.g., 1988, 1994, 2003, and 2011). The laws give a wide range of powers to the more representative trade unions to enable them to fulfil their function of defending workers' rights: authority for collective negotiations, both to approve collective agreements binding on workers and employers alike as to make National Consensus Agreements with the government, be informed by the government on the contents of the budget, etc. For its part, the Confederación Española de Organizaciones Empresariales (The Spanish Confederation of Business Organizations), founded in 1977 and consisting of more than 200 territorial and sectoral organizations, represents the interests of the employers.

§3. Miscellaneous: Referendums and Popular Initiatives

104. The Spanish Constitution incorporates several techniques for direct participation, such as the popular legislative initiative and the referendum, albeit with a degree of caution to avoid the excessive undermining of parliament and the political parties and to prevent their being used demagogically by anti-system groups. While that position was understandable in 1977 and 1978, when the political parties were very weak, today, it is a precaution that is difficult to accept for a democracy that describes itself in the Preamble to the SC as 'advanced'. The popular legislative initiative can be exercised by 500,000 Spaniards in matters not reserved for organic law or dealing with financial or international affairs. The high number of signatures required has ensured that only a few propositions of law under this popular initiative have been put forward to Congress. The development made by the Organic Law 3/1983 added certain other procedural requirements in addition to this large number of signatures, such as the period of six months to gather the signatures, which in practice made it difficult to exercise this popular initiative. For this reason, Organic Law 4/2006 lengthened this period to nine months and established other mechanisms to benefit popular participation, such as the recognition of the electronic signature and the payment of a greater subsidy for the costs involved to the promoting Commission. In spite of these improvements, popular legislative initiatives are not very frequent, to a large extent due to the great extension of the prohibited subjects, which places us in a political system very controlled by the parties, very different from the Swiss participatory system, where the popular initiative can even be exercised to amend the Constitution. Moreover, these popular Swiss initiatives of constitutional amendment must be voted in a referendum without parties being able to prevent it. In Spain, by contrast, the vast majority of the hundred or so citizens' initiatives that have obtained the required 500,000 signatures have been rejected by Congress, so to date, only three have been transformed into law, two of which ended their legislative route successfully for their promoters: Law 8/1999, *de reforma de la Ley de Propiedad Horizontal* (Law on Horizontal Property) and Law 18/2013, 12 November, *para la regulación de la Tauromaquia como patrimonio cultural* (For the Regulation of Bullfighting as Cultural Heritage), the first law to be signed by the electronic signature, and Law 19/2022, *para el reconocimiento de personalidad jurídica a la laguna del Mar Menor* (on the recognition of the legal personality of the Mar Menor lagoon).[17]

105. Article 92 allows the Congress of Deputies to authorize the king, at the suggestion of the president of the government, to summon a 'consultative referendum' on political decisions of particular importance. In the first twenty-five years of the Constitution's existence, the only decision submitted to the referendum was whether Spain should remain in NATO in 1986, a proposal of the Socialist government in fulfilment of its election programme, which gained a tight majority of 48%–52% (with more than 40% abstention). Unlike in other States, the adhesion to the European Community and subsequent reform treaties have not been submitted to a referendum. A possible explanation for this lack of popular consultation is that the political elite, like the population in general, is strongly pro-European; since Spain's incorporation into the EEC, the parliament has almost unanimously approved any legislation in this matter, including the most important ones, such as Constitutional reform and nearly ten organic laws authorizing treaties. In a break with that tradition, in April 2003, all the political forces of the parliament agreed to submit the signing of the European Constitutional Treaty to popular ratification; it was held on 20 February 2005 with an overwhelming triumph (76% of the votes cast), though with a very high number of abstentions (57%).

106. The Constitution also gives the municipalities the power to hold popular consultations with the previous consent of the State (Article 149.1.32). The Regulator of the Bases of the Local Regime (LBRL) develops this mandate by establishing that the municipal plenary session can agree, by absolute majority, to submit to a popular vote on local affairs of special importance, except those relating to the local Inland Revenue, always with the previous authorization of the national government. This provision is clearly a minimum precaution to prevent political forces opposed to the parliamentary majority from convoking referendums against government policy. In spite of this, and protected by the right of freedom of speech, some Municipal Councils carry out local consultations on matters of national policy that, logically enough, have no binding effect but enjoy some repercussion in the press.

---

17. A complete account of all popular initiatives can be seen on the official web page of the Central Electoral Council, www.juntaelectoralcentral.es.

The Catalan Autonomous Statute of 2006 establishes the right of the Catalans to promote popular consultation by the Generalitat and the municipal authorities in matters concerning their respective competences, in the form and under the conditions established by the law (Article 29), so that the Generalitat has to lay down its legal regime, with the exception of what is stipulated in Article 149.1.32 of the Constitution (Article 122). This provision has been interpreted by the Constitutional Court in the sense that the competence to regulate (and not only call) any referendum is the obligation of the State, while the Generalitat can regulate surveys, public hearings, forums of participation, and any other instrument of popular consultation that is not a referendum.[18] Beyond the legal polemic, this article has caused great political controversy in that it could be understood as serving as a legal ground to call a referendum on the link between Catalonia and Spain, defended by some nationalist forces. They claimed it was analogous to the referendums on the sovereignty of Quebec held at the end of the last century. Other Statutes of the neo-autonomous State also claimed the possibility of making popular consultations but clearly ensured State competence to regulate referendums, so avoiding the invasion of the State's competence (Article 50 of the Valencia Statute, Article 78 of the Andalusian, Article 71.27 of the Aragonese, etc.). Precisely, in September 2017, the Catalan Parliament passed a law to hold a referendum in which citizens would be asked, 'Do you want Catalonia to be an independent state in the form of a republic?' This law was quickly appealed before the Constitutional Court, which declared it contrary to the Constitution (STC 114/2017, 17 October) as well as the decree calling the referendum for 1 October (STC 122/2017, 31 October).

18. STC 31/2010, 28 June, case *Reforma del Estatuto de Autonomía para Cataluña*. Previously, in STC 103/2008, 11 September, the Constitutional Court had established that the referendum is defined by its content ('That consultation whose object is strictly related to the opinion of the electoral body and externalized through an electoral procedure') and not because of the name it is given, in such a way that its authorization is the exclusive competence of the State (Art. 149.1.32ª SC). It thus declared unconstitutional and null and void the Law of the Basque Parliament 9/2008, 27 June, on the convening and regulation of a popular referendum in order to gather public opinion in the Autonomous Community of the Basque Country on the opening of a negotiation process to achieve peace and political normalization.

Chapter 2. Head of State

§1. Designation

107. The 1978 Constituent Assembly did not have much doubt about accepting, first, the monarchy as the form for the Head of State (Article 1.3 SC) and, subsequently, keeping the king designated by the Francoist parliament, Don Juan Carlos de Borbón, who was declared the 'legitimate heir of the historical dynasty' (Article 57 SC), since his attitude towards facilitating the transition from dictatorship to democracy meant that the great majority of the political parties considered this to be a factor of political union and stability. In this way, the House of Bourbon (Figure 2), which from 1700 had ruled with more than one interruption[19] and, lacking public support, had been dethroned in 1930, has not only returned to reign again but has done so with wide political and social backing, although in Spain, unlike Italy in 1946, the citizens have never been directly and independently consulted about the alternative between republic or monarchy; indirectly, it has been endorsed by the citizens when voting in the referendum for the ratification of the Constitution (*see* paragraph 20).

108. The order of succession established in Article 57 of the Constitution is the traditional form that goes back to the Partidas (Mandates) of Alfonso X el Sabio (the Wise) in 1265: 'The succession to the throne shall follow the regular order of primogeniture and representation, the first line always having preference over subsequent lines; within the same line, the closer degree over those more remote; in the same degree, the male over female and in the same sex, the elder over the younger.' Translating this to ordinary language and applying it to the present Royal Family, this provision has meant that Felipe VI has inherited the throne, although his sisters (Elena and Cristina) are older than he is. And as everybody in Spain knows, when Felipe VI acceded to the throne on 19 June 2014, his older daughter, Leonor, became the Princess of Asturias. Evidently, this provision, while not so cruelly discriminatory as the Salic law, results in a preference for men over women, which is not only anachronistic at this historical moment but cannot, in the long term, benefit the monarchy, an institution that is already rather out of step with the values of equality prevailing in democratic societies.

The heir to the Crown is given the official title of *Príncipe/Princesa de Asturias* (Prince/Princess of Asturias), which dates back to 1388, and the 'other titles traditionally linked to the successor' (Article 57.2 SC); these titles applied to the current heiress are: *Princesa de Gerona, Princesa de Viana, Duquesa de Mont-Blanc, Condesa de Cervera and Señora de Balaguer (Princess of Girona, Princess of Viana, Duchess of Montblanc and Lady of Balaguer).*

---

19. From 1808 to 1813 José I, Napoleon's brother, was king of Spain although the Cadiz parliament did not accept his legitimacy and he was able to maintain himself in power only by the occupation of the French troops. In 1870 parliament proclaimed Amadeo de Savoya king and on his abdication that same year, the First Republic of short and uncertain existence, was established.

Figure 2 Genealogy of the Kings of Spain

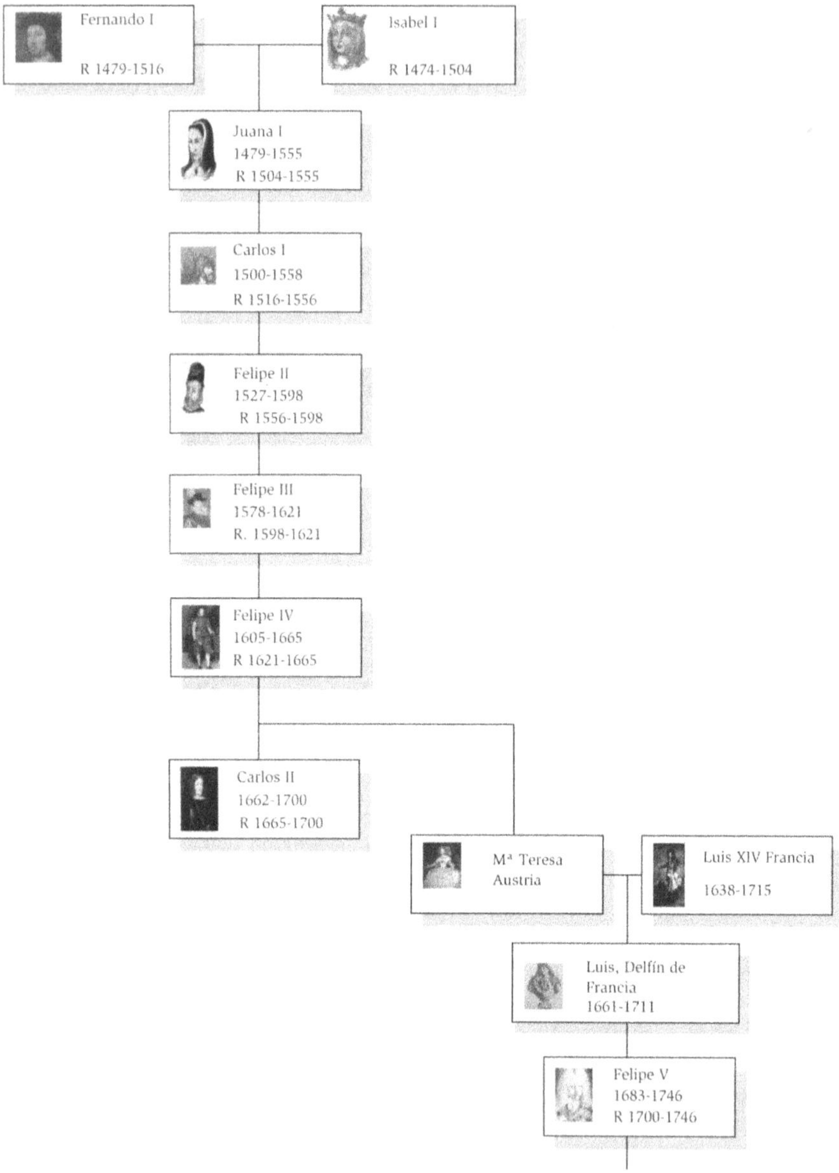

Luis I
R 1724-1724
1707-1724
Fernando VI
1713-1759
R 1746-1759
Carlos III
1716-1788
R 1759-1788
Carlos IV
1748-1819
Fernando VII
1784-1833
R 1808; 1814-1833
Isabel II
1830-1904
R 1833-1868
Alfonso XII
R 1788-1808
Alfonso XIII
R 1870-1885
Don Juan
Conde Barcelona
1913-1993
Juan Carlos I
1938-
R 1975-2014
Felipe VI
1968-
R 2014-
Leonor,
Princesa de
Asturias
2005-

109. Farsightedly, the Constitution stated that if there were no heirs according to these criteria, the parliament should appoint the successor as is 'in the best interests of Spain'. Likewise, it stipulated that abdications, renunciations, or any doubt 'in fact or law that may occur in the order of succession to the Crown shall be resolved by an organic law'. In fact, the abdication of King Juan Carlos I was affected by a single law or single case, Organic Law 3/2014, 18 June, 'by which the abdication of King Juan Carlos I was made effective'. In my opinion, this formula is a little ambiguous as it does not make clear that in certain situations – absolutely exceptional, of course – the parliament could refuse to accept abdication. At the same time, the *Cortes* amended the LOPJ to give Juan Carlos special jurisdiction at the Supreme Court, as he lost his inviolability when he abdicated. With good sense, the other members of the royal family also received this special jurisdiction: the Civil and Criminal Chambers of the Supreme Court 'will process and try civil and criminal actions, respectively, lodged against the queen consort or the consort of the queen, the princess or prince of Asturias and his or her consort, and against a king or queen who has abdicated and his or her consort' (Article 55*bis* LOPJ). A difference between this and historical Spanish constitutions is that now, neither the king nor his heirs need any type of parliamentary authorization to contract marriage; however, Article 57.4 of the 1978 Constitution lays down that any person having the right of succession to the throne who contracts a marriage expressly prohibited by the king and the parliament shall be excluded from the succession to the Crown.

110. The succession to the Crown is automatic as soon as it is vacant due to the death of the king or any other cause, but for the monarch to be able to fully exercise his functions, a solemn act before parliament is required in which the king must swear an oath promising to faithfully carry out his duties, to obey the Constitution and the laws and ensure that they are obeyed, and 'to respect the rights of citizens and the Autonomous Communities' (Article 61). Thus, in the case of Felipe VI, on 19 June 2014, he attended the parliament to swear the oath and then to be proclaimed king of Spain.

111. In the event that the king is a minor or is unable to reign, Article 59 of the Constitution sets out that his father or mother shall exercise the regency. In the absence of parents, the adult relative nearest in succession shall do so, and if there is no one, parliament shall appoint a regency that can consist of one, three, or five persons. The regent shall have the same powers as those given to the king by the Constitution, although they shall be exercised in his name and shall cease when he becomes of age or regains his capacity to rule. The Constitution entrusts no specific function to the regent in relation to the King; on the contrary, it establishes the post of tutor, who can only be the regent if he/she is the parent or another direct ascendant of the King. The guardianship of a minor depends, in the first place, on the testamentary dispositions of the late King, and if no one is appointed, the surviving spouse shall be tutor during widowhood; by default, parliament shall make the appointment.

§2. LEGAL STATUS OF THE KING

112. Following the text of the Belgian Constitution, Article 56.3 of the Spanish states that the king is inviolable and not subject to responsibility. This means that no type of proceedings, civil or criminal, can be initiated against him. This prohibition has historically been understood in a broad sense: both for his public acts, carried out as Head of State, and private acts, carried out as a private person. Inviolability also includes the impossibility of carrying out any political control in the *Cortes*, much less in the Assemblies of the Autonomous Communities. For example, the Catalan Parliament attempted in 2018 and 2019, first with the approval of a resolution condemning 'the position of King Felipe VI, his intervention in the Catalan conflict and his justification of the violence by the police forces on 1 October 2017' and then with another resolution creating a commission of enquiry into the monarchy. The two parliamentary resolutions were unanimously declared unconstitutional by the judges of the Constitutional Court (SSTC 98/2019, 17 July and 111/2019, 2 October). But, as in a democracy, powers without responsibility cannot exist, and the same article adds that his acts must be endorsed if they are to have validity. Thanks to this technique of endorsement, the political responsibility for the king's acts is transferred to the person who endorsed them; therefore, although formally they are the king's acts, he/she who takes the material decision – and is responsible for it – is the person who countersigns it (express endorsement), or who is present when the king makes a speech, visits an institution, etc. (tacit endorsement) The Christmas message that the king gives every year on television partially breaks this scheme because he writes it himself, although he first sends it to the president of the government. As all the parties consider it to be the work of the king – and praise or criticize it based on this assumption – it does not seem logical to consider that there is a tacit endorsement. By Constitutional custom, it allows the king to give his opinion on the Spanish political situation based on the function of arbitrating and moderating the institutions attributed to it by Article 56.1 of the Constitution. Finally, common sense (called *epiqueya* in the Spanish legal jargon) points out that some personal acts referred to in the Constitution do not need endorsement, although this does not expressly exclude it, such as the abdication itself (which, of course, has to be accepted) by parliament), the prohibition of marriage to the successors (Article 57.4), and the appointment of the guardian of the minor king in his will (Article 60.1). Article 64.1 of the Constitution establishes that the king's actions will be endorsed by the president of the government and, when appropriate, by the competent ministers. When it is a question of the proposal of the candidate for the presidency of the government and subsequent appointment, the President of Congress makes the endorsement. According to the Constitutional Court, the wording of this article prevents other persons from endorsing the King's acts, so the appointment of presidents of the Autonomous Communities made by the king must be endorsed by the president of the government (STC 5/1987, 27 January, case *Lehendakari I*). While this may be an impeccable literal interpretation, in my opinion, it would have been more consistent with the role of the king as a symbol of the unity of the State and with the ultimate logic of the technique of endorsement (to show the organ responsible for the King's actions) if this appointment was endorsed by the President of the Autonomous Parliament.

113. The king needs no endorsement for his private acts, beginning with the administration of his personal wealth; neither does he need it for the distribution of the total sum that he receives annually from the State for 'the maintenance of his Family and Household' nor for the appointment and dismissal of civil and military members of it (Article 65). However, in practice, the custom has arisen for the President of the Government to endorse the appointment of the Head of the Royal Household. This 'courtesy endorsement' is undoubtedly a logical attitude both because it facilitates a smooth relationship between the government and the king and because it is consistent with the monarch's status of inviolability and non-responsibility. In this same line of making the functioning of the Royal Household more similar to the rest of the administrations, its legal regime has been modified, especially with the Royal Decrees 434/1988, 6 May, on the restructuring of the House of HM the King; 999/2010, 5 August, and 297/2022, 26 April, which modified the previous one in order to advance the principles of transparency, accountability and publicity 'in line with the Crown's commitment to society to observe an upright, honest and transparent conduct' (from the Explanatory Preamble of Royal Decree 297/2022). These decrees legally consolidate the functions of the Comptroller of the Royal Household, a figure created in 2007 by King Juan Carlos, similar to what happens in all public administrations. Besides, Law 19/2013 of Transparency included – not without prior debate – the Royal Household amongst the administrations submitted to it, for which it is obliged to offer on its website the institutional and economic information that this law demands. Even so, the Royal Household is not subject, like the rest of the administrations, to the external control of the Court of Auditors, although the aforementioned Royal Decree 297/2022 establishes that a collaboration agreement will be signed with the Court of Auditors to carry out an annual external audit.

Finally, Law 23/1982, 16 June, regulating the National Heritage, establishes the legal regime of state property destined for the use of the king and his family members and that has been historically linked to the monarchy, as are the palaces of Oriente and La Zarzuela in Madrid, the Royal Palace of San Lorenzo de El Escorial, and the Palacio de la Almudaina in Palma de Mallorca.

§3. Functions of the King

114. The parliamentary monarchy established by the Spanish Constitution means, in the proverbial phrase of Adolphe Thiers, that the king 'reigns, but does not rule' (*see* paragraph 24). The role the Constitution reserves to him is that of an integrating element of Spanish society: 'The King is the Head of State, symbol of its unity and permanence, he arbitrates and moderates the regular functioning of its institutions, assumes the highest representation of the Spanish State in international relations, especially with the nations of its historic community and exercises the functions that the Constitution and the laws expressly attribute to him' (Article 56). But these specific functions, enumerated in Articles 62 and 63 of the Constitution, have a solid content that depends not on the monarch's will but also on other organs:

(1) To sanction and promulgate laws: an act for which the Constitution gives him a period of fifteen days (Article 91), with no possibility of a veto, as was traditional in our liberal Law.

(2) To summon and dissolve the general parliament and to call elections in the terms set out in the Constitution so that, in fact, these decisions are taken by the President of the Government (Article 115 SC) or the king does them following the constitutional mandate that obliges him to dissolve parliament and call new elections in the event that Congress cannot nominate a president in the period of two months from its constitution (Article 99.5 SC).

(3) To call a referendum in the cases envisaged by the Constitution, in which either a referendum must be held when the requirements fixed by the Constitution are met (Articles 151, 167 and 168) or when the President of the Government decides, and the parliament so authorizes (Article 92).

(4) To propose the candidate for President of the Government and, in turn, appoint him as well as put an end to his functions in the terms stipulated in the Constitution. Some commentators have wanted to see, in this provision, a substantial arbitrating power in which the King, in the event of an election not giving a clear majority, could freely choose between various aspirants. However, far from being able to propose whom he considers appropriate to preside over the government, the king must designate the person who can obtain the investiture in Congress. For that, in practice, he always proposes the candidate of the party with the most seats, except in February 2016, when previous consultations with the party leaders, the candidate of the party most voted for (Mariano Rajoy of PP) 'declined' King Felipe VI's proposal. So, the king proposed the candidate of the second party (Pedro Sánchez of PSOE).

(5) To appoint and dismiss the members of the government at the request of its president. The very wording of this and the subsequent three functions make any comment on the King's decision in each of them unnecessary.

(6) To expedite the Decrees agreed upon in the Council of Ministers, to confer civil and military posts, and to grant honours in accordance with the laws. Specifically, other constitutional articles empower the king to make the following appointments:
   - the twenty members of the General Council of Judicial Power (GCJP), the president of the Supreme Court and the Attorney General (Articles 123, 124 and 125);
   - the presidents of the Autonomous Communities (Article 152);
   - the twelve members of the Constitutional Court (Article 159).

(7) To be informed of affairs of State and, for this purpose, to preside over the sessions of the Council of Ministers, when thought appropriate, at the request of the President of the Government.

(8) The Supreme Command of the Armed Forces, although this command is not direct and effective since the government is responsible for directing the military administration and the defence of the State (Article 97).

(9) To exercise the prerogative of pardon in accordance with the law, as he cannot authorize general amnesties. The venerable Law on Pardons of 1870, modified in 1988, attributes the decision to the government. For many years it was considered a political act without jurisdictional control, although, in the 2010s,

the Supreme Court changed its mind and began to control them 'in the regulated aspects of the procedure'. In its opinion, in order not to fall into arbitrariness (prohibited by Article 9 of the Constitution), the government must explain the reasons of justice and equity that justify a pardon against the report of the sentencing court (STS (3) 5997/2013, 20 November).

(10) The honorary patronage of the Royal Academies.

(11) Functions of international representation exercised following the indications of the government or parliament: accreditation of ambassadors, the signing of treaties, declaration of war and peace.

Surveying this range of specific functions, the integrating, symbolic role designed for the king by the Constitution can be clearly appreciated. However, as Article 56 of the Constitution points out that 'he arbitrates and moderates the regular functioning of the institutions' it is possible that, in exceptional situations, those concrete powers would allow him not only to advise and influence, *auctoritas*, but also to exercise specific powers to ensure the return to a democratic situation. In this way, it is possible to give a legal framework to the extraordinary speeches that kings have given in exceptional situations. Such as the 'Institutional Message from His Majesty, the king on 3 October 2017' by Felipe VI, which arose from the illegal referendum on independence held in Catalonia on 1 October (which, according to the press, was drafted by the king, although President Rajoy accepted it beforehand and the head of the opposition, Pedro Sánchez, was also informed of it). Or that of King Juan Carlos on 23 February 1981, when an armed group kidnapped the government and Congress in a plenary session: the king, who holds the Supreme Command of the Armed Forces, was able, in this exceptional circumstance, to give orders directly to the military captains, with no endorsement, to guarantee the Rule of Law.[20]

20. Ángel Garcés Sanagustín, *La caracterización jurídico-pública de la Corona* (Madrid: Iustel, 2021), 61 et seq.

Chapter 3. The State Legislature

§1. The Composition of Parliament

I. Imperfect Bicameralism

115. The Spanish Constitution, maintaining a tradition that dates back to the Middle Ages, calls the legislative State power '*Cortes*', although the word 'General' is now added. It consists of two Chambers, the Congress of Deputies and the Senate, although the latter is no longer the elitist and conservative Chamber of our constitutional history but rather corresponds to the design of compound States where the Senate is formed – as Article 69 SC proclaims – as 'the Chamber of territorial representation'. In spite of this definition, the Constitution is far from the formula for a perfect or egalitarian two-chamber system, where both Chambers have similar powers, as in Italy, Belgium, and other compound States (not to mention the pre-eminence of the Senate in the US), because it attributes a predominant role to the Congress of Deputies in a good number of matters. These include draft bills and propositions of law that are first processed in Congress, and if the Senate should modify them, they are returned to Congress for these changes to be ratified (Articles 88 and 90 SC); in case of conflict in the passing of laws Congress can overturn the Senate's veto by an absolute majority or, after two months, by a simple majority (Article 90); only Congress validates Decree-laws and invests and censures the President of the government (Articles 82, 99 and 113), etc.

116. All the important political forces agree on the need to reform this imperfect bicameralism so that the Senate can better carry out its role as the Chamber representing territorial interests. Thus, in 1994 the Senate approved its new Standing Orders in which, amongst other reforms, it created a 'General Commission of Autonomous Communities' and permitted the Governing Councils of the Autonomous Communities to take part in this Commission. Since then, the need to make more profound changes, including the reform of the Constitution itself, has been put forward on several occasions, but while all parties agree on the need for reform of the Senate, the consensus that led to the approval of the Constitution cannot be recaptured. The Report of the Council of State of February 2006 (*see* paragraph 57) considered that the reform of the Constitution should reinforce the position of the Senate in the Autonomous State, both in the procedure for passing laws that influence the Autonomies (e.g., the laws of delegation of Article 150 of the Constitution should begin the process in the Senate) and in its role as a place of territorial meeting and cooperation, especially in relation to the drafting of Communities' law and its development, application, and enforcement. According to the Council of State, this new Senate would consist of a minimum of six senators elected by each Autonomous Community plus another senator for each 1 million inhabitants and for each Province. They should be elected by universal, free, direct, and secret ballot by the voters of each Autonomous Community on the same date as the autonomous elections. But the political future following the publication of the report has occurred in fields different from those of the reform of the Senate, so until today, the only things that have better reflected the territorial character of the Senate have been, on the one hand, the passing in July 2010 – with great controversy and the vote against of PP – of a reform of the Standing Orders to permit, in certain conditions, the use of the official languages of the Autonomous Communities in the Senate's daily activities and on the other hand, to reform, in – 2007 – the LOTC to establish that the Judges of the Constitutional Court chosen by the Senate will be from amongst those proposed by the Autonomous Legislative Assemblies (*see* paragraph 196). Both initiatives were at first opposed by PP, which, however, did not repeal them in later years when it had enough seats in parliament to do so.

II. The Congress of Deputies

117. The Congress of Deputies is the Chamber of popular representation, which consists of a minimum of 300 and a maximum of 400 deputies, chosen by universal suffrage, free, equal, direct, and secret in provincial electoral districts, through a system of proportional representation for a period of four years, although it can be shorter if the President of the Government dissolves the Chamber earlier (Article 68 SC).

To a great extent, what the Constitution did was to establish the electoral system under which the constituent assembly that drafted it had been elected, thus complying with what has been called the law of electoral inertia, by which legislative powers tend to make definitive the provisional laws under which they themselves had been elected.

The Organic Law on the Regulation of General Elections (LOREG), in its development of the constitutional mandates, followed this law of inertia and ratified all the essential elements that had marked Decree-law 20/1977, 18 March, on Electoral Norms. Thus, it maintained the number of deputies in Congress at 350, did not modify the number of a minimum of two deputies in each province, and divided the seats between the candidates by employing the formula of the highest average, or the D'Hondt formula, which takes its name from the Belgian professor who invented it. Also maintained was the 3% of votes per electoral district for a candidate to take part in the share-out of seats, although this barrier only acts as a brake in the big electoral districts of Madrid and Barcelona but not in the others, where a much higher percentage would have been needed to get a deputy.[21] The system of closed blocked lists was also taken from the Decree-law, meaning that the voter cannot vary the order in which the candidates are presented, so reinforcing the role of the parties in the political system.

118. In Spain, there are fifty provinces plus the Autonomous Cities of Ceuta and Melilla (each elects one deputy). The number of 248 seats to be divided between the provinces according to population is insufficient to compensate for the inequality of population and to enable the relationship between the number of inhabitants and deputies to be similar in all the provinces. The contrast between the most and

21. Of the thirteen general elections held until now, this provincial barrier has only worked once: in the 1993 elections, CDS did not win the seat that the deputy would have won with 2.9% of the votes cast in Madrid.

the least populated provinces is truly extraordinary: in the November 2019 elections, the province of Madrid had thirty-seven deputies for its 6,755,828 inhabitants and Barcelona thirty-two seats for its population of 5,639,524, giving, in rounded terms, 180,000 votes for each seat. However, the two deputies for Soria represent 89,420 inhabitants, only 45,000 inhabitants per deputy. For this reason, the least populated rural districts are over-represented while the urban areas are under-represented, and so the value of a vote depends on residence: a vote cast in Soria is *worth* four times more than one cast in Madrid or Barcelona.

In this way, the 'equal' suffrage guaranteed by the Constitution excludes the nineteenth-century techniques invented to give greater weight to the opinion of certain people (such as the 'plural vote' that allowed people, who satisfied certain requisites, to cast more than one vote, or the 'multiple' that permitted property owners to vote in the various districts in which they had property); it does not mean a strictly mathematical equality of each vote in the whole of the State but rather that this equality is produced within each electoral district. To eliminate this disproportion in the value of votes, LOREG could increase the number of deputies to 400 and initially grant only one to each province so that the distribution of seats according to population would be much better than it is now.

119. The size of the constituency, determined by the number of deputies elected in each of them, also affects the proportional system of the election because most of them are small, choosing six deputies or less (in the last elections, thirty-five, of which eleven choose only three or fewer deputies) and, for purely mathematical reasons, the effect of the D'Hondt formula is to favour the two most voted parties, and so the third party has no possibility of obtaining a seat. Thus, the two major Spanish parties, PP and PSOE, win a greater number of seats than they would if the system were strictly proportional. The parties with strong regional support (such as PNV and CiU) are not prejudiced by this system. The big losers are the *third parties* that have similar support throughout the country (IU especially), that end up not only obtaining fewer seats than they would be entitled to under a strictly proportional system but with even fewer deputies than other parties with fewer votes, but which are more concentrated territorially (Table 5).

Table 5 Percentage of Votes and Seats in the Elections to Congress

Partidos	*1977*		*1979*		*1982*		*1986*		*1989*		*1993*		*1996*	
	% vot	*% esc*	*% vot*	*% esc*	*% vot*	*% esc*	*% vot*	*% esc*	*% vot*	*% esc*	*% vot*	*% esc*	*% vot*	*% esc*
AP-PP	8.1	4.6	6.0	2.6	26.5	30.6	39.2	44.6	26.1	30.0	25.1	28.9	34.6	39.4
PSOE	29.2	33.7	30.5	34.9	48.3	57.7	38.0	40.3	44.3	52.6	39.9	50.0	39.1	45.4
Podemos														
Ciudadanos														
PCE-IU	9.4	5.7	10.7	6.3	4.0	1.2	9.5	5.4	3.8	1.7	8.0	4.0	8.1	4.3
UCD	34.5	47.4	35.0	48.0	6.5	3.1								
CDS					2.9	0.6			9.2	5.4	8.0	4.0		
ERC	0.8	0.3	0.7	0.3	0.7	0.3	0.7	0.3					0.8	0.3
CiU	2.8	3.1	2.7	2.3	3.7	3.4	4.6	4.6	5.1	5.1	5.1	5.1	5.0	4.9
PNV	1.6	2.3	1.5	2.0	1.9	2.3	1.3	1.4	1.5	1.7	1.2	1.4	1.3	1.4
HB-Bildu			1.0	0.9	1.0	0.6	0.7	0.6	1.1	1.4	1.1	1.1	0.9	0.6
Otros	13.6	2.9	11.9	2.7	4.5	0.2	6.0	2.8	8.9	2.1	11.6	5.5	10.2	3.7
Totales	100.0	100.0	100.0	100.0	100.0	100.0	100.0	100.0	100.0	100.0	100.0	100.0	100.0	100.0

Partidos	*2000*		*2004*		*2008*		*2011*		*2015*		*2016*		*2019(A)*		*2019(N)*	
	% *vot*	% *esc*	% *vot*	% *esc*	% *vot*	% *esc*	% *vot*	% *esc*	% *vot*	% *esc*	% *vot*	% *esc*	% *vot*	% *esc*	% *vot*	% *esc*
AP-PP	45.2	52.3	38.3	42.3	41.7	44.0	48.9	53.1	29.7	35.1	34.1	39.1	29.9	35.1	28.9	34.3
PSOE	34.7	35.7	43.3	46.9	45.8	48.3	31.5	31.4	23.0	25.7	23.4	24.3	17.4	18.9	21.5	25.4
Podemos								0.0	21.6	19.7	21.8	20.3	10.7	6.9	15.6	14.9
Ciudadanos								0.0	14.6	11.4	13.5	9.1	14.9	12.0	13.4	10.0
PCE-IU	5.5	2.3	5.1	1.4	3.9	0.6	7.6	3.1	3.8	0.6			16.5	16.3	7.0	2.9
UCD																
CDS																
ERC	0.9	0.3	0.7	3.3	1.2	0.8	1.2	0.9	2.5	2.6	2.7	2.6	4.1	4.2	3.7	3.7
CiU	4.3	4.3	3.3	2.9	3.2	2.9	4.6	4.6	2.3	2.3	2.1	2.3	2.0	2.0	2.3	2.3
PNV	1.6	2.0	1.7	2.0	1.2	1.7	1.5	1.4	1.3	1.7	1.2	1.4	1.6	1.7	1.6	1.7
HB-Bildu							1.5	2.0	0.9	0.6	0.8	0.6	1.0	1.1	1.2	1.4
Otros	7.8	3.1	7.6	1.2	3.0	1.7	3.3	3.4	0.3	0.3	0.3	0.3	1.9	1.7	5.0	3.4
Total	100	100	100	100	100	100	100	100	100	100	100	100	100	100	100	100

Source: Calculated on the basis of Tables 1 and 4. The percentages of votes obtained by each party on the total of votes of parties that won seats, if calculated over the total of valid votes (plus votes in blank and votes cast for candidates who did not obtain seats) or votes issued (plus null votes); the difference between the percentage of votes of each party and the seats won would be greater for the parties benefitting from this system and would minimize it for those harmed by it.

120. The Constitution remits to an organic law the regulation of the procedural aspects of the elections (organization of the electoral administration, presentation and declaration of candidates, the electoral campaign, etc.) merely stating that the verification of the acts and credentials of the members of both Chambers shall be submitted to judicial control (Article 70), a provision that wisely broke with Spanish constitutional history and that assigned this control function to the Chambers themselves, which, at times, caused some confrontations between majority and minority.[22] LOREG has continued this line and established an independent electoral administration whose decisions, moreover, can be legally appealed. As a result, the old problems of electoral manipulation are now a thing of the past. From this set of procedural aspects of the elections to Congress, it is worth mentioning the regulation that was made in 2011 for the presentation of candidates: until then, LOREG allowed all the parties to submit lists without any special requirement. However, the new wording of Article 169.3 stipulates that those parties that had not obtained parliamentary representatives in the previous elections will need a minimum of 0.1% of the signatures of the voters registered in the electoral roll of each constituency in which they wish to appear. This requirement prevented the participation of some parties in the 2011 elections, which filed appeals of unconstitutionality. These were dismissed by the Constitutional Court as it considered that it was an admissible restriction of the right to present candidates because it has the objective of rationalizing and optimizing the electoral process that can be 'affected by the excessive proliferation of inadequate candidates, for whatever reasons, of support or roots in the electoral body' (STC 163/2011, 2 November, case *Partido Humanisa*). This reasoning was later upheld by the ECtHR in its Decision of 26 May 2015 on inadmissibility of the appeal 30537/12, case *Soberanía de la Razón v. Spain.*

III. The Senate

121. Article 69 defines the Senate as the 'Chamber of territorial representation' chosen, as is Congress, for four years. For its composition to reflect this definition, the Constitution assigns equal numbers of senators to all the provinces without taking into account the differences in population (which, in extreme cases such as Madrid and Soria, are enormous, in the ratio of 76:1 in 2019) and sets out that each Autonomous Community shall designate one senator furthermore with one for each 1 million inhabitants. Each province elects four senators, except in the three island provinces where the constituencies are the islands: three senators in each of the big ones (Gran Canaria, Tenerife, and Mallorca) and one each in the small ones: Ibiza-Formentera, Menorca, Fuerteventura, Gomera, Hierro, Lanzarote and La Palma. The cities of Ceuta and Melilla each choose two senators. As these cities only elect one deputy, there is the paradox that they have more representation in the Senate

22. The extreme case occurred in the February 1936 elections, where the majority annulled the elections in various constituencies where the opposition parties had won. It was precisely by this annulment that the participants in the 18 July uprising found a 'legal' argument to attack the legitimate government of the Republic. *See* the *Dictamen de Comisión sobre ilegitimidad de poderes actuantes el 18 de Julio de 1936* (Barcelona: Editora Nacional, 1939), 43 et seq.

than in Congress, which also happens in the nine provinces that choose three deputies. In total, these senators, elected by universal, free, equal, direct, and secret vote in 59 constituencies (47 provinces + 10 islands + 2 cities), amount to 208. They are voted for, as provided for by LOREG, under a majority system of restricted plural vote: each elector can vote for a maximum of three candidates in provincial constituencies, two in Gran Canaria, Mallorca, Tenerife, Ceuta and Melilla, and one in the other island electoral districts. Logically, a system like this benefits the party most voted for, and so the winning party in each election has always obtained the absolute majority of senators.

122. The regional senators are designated by the Legislative Assemblies of the Autonomous Communities according to the systems established by their respective Statutes, although always respecting the principle of proportional representation of the different political forces of which it is composed (Article 69.5 SC). Although at the founding of the Autonomous State, most Statutes demanded that to be designated as a senator, a person had first to be a member of his own assembly, this has been repealed in the later reforms of the Statutes because practice has shown that the Autonomous Parliaments have a great amount of work, and it is difficult to serve in both institutions at once. To fix the total number of senators for each Autonomous Community in each Legislature (one plus one for every million inhabitants), the voters' list in force at the time of the previous election to the Senate is used (Article 169 LOREG). At present, there are 57 senators designated by the Autonomous Communities (Table 6), which added to the 208 senators directly elected in the provincial constituencies, resulting in the Senate being composed of 265 senators. Simply by comparing the number of autonomous senators with the senators directly elected by the provinces, it will be seen how far from ideal the present makeup of the Senate is for a Chamber of territorial representation because it assigns four times more senators to the provinces than to the Autonomous Communities when these are the territorial bodies that have recognized political autonomy, qualitatively distinct from that of the provinces. This system of two classes of senators established by Article 69 of the Constitution was justified in 1978 when it was not known if all the Spanish territory was going to form Communities, but now there are seventeen Communities of great political importance and a constitutional reform to reflect this new circumstance is needed.

Table 6 Number of Senators Designated by the Autonomous Communities in Each Legislature

Autonomous Community	*I Legislature (1979–82)*	*II (1982–1986) And* III (1986–1989)	*IV (1989–93)*	*V (1993–96)*	*VI (1996–2000)*	*VII (2000–04) and VIII (2004–08)*	*IX (2008–11),*	*X (2011–15) XI and XII (2016–2019)*	*XIII (2019) and XIV (2019–)*
Andalusia		7	7	7	8	8	9	9	9
Aragon		2	2	2	2	2	2	2	2
Asturias		2	2	2	2	2	2	2	2
Balearic Islands		1	1	1	1	1	2	2	2
Canary Islands		2	2	2	2	2	3	3	3
Cantabria		1	1	1	1	1	1	1	1
Castilla-La Mancha		2	2	2	2	2	2	3	3
Castilla y León		3	3	3	3	3	3	3	3
Catalonia	7	6	6	7	7	7	8	8	8
Extremadura		2	2	2	2	2	2	2	2
Galicia		3	3	3	3	3	3	3	3
La Rioja		1	1	1	1	1	1	1	1
Madrid		5	5	5	5	6	7	7	7
Murcia		1	2	2	2	2	2	2	2
Navarre		1	1	1	1	1	1	1	1
Valencia		4	4	4	5	5	5	6	5
Basque Country	3	3	3	3	3	3	3	3	3
Total	10	46	47	48	50	51	56	58	57

Source: The Senate and the author.

§2. Legal Status of Members of Parliament

I. Mandate of Members of Parliament

A. Nature of the Parliamentary Mandate

123. Following the habitual guidelines of representative democracies, the Constitution lays down that Members of parliament are not bound by an imperative mandate (Article 67.2). As no express distinction is made, it follows that the autonomous senators, chosen by their assembly, are also governed by the representative mandate, and so, in theory, each and every Member of Parliament can think and vote freely. This freedom of the autonomous senators that guarantees the representative mandate prevents an Autonomous Community from establishing a procedure for the Assembly to revoke the senators elected by it due to the 'loss of confidence', as was intended by the Law of the Valencian Parliament 10/2016, 28 October (STC 123/2017, 2 November). In practice, the parties exercise, quite naturally, 'party discipline' since, not in vain, Spanish politics – and the electoral system – do revolve much more around the parties and their leaders than individual members.

The importance of the parties is such that the Standing Orders of Congress and the Senate require all deputies to belong to a Parliamentary group, making them the subject of much parliamentary activity. The Standing Orders of Congress demand a minimum number of fifteen deputies to form a parliamentary group, which is reduced to five if it has won 5% of the votes in all of Spain or 15% of the votes in the electoral districts in which it has presented candidates, a logical measure designed to enable territorial groups to have their own group. Any deputy who does not voluntarily join a Group is automatically assigned to the 'mixed group'. The Standing Orders of the Senate are similar, demanding ten senators, although the 'territorial groups' can be created within each Parliamentary group. To avoid fraud and to reinforce internal party cohesion, both Standing Orders prohibit the setting up of a separate parliamentary group of Members of parliament belonging to the same party or electoral coalition and who, at the time of the elections, belonged to political formations that were not presented as such to the electorate.

B. Acquiring and Losing the Status of Member of Parliament

124. Article 68.5 of the Constitution lays down that all Spaniards who have full use of their political rights (in principle, all those over the age of 18, which the Constitution itself stipulates is the age of majority, Article 12) shall be voters and eligible for election to Congress. No similar article establishes this same relationship between voters and the right to be elected in the case of senators; however, LOREG does do it, so avoiding the traditional techniques (age, educational level, etc.) designed to give a conservative bias to the second Chamber. For their part, most of the Autonomy Statutes demand that the autonomous senators be members of their Legislative Assemblies.

While the Constitution does not establish any special requirement for an elector to be a candidate, it does lay down who is ineligible, preventing persons occupying certain public offices from presenting themselves to the electorate and so ensuring democratic elections by preventing those persons from using their office for their own benefit. Article 70 remits the causes of ineligibility to the law, starting from a minimum catalogue that it itself establishes:

(a) members of the Constitutional Court;
(b) high officers of the State administration as determined by law, except for members of the government;
(c) the Ombudsman;
(d) magistrates, judges, and prosecutors on active duty;
(e) professional military, members of the armed forces, security corps, and police on active duty;
(f) members of Electoral Commissions.

Article 6 of LOREG sets out these cases of ineligibility, specifying high offices, including the royal family, and, on its own, adds (since its reform in 2003) an assumption designed to avoid the inclusion of persons convicted of terrorism in the first instance but who were appealing their conviction, meaning that they were not deprived of political rights even if they were in provisional prison: those 'convicted by sentence, even if it is not firm, for crimes of rebellion, terrorism, or against the Institutions of the State when the same has established the penalty of disqualification for the exercise of the right of passive suffrage in the terms foreseen in the penal legislation'. In this way, Herri Batasuna was prevented from including terrorist defendants on its lists. As already mentioned, that year, 2003, Batasuna was itself declared illegal (*see* paragraph 97).

125. In order to acquire the status of a Member of Parliament, deputies- and senators-elect must meet certain, purely bureaucratic, administrative requirements (such as completing a declaration as to their activities and assets) and must promise or swear to accept the Constitution, as required both by LOREG and the Standing Orders themselves. This has given rise to various political and legal disputes since members-elect of minority parties, such as Herri Batasuna (from the Basque Country) and the Bloque Nacionalista Galego (from Galicia), have shown themselves unwilling to respect the Constitution. The Constitutional Court accepted the constitutionality of this requisite considering that, in default, the deputy- or senator-elect could not acquire the full status of a Member of Parliament, meaning that although the mandate was not extinguished, its rights and privileges could not be exercised (STC 119/1990, 21 June, case *Idígoras*).

126. The parliamentarians lost their status at the end of the mandate, which occurs four years after the election or on the day of the dissolution of the House (arts. 68.4 for the Congress and 69.6 EC for the Senate). Even autonomous senators lose their status and must be re-appointed by the Legislative Assemblies. The king may dissolve either of the two Houses at the proposal of the President of the Government or if the Congress fails to elect a President within two months of its constitution. While the new elections are being held, the members of the Permanent Deputations do not lose their parliamentary status. The Standing Orders of both

Chambers set out other causes for the loss of this status, such as personal reasons (death, resignation) as well as by judicial decision annulling the election or condemning the member to the penalty of disqualification from public office. A member can be provisionally suspended from office for disciplinary reasons, a decision that must be adopted by the plenary session of each Chamber, and when a charge is brought against a member. This status can also be lost through incompatibility by accepting another public office that the Constitution or LOREG does not allow to be held simultaneously. The evolution of the LOREG in its different modifications when it comes to regulating the incompatibilities of deputies and senators has been that of a progressive hardening, currently establishing a large number of prohibitions: all cases of ineligibility (therefore, all senior officials, except ministers and secretaries of state), working as a civil servant, forming part of boards of directors of companies that are contractors of any public administration, and in general, all private activities that are not directly related to the administration of their assets or that are not artistic and literary creation, etc. (Articles 155 et seq. LOREG). The aim of this concept of incompatibility is different from that of ineligibility since while the former is intended to guarantee the fairness of the electoral process, the latter defends parliament's independence by avoiding the simultaneous holding of posts. Therefore, their legal consequences are different; in the case of a member being ineligible her/his election is nullified. However, if the allegation is one of incompatibility, the member does not lose the seat automatically but has a period of days in which to choose between offices. If he/she does not do so, he/she will automatically lose his/her parliamentary status (Article 160 LOREG).

II. Individual Parliamentary Prerogatives

A. Concept

127. Prerogatives are legal concepts designed to guarantee the independence of parliament against other powers and, therefore, they are collective: the right of the totality of deputies, as individuals, of each one of its members. They are not the particular rights of specific citizens but guarantees to protect members in the exercise of their parliamentary duties, so not only can they not be thought of as privileges, but their legal interpretation has to start from that objective purpose of guaranteeing the legislative function so as not to extend them unduly and thus convert them into privileges. The Constitution sets out three typical individual prerogatives of Spanish parliamentary law: inviolability, immunity, and special jurisdiction (Article 74).

B. Inviolability

128. Inviolability is not being legally accountable for opinions expressed during parliamentary acts and for the votes cast in the exercise of office, even after the mandate has ended. It is an absolute guarantee since it prevents any legal proceedings whatever (whether civil, criminal, administrative, or labour), having its cause in parliamentary activity; it is perpetual or permanent in that proceedings cannot be commenced for those opinions even though the member has ceased to be so. As the purpose of inviolability is to guarantee the liberty of the member in the exercise of her/his office, it protects all opinions expressed in the course of parliamentary duties, in or outside the Houses of Congress or the Senate. However, it does not protect those opinions stated in non-parliamentary duties (STC 51/1985, 10 April, case *Castells*). Logically, this inviolability also protects the reproduction of the opinions of deputies made in the course of parliamentary duties, whether or not the method of diffusion is official (Daily Publication of Sessions, press, etc.).

C. *Immunity*

129. Immunity, whose precedents in Spain date back to the *Siete Partidas* of Alfonso X the Wise, has two effects: it prevents the initiation of criminal proceedings against and the detention of a member without the previous authorization of parliament, except in case of *in flagrante delicto*. Unlike inviolability, immunity protects the member from any criminal process regardless of whether it is alleged to have been committed in the exercise of office or not. If in this aspect, immunity can be said to be wider than inviolability, in the other two, it is more restricted: (a) immunity only applies to penal matters and not to other legal proceedings, not even when a civil suit for defamation arises out of a member's political declarations that are not covered by inviolability (STC 9/1990, 18 January, case *Suplicatorio civil*); (b) moreover, immunity ceases the moment in which the member loses that status so that the accusation against her/him can be renewed. But the most important difference between this and inviolability is its very nature; while the latter is absolute, automatically and permanently protecting the member, immunity is only temporary while he/she is a member of parliament and can also be lifted if the plenary session of the Chamber so decides. The Constitutional Court has changed the historical meaning of the *suplicatorio*, the Supreme Court petition asking parliament to waive a member's parliamentary immunity so that he/she can be prosecuted: before, it was considered that its granting was a free action of the plenary, that needed no type of reasoning; now, however, the Constitutional Court demands that the refusal of the *suplicatorio* is reasoned because refusal is only justified if behind that petition there lies a political persecution, the only case in which the Chamber could deny it (STC 206/1992, 27 November, case *González Bedoya*). In practice, this doctrine means that it is difficult for the Chambers to deny a *suplicatorio* for it would imply, one way or another, that they considered that the Supreme Court was taking part in a political operation against a specific member. Therefore, both the Congress and the Senate have granted all the requests that the Supreme Court has presented to them, which are already approaching a hundred.

D. Special Jurisdiction

130. Special jurisdiction assigns criminal proceedings against deputies and senators exclusively to the Supreme Court. In reality, this prerogative is not only a guarantee for members of the legislative power but also for the judicial since the jurisdiction makes it difficult for pressure to be brought against the trial judge. In return for this balance of powers, the members, unlike all other accused, do not have the right to appeal against the sentence of the Criminal Division of the Supreme Court, which is perhaps a failure of our procedural system but does not amount to a breach of the Constitution (STC 51/1985, 10 April, case *Castells*). In any case, the member can avoid this by resigning as soon as proceedings are initiated against her/him, a practice that has become commonplace in recent years.

III. Rights and Duties of Members of Parliament

131. While not strictly speaking about guarantees for members against external interference, the Standing Orders of Congress and the Senate include a set of rights and duties of the members to ensure that they properly fulfil their duties as representatives of the citizens: the right duty to attend, with voice and vote, the plenary sessions and those of the committees of which they form part, the right to belong to at least one committee, the power to demand data, reports, information, etc., from the public administrations. The right to a salary for parliamentary work deserves a special mention for, perhaps as a tribute to the old liberal parliamentary system in which it was considered to be an honorary function, the Standing Orders recognize this right in a periphrastic phrase: 'The Deputies shall receive an allowance to enable them to carry out their duties efficiently and worthily' (Article 8 RCD).

IV. Collective Prerogatives

132. Article 72 of the Constitution sets out the collective prerogatives of the legislative power, which are designed to guarantee its independence, particularly from the government:

(a) Regulatory autonomy so that each Chamber has the capacity to draw up the legal norms that regulate its organization and functioning.[23] The Constitution orders that both the Standing Orders and their reform shall be passed by an absolute majority, a prudent provision to make sure that the *rules of the game* have a wide political backing. The Standing Orders of both Chambers are norms deriving directly from the Constitution that reserves to them certain matters, such that they shall be 'assimilated to the laws and provisions with the force of

23. The differences between a dictatorship and a democracy can also be seen in these apparent *details*. During Franco's reign, the more than submissive parliaments were not even allowed to draft their Standing Orders themselves but had to do it 'in agreement' with the government.

law' (STC 118/1988, 20 June, case *Roca*). For this reason, they may be subject to an appeal of unconstitutionality (see paragraph 201).

(b) Administrative autonomy, which is embodied in the capacity of both Chambers to pass, by common accord, the regulation of the legal system of its civil servants in the Statute of Personnel of Parliament.

(c) Budgetary autonomy, which involves the autonomous approval of their budgets, without the government, which has the exclusive right to initiate budgets, being able to intervene in this matter.

(d) Self-governing autonomy, which permits each Chamber to choose its respective Presidents and the other members of its committees. Halfway between this and administrative autonomy is the competence of the President to exercise all administrative powers and police authority inside the Chamber.

(e) Article 72.3 specifies that the Presidents of Congress and the Senate exercise all administrative and police powers within their respective seats. Therefore, they are responsible for the security personnel in charge of maintaining order. Thus, the solemn declaration of Article 66.3 is made concrete: 'The Cortes Generales are inviolable', the form in which the constituent assembly took up the traditional immunity of the seat, under which no authority, civil or military, can enter the interior of parliamentary buildings without the authorization of their president, and which has been embodied in the Criminal Code in various crimes of invasion of parliamentary seats (Articles 493–499).

§3. Functions of Parliament

I. The Legislative Function

133. Article 66 of the Constitution, after stating that parliament represents the Spanish people, specifies that it exercises the legislative power of the State, approves the budget, controls the actions of the government, and has the other competences assigned to it by the Constitution. In this way, it brings together the three classic functions of parliament, legislative, budgetary, and controlling; to these, it adds others, as we shall see when scrutinizing the constitutional text, beginning with its representative function, the election of the President of the Government and other members of the institutional organs, etc.

As was seen when studying the sources of Spanish law (*see* paragraph 67), the legislative function is carried out by the drafting of various classes of laws under various legislative procedures and with varying contents, which were there grouped into ordinary, shortened, and special procedures. In the modern democratic state, the importance of the legislative procedure, with its basic characteristics of publicity and debate, lies not so much in the ability of some deputies to convince others in the collective search for the general interest but rather as a form of democratic control in which the majority must debate the norms it approves with the minority, publicly explaining its reasons so that the minority can criticize. Specifically, the Standing Orders of Congress and the Senate regulate, in detail, the different legislative procedures. If in the liberal State, the *iter legis* was conceived of as a not over-formal procedure governed by the principles of publicity and discussion, in the present democratic State, it is regulated in some detail by the Constitution and parliamentary Standing Orders as a further display of the rationalized parliamentary system that not only favours the stability of the government but also acts as a guarantee of political and social pluralism. This idea of legislative procedure as a guarantee is the fundamental reason justifying the validity and utility of the reserves of law, the constitutional mandates to the Courts (and in their own spheres, to the Autonomous Assemblies) so that they themselves regulate a specific matter, without the possibility of delegating it to the government. If it were not so, in a party State in which the will of the parliamentary majority coincides with that of the government and the division of powers has been substituted by the separation of functions, the reserve of law would have no sense.

134. In general, the legislative procedure has three phases, initiation, deliberation, and publication. Article 87 of the Constitution assigns the legislative initiative to the government, to Congress, to the Senate, to the Assemblies of the Autonomous Communities, and to 'not less than' 500,000 citizens. Totally consistent with the leadership of the government in the Spanish parliamentary system, governmental initiative is the most common, and the Constitution itself is responsible for giving it preference, both symbolically (its initiatives are called 'bills', while the others are denominated as 'proposals of law') and practically, giving bills priority over proposals (Article 89) and reserving to the government the initiative in matters of economic planning and the budget (Articles 131 and 134). Furthermore, Article 134.6 EC gives it the power to veto all bills and legislative amendments that involve an increase in expenditure or a decrease in budgeted revenue. However, this veto can be controlled by the Bureau of the House to verify that the vetoed legislative initiative has a 'direct and immediate, and therefore current, and not merely hypothetical' connection with the Budget in force (STC 34/2018, 12 April, case Budgetary veto on the suspension of the timetable for implementing the LOMCE). The Constitution specifies that bills shall be approved by the Council of Ministers and sent to Congress with an exposition of reasons, thus marking the role of Congress as being more important than that of the Senate. The deliberative phase commences in Congress with the opening of a period for the presentation of amendments; if there are any amongst them that deal with the totality of the bill (as is usual), they are debated in a plenary session, and then the text of the bill is remitted to a Commission that chooses a committee (made up of representatives of all political groups) that decides what amendments to accept and what to reject. In turn, this 'report' of the committee is debated in the Commission, where the text of the draft bill and its amendments are voted on drafting an 'opinion' that is submitted to the plenary. Once the plenary session of Congress has debated and approved the bill, it is sent to the Senate for approval, veto by absolute majority, or amendments within two months, which can be shortened to twenty days if the government or Congress declares it to be an urgent bill. While the veto has only occurred on very few occasions (for example, in the vote on some controversial laws of the 8th and 9th Legislature, such as the modification of the Civil Code to allow same-gender marriages in 2005), the introduction of amendments is very common. This change is not so much a sign of a confrontation between Congress and the Senate but rather a continuation of dialogue and negotiation between the parties. In any case, if the Senate approves a veto, Congress can ratify the bill by an absolute majority (which to date has always been the case in the few vetoes that have been approved), and in the case of amendments, the Constitution establishes that the text must return to Congress so that it can accept or reject them by a simple majority (in the case of ordinary laws) or an absolute majority (organic laws).

Once approved, a bill or proposal of law is sent by the President of Congress (or the Senate, if that House does not support amendments) to the President of the Government in order that the king, within fifteen days, gives his assent, promulgates it, and orders its publication, with the endorsement of the President of the Government. All this activity of the king is entirely obligatory as the Constitution does not permit him to veto a law or refuse his signature.

II. The Budgetary Function

135. At the beginning of the constitutional system, the budgetary function was thought of as distinct from the legislative, and even today, most constitutions maintain this distinction, as does Article 66 of ours. However, the budget is approved by a law that only differs from the rest by certain peculiarities of procedure and content that are derived directly from the special features of the legislative procedure. Article 134 of the Constitution determines these; the government has the exclusive responsibility for initiating the annual budget. Thus, the government must present the draft budget at least three months before the expiry of that of the previous fiscal year, which in Spain corresponds to the natural year, and so the draft is usually presented in mid-October. The budget bill is processed in preference to other legislation, and the amendments that involve an increase in expenses or a decrease in revenue require the government's approval in order to be processed. In addition, the budgetary stability laws have established a preliminary requirement since 2002:[24] every year, the government – considering its forecasts on the evolution of the national economy – has to put forward to parliament the 'aim of budget stability' for the three following years, whose function is to set a 'ceiling of expenditure' of the General Budgets. For example, in September 2021, *Cortes* approved the deficit target for the period from 2022 to 2024, which was set at 5% of GDP for 2022, 4% for 2023 and 3.3% for 2024. Furthermore, the expenditure ceiling for 2022 was set at 1969.142 billion, 1.4 billion more than in 2017. These high deficit figures are due to the increase in expenditure resulting from the fight against the COVID-19 pandemic.

136. The budget must include the totality of the expenditure and revenue of the public sector, and the Constitution expressly forbids it to create new taxes (Article 134.7 SC), a prohibition that the Constitutional Court has interpreted literally in

24. The first Law that established this requirement was Law 18/2001, 12 December, General Budgetary Stability, which has been modified so often that it was substituted by Royal Legislative Decree 2/2007, 28 December. At present Art. 15 of the Organic Law 2/2012, 27 April, *de Estabilidad Presupuestaria y Sostenibilidad Financiera* (Budgetary Stability and Financial Sustainability), is in force. It has the rank of an organic law because it was passed as a development of Art. 135 SC, reformed in 2011.

such a way that the creation of a new tax is unconstitutional (Article 31.1 SC), but not the creation of a 'personal or property contribution for public purposes' (Article 31.3. SC) which enables, for example, the budget law to oblige pharmaceutical companies to make a discount of up to 5% on sales to Social Security, because it is not a tax but a property contribution resulting from the 'exercise of an activity that is part of a sector regulated by the State, both in the pricing of pharmaceutical specialties, and in the determination of the commercial margins of the pharmacies that dispense them'.[25] In the first years of the democracy, the government took advantage of this bill to modify many substantive laws, a practice that was appealed to the Constitutional Court, which only permits it when it deals with matters that have a direct relation to expenses or revenue or with the criteria of economic policy and, in addition, of that its inclusion in the budget is 'a complement for the better and more efficient execution of the budget' (STC 178/1994, 16 June, case *Presupuestos Generales del Estado para 1990*). However, the custom of approving an omnibus law modifying many others has not been lost since the government, every year, remits, together with the budget, another bill in which this type of provision (law of 'accompaniment') is included. Although this manner of legislating is not the most technically correct, the Constitutional Court declared that 'there is no precept in the Constitution that prevents laws from having a heterogeneous content', and so these 'complex laws' are perfectly Constitutional (STC 136/2011, 13 September, case *Ley 50/1998 de medidas fiscales, administrativas y del orden social*). The Socialist Government, in 2004, refused to present a draft bill jointly with the 2005 budget, a decision that it maintained in the following years, as did the PP Government subsequently. It was not so in various autonomous governments (like Andalucía and Madrid), where they continued using it with total normality. Logically, the Constitutional Court has transferred its doctrine on state budget laws to these regional laws and therefore considers that they do not violate legal certainty 'however inadvisable such a practice may seem technical' (STC 161/2019, 12 December, case *Ley de la Asamblea Regional de Murcia 10/2018, de aceleración de la transformación del modelo económico regional*).

III. The Function of Creation and Controlling the Government

137. The system of government in a parliamentary monarchy is based on the relation of trust or confidence between parliament and the government it elects, expressed both through that election, resulting in the *investiture* of the President, as in the possibility of removing it from office by means of a *motion of censure* or rejecting a *vote of confidence* (*see* paragraph 150). In addition, the Constitution establishes a series of parliamentary techniques that allow parliament habitually to control the executive's actions. Logically, these control techniques are, in practice,

25. STC 44/2015, 5 March, case *Presupuestos Generales del Estado para 2005* and STC 62/2015, 13 April, case *Disposición adicional cuadragésima octava de la Ley 2/2004, de presupuestos generales del Estado para 2005*. The difference between tax and property contribution (a more generic concept, characterized by its coactivity), was fixed by the Constitutional Court in its judgment STC 185/1995, 14 December, case *Ley de Tasas y Precios Públicos*.

used for this purpose almost exclusively by the opposition parties, for when they are employed by the majority, it is usually to give publicity to some specific act of the government:

(1) The questions are put by deputies or senators to a particular individual and deal with concrete matters. The parliamentarians may request written or oral answers. In this case, a brief debate may occur between the questioner and the government member who answers. Article 111 of the Constitution requires a weekly minimum time to be set aside for questions and interpellations, which has been fixed at two hours by the Standing Orders
but which, in practice, is normally longer since, traditionally, all Wednesday mornings are given over to it. In the Senate, Tuesday afternoon is devoted to questions.
(2) Interpellations are qualified questions that can result in a motion which, if approved, is a mandate to the government to carry out a certain action. The difference between these and questions, not always easy, lies in their content which is broader, dealing with 'the reasons or proposals of the executive's conduct in matters of general policy, either of the government or of some ministerial department' (Article 181 RCD). Unlike questions, interpellations – which can be presented by deputies, senators, or parliamentary groups – are always presented in a plenary session of the respective Chamber and give rise to a debate in which all parliamentary groups take part.
(3) The requests for information and for the presence in the Chamber of members of the government (Articles 109 and 110 SC) are instruments of control insofar as they provide information to the Members of Parliament and to public opinion since publicity, as we have known since Kant, is the primary method of control. The possibility of members of the government attending parliament to give information has had the unforeseen effect of being the channel for the importing of a technique characteristic of presidential systems: the debate on the State of the Nation in Spain, made annually in the Congress of Deputies. In the Senate, a debate on 'the State of the Autonomies' takes place, in which the Presidents of the Autonomous Communities can participate (Article 56*bis* RS).
(4) The investigating Commissions are set up to investigate 'any subject of public interest' (Article 76 SC). The Standing Orders of both Congress and the Senate require these Commissions to be approved by a majority, a requirement unanimously criticized by the specialists and by the political parties when they are in opposition because it is illogical to leave an investigation of the actions of the government or those of its agents in the hands of the government itself (by means of the parliamentary group that supports it). The result of the investigation is embodied in a report that must be approved in a plenary session of each Chamber, but this is not binding on the courts. The value of these Commissions lies in the fact that they have the power to compel any citizen to appear before them who risks a penal sanction for disobedience by refusing to do so; therefore, the importance of the score of Commissions of investigation

set up by parliament to control the government lies not so much in their conclusions as in the appearance of senior public officials who have had to submit themselves to the questions of opposition members of parliament.

(5) The motions (linked to a previous interpellation) and proposals not of law are conceived in the Standing Orders as instruments to force the action of the government, which in large measure we can also consider an instrument of control, in that they are indications of a specific action that the government should carry out. In particular, parliamentary use has created the motion of 'reprobation' through which a Chamber shows its displeasure with a certain minister; although, even if approved, it has no legal value since only the President of the Government can appoint and dismiss ministers (Article 100 SC). Likewise, suppose the government does not follow the indications of a motion or proposal. In that case, it cannot be judicially demanded to do so, as the agreement of the chamber 'exhausts its effects' in the adoption of the agreement and lacks binding legal value for 'subjects or bodies that do not form part of the Chamber that adopts it' (STC 40/2003, 27 February, case *Inadmisión proposición no de ley sobre requerimiento de informe al Tribunal Vasco de Cuentas*).

IV. Other Functions

138. In a good number of its articles, the Constitution assigns other functions to parliament, which will be treated in more detail in other parts of this work and which, without wishing to explain them all, can be grouped into two sections:

(1) the selection of members of other constitutional bodies (the Constitutional Court, the GCJP, the Court of Auditors, the Ombudsman) that several laws have added to (the Central Electoral Board, the Spanish Radio and Television Council, etc.);

(2) the prior authorization to enable public powers to carry out certain acts, such as the authorization for the king to declare war (Article 63.3 CE), the ratification of certain international treaties and agreements, and the authorization for the Autonomous Communities to conclude collaboration agreements (*see* paragraph 62). Apart from these main groups of functions, Congress authorizes the state of emergency (*see* paragraph 449), the calling of referendums, etc. For its part, the Senate must give its authority for the government to carry out *state coercion* against a specific Autonomous Community that fails to fulfil its constitutional obligations (*see* paragraph 277).

§4. THE OPERATION OF PARLIAMENT

I. The Internal Organization of the Chambers

A. The Organs of Government

139. Article 72 of the Constitution points to the President and the Bureau as the organs of government of the Chamber, so attaching it to the collegiate parliamentary model of direction characteristic of continental Europe as opposed to the British model with one person (the Speaker) in charge of the Chamber:

(1) The President of each Chamber is chosen by all its members in a secret ballot and by an absolute majority in the first ballot, which so far is what has always occurred, almost always choosing a member of the parliamentary majority in both Chambers. The Constitution and the Standing Orders confer on the holder of this post a considerable number of functions: direction of parliamentary debates, administrative powers and the policing of the Chamber, interpretation of the Standing Orders, relations with the administration to process members' requests for information, etc. The President of Congress presides over joint meetings of Congress and the Senate and has the duty of transmitting to the plenary session of the lower Chamber the king's proposal of the candidate for President of the Government (Article 99 SC).

(2) The Bureau, of which the President forms part, is the organ of collegiate direction, also chosen by secret ballot by all the members of the Chamber by a system of limited voting, with the aim of enabling representatives to be chosen from all political groups. That of Congress is wider than that of the Senate, being made up of a President, four vice presidents, and four secretaries (Article 30 RCD), while the Senate has a President, two vice presidents, and four secretaries (Article 5 RS). The Bureau's functions include drawing up the parliamentary budget and directing its implementation, approving the members of staff, etc. Particularly important amongst these is the declaration of the eligibility, or not, of the documents, which must be done following a legal criterion of compatibility with the provisions of the Standing Orders of each Chamber. Traditionally, the division of powers meant that these decisions could not be reviewed by the courts (*interna corporis acta* theory); however, the LOTC allows them to be appealed before the Constitutional Court, which has led to the annulment of some very arbitrary majority decisions, not based on legal arguments but political expediency. Thus, for example, the decision of the Bureau of the Congress not to admit a request for a hearing requested by the Socialist Group (STC 89/2005 of 18 April, case *Inadmision solicitud de comparecencia del Fiscal especial antidroga*), the refusal of the Bureau of the Valencian Parliament to process twenty-nine questions from the Socialist Parliamentary Group (STC 44/2010, 24 July, case *Inadmisión de preguntas sobre el caso Gurtel*), etc.

(3) The Board of Party Spokespersons, which is not expressly recognized in the Constitution, has become, in parliamentary practice in both Chambers, an organ of political direction since – as its name indicates – it is formed of the

parliamentary leaders and a representative of the government can attend it. The Board participates in the Chamber's major procedural decisions (fixing commissions, programming the general lines of action, etc.) and is the most politically contentious and with the greatest repercussion in the press: fixing the agenda. To reflect the weight that each parliamentary group has within the Chamber, the vote of each party spokesperson is proportional to the number of deputies he or she represents (weighted vote).

B. *Plenary Sessions and Commissions*

140. Article 75 of the Constitution states that the Chambers can function in plenary sessions or Commissions. The plenary sessions of each Chamber consist of all its members, and it takes the decisions that the Constitution assigns to Congress and the Senate. The Commissions are the organs that prepare those decisions, being either permanent (those included in Standing Orders tend to adapt themselves to the structure of ministerial departments), or 'not permanent', or ad hoc, created to perform a specific task, such as that of investigating a particular matter. The number of members is fixed at the beginning of each legislature, so for the XIV Congress, there are 37 members, the Senate, 29. The Mixed Congress-Senate, 39, and the General Commission of the Autonomous Communities, 59. The Commissions are made up proportionately to the members of each parliamentary group, and each one chooses a president and committee members, similar to the plenary sessions. However, here a member of the majority does not always preside since the custom has arisen of permitting certain Commissions (such as that of the budget) to be presided over by members of the opposition.

As the Commissions have the function of preparing the work of the plenary session, traditionally, they work without the presence of members of the public; however, the Standing Orders of both Chambers permit journalists to attend Commission sessions, a decision that has the paradoxical effect that, although it increases the transparency of the legislative process it does so at the cost of weakening the Commission's role as the place that sometimes facilitated a discreet agreement between members, which has now moved to the previous committee meeting or, more usually, to somewhere outside parliament. The Spanish Constitution – following the Italian one of 1947 – enables the plenary session to delegate to permanent Legislative Commissions the approval of bills and proposals of law provided that they do not deal with constitutional reform, international questions, organic or basic laws, and the General Budget of the state, an authorization of which generous use has been made in daily practice.

C. *The Permanent Deputations*

141. Since the Cadiz Constitution of 1812, the Spanish constitutional system has been concerned with endowing parliament with a measure of permanence, granting it equality with the government. Article 78 of the Constitution, faithful to this tradition, orders that in each Chamber, a Permanent Deputation shall be set up, formed of a minimum of twenty-one members in proportion to the composition of each parliamentary group. In recent legislatures, the respective Congress and Senate Committees have set 68 deputies and 35 senators, distributed amongst the groups according to the number of members of each group. Logically, the parties designate their leaders and the most important parliamentarians. Article 78 itself determines the functions of the deputations: to oversee the powers of the Chambers when they are not in session or when they have been dissolved. In this latter case, the Deputation of Congress additionally has to validate Decree-laws and carry out the functions of the plenary in relation to states of emergency.

II. The Operational Norms

A. *Norms of the Parliamentary Timetable*

142. In order to comply with the constitutional declaration that parliament represents the Spanish people, it is necessary that the mandate given to Members of parliament on their election is for a limited period. The Constitution employs two classic concepts for the temporal organization of parliamentary work:

(1) The legislature is the period of time that runs from the beginning to the expiry of the parliamentary mandate, established by the Constitution as four years (Articles 68.4 and 69.6), which can be shortened in the case of an early dissolution of the Chamber, either by the decision of the President of the Government or because a new president cannot be chosen (Article 99), or the extraordinary procedure of constitutional reform so demands (Article 168). As a precautionary measure, Article 68.6 of the Constitution requires that the Congress-elect should be convened within twenty-five days of the holding of the elections. Therefore, the date of the summoning of Congress within this period is set out in the very Decree calling the elections that is signed by the king and endorsed by the President of the Government (or exceptionally by the President of Congress if a new President has not been chosen).

(2) The sessions are the periods of work of a Chamber within each legislature, which according to Article 73.1, are two periods a year, the first from September to December and the second from February to June, although outside these periods, the Chambers can hold extraordinary sessions. In my opinion, on this particular point, the 1978 Constitution would have been more up-to-date if it had abandoned – as has, for example, the Bonn Fundamental Law of 1979 – the tradition of parliamentary law, for it makes no sense nowadays to keep to the parliamentary timetable designed at the beginning of the nineteenth century, when there was far less legislation and when the most rapid means of communication was a galloping horse.

B. The Norms of Debates and Voting

143. For the Chambers to meet and their actions to have validity, it is necessary for them to be in a regular session and with the attendance of the majority of their members (Article 79.1 SC); this constitutional provision has resulted in a considerable number of articles in the Standing Orders on the matters to be dealt with and the way of doing it (agenda, submission of documents, times of the debates, circumstances in which the sessions can be held in camera, etc.), all designed with the evident aim of facilitating parliamentary work, avoiding both that the majority should take advantage of their situation as that the minority should delay and obstruct it.

As a general rule, for Congress to operate and for its agreements to be valid, Article 79.2 of the Constitution requires a majority of members to be present without prejudice to the special majorities established by the Constitution, the organic laws, and Standing Orders. Thus, three classes of majorities can be distinguished for the validity of parliamentary agreements (voting quorum):

(1) A simple or ordinary majority: when more Members of Parliament vote in favour of one view rather than the opposite (let us say more votes in favour of an amendment of a bill than against), but considering that for the agreement to be valid, the numbers attending must exceed half plus one of the members adopting the agreement. (quorum of attendance).
(2) Absolute majority: half plus one of the total number of members composing the organ (therefore, abstention and absences count against).
(3) Qualified majorities: for example, the three-fifths of each Chamber for the selection of members of the Constitutional Court or the ordinary reform of the Constitution and the two-thirds required for the extraordinary reform procedure.

Chapter 4. The Executive

§1. The Constitutional Form of the Government

144. As in other parliamentary systems, the Spanish government has passed from being in a subordinate position in the institutional structure of the division of powers to occupying the central place in the political system for a variety of reasons that go from the creation of a social state, which demands an interventionist state inevitably directed by the executive power, to reasons of simple electoral politics, such as the attenuation of ideological differences and the growing role of the leaders. Thus, in historical Spanish Constitutions, the executive power was established in 'the King and his ministers', and it was not until the 1931 Constitution that there was for the first time a Title referring to the government as distinct from the Head of State, although he could freely appoint and dismiss the President of the Government. The 1978 Constitution, taking a further step in the country's historical evolution, not only regulated it in a Title distinct from that of the king but also asserted that the government alone holds the executive power in the State and expressly declared that the government directed domestic and foreign policy (Article 97). In this way, the evident practice of modern parliamentary systems is recognized in that the fundamental division of powers is not only that between the government (with the parliamentary majority that maintains it) and the opposition but also – in contrast to the abstract model of the parliamentary system – it is the government that predominates over parliament.

Almost parallel to the revaluation in the role of the government in the political system, there has been, throughout Europe, an increase in the power of the President of the Government, who has passed from being *primus inter pares* to the outstanding leader who chooses the ministers, a reality reflected in the Spanish Constitution in a series of articles that assign to her/him a special importance (beginning by being the only one chosen by Congress). In practice, in our daily political life, the role of the President has slowly continued to increase to the point that Law 50/1997 on Government has recognized, arousing no particular controversy, that 'presidential direction' is one of the functions of government.

§2. The Composition of the Government

I. The Members of the Government

145. Article 98 of the Constitution states that the government shall consist of the president, vice president or vice presidents, ministers and, in some cases, such other members as the law may establish. However, the law has never amplified this definition, nor has it fixed a rigid composition for the government, enabling the President to decide on the number, denomination, and scope of the competences of the ministries (Article 57.3 LRJSP). The law does, nevertheless, distinguish between two classes of ministers: those who are heads of a department, that is, in charge of a hierarchical administrative organization and those who are not, known as 'ministers without portfolio' (Article 4 LG), although in recent times these types of ministers have not been appointed. The most common practice followed by the Presidents of Government has been to appoint one or two vice presidents (one political and the other for the economy when there have been two) and a number of ministers, usually less than twenty. In daily political language, 'government' is used in a wider sense than in a strictly legal meaning since it usually refers not only to the ministers but also to the Secretaries of State and, in general, to all senior officials that the government can appoint at will.

II. The Election of the President of the Government

146. The Constitution regulates, in detail, the procedure by which Congress grants the 'investiture' of the President. The use of this archaism is rather ironic because the prolix regulation of the procedure to choose the President set out in Article 99 – and which is completed in new provisions in the Standing Orders of Congress – was totally unknown in our constitutional history. Moreover, possibly the will of the 1978 Constituent Assembly in drafting this article was to cut, root, and branch the former practice of the Heads of State – both in the monarchy and in the Republic – of adopting an active role in the designation of the President of the Government, without strictly abiding by the will of the deputies.

147. Article 99 of the Constitution provides that after each renewal of the Congress of Deputies and in other constitutional situations in which there is no President (resignation, death), the king shall propose a candidate for the Presidency of the Government after consulting with the representatives designated by the political groups with parliamentary representation. On the eleven occasions that King Juan Carlos 1 had to propose a candidate (after ten general elections and one resignation), these consultations were little more than protocol because the party with most deputies, either alone or as a result of pacts with other parties, had always won a majority favourable to its candidate. However, on none of the four occasions in which King Felipe VI has had to propose a candidate to date (twice in 2016 and twice in 2019) has there been a candidate who had that majority in principle, which is why the consultations took on an unprecedented relevance in our democracy.

The candidate proposed by the King, through the President of Congress, submits the political programme he intends to follow (which in parliamentary practice means that the names of future ministers are also indicated) and then there is a debate where each parliamentary group makes its position clear. Later a ballot is taken that is not secret – unlike the practice in other parliaments, such as the German and the Italian – but 'in public and aloud'. To be invested President, the Constitution requires the candidate to obtain an absolute majority of the members of Congress (176 out of 350, therefore); if he/she does not get this majority, the candidature is re-submitted to a second ballot where a simple majority is enough. If this is still unsuccessful, the King must propose new candidates who undergo the same procedure, and if none of these manages to obtain a majority within two months from the first ballot for the investiture, the king shall dissolve both Chambers and call new elections with the endorsement of the president of Congress. These provisions for dissolution and new elections had remained untried in Spanish democracy until the eleventh legislature when it was impossible to obtain a government with sufficient backing, and the king had to call elections in May 2016. This situation was repeated in 2019, when Pedro Sánchez, the candidate of the party with the most seats (PSOE), did not obtain an absolute majority in the first round or a simple majority in the second round. Until then, all presidents had been chosen on the first vote, except for Leopoldo Calvo Sotelo in February 1981 and José Luis Rodríguez Zapatero in April 2008; in both cases, they were elected on the second vote (Table 7).

Table 7 Investiture Sessions

Legislature	*Date of Investiture*	*Candidate*	*Votes*			*Parties in Favour*
			Yes	*No*	*Abs*	
Constituent Assembly (77–79)	(4-7-77)[26]	Adolfo Suárez				
1 (79–82)	30-3-79	Adolfo Suárez	183	149	8	UCD, PAR, UPN
	25-2-81	Leopoldo Calvo Sotelo	186	158	0	UCD, CD, MC, Mix
2 (82–86)	1-12-82	Felipe González	207	116	21	PSOE, EE, Mix
3 (86–89)	23-7-86	Felipe González	184	144	6	PSOE
4 (89–93)	5-12-89	Felipe González	167	165	6	PSOE, AIC
5 (93–96)	9-7-93	Felipe González	181	165	1	PSOE, CiU, PNV
6 (96–00)	4-5-96	José Mª Aznar	181	166	1	PP, CiU, CC
7 (00–04)	26-4-00	José Mª Aznar	202	148	0	PP, CiU, CC
8 (04–08)	16-4-04	José Luis Rodríguez	180	148	19	PSOE, IU, CC,
9 (08-11)	11-4-08	José Luis Rodríguez Zapatero	169	158	23	ERC, BNGPSOE
10 (11-15)	20-12-11	Mariano Rajoy	187	149	14	PP, UPN, FA

26. The King, in light of the electoral results, ratified Adolfo Suárez; there was no investiture as such.

Legislature	*Date of Investiture*	*Candidate*	*Votes*			*Parties in Favour*
			Yes	*No*	*Abs*	
11 (16-16)	4-4-2016	Pedro Sánchez-Castejón (Not chosen)	131	291	0	PSOE, Ciudadanos
12 (16-19)	29-10-16 01-06-18	Mariano Rajoy (motion of censure) Pedro Sánchez	170 180	111 169	68 1	PP, Cs PSOE, Podemos, PDeCAT, ERC, PNV, Bildu
13 (19-19)	23-07-19 25-07-19	Pedro Sánchez (Not chosen)	124 124	170 155	52 67	PSOE
14 (19-)	5-01-20 7-01-20	Pedro Sánchez	166 167	165 165	18 18	PSOE, Podemos, PDeCAT, ERC, PNV, Bildu

III. The Appointment of the Other Members of the Government

148. According to Article 100 of the Constitution, the other members of the government are appointed and dismissed by the king at the proposal of the president. There is no need to point out that the king has no power of autonomous appointment beyond the advice and recommendations he can make as a person of influence, but he cannot refuse to accept the names put forward by the president. Equally, other institutions do not have the competence to dismiss ministers since Article 100 is strict in assigning this competence to the President of the Government, and there is no provision similar to Article 64 in the 1931 Constitution, which permitted votes of censure in parliament against specified ministers. In practice, Congress has created the motion of 'reprobation' to criticize the conduct of a minister, but it has no binding force on the president. Yet the limitations on the President when forming the government are real, either because he/she has won the investiture through the support of various parties and a coalition government has to be formed (which has not occurred in the national governments but has in many regional ones) or because the internal circumstances in the party (political currents, territorial origins, etc.) must be taken into account. Since the Organic Law 3/2007, 22 March, on the effective equality of women and men, the president has had a further legal limit: the principle of 'balanced presence of men and women' in public offices requires him to share the ministries equably between both sexes.

IV. The Resignation of the Government

149. The government resigns after the holding of the general elections in the event of losing the confidence of parliament (either through the passing of a motion of censure or a vote of no-confidence) or the resignation or death of its president. The motion of censure, regulated by Article 113, is technically known as *constructive* in that the group of deputies that present it (10% of the Chamber) must include the name of an alternative candidate, and the motion can only succeed if approved by the absolute majority of the members of Congress. This form of motion, taken from the Bonn Fundamental Law, is due to the desire to prevent the purely negative coalitions of the liberal parliamentary systems in which the various groups agreed only on the wish to get rid of a government but were incapable of agreeing on the formation of a government. In the three first cases in which the motion of censure has been used in Congress, the proposers did not do it to try to overthrow the government (they always knew in advance that they would not win) but to show a public opinion that an alternative did exist. On the contrary, at the end of May 2018, the socialist leader Pedro Sánchez presented a motion of censure against Mariano Rajoy, which did succeed (Table 7). In October 2020, Vox presented another motion of censure with no chance of success in gaining publicity, as its fifty-two deputies only supported it.

150. The vote of confidence can be presented, under Article 112, by the President of the Government after deliberation by the Council of Ministers and only on the programme or a declaration of general policy. Confidence will be understood as granted when there is a simple majority vote of the deputies in favour. This provision avoids the vote of confidence being binding, as in France, on a specific normative text so that the government cannot use this *threat of suicide* to discipline a reluctant majority into approving a determined text. If to this limitation is added the fact that in Spain, one party, backed by a disciplined party group, has always governed, it will be understood why a vote of confidence has only been presented twice and won without problems by the President. The first occasion was in October 1980 by President Adolfo Suárez, whose party had many problems with internal cohesion, so much so that the President himself resigned a few months later, in February 1981. The other time was in April 1990 when the Socialist President Felipe González presented a question of confidence to demand a 'special policy of dialogue' to enable him to carry out a competitive economy in the framework of the EU without borders, to boost foreign policy and advance the chapter of the Autonomous Communities.

§3. Legal Status of Members of the Government

151. The Constitution does not establish any personal requirements in order to form part of the government, although the wording of Article 13 (foreigners) and Article 23 (right of participation in public affairs) must imply that, at the least, majority of age and Spanish nationality are necessary. These requirements were given expression in Article 11 of the Law on Government, which repeats that the candidate for office shall enjoy the rights of active and passive suffrage as well as not being disqualified from exercising public employment or office under a final legal judgment.

152. Article 98 of the Constitution establishes the minimum regime of incompatibilities for members of government, ordering that they shall not exercise representative functions other than those of the parliamentary mandate itself, nor any other public function that does not derive from office, nor any professional or mercantile activity whatever. The detailed regime of incompatibilities is remitted to a law (Article 98.4). Law 3/2015, 30 March, regulating the exercise of senior positions in the General State Administration strengthened the strict regime of incompatibilities which had been established by previous similar laws in 1995 and 2006. Thus, they must be honourable people 'with the appropriate training and experience in the field' (a somewhat evanescent requirement if we read some of the ministers' CVs). Furthermore, it is declared incompatible for members of the government and other senior officials to hold stakes of more than ten per cent in companies that have contracts with the state, regional or local public sector; it is prohibited for senior officials to carry out private activities related to cases on which they have issued a decision in the exercise of their office for two years following the date of their resignation, etc.

153. The members of the government are, logically, responsible for their acts, both politically and legally. Article 108 of the Constitution determines that political responsibility is global, that the whole government is 'collectively accountable for its political management before Congress'. It has already been pointed out how that accountability, which does not result from the breach of any norm but from the exercise of office in such a way as to deserve parliamentary reproach, materializes in the motion of censure and as motions of individual reprobation (that have no other value than to censure the minister's conduct but have no legal force to dismiss him).

154. Legally, the responsibility of ministers is controlled by the Courts, especially those of the Contentious-Administrative legal system, which supervises the legality of the acts of the administration. In the case of a criminal process, Article 102 establishes a special jurisdiction for members of the government: the Criminal Division of the Supreme Court. The reasons for the balance of powers that were referred to when studying the special jurisdiction of Members of parliament are equally applicable here (*see* paragraph 131). If the charge is of treason or any crime against the security of the State in the exercise of his functions, it can only be brought through the initiative of one-fourth part of the members of Congress and with the approval of an absolute majority in a plenary session. This is a precaution, with its roots lost in history, to guarantee that only when sound reasons exist can such politically charged criminal proceedings be launched.

§4. Functions of the Government

I. The Political Direction of the State

155. Article 97 of the Constitution enumerates the basic functions of the government and provides that it 'directs the domestic and foreign policy, the civil and military administration and the defence of the State. It exercises the executive function and the regulatory power in accordance with the laws'. As shown by the separation of the phrases by a full stop, there is a marked difference between the purely political function of direction, barely formalized, and the executive function, subject to law. The mentions made by the Constitution of the direction of domestic and foreign policy and of the civil and military administration, as well as the defence of the State, are concrete expressions that, in a better world, would not be necessary made by the constituent assembly to avoid interpretations of the Constitution that today nobody would maintain. However, in 1978, they were theories with no few followers, such as the military command being independent of the government and the direct power of the king over the armed forces. These theories could find support in certain constitutional articles, such as Article 62, which lists amongst the King's functions that of Supreme Commander of the Armed Forces, and Article 8, which states that the mission of the Armed Forces is to guarantee the sovereignty and independence of Spain, to defend its territorial integrity and constitutional system. If a theory of military autonomy is incompatible with a democratic State worthy of the name, Article 97 makes it completely unsustainable.

156. To enable the executive to carry out its function of political direction, the Constitution assigns to it a series of competences such as the approval of Decree-laws (Article 86), legislative initiative (Article 89), initiating and negotiating treaties (Article 94 SC and Article 5.1.d of LG), economic planning (Article 132), budget initiatives, and the implementation of the budget (Article 134). Equally, it can carry out this function through certain constitutional competences in relation to other constitutional bodies; thus, the government can adopt measures to force compliance with the obligations of Autonomous Communities (Article 155); it even has the competence to nominate the State Public Prosecutor (Article 124) and two judges of the Constitutional Court (Article 159). This function of political direction does not end with all the competences given by the Constitution and the Laws on Government, but rather it is a function it exercises in multiple other acts, many of them with no direct legal consequences: awarding honours and distinctions, mediating discourses in which the ministers put forward their vision of the general interest, supporting social acts by their attendance, etc.

157. The general characteristic of the acts emanating from the function of political direction means that they are subject to very limited legal control: it is difficult for the government to break the law by presenting a specific bill on a matter but leaving the legal regulation of other matters to another day, to include certain public investments in the budget but omit others, to appoint a lawyer of recognized prestige as a judge, etc. Even the Constitutional Court has recognized that to decide when there is an extraordinary and urgent necessity justifying the approval of a

Decree-law is a political decision that cannot be controlled by the Constitutional Court, except 'on the assumption of abusive and arbitrary use, without interfering in the decision of the government, since to do so would alter the assumptions on which the democratic constitutional order is based' (S111/1983, 2 December, case *RUMASA I*). However, recently, it seems willing to be more demanding when admitting governmental arguments to justify urgency (*see* paragraph 74).

II. The Executive Function and the Regulatory Power

158. Through the executive function, the government carries out the laws approved by parliament. In a social State such as Spain, the executive function entails the management of public services and the handling of a budget of gigantic proportions (the General Budget for 2022 exceeded EUR 240,375 million). The Constitution expressly refers to the regulatory power habitually employed to give normative completion to State laws (parliamentary regulations or development laws), that is to say, as part of the executive function, but the regulatory power enables the government to approve independent regulations to regulate a matter that is not subject to the reserve of law and, in particular, to approve administrative regulations designed to organize the services of the administration.

159. The degree of legal control resulting from the government's executive function is much tighter than over its political acts, though not reaching the point of converting the government into a mere administrator lacking the capacity to make innovations and decisions; and so if today no one can maintain, in all its crudeness, the phrase, 'You keep the Laws and leave me the Administrative Regulations' pronounced in the nineteenth century by the Conde de Romanones, it cannot be said that members of the government, who have the responsibility for doing so, are indifferent to the execution of the laws. Perhaps the best example is Royal Decree 2393/2004, 30 December, passed by the Socialist government to develop Organic Law 4/2000, 11 January, on the rights and freedoms of foreigners, which had been approved by the *Cortes* when the Popular Party had an absolute majority. However, contrary to what that party had envisaged when it passed the law, the socialist regulation opened a regularization procedure for undocumented immigrants that allowed the normalization of more than 600,000 people.

III. Functions of the President of the Government

160. The leadership of the President of the Government envisaged by the Constitution and reinforced by the Law on Government and Spanish practical politics has its logical expression in the specific functions attributed to him by the legal system, beginning with the appointment, direction, and coordination of the other members of the government. Article 2 LG sets out the functions given by the Constitution, adding others that are the logical consequence of his pre-eminence and that, to a great extent, are implicit in it, such as representing the government, establishing its political programme, calling and presiding over and fixing the agenda for the meetings of the Council of Ministers, resolving the conflicts of power between ministers, and giving instructions to other members of the government. Legally, the most important of these functions is the authority to create, modify, and abolish ministerial departments, which is usually done when making a new government, a moment used to reform the structure of the government and to reorder the main administrative services of the State.

In relation to other constitutional bodies, the President of the Government has the competence for a series of acts, analysed in more detail in other parts of this work: to endorse the more important acts of the king (Article 64.1 SC); to propose to the king the holding of a consultative referendum, with the previous authorization of Congress (Article 92); to present a vote of confidence to Congress (Article 112); to dissolve parliament or only one of the Chambers (Article 115 SC); and to present the appeal of unconstitutionality before the Constitutional Court (Article 162.1 SC). Moreover, the president has other functions entrusted to him in other laws, such as the direction of the defence policy and the management of crises under the Organic Law of National Defence (LO 5/2005 17 November).

IV. The Caretaker Government

161. The government ceases to be in office following elections, loss of parliamentary confidence or the resignation or death of its President. However, the outgoing government will continue 'in office' (Article 101.2 CE) until the new government takes office, which usually takes around a month after the elections. By pure democratic logic, a caretaker government cannot fully develop its activity during this period, even if the Constitution does not expressly specify its restrictions. It must limit itself to maintaining the functioning of the State so that the new government can carry out the policy it deems appropriate. An expressive phrase used in the ecclesiastical sphere: 'Sede vacante, nihil innovetur'.

In 1997, the Government Act legally established what had been standard practice: the caretaker government will limit itself to the 'ordinary business of public affairs', refraining from adopting other measures, except in cases of urgency or duly accredited general interest, and will be obliged to facilitate the normal development of the process of forming the new government and the transfer of powers (Article 21). In addition to this general principle, the Law specifies certain functions that the government cannot perform (such as the presentation of bills or the approval of legislative decrees). Likewise, it limits the functions of the President of the Government, who cannot dissolve the *Cortes*, raise the question of confidence and propose to the king the calling of a consultative referendum. These excluded functions all stem from the 'political direction' that Article 97 SC attributes to the government in such a way that the indeterminate legal concept of 'ordinary business' in the Law can be understood as referring to the administrative direction of the State attributed to it by Article 97 itself. It was not so right when it granted the extradition of a person to Italy, as the Supreme Court ruled (STS (3) 5369/2005, 20 September), and it is debatable whether it was correct when it refused to grant a pardon, although the Supreme Court endorsed this decision (STS (3) 5369/2005, 2 December). Without controversy, it has been accepted that the caretaker government can issue decree-laws (such as Decree-Law 1/2016 of 15 April) to meet urgent needs and that the caretaker president can appeal regional laws that he considers unconstitutional (such as IR no. 7870-2014 against the Law of the Parliament of Catalonia 4/2014, on the tax on deposits in credit institutions, which gave rise to STC 111/2015 of 28 May). There was much controversy in the failed XI Legislature (January–May 2016) over the control the *Cortes* could exercise over the caretaker government. Thus, according to Rajoy's then-caretaker government, the *Cortes* could not exercise any control since they had not granted it their confidence; on the contrary, in the opinion of Congress, the government was subject to the control of the Houses in the ordinary acts it carries out under Article 21 of the LG. This discrepancy led the Congress to file a conflict between constitutional bodies 'about the fact that the caretaker Government was not subject to control initiatives by the Congress of Deputies', which the Constitutional Court ruled in its favour because 'the Cortes Generales cannot be denied the exercise of the control function attributed to them by Article 66.2 EC because the caretaker government is not carrying out any activity, insofar as, as we have seen, it continues to do so'. In the specific case that gave rise to the conflict, the government activity consisted of the meeting of NATO Defence Ministers held on 10 and 11 February 2016 in Brussels, which the government refused to explain in a request for a hearing requested by several congressional groups (STC 124/2018, 14 November).

§5. The Operation of the Government

162. According to the LG, its functioning is based on three principles: presidential direction, collegiality, and the departmental principle. We have already seen how the principle of presidential direction is embodied in a series of functions that allow the President to determine the political direction that the government and each minister must follow. The Law authorizes the President to delegate some of his competences, an authorization usually employed to assign the functions of coordination of ministers to the vice president.

The departmental principle implies that the ministers are responsible for developing government policy within the ministry, such that the minister is both administrator – the head of a department – and a politician to whom a considerable number of competences are assigned: regulatory power in the matters of the department, determining the aims of the ministry and assigning the resources necessary for their implementation, appointing and dismissing holders of managerial posts in the ministry, resolving administrative appeals made against the resolutions of the senior members of the ministry, etc. (Article 61 LRJS).

163. The principle of collegiality means that for the government to adopt decisions as an entity, it must meet to express its collective opinion in those matters assigned to it by the Constitution and brought together in Article 5 of the Law on Government: approval of bills, approval of Decree-laws, agreement of the negotiation, signature of treaties, etc. The Spanish tradition, included in several constitutional Articles (62,112, 115 and 116), designates this meeting as the Council of

Ministers. The Law on Government specifies that the president shall call it, and it is usually held weekly, every Friday. Unlike the legislative procedure, which is strictly regulated and public, the deliberations of the Council are secret (Article 5.3 LG), and few indications about the agenda, fixed by the president, and the content of the acts of the meetings are given (Article 18 LG). For this reason, the rules of the functioning of this body are not so much based on legal provisions as on custom and, above all, on the leadership of the president, who, in the unlikely event of a vote being called for on any question in the Council, could make his own the phrase Abraham Lincoln pronounced in a meeting of the American government 'seven votes against and one in favour, proposal carried'.

The Council of Ministers, at the proposal of the president, can create Delegate Commissions with the purpose of studying and presenting joint proposals to the Council on matters of the various departments or to resolve those affairs that, because they affect more than one ministry, cannot be resolved in Council. At the present time, there are six Delegate Commissions: Economic Affairs, National Security, Matters of Intelligence, Scientific and Technological Policy, Equality Policy, and Cultural Affairs. A very important body to support the government is the General Commission of Secretaries and Undersecretaries of State, presided over by a vice president, who prepares the sessions of the Council of Ministers.

§6. The Public Administration

164. The 1978 Constitution was the first one in Spanish history to designate one of its Titles, 'Government and Administration', so recognizing the importance for the state of this network of administrative bodies in charge of carrying out the executive function and without which the laws could not be implemented in society. But yet, the duality of the Title makes us reflect on the different levels on which government and administration operate; while the former is characterized by its power to decide freely on the political aims that the state should pursue, the administration, in the words of Article 103 SC 'serves the general interest with objectivity and shall act in accordance with the principles of efficacy, hierarchy, decentralization, deconcentration and coordination, being fully subject to justice and the law'.

165. The administration is, to put it graphically, the tool that the democratic government uses to carry out its policy, but that tool has been previously fixed in the law and is strictly subject to it in two aspects: in its external aspect, which obliges it to act impartially, and in its own formation and composition since Article 103 of the Constitution not only states that the organs of the State administration are 'created, governed and coordinated in accordance with the law' but adds that the Statute of civil servants shall be established by law and must regulate access to the civil service in agreement with the principles of merit and ability. The logical corollary of this subjection of the administration to the law is the legal control of its acts, as set out in Article 106 of the Constitution. The law most relevant in making this control effective is Law 29/1998, on regulating the Contentious-Administration Jurisdiction.

166. Law 40/2015, 1 October, on Legal Regime of Public Sector (LRJSP) regulates the general administration of the State, differentiating between the central bodies, the territorial bodies – with the Government Delegate in each Autonomous Community at its head – and institutional administration. This law complements Law 39/2015, 1 October, on Common Administrative Procedure of Public Administrations, which, as its name indicates, regulates the procedure of the actions of administrations in relation to private individuals. Other relevant laws in the legal configuration of the State administration are Organic Law 2/1986 on the Corps and Security Forces of the State and Law 6/1980, 1 July, which establishes the basic criteria of national defence and military organization. These and many other laws relevant to civil and military administration have accomplished various constitutional mandates, especially those such as Articles 93 and 104 that have put the Armed Forces and the security service under the direction of the democratic government. Examples are the Organic Law 4/2010, 20 May, on the disciplinary regime of the national police force, and Law 39/2007, 19 November, on the military career.

Chapter 5. The Judiciary and the Constitutional Court

§1. The Judicial Power in the Constitution

I. Jurisdictional Power

167. Judicial power is defined, in de Tocqueville's words, by three characteristics:

> The first characteristic of judicial power in all nations is the duty of arbitration. An action must be brought to obtain the decision of a judge. The second characteristic is that it is pronounced on special cases and not upon general principles. Its third characteristic is its inability to act unless it is appealed to, or until it has taken cognizance of an affair.[27]

This brilliant summary of the features of judicial power allows us to understand its peculiarities and its differences from the other two, starting from its lack of autonomous will ('a nothing power', Montesquieu called it): the courts when passing a sentence do not express their own will but that of the law, from which they receive their legitimacy to bind the citizens who take part in the proceedings. The function of judicial power is not to direct and regulate society, the purpose of the political activity of the other powers, but to ensure compliance with the laws that society has given itself through its representatives, independently of the individual will of its addressees and of their particular circumstances, according to the principle of equality before the law. That is to say, as Alexander Hamilton saw, and as history has shown, the main task of the judges is to guarantee legal certainty, essential for the existence of the Rule of Law.

168. For this feature of guaranteeing an impartial application of the law in situations of conflict, the technical aspect is predominant in the judicial power: its members must have good legal training to resolve the controversies posed, both in the interpretation of the norms as in making the correct fit between them and the facts, the application of the law. Thus, unlike the other powers in a democratic State, the members do not need to be chosen by the citizens, and they can fulfil their role indefinitely, without the necessity of changing them, as with the other powers, as a means of adapting their composition to the changing will of society. Finally, the fact of having to resolve disputes on the application of law in concrete cases means that the judicial power must consist of a great many courts, and so it can be said that this is a diffuse power, while the legislative and executive are concentrated.

169. The Spanish Constituent Assembly was very conscious of the role of the courts in the State of Law; therefore, from the first moment, they considered that it was a question of the power of the state and not merely a public service. Thus, they

27. Alexis de Tocqueville, *Democracy in America* Vol. I, 136-137 (Saunders and Otley).

did not employ the expression 'Administration of Justice' (traditional in our moderate Constitutions) and followed the progressives by devoting Title VI to 'Judicial Power'.[28] This title establishes its main lines and sets out, with vigour unknown in our constitutional history, a series of techniques oriented to guarantee that the judges and magistrates would exercise jurisdictional power impartially, summed up in the fives principles of being subject to law, independence, responsibility, unity, and exclusivity of jurisdiction. We shall look at each one of them, superficially at least.

II. The Democratic Legitimacy of Judicial Power: The Principle of Submission to the Constitution and the Law

170. Article 117.1 of the Constitution states that 'justice emanates from the people and is administered in the name of the King by judges and magistrates who are members of the Judicial Power, independent, irremovable, responsible and subject only to the rule of law'. This definition establishes the Spanish and European tradition of a corps of civil servants entrusted to administer justice; later, in Article 122.1, it even specifies that it is a 'single body' as a way of underlining the similar position of every person charged with exercising jurisdictional power, albeit divided into various categories, basically two. These are judges (the lower rank who are heads of one-person organs) and the magistrates (higher, normally appointed to multi-person organs, the courts). But furthermore, Article 117 establishes very clearly that the legitimacy of the courts emanates from the people, those who approved the Constitution, who assigned jurisdictional power, and who, by electing the legislators, determined the norms that the courts must apply when resolving legal conflicts, independently of their own personal or political viewpoints.

171. According to the literal wording of Article 117, the judges are subject only to the 'rule of law'; however, if we remember that Article 9.1 of the Constitution states that 'the citizens and the public powers are subject to the Constitution and to the rest of the legal order', it becomes necessary to also include within this 'law' the Constitution, the supreme norm of the legal order, as Article 5 LOPJ expressly declares, which imposes on judges and courts the obligation to interpret and apply the laws and regulations according to the constitutional precepts and principles 'in agreement with their interpretation resulting from the judgments of the Constitutional Court in all classes of proceedings'. The possible conflict between a law and the Constitution that can be presented to the judges is resolved in Article 163 through the question of unconstitutionality, as the judicial bodies may consult the Constitutional Court on the validity of any law that they must apply during a trial and which they consider unconstitutional (*see* paragraph 203). Similarly, suppose they consider that a Spanish law they must apply may be contrary to European law,

28. The exceptions to these equivalents 'Administration of Justice = moderate Constitution; Judicial Power = progressive Constitution' was the very progressive 1,812 Constitution that under the rubric 'on Courts and the Administration of Justice' in its Title V shaped a judicial power that was remarkably advanced for its time.

they may submit a preliminary ruling to the CJEU, or they may not apply the Spanish law. This produces the paradox that a judge or court may decide on its own not to apply a law if it considers it contrary to European law but may not do so if it considers it contrary to the Constitution (*see* paragraph 66).

III. The Principle of Independence

172. There is no need for much theoretical reflection to justify the judge's independence as a guarantee of impartiality in the application of the law, an essential component of legal certainty in a democratic State since, as Loewenstein said in a lapidary phrase, 'the law is the judge's only master'. In the absolutist State, the administration of justice depends on the final instance of the king's will; therefore, judicial independence has been thought of in a democratic State as, above all, independence from the executive power, but nowadays, it has been widened to include both public and private powers and even the judicial power itself, for every judge and court is independent of 'all those in the exercise of its jurisdiction' (STC 108/1986, 29 July, case *Ley Orgánica del Poder Judicial-II*). To guarantee this independence, the Constitution itself establishes the irremovability of judges and reserves to law the creation, operation, and government of the courts (the functional aspect of judicial independence), as well as the status of judges and magistrates (the personal aspect). This status is regulated by the LOPJ by a strict system of guarantees as well as limitations and prohibitions, particularly important amongst which are those not belonging to a political party or trade union, as established by the Constitution itself (Article 127.1), although from 2012 the LOPJ permitted judges to hold political office with the same legal regime as other civil servants (in special services, that is, that they maintain the position that they had, and the years that they have been in political life is treated as if they had been in the judiciary), provided that they did not belong to a political party, which in my opinion is a clear Constitutional fraud. Article 122 of the Constitution reinforces those personal and functional aspects of judicial independence with the creation of the GCJP as its 'governing organ'.

IV. The Principle of Responsibility

173. In a democratic State, there cannot exist a public power invested with the degree of independence enjoyed by the judiciary without responsibility. So, it is usually said that responsibility is the reverse of judicial independence. This responsibility is embodied in various legal techniques, beginning with criminal responsibility for the crime of perverting the course of justice to sanction judges who knowingly pass unjust judgments (Articles 446–449 Criminal Code). The LOPJ also regulates their civil responsibility when, by deceit or fault, they cause damage or harm in the exercise of their functions, and disciplinary responsibility when they fail to fulfil their duties as judges (Articles 411–427), although this one, unlike the other two, does not extend to going into the merits of their decisions, since this would break judicial independence as the GCJP, the sanctioning body, is not jurisdictional.

This explains why in some cases where a judicial decision has aroused a certain degree of controversy in society (such as granting provisional liberty to alleged terrorists) and a sanctioning complaint has been made by the General Council against the judge, it has always had to be withdrawn/adjourned *sine die*: only the duty judge could be required to hold criminal responsibility, but not a disciplinarian one.

V. The Principle of Jurisdictional Exclusivity

174. A correct delimitation of the functions of the powers requires that only the judicial power can pass judgment and carry out the sentence, as laid down by Article 117.3 of the Constitution, which reserves to law the norms of competence and procedure of jurisdictional bodies, so avoiding arbitrariness in the determination of the judge who must have knowledge of the matter. The principle of exclusivity means that in Spain, unlike what has traditionally occurred in France and the other 'civil law' States, the public administration is totally controlled by the courts and is forbidden to exercise jurisdictional functions, as happened under Franco. However, due to certain historical inertia, some administrative bodies have still kept the name of the *court*, such as the Central Economic-Administrative Court, attached to the Ministry of Exchequer (Finance), whose existence can be traced back to 1881. In pure constitutional logic, and however much these bodies resolve the claims according to Law, those names should be changed to avoid any confusion about their true nature.

175. If the judiciary's monopoly of jurisdiction is the positive part, the negative is the prohibition against exercising any non-jurisdictional functions except 'those expressly assigned by law to guarantee any right' (Article 117.4 SC). That same inertia has led to such a lax understanding of this mandate of exclusivity and of the separation of powers itself that the judiciary continues to participate in most of the administrative bodies where it was doing so in the time of Franco, such as Compulsory Purchase Tribunals (Law of Compulsory Purchase, 1954). Some new laws have even increased the participation of judges in administrative bodies, undoubtedly with the commendable intention of improving their independence. For example, judges participate in the electoral administration and the provincial video surveillance commissions. However, a good division of powers is not helped either by the possibility that the same legal act can be carried out by the administration or by the Judiciary, as happened from 1994 to 2011 with civil marriages, which the Civil Code allowed to be celebrated before the judge in charge of the registry or before the mayor of the locality. Fortunately, judges lost that competence with Law 20/2011, 21 July, on the Civil Registry. This Law was a step forward in the direction of a correct division of functions between the Judiciary and the executive, as it put an end to the pre-constitutional regime of this registry, which was managed by judges, but whose decisions could be appealed administratively before the Director General of Registers. With much more constitutional logic, the new Law completely de-judicializes the management of the registry, which becomes a function of the Ministry of Justice (albeit in coordination with the Autonomous Communities that have executive powers over the material resources of the Administration of Justice). However, its implementation caused quite a few problems to the point that its full entry into force did not occur until 30 April 2021, but not before being modified by Law 6/2021, 28 April.

VI. The Principle of Jurisdictional Unity

176. Article 117.5 declares that 'the principle of jurisdictional unity is the base of the organization and operation of the Courts', although there is a nuance when it adds that 'the law shall regulate the exercise of military jurisdiction within a strictly military framework'. Without a doubt, the constituent assembly wanted to modify the system of punitive organs of Franco's regime, with its special (labour) and exceptional (military) jurisdictions as well as other repressive mechanisms that the assembly expressly abolished in other articles, so abolishing the Court of Honour and other exceptional tribunals (Articles 26 and 117.6 SC). At present, the LOPJ distinguishes between the Civil, Criminal, Contentious-Administrative, and Employment 'jurisdictional divisions'. It maintains military jurisdiction, although it has reduced the number of acts classified as military offences in the Military Penal Code and in the case of a state of siege (Article 9 LOPJ), at the same time as integrating it in the ordinary jurisdiction to the point of establishing a 'Military Division' (the fifth) within the Supreme Court. Article 136 of the Constitution also grants 'jurisdiction over accounts to the Court of Auditors, a fiscal body of the general parliament with jurisdictional functions to determine accounting responsibilities of those in charge of managing public funds' (*see* paragraph 218).

177. The Constitution has understood jurisdictional unity in such a way as to prevent the Autonomous Communities from having their own judicial power since Article 122 reserves its regulation to LOPJ and Article 149.1 SC includes the administration of justice amongst the exclusive competences of the State. However, and as a reflection of the Autonomous State, the Constitution recognizes in its article 152 the existence of High Courts of Justice in the first-rank Communities. The LOPJ has not only made these courts general throughout the autonomous regions but, while keeping them as state organs, allows a system of collaboration between the Legislative Assembly of the respective Autonomous Communities and the GCJP to appoint one magistrate out of every three who makes up the civil and criminal divisions of these Courts.

§2. The Spanish Judicial Organization

I. The Organizing Criteria of the Court Scheme

178. In order to structure a judicial power that is single but dispersed in a multitude of organs, the LOPJ sets out a 'ground plan' of the courts using the criteria of territoriality and hierarchy. The criterion of specialization according to subject matter divides the jurisdiction into four jurisdictional divisions: Civil, Criminal,

Contentious-Administrative, and Social. The Civil is a catch-all division in that it deals not only with matters that belong to it but also with all those that are not expressly assigned to any other jurisdictional order (Article 9.2 LOPJ). Moreover, as we already know, there is military jurisdiction, and accounts are the exclusive province of the Court of Auditors. On the other hand, within each jurisdictional division, there are highly specialized courts; thus, within the civil jurisdiction, there are the commercial courts, and within the criminal jurisdiction, there are the juvenile courts and the penitentiary courts, which are responsible, respectively, for judging crimes committed by persons over fourteen and under eighteen years of age and for overseeing the correct execution of penitentiary legislation. In a particular situation are the Courts for Violence against Women; since they are specialized criminal courts, they also have essential civil competences.

II. The Territorial Division of Judicial Power

179. Article 30 of the LOPJ applies the criterion of territoriality, dividing the State for legal purposes into municipalities, local courts, provinces, and Autonomous Communities. Of these four divisions, three coincide with the administrative divisions, so their limits need not be marked out for the legal organization. However, a specific demarcation is required for areas of the local courts, which are made up of one or more bordering municipalities belonging to the same province (Article 32 LOPJ). The scope of the local courts is fixed by state law, although Autonomous Communities have the capacity to make representations to the government before it draws up the corresponding bill (Article 35 LOPJ).

The organization of the courts, territorially speaking, is generally as follows:

(a) Municipalities that are not capitals of local court areas: one Judge of the Peace.
(b) Local Courts: one or several courts of first instance (civil) and examining magistrates' courts.
(c) Provinces: Provincial Court and Criminal, Contentious-Administrative, Social, Penal Supervision, Juvenile, and, from September 2004, Commercial Courts.
(d) Autonomous Communities: High Court of Justice, with Civil, Criminal, Contentious-Administrative, and Social Divisions.
(e) State: National High Court, with Criminal, Contentious-Administrative, and Social Divisions and the Supreme Court. The latter, with its seat in Madrid, has jurisdiction over all of Spain and, as Article 123 SC states, is the highest jurisdictional organ in all orders, except in matters of constitutional guarantees, which is, of course, assigned to the Constitutional Court. The Supreme Court consists of five divisions: (1) Civil, (2) Criminal, (3) Contentious-Administrative, (4) Social, and (5) Military.

III. The Judicial Hierarchy

180. The criterion of hierarchy generally coincides with geography to organise the distribution of courts throughout the country, in that the bigger the territory, the greater the hierarchy. However, hierarchy in the legal sense is not the same as it is understood in the administration or in society in general, as the power to give orders to subordinates. Legal hierarchy means that the higher court has the capacity to confirm, revoke, or modify a judgment of an inferior one when the parties to a process appeal that decision, following the procedures established by law, but judicial independence even prevents the higher court from directing the inferior, from making a general or specific ruling on the application or interpretation of the legal system that it must make in the exercise of its jurisdictional function (Article 12 LOPJ).

The system of two levels, through which the superior judicial organ (or court *ad quem*) is allowed to review the decision of the lower (*ad quo*), is a guarantee for the citizens against possible errors or arbitrariness of the judiciary, which is expressly established in the criminal field in Article 14.5 of the International Covenant on Civil and Political Rights 1966 (ICCPR) and which has been extended by the Spanish legal system to the great majority of cases (*see* paragraph 414). Furthermore, the appeals system responds to the idea of uniformity in the application of law since if there is only one law, it is logical that there is only one interpretation. The Supreme Court is in charge of watching over this uniformity in the application of law, a task it carries out through its judgments in all processes and, especially, those given on appeals of cassation, which were designed as a way of achieving this unity in the interpretation of law.

§3. The Government of the Judiciary: The GCJP

I. Justification

181. The Constitution establishes a series of guarantees to enable the judiciary to make its decisions with independence, but as they remain civil servants, the government can influence them through the two major weapons that it can wield against all government employees: disciplinary power and the system of promotion and transfer. Therefore, and following the tendency of several of our neighbouring States, such as France, Italy and Portugal, the Constitution created the GCJP as the 'governing order' of judicial power (Article 122) so that it is competent to apply the Statute of judges and magistrates to all.

II. Composition

182. Article 122.3 states that the GCJP shall consist of the President of the Supreme Court, who shall preside, and of twenty members nominated by the king for a period of five years. Of these, twelve are to be chosen from judges and magistrates of all judicial categories, in the terms established by the organic law, four nominated by the Congress of Deputies and four by the Senate, in each case chosen from amongst lawyers and other jurists by a majority of three-fifths of the members of the Chambers. The way of choosing these twelve judges has been a source of bitter controversy in Spain. So, its first regulations in 1980 organized direct elections under which the judges chose their representatives. In 1985 the LOPJ changed this system to one where parliament made the selection: Congress and the Senate each chose six judges by a three-fifths majority, a system that PP appealed to the Constitutional Court. The Court held that the Constitution did not require that the twelve representatives from the judiciary be chosen 'by' the judges but 'from among' them (STC 108/1986, 29 July, case *LOPJ*). In 2001 the two most important parties in the parliamentary spectrum, PP and PSOE, reached a 'pact on Justice', which amongst many other matters, modified the system of electing the twelve representatives by finding a hybrid between the previous two, which was slightly changed in 2013: parliament would continue to designate them, but it would choose between the candidates presented by the professional associations of judges or by twenty-five magistrates. Therefore, at present, all the representatives, whether the twelve from the judiciary or the eight jurists of recognized prestige are chosen by parliament on the basis of ten by each Chamber by a three-fifths majority, which in effect is by agreement between the two main parties.

183. In their first, or constituent, meeting, the twenty members of the GCJP choose the President of the Supreme Court and of the GCJP from amongst the professional lawyers or jurists of recognized competence with more than fifteen years seniority in their career or the exercise of their profession. The LOPJ requires the decision to be adopted by a three-fifths majority of the members (twelve out of twenty) and the practice followed until now is that of always designating a jurist.

The President is the only member of the Council that can be re-elected only once, although, in practice, this has still not occurred.

In the same constituent meeting, the vice president is selected, also by a three-fifths majority, but now only amongst the judicial representatives, and so the plenary session of the GCJP consists of twenty-one members. Other bodies of the Council are the Permanent Commission, the Disciplinary Commission, and the Qualifications Commission, each formed by five members and basically with the duty of preparing the work of the plenary sessions.

184. The 2006 Statute of Autonomy of Catalonia establishes the Council of Justice of Catalonia as the 'governing body of the judiciary in Catalonia'. As the government of the judiciary is clearly a matter of state competence and its logical regulatory place is the LOPJ, the Statute tries to overcome this antinomy by stating that 'it shall act as a decentralised body of the General Council' and 'in accordance with the provisions of the LOPJ'. However, the Statute itself attributes to it some powers (such as participation in the appointment of presidents of judicial bodies and disciplinary functions) which have been declared contrary to the Constitution by the Constitutional Court because they condition the freedom of the organic legislator to whom the Lex legum has reserved the regulation of the Judiciary (STC 31/2010, 28 June, case *Reforma del Estatuto de Autonomía para Cataluña*). As this is formal unconstitutionality, in that the Statute is not the appropriate source, nothing prevents the LOPJ from being changed in the future in order to create these autonomous Councils of Justice, which have also been included in the amendment of other Statutes, such as the Valencian, Andalusian and Aragonese, although without attributing powers to them and referring their regulation to State legislation.

III. Functions

185. Article 122.2 of the Constitution defines the Council as the 'governing organ' of judicial power. However, the functions of *government* of the GCJP are not comparable to those of the government of the nation because the Council, which is not a jurisdictional body, cannot carry out the function of 'political direction' of the judiciary and is not responsible for the material and human resources assigned to the courts, which depend on the government or, in some Communities with competence in the matter, on the autonomous governments. Its purpose is rather to reinforce the independence of the judiciary so that when Article 122.2 SC remits the determination of the Council's functions to the LOPJ, it specifies that, as a minimum, it shall establish (*inter alia*) the system of appointments, promotion, inspection, and the disciplinary regime.

Nor is there a parallel between the responsibilities of the *government* of judicial power and that of the government of the nation; unlike the latter, it is subject to no political control beyond that of having to submit an Annual Report to parliament on the activities and operation both of the Council itself and that of the courts and tribunals, as well as the need for personnel, facilities, and resources. The Chambers can debate the content of this report and approve the motions that it deems necessary (Article 109 LOPJ). In practice, the President of the GCJP presents the report to the Commission of Justice and Internal Affairs of the Congress of Deputies, whose members can ask questions they consider relevant and put forward proposals, which are debated in the plenary session of Congress (Ruling of the President of Congress, 4 April 1984 on the parliamentary procedure of the Annual Report of the GCJP).

However, in the exercise of their functions, there is a parallel with the political institutions and not to the government of the nation but to parliament: the members of the Council, regardless of origin, tend to group themselves according to their political ideology and to vote in bloc such that it is usual to speak of the 'conservative' and 'progressive' sectors, identified, to a greater or lesser degree, respectively with PP or PSOE.

186. The main task of the GCJP is that of ensuring the independence of the judiciary in the exercise of their judicial functions; thus, if a judge is anxious or concerned about it, he/she can report the matter to the Council for it to take the relevant measures (Article 14 LOPJ). Furthermore, the Council has a good number of specific functions designed to maintain this independence and, at the same time, enable the judicial power to fulfil its duty of public service in the Administration of Justice. These functions of the Council are listed in Articles 107 et seq. of the LOPJ and can be grouped as follows:

(1) The professional career of the judges and magistrates: appointment; provision of placements and promotions, although for the most part, these are regulated in accordance with set criteria and the discretion of the GCJP is limited to certain posts, such as the magistrates of the Supreme Court, the Presidents of High Courts, and the Provincial High Courts; administrative situations of the judges (leave of absence, permissions, etc.).

(2) Inspection of Courts and buildings as a Disciplinary Regime, which is carried out through the opening of a disciplinary file/dossier to establish the scope of the conduct of the judge or magistrate, which can be sanctioned by forced transfer or separation from the service.
(3) Training of judges for which the Council has a judicial school with its headquarters in Barcelona.
(4) Appointment by a three-fifths majority of two magistrates of the Constitutional Court.
(5) Reporting on proposals for bills related to justice, such as procedural law and those concerning the status of the judges. It is also the duty of the Council to report on the appointment of the Attorney General designated by the government.

§4. Popular Participation in the Administration of Justice

187. The Spanish Constitution maintains the European tradition of assigning the Administration of Justice to a professional body of civil servants whose democratic legitimacy comes from their submission to the Constitution and the Law, but the Constitution itself does not exclude the possibility of more direct participation by the citizens, through popular action (generously recognized in most criminal proceedings and many administrative ones concerned with town planning, environment, etc.), participation in juries, and in the customary courts (Article 125 SC). The customary courts are almost extinguished now in Spain, as shown by the fact that in 1985 the LOPJ only expressly mentioned one (the Tribunal de las Aguas de Valencia). However, in successive amendments, three others have been added, also on the Mediterranean coast: the Consejo de Hombres Buenos de Murcia, the Tribunal Privado de las Aguas de Orihuela and the Tribunal del Comuner de l'Horta d'Aldaia (Article 19).

188. In a country such as Spain with little tradition of the jury (and what does exist is none too positive) and with professional judges and magistrates who guarantee a technical and impartial justice, it is no surprise that neither when drawing up the Constitution nor after was there any great political and social concern favouring this form of popular participation in the Administration of Justice. In the drafting of the text, the concept of the jury was introduced at a very late stage, in the Constitutional Commission of the Senate, and was restricted to criminal trials; not compulsory but rather optional for the legislator ('they may … participate', says Article 125 SC). Subsequently, none of the major political parties had this amongst their priorities, and the question was delayed until the passing of Organic Law 5/1995 on the Tribunal of the Jury, a law with certain technical failings that caused it to be reformed very shortly after it was passed (Organic Law 8/1995).

189. The Law on the Jury has designed a Tribunal of nine members, adult citizens with the full exercise of their political rights who know how to read and write and are not specialists in law, plus a magistrate who presides but does not take part in their deliberations. This formula maintains the historical Spanish tradition and does not follow the line of the mixed jury, made up of both judges and laypersons, seen in France and other civil law countries. The jurors are chosen by lot, and their participation is viewed as a right to take part in public affairs and also a civic duty. The verdict of the jury determines whether or not the facts have been proved and, if so, whether the accused is guilty or 'not guilty' (an expression that, for its Anglo-Saxon influence, the Law prefers to the traditional 'innocent') for which seven votes in favour are needed. On that basis, the magistrate passes sentence, which can be appealed to the respective High Court of Justice. The jury is competent to judge a total of twelve crimes grouped as crimes against the person (such as murder), liberty and security (threats), arson, and those committed by civil servants in the exercise of office (the most numerous group: bribery, peddling political favours, etc.). These twelve crimes have been selected because the typical actions involved are not unduly complex or ones in which the legal elements are especially suitable for evaluation by citizens who are not legal professionals.

190. Citizens have another way of taking part in the Administration of Justice, namely as Justices of the Peace, the first level of the judicial structure in those municipalities where there is no Court of First Instance. The Justice of the Peace is a layperson appointed for a period of four years by the Government Division of the High Court of Justice on the proposal of the plenary session of the Town Council by an absolute majority of the vote. The Justice of the Peace is in charge of the Civil Register and hears, at first instance, criminal offences and minor civil matters. In general, he/she is subject to a similar regime of incompatibilities as a professional judge (Articles 90 et seq. LOPJ).

§5. The Prosecutor General of the State

191. The Prosecutor General of the State, whose roots possibly go back to the *Siete Partidas* of 1265, has been considered in Spanish Constitutional history as an organ of government and not part of an independent judicial power. The 1978 Constitution expressly includes it in the Title on judicial power and gives it a certain autonomy from the government but does not integrate it into judicial power, rather making it – in the words of the LOPJ – into a cooperating organ in the Administration of Justice, with the mission of promoting the defence of legality, the rights of the citizen, and the public interest protected by the law, either ex officio or at the request of interested parties, as well as 'to watch over the independence of the Courts and procure before them the satisfaction of social interest' (Article 124.1 SC).

192. But if the Prosecutor General of the State is not part of the judicial power, neither can we say it is, purely and simply, integrated into the administration since, according to Article 124.2 of the Constitution, it exercises its functions by means of its own organs in conformity with the principles of unity of action and hierarchical dependence, subject in all cases to those of legality and impartiality. Law 50/1981, on the Organic Statute of the Prosecutor General (heavily modified by Law 27/2007) reinforces its independence with a set of guarantees and incompatibilities similar to those of the judiciary, to the point of declaring – with evident exaggeration – that the ministry is 'integrated with functional autonomy in the judicial power'. However, the government has a measure of control: it is responsible (as required by Article 124.4 SC) for the appointment of the Public Prosecutor of the State, although the change in 2007 strengthened the mechanisms of independence of this Public Prosecutor (who is appointed for four years which cannot be renewed); the reasons for cessation are evaluated, and before the appointment, he/she must appear before a Commission of Congress so that 'the merits and suitability of the candidate can be assessed'. In practice, it is an office totally at the disposition of the government; if to this is added the fact that the government can tell the Public Prosecutor to 'take an interest' in certain actions and that under the principle of hierarchy, the Public Prosecutor of the State is competent to determine promotion within the prosecuting career and can give orders and instructions to the other prosecutors, it will be understood that the influence of the government on the Prosecutor General of the State is much greater than over the judicial power.

§6. The Constitutional Court

I. Constitutional Nature and Position

193. The 1978 Constituent Assembly had few doubts about the need to create a Constitutional Court that would watch over the normative force of the Constitution, for which reason it endowed it with a wide range of competences; left behind was the reluctance of the Second Republic when it hedged the creation of the Court of Constitutional Guarantees around with so many cautions to avoid installing a 'dictatorship of lawyers'. By acting in this way, the Spanish Assembly was simply following in the wake of Germany and Italy, who, after the Second World War and the profound rupture of their democratic principles by their respective dictatorships, came to be convinced that Constitutional Courts were a guarantee of democracy. With the logical exception of the United Kingdom and other old democracies, Europe today has ended by losing the absolute confidence it had in law and the democratic legislator, and has admitted, as de Tocqueville pointed out, that the judicial control of constitutionality is 'one of the most powerful barriers which has ever been devised against the tyranny of political assemblies'.[29]

194. The Spanish Constitution has also followed the Bonn Fundamental Law of 1949 in creating control of concentrated constitutionality in the hands of a body distinct from that of judicial power. Most European states have not taken the diffuse model of the US by which any court can refuse to apply a law that it considers contrary to the Constitution. Following the design of Hans Kelsen after the First World War, the control of constitutionality has been conceived of as a different function from the judicial that, therefore, demands its own organ directly shaped by the Constitution.

29. Alexis de Tocqueville, *De la démocratie en Amérique*, *supra*, 148.

Moreover, the Constitutional Court is chosen by a different process from that used to select judges, in that the main political actors (especially the parties) play a decisive role in the designation of the members of the Constitutional Court. To a great extent, this is a side effect of the idea of the Constitution as a pact between the great political and social forces of a country that reserves the designation of the organ that, in the last instance, controls the fulfilment of that pact. Thus, we can say that the Constitutional Court is a *contra-majority* organ in the sense that its main function is to ensure that the majority does not break the constitutional pact to the prejudice of the minority. This control of the majority is projected not only in the relationship between the parliamentary groups properly so-called but also assigns it the role of guarantor of fundamental rights (so indirectly also controlling the judicial power) and, with it, the arbiter of legal conflicts between the central State and the Autonomous Communities.

II. Composition and Structure of the Constitutional Court

195. The Constitution regulates, in great detail, both the composition and the status and functions of the Constitutional Court, so highlighting its central role, more important than the other organs with constitutional relevance that the *Lex legum* merely mentions, remitting their regulation to law. Article 159 of the Constitution states that the Constitutional Court is composed of twelve members appointed by the king, four of whom shall be nominated by Congress with a three-fifths majority, four by the Senate with an identical majority, two at the proposal of the government of the nation, and two by the GCJP. The members are appointed from amongst Spanish citizens, who are magistrates, prosecutors, university professors, civil servants, and lawyers, all of whom must be jurists of recognized competence with at least fifteen years of professional experience. Tradition indicates that, at the least, the two chosen by the GCJP shall be judges. Organic Law 6/2007 modified the LOTC such that, amongst other issues, it laid down that the four judges chosen by the Senate have to be amongst the candidates presented by the Legislative Assemblies of the Autonomous Communities in the terms established by the Standing Orders of the Upper Chamber. This can be summarized as that each assembly must propose two candidates. The PP presented appeals of unconstitutionality against both the new draft of the LOTC and the Senate's Standing Orders as limiting the Upper Chamber's power of decision, a power not subject to such a condition in Article 159 of the Constitution. The Constitutional Court dismissed both appeals, the first because the aim of permitting the participation of the Autonomous Communities in the initial phase of the selection of judges held by the Senate was not contrary to its configuration as an organ of territorial representation (STC 49/2008, 9 April, case *Artículo 16 LOTC*); the second, as being against the Senate's Standing Orders, was also rejected, although it made an interpretation in accord with the *Lex legum* of Article 184.7 of the Standing Orders. Under this, if the majority of three-fifths needed to choose the four magistrates from amongst the candidates proposed by the Autonomous Assemblies was not obtained in the Upper Chamber, the Senate could freely vote for other jurists for the vacant places (STC

101/2008, 24 July, case *Artículo 184.7 del Reglamento del Senado*). That interpretation permitted, for example, that in 2010 the Senate chose three magistrates proposed by the Autonomous Assemblies while the fourth was at the direct initiative of a parliamentary group, the PP.

Their appointment is for a period of nine years, and the Court is renewed by thirds every three years, which obliged them to be chosen by lot on the first two occasions that the Court had to be renewed (1983 and 1986). This periodic renovation permits the composition of the principal interpreter of the Constitution to adapt to the changes that, by virtue of democratic processes, are produced in the constitutional bodies in charge of designating them.

196. For magistrates to be able to carry out their task, which to a large extent is that of resolving political disputes through legal techniques, their impartiality must be guaranteed, and so the Constitution declares that they are independent and irremovable and lists the same incompatibilities as for the other members of the judicial power, with one exception: instead of prohibiting membership of a political party in general, Article 159.4 SC limits itself to forbidding them to play 'a management role in a political party or trade union or (take) any employment in their service'. Organic Law 2/1979 on the Constitutional Court (LOTC) reinforces this legal status of constitutional magistrates with several measures, perhaps the most important of which is the prohibition on re-election. Without a doubt, once the Constitution rejected the American technique of appointment for life (the best form of guaranteeing independence), the impossibility of re-election after the long period of nine years for which they are appointed is a good method of ensuring magistrates' independence.

197. The LOTC determines the internal structure and operation of the Constitutional Court, which works in a plenary session, made up of its twelve members and in two Chambers, each with six magistrates. For more than twenty-five years, the plenary was in charge of resolving the litigation on the control of the constitutionality of norms with the force of law while the Chambers tried appeals on the grounds of unconstitutionality, and the four sections, each made up of three judges, decided on the admissibility of appeals. However, the reform of 2007, designed to make the Court's functioning smoother, has modified this sharing of functions in the following way:

(a) The plenary exercises control over:
- the preliminary appeal of unconstitutionality of international treaties and the drafts of Autonomous Statutes;
- the appeals of unconstitutionality against the laws and other norms with the force of law and the complaints and questions on tax matters against the Basque regional provisions; except those that merely apply jurisprudence, which the plenary will send to the Chambers specifying the constitutional doctrine to be applied in that case;
- questions of constitutionality reserved to it: the others being referred to the Chambers according to objective turns;

  - conflicts of competence between the State and the Autonomous Communities, or amongst them;
  - the challenges envisaged in Article 161, Subsection 2 of the Constitution;
  - conflicts in defence of local autonomy;
  - conflicts between constitutional bodies of the State.

(b) The Chambers hear appeals for constitutional protection of fundamental rights and the actions and questions of unconstitutionality submitted to the plenary. However, if such a court considers it necessary to depart from the doctrine of the Constitutional Court, the question shall be submitted to the plenary for its decision.

(c) The sections decide on the ordinary dispatch of business and on the admissibility of constitutional procedures. Moreover, it can now resolve appeals for constitutional protection of fundamental rights remitted to them by the courts.

The plenary chooses its President from amongst its members for a period of three years, with the possibility of re-election by secret ballot. Except in the case of the first President, the custom has arisen of choosing a magistrate who is in the last third of his mandate, so there has been no question of re-election. However, since its reform in 2007, the LOTC stipulates that the mandate of the president shall be extended, if not renewed, as a judge until the moment when that renewal occurs. Equally, the plenary chooses its vice president who substitutes for the president when s/he is absent, or the post is unfilled or for some other legal reason; the vice president is also the president of the Second Chamber, the president of the full Court presiding in the First Chamber. In both Chambers, the presidents have a casting vote in the event of a tie, which the president of the plenary has had to use on several occasions, the most important being STC 111/1983, 2 December, in which the Court upheld the constitutionality of Decree-law 2/1983 on the expropriation, on the grounds of public utility, of the banks and other companies that made up the Rumasa Group.

§7. Competences of the Constitutional Court

I. The Control of the Constitutionality of Laws and Norms with the Force of Law

A. *General Aspects*

198. In Kelsen's scheme of jurisdictional defence of the Constitution, the appeal of unconstitutionality against laws was the typical competence of the 'guardian of the Constitution' and is recognized as the primary competence of the Constitutional Court by Article 161 SC. However, Kelsen's scheme, in which this control is only initiated at the instance of political organs, was modified in Austria itself in 1929 to permit the ordinary and the Constitutional Courts to collaborate, a tendency which has been maintained in most European Constitutions, including the Spanish. Judges and courts have the capacity to present questions on unconstitutionality when they have to apply a norm with the force of law which they consider to be contrary to the *Lex legum*. Judging the constitutionality of a law in relation to the case in hand in which the interests of specific persons are at stake is known to the doctrine as concrete control, in contrast to the abstract control of the appeal of unconstitutionality, in which the appellants – at least in principle – have no other object than to maintain the supremacy of the Constitution. Due to the collaboration between the ordinary and Constitutional Courts, the Spanish system of constitutional control assigns to the ordinary jurisdiction a role in guaranteeing the constitutionality of the laws, as happens in the diffuse North American system; however, the essential feature of concentrated control does not entirely disappear: the monopoly to declare that a norm is within the law lies exclusively in an organ not integrated into the judicial power, the Constitutional Court.

199. The LOTC details the norms that can be the subject of constitutional control, either by way of appeal or by a question posed by a judge, and they are as follows:

(a) The Statutes of Autonomy and other Organic Laws.
(b) Other provisions with the force of law, without prejudice, in the case of Legislative Decrees, to the control, that the laws of delegation themselves may stipulate in favour of the Courts, although in practice, no law has ever established such control. The LJCA does establish a general control by the ordinary courts when they go beyond the limits of delegation (*see* paragraph 73).
(c) International treaties.
(d) The Standing Orders of the Congress, the Senate and autonomous parliaments.
(e) The Laws and norms with the force of law of the Autonomous Communities.
(f) The Standing Orders of the Legislative Assemblies of the Autonomous Communities.

Organic Law 1/2010, 19 February, introduced into LOTC a Fifth Additional Provision which attributed to the Constitutional Court the exclusive control of some new norms: the Fiscal Foral (local) norms of the Territories of Álava, Guipúzcoa, and Vizcaya; it was this very same Organic Law 1/2010 that modified Article 9 of the LOPJ and Article 3 of Law 29/1998, *reguladora de la Jurisdicción Contencioso-administrativa* to exclude these *foral* norms from the control of the Contentious-Administrative courts. To justify this change of legal regime, the Preamble to the Organic Law turned to comparative reasoning: if the State courts and those of the Foral Community of Navarra were fixed by law and could only appeal to the Constitutional Court, the law-making capacity of the Basque Foral Provincial Councils (Deputations) which has an autonomy based on the First Additional Provision of the Constitution (which grounded the Navarre Autonomy) should not be more 'fragile' than those of the State and Navarra. This reasoning did not convince various neighbouring Autonomous Communities (governed by the PP), who lodged their corresponding appeals of unconstitutionality that the Constitutional Court rejected because, although it accepted that these *foral* norms had the legal nature of regulations, it considered that they were supported by the First Additional Provision of the Constitution and substituted 'in the historic territories to the legislative provisions of the State in tax matters', and that singularity justified the legislator being able to exclude them from the ordinary control of the regulations by the courts (Article 107 SC). Thus, it used the clause of Article 161.1 d) of the Constitution to attribute it to the Constitution itself through a procedure similar to that of the appeal of unconstitutionality. However, the Constitutional Court made an interpretation of Organic Law 1/2010 in accordance with the Constitution to clarify that it would only control the adaptation of those foral norms to the Constitution and the block of Constitutionality, but the ordinary courts would control those norms 'when the contradiction occurred with norms distinct from that block (as happened with international treaties and conventions, with the norms of fiscal harmonization of the EU or the laws of the Basque Parliament)' (STC 118/2016, 23 June, case *Normas Forales Fiscales*).

200. Judgments pronounced in proceedings for unconstitutionality take effect in the particular case and in general from the moment of their publication in the Official State Gazette (Article 164.1 SC), that is to say, when no form of appeal can be lodged (things judged to be formal) and no other proceedings can be proposed in which the question being litigated can be opened up again after the Constitutional Court has pronounced a final judgment (a thing considered material). Moreover, Article 5.1 of the LOPJ orders judges to apply the laws and regulations according to the precedents established by the Constitutional Court. The Court can declare the unconstitutionality of the precepts challenged based not only on the articles cited in the proceedings but also any other it deems violated. This is much more so if they are from other normative texts, whose most evident and paradoxical effect occurred in STC 31/2010, where the Constitutional Court declared various articles of the Catalan Autonomous Statute of 2006 unconstitutional without having been able to do the same with other similar articles in other Autonomous Statutes (*see* paragraph 29). In the Autonomous State, not only the Constitution itself will be taken into account but also the 'whole block of constitutionality', in which the Statutes of Autonomy and other laws delimiting competences are included.

The judgments that declare the unconstitutionality of the precepts challenged shall pronounce their nullity, with the result that they are removed from the legal system in general from the moment of their publication (*ex nunc*). However, the LOTC itself states that the sentence takes effect from the moment in which the unconstitutional norm was approved (*ex tunc*) when dealing with criminal proceedings or contentious-administrative cases that carry a sanction since annulling the norm results in a reduction in the sentence or sanction. On some occasions, the Court does not declare the unconstitutionality of the norm but requires a certain interpretation of it *conforming to the Constitution*, ruling out other possible, normally more evident, ones.

B. The Appeal of unconstitutionality

201. According to Article 162 of the Constitution, the appeal of unconstitutionality can be lodged by the President of the Government, the Ombudsman, fifty deputies, fifty senators, the executive corporate bodies of the Autonomous Communities, and their Legislative Assemblies. The LOTC has restricted the authority of these two autonomous bodies to lodge actions against laws, provisions, or acts with the force of law to those that may affect their own sphere of autonomy. The Constitutional Court has accepted the constitutionality of that restriction even though at first it interpreted it strictly as a defence of its own competences, but from the decision in STC 199/1987, it has given it a much wider interpretation and practically admitted all challenges made by the autonomous bodies.

The appeal of unconstitutionality is lodged by way of a petition addressed to the Constitutional Court within the period of three months from the publication of the norm with the status of law. The petition must set out the articles of the contested norm as well as the constitutional precepts that are alleged to have been violated. Once admitted for process, the petition, which does not generally suspend the validity of the norm, is sent by the Court to Congress and the Senate, to the government and, when appropriate, to the executive and legislative organs of the Autonomous Communities. All these organs may be officially represented and make declarations. Trying to lessen the litigation between the State and the Autonomous Communities, Organic Law 1/2000 modified the LOTC to enable the President of the government and the regional Governing Councils to lodge this action within the period of nine months, always provided that both parties agree to open negotiations to resolve the discrepancies caused by the new norm. Regrettably, after the approval of this law, there have only been very few of these negotiations, while the number of appeals of unconstitutionality due to disputes over competences has increased notably.

C. The Question of Unconstitutionality

202. As we have already seen, the 1978 Constitution transformed the strict conception of the 'Rule of Law' in that of the Rule of Law and the Constitution, since although Spanish Courts cannot refuse to apply a norm with the status of law passed after the *Lex legum* (it can, however, do so with one passed prior, by virtue of the principle of temporality), they have the capacity to bring the matter before the Constitutional Court by way of a question of unconstitutionality when in a particular action they consider that a law applicable to the case and on whose validity the judgment depends, is unconstitutional (Article 163 SC). The judge or the court presenting the question may not limit itself to expounding its doubts or to transmitting the opinions of the parties but must give an opinion grounding the unconstitutionality of the norm and explaining its importance for the resolution of the case in hand. This decision of whether or not to present the question of unconstitutionality is a matter solely for the judge or the court; however, if one of the parties to the proceedings asks that it be presented, the court must either present it or give good reasons for not doing so, since if it simply limits itself to rejecting the request without reasons its rejections will enable the question to be referred to the Constitutional Court as it would be violating the effective legal protection of the party (STC 222/2015, 2 November, case *Garmendia Larrañaga*). Finally, this question is presented – as required by the LOTC – once the action has been concluded and before the expiry of the period for giving judgment and after hearing the Parties and the Prosecutor General of the State.

The Chambers or, where relevant, the Sections may present a question to the plenary if they consider that an appeal for constitutional protection of fundamental rights should be granted because the applicable law violates a fundamental right. As with a question presented by the ordinary courts, the internal question or *self-question* is presented before the judgment is given, and the time limit to give the judgment is suspended until the plenary has given its decision. This procedure was set out in the reform made by Organic Law 6/2007 since the original wording of Article 55.2 of the LOTC stipulated that the self-question should be submitted after judgment was passed. However, this could cause a disagreement between the opinion of a Chamber and the plenary. This has been criticized by most constitutional academics, including in the first edition of this book.

II. The Preliminary Appeal of Unconstitutionality of Treaties and Autonomous Statutes

203. As we have just seen, Article 27 of the LOTC expressly includes treaties amongst the norms that may be unconstitutional, thus guaranteeing the hierarchical superiority of the Constitution in the Spanish legal order, determined by the Constitution itself by requiring its reform for the conclusion of treaties that contain stipulations contrary to its precepts (Article 95.1 SC). But the nature of treaties, being international and yet controlled by domestic law (*see* paragraphs 61–62), justifies the Constitution providing a mechanism whereby the Constitutional Court may be consulted to see if the treaty is consistent with the Constitution before it is ratified. According to the *Lex legum*, the only organs that can legitimately initiate this prior control are the government and the two Chambers of Parliament. The correct moment to petition the Constitutional Court for its opinion is before the giving of consent and always providing that the text is definitive. The opinion issued by the Court in this process is not legally binding, nor yet a judgment, and so it is called a 'Declaration'. The effect of that declaration is completely binding on the state powers, and so if the Constitutional Court deems that there is a contradiction between the Constitution and the treaty to be ratified, there remain only two solutions: either to reform the Constitution or not to give definitive consent (Declaration 1/1992, 1 July, case *Tratado de la Unión Europea*).

204. The first text of the LOTC in 1979 used the authorization of Article 161.1(d) of the Constitution to establish a prior appeal of unconstitutionality against the Statutes of autonomy and the other organic laws (Article 79) which, by preventing the entry into force of these rules until the Constitutional Court's ruling, legally constituted an exception to the Presumption of Constitutionality of the laws and is a politically powerful weapon for the minority dissatisfied with the content of certain organic laws. For that reason, in 1985, the socialist majority in parliament approved a modification of the LOTC that suppressed this appeal, and although the PP was very opposed to it (to the point of presenting a prior appeal of unconstitutionality, which logically was rejected in STC 66/1985, 23 May), the truth is that PP did not reinstate it in its eight years of government from 1996 to 2004. This was because it was not at all relevant to develop the government programme with which it had won the elections. However, the subsequent processing of the reform of the Statute of Autonomy of Catalonia, which was endorsed by the citizens of Catalonia in June 2006 and subsequently appealed by the PP before the Constitutional Court, which declared it partially unconstitutional (*see* paragraph 29), highlighted that it might be useful to recover it at a time when the consensus had broken down in the deployment of the Autonomous State. This was so, although only against the draft Statutes, allowing the Court to rule before the electoral body did so. The appeals of unconstitutionality were used more deeply against other Statutes, such as the Andalusian (STC 30/2011, 16 March), that of Castilia-Leon (STC 32/2011, 17 March), and of Aragon (STC 110/2011, 22 June), in such a way that Organic Law 12/2015 recovered the previous appeal for the drafts of Organic Law of Statute of Autonomy by means of the modification of Article 79 of the LOTC. The purpose of this prior appeal is to challenge the final texts of the draft Statutes or the proposed amendments. Therefore, it will be presented after its processing in both Chambers of Parliament and before its endorsement by the citizens if this is necessary. Its procedure is governed by the general rules provided for appeals of unconstitutionality, with only two specific mandates: the period for filing the appeal is only three days, and the Constitutional Court itself has a non-extendable period of three months to issue its ruling. The law specifies that it will not produce the effect of res judicata, for which reason it will be possible to file an appeal of ordinary unconstitutionality against the Organic Law that approves the Statute. Logically, if a draft Statute that has to be submitted to a referendum is used and the Constitutional ruling is dismissed, the draft will be submitted to a referendum; if, on the contrary, it is the Court that approves it, the LOTC orders that the procedure cannot proceed without the Articles declared unconstitutional 'having been deleted or modified by Parliament'. In my opinion, this allows some margin of manoeuvre for the legislator that is not seen to be forced to submit to the electorate the text refined by the ruling of the Constitutional Court. So, it can modify the draft Statute while always considering the doctrine set by the Court.

III. The Conflicts of Competences and the Government's Challenge to the Provisions and Resolutions of the Autonomous Communities

205. The government of the nation and the Governing Councils of the autonomous legislatures may lodge appeals of conflict of positive competences within two months against the provisions, rulings, and acts emanating from the organs of State or from the Autonomous Communities when they consider that they do not respect the block of constitutionality. The great majority of these conflicts are between the State and one or more Communities and only very exceptionally between the Communities inter se.

The LOTC imposes a prior condition to facilitate agreements between the parties, although its regulation is not the same for all: while the autonomous executive must compulsorily fulfil this requirement, for the government, it is merely optional. If the disputed competence that gave rise to the conflict originated in law, then the conflict will be processed as an appeal of unconstitutionality (the petition sent to Congress and the Senate, to the corresponding Legislative Assembly, etc.), which permits norms with the status of law to be declared unconstitutional in this proceeding of conflict of competences. The judgment that resolves the conflict must determine to whom the disputed competence belongs and, where appropriate, the nullity of the provision, ruling, or act causing the conflict. Private individuals may lodge allegations of negative conflicts when none of the bodies, State or autonomous, to which they have made a request considers itself competent to resolve any claim. These types of conflict are little more than anecdotal since, in more than thirty years of existence, the Constitutional Court has only given three judgments of this type. Curiously, in all three cases, the Court denied that the conflict was, in fact, negative, and so it was not the appropriate tribunal and sent the appellants to the ordinary jurisdiction. And completely unknown, at least until now, is the negative conflict that the state could present, claiming that a specific competence was that of an Autonomous Community, which it was refusing to exercise (Article 71 LOTC). The reverse possibility that the Autonomous Communities can lodge a negative conflict does not exist, which without a doubt would be useful, given that at present, there is no jurisdictional instrument to resolve disagreements between the state and a Community in questions of transfers of services and civil servants (*see* paragraph 228).

206. Article 161.2 of the Constitution permits the government to challenge before the Constitutional Court the provisions and rulings adopted by the organs of the Autonomous Communities with the effect of suspending the provision appealed. The LOTC has developed this constitutional precept as a residual instrument in relation to appeals and conflicts so that through it, illegal acts that supposedly breach the Constitution may be appealed when, due to its political content, it is more appropriate for constitutional rather than ordinary jurisdiction to control it. This residual power has given rise to a very low number of this type of process.[30] However, Article 161.2 SC is much more important in the Autonomous State than could be deduced from the number of cases because Articles 30 and 62 of the LOTC permit the government to lodge appeals of unconstitutionality and conflicts of competences, so causing the suspension of the operation of the norm or the application of the act complained of, although the Court must ratify or lift the measure within five months. All the governments that Spain has had since the Constitution – without distinction of party – have systematically used this power.

IV. The Conflict of Power Between Constitutional Bodies

207. The LOTC creates a procedure to resolve the conflicts between the government and Congress, the Senate, or the GCJP or between any of these organs *inter se*

30. The government had hardly used this procedure until 2015 when it challenged the resolution of the Parliament of Catalonia 1/XI, of 9 Nov. 2015, on the 'start of the political process in Catalonia as a consequence of the election results of 27 September 2015' which led to STC 259/2015, of 2 December. However, the attempt by the majority of members of the Catalan Parliament to proclaim independence forced him to use it several times in the following years. Vid. Josu De Miguel Bárcena, *Justicia constitucional y secesión: El caso del proceso soberanista catalán* (Reus, 2019).

with the aim of guaranteeing 'the existence of the Constitutional structure conceived as a system of relationships between Constitutional bodies endowed with their own competences' and to preserve 'the respect for the plurality or complexity of the Constitutional structures' (STC 45/1986, 17 April, case *LOPJ-I*). The procedure commences with an application to the plenary of the organ that considers its sphere of powers prejudiced after previously requiring, in vain, the encroaching organ to modify its action or inaction. As in the cases of conflicts of competences, the Constitutional Court must determine the disputed power, using not only what is set out in the Constitution but also the organic laws that assign competences to constitutional bodies to do so. In practice, this process has been used very seldomly; moreover, the first time a conflict of powers was presented, the Constitutional Court ruled that it was not a real conflict: the General Council of the Judiciary understood in 1985 that the new form of election of the twelve judicial members of the Council that established the LOPJ invaded its powers, but in the aforementioned STC 45/1986 the Constitutional Court concluded that as this new form of election (the twelve by the courts and not by the judges) was established in law, the appropriate way was the appeal of unconstitutionality and not conflict. In the second process, there was no doubt that this was a genuine conflict of powers: in November 1995, the Senate Bureau (with a majority of the PP) did not accept the declaration of urgency that the government had made to process the draft Organic Law on regulation of the voluntary interruption of pregnancy, a decision that the government (PSOE) appealed on the grounds that it was a violation of the jurisdiction attributed to it by Article 90.3 of the Constitution. Evidently, the Constitutional Court agreed with the government unanimously, but only after five years (STC 234/2000, 3 October).

V. Conflicts in Defence of Local Autonomy

208. The 1978 Constitution, faithful to the design of classic constitutional justice, failed to provide any procedure to permit local bodies to challenge laws that they considered contrary to their local autonomy. However, in the subsequent years, the idea grew that it would be desirable to grant this, mostly after the adoption of the European Charter of Local Autonomy in 1985, which established that local bodies must have a way of legal appeal available for the defence of their competences. The simplest formula for this proposal, well adapted to the Constitution, is none other than the reform of Article 162 to permit the municipal and Provincial governments to have the right, under certain conditions, to lodge an appeal of unconstitutionality. But as, in Spain, there is a general prejudice against modifying the Constitution; in the end, the open clause of Article 161.1.d was used to force the creation of a complex constitutional procedure established by the Organic Law 7/1999, a modification of the LOTC.

209. The conflict in defence of local autonomy allows local bodies (in number varying according to the scope of application of the contested norm) to appeal the laws and norms with the force of law of the State and of the Autonomous Communities that attack local autonomy. The procedure thus initiated has the exclusive aim of determining whether or not that autonomy has been damaged. If the decision is provisional, then the plenary of the Constitutional Court will pose an internal question of unconstitutionality that will give rise to a new judgment in which it can now be declared if the State or autonomous norm appealed is contrary to the Constitution.[31] Despite the impetus with which the local representatives demanded this legal instrument, it has not been much used. Thus, until 2017 the Constitutional Court has only given eleven judgments on these conflicts, almost one every two years since the procedure was instituted in 1999.

VI. Conflicts in Defence of Foral Autonomy

210. The same Organic Law 1/2010 that introduced the action mentioned above against the provincial tax rules into the LOTC also added a procedure whose purpose is to resolve conflicts in defence of the regional autonomy of the Historical Territories of the Autonomous Community of the Basque Country against State norms with the rank of law. These conflicts are processed by the procedure for positive conflicts of competence and can be filed by the Provincial Councils and the General Councils of the Historical Territories of Álava, Guipúzcoa, and Vizcaya. And just as with shielding the fiscal rules, the neighbouring Autonomous Communities also filed a constitutional appeal against this new procedure, which the Constitutional Court rejected in STC 118/2016, 23 June, because it is not an unfounded privilege of these provinces over those of the common regime but that the First Additional Provision of the Constitution supposes that 'the Basque historical territories enjoy a singularity that materializes in a different and wider scope to that conferred on the provinces of common regime'. For that reason, this new procedure before the Constitutional Court is justified as a way 'to guarantee in a particularized way different institutions that respond to different circumstances and purposes' (FJ 4). Interestingly, in practice, it does not seem that the historical territories feel much attacked by state laws: to date, they have not interposed a single conflict action in defence of the autonomy of the provinces.

VII. Appeals for Constitutional Protection of Fundamental Rights

211. The jurisdictional protection of fundamental rights is the duty of the courts in all types of proceedings. In addition, Article 53.2 of the Constitution stipulates that the rights recognized in Section I of Chapter II are protected before the ordinary courts by a procedure based on the principles of preference and speed. Second, this same article creates the appeal of unconstitutionality to the Constitutional Court for the defence of those rights and for 'the objection of conscience recognized in

31. This artificial division into two decisions of what is really only one process has no logical explanation beyond trying to differentiate as much as possible between the conflict in defence of local autonomy and the appeal of unconstitutionality. I have tried to explain this idea in Agustín Ruiz Robledo, *El conflicto en defensa de la autonomía local*, in *Modificaciones y panorama actual del Régimen Local Español* 113–149 (Federico A. Castillo Blanco ed., CEMCI 2000).

Article 30' This last provision has become obsolete as Law 17/1999, 18 May, abolished compulsory military service from 31 December 2002.

212. The subsidiary character of the appeal for constitutional protection of fundamental rights with regards to appeals to the ordinary jurisdiction is at the base of Article 123 SC when it proclaims that the Supreme Court is the highest jurisdictional organ in all 'orders, except in matters concerning constitutional guarantees', which logically are matters for the Constitutional Court, although we must not forget that their decisions can be challenged before the ECtHR when the conditions set out in the ECHR are met. In practice, the appeal against human rights violations has enabled the Constitutional Court to incorporate constitutional rights throughout the legal system and to ensure that the activities of all public powers are adapted to the Constitution, especially those of the ordinary courts, who have ended by applying the Constitution in their daily work, far from the idea of a programmatic text with scant practical influence. This function of the Constitutional Court, which is statistically the most numerous cases (more than 95% of the cases brought before this Court are appeals on the grounds of unconstitutionality), has led to friction and disagreement with the judicial power, which has had two moments of maximum public expression: (a) in February 1994 when the majority of the judges of the First Court of the Supreme Court, disagreeing with a decision of the Constitutional Court, STC 7/1994, which had overruled one of its decisions, agreed to ask the king to exercise his role as moderator between institutions. After the wave of criticism that this provoked, the judges must have changed their opinion because the petition was never formalized; (b) on 23 January 2004, the Court of the Civil Jurisdiction of the Supreme Court condemned eleven judges of the Constitutional Court in serious negligence in the exercise of their functions, which caused a tough accord in the plenary of the Constitutional Court on 3 February 2004, on the invasion of constitutional jurisdiction. To prevent these confrontations, so unedifying in the eyes of the public, Organic Law 6/2007 sets out several measures, amongst which are that the decisions of the Constitutional Court cannot be challenged by any organ of the State.

213. The breaches of fundamental rights recognized in Articles 14–29 have to result from the provisions, legal acts, or simply the conduct of public powers of the State, Autonomous Communities or other public bodies, or their servants and agents; therefore, appeals against foreign public powers or the authorities of the EC (STC 64/1991, 22 March, case *APESCO*) will not lie. Breaches of fundamental rights committed by individuals can be indirectly controlled by the Constitution as long as the ordinary courts have not previously considered them (STC 18/1984, 7 February, case *Caja de Ahorros de Asturias*). In short, the only claim that can be asserted in this appeal is the restoration of the rights originating the appeal, but not other aspects that could be of interest to the appellants; thus, for example, if the Court grants the protection to a trade unionist who has organized a strike to demand improvements in occupational safety, it will declare the violation of the right to strike and will qualify the dismissal as radically null but will not calculate the economic compensation to which he is entitled, if the employing company has made any other violation of labour legislation or occupational health and safety, etc.

At present, there are five modalities of the appeal for constitutional protection of fundamental rights, three established by the Organic Law of the Constitutional Court and two by the Organic Law of the General Electoral System, depending on the institution to which the violation of fundamental rights is imputed:

(a) against parliamentary decisions (Article 42 LOTC);
(b) against governmental and administrative decisions (Article 43 LOTC);
(c) for constitutional protection of fundamental rights against judicial decisions (Article 44 LOTC);
(d) against the Agreements of the Electoral Boards on the proclamation of candidates (Article 49.3 LOREG);
(e) against the Agreements of the Electoral Boards on proclamation of the elected and election and proclamation of presidents of local Corporations (Article 114.2 LOTC).

The right to bring such an appeal is very wide, and every natural or legal person with a legitimate interest may do so, as can the Ombudsman and the Prosecutor General of the State. The ministry intervenes in all the processes of the appeal on these grounds to defend legality, citizens' rights and the public interest protected by law. Exceptionally, public administrations can also appeal in the few cases where they hold rights to which this form of appeal is applicable (such as that of effective guardianship). However, the remedy for constitutional protection of fundamental rights is a subsidiary remedy; that is to say, in order to be able to bring it, it is necessary to have previously exhausted all the previous judicial procedures as well as invoking it as soon as possible, for the violation of the fundamental right that the appellant seeks to assert before the Constitutional Court. For reasons that I personally cannot understand, the terms established by the LOTC to file the appeal for constitutional protection of fundamental rights are different depending on the modality in question: against governmental or administrative decisions, it is twenty days; against judicial decisions, it is thirty days, while it is extended up to three months for the remedies of constitutional protection of fundamental rights against parliamentary decisions not invoking the law. It is understandable that the deadline is only three days in the case of the constitutional protection of fundamental rights under LOREG because the purpose is that if the appeal is successful, the candidates can participate in the elections.

The procedure for admitting the appeal for hearing, which in other constitutional matters is almost automatic, becomes an obstacle that is difficult to overcome in these cases and much more so since the reform of the LOTC of 2007. This modified the requirement in order to reduce the Court's overwhelming caseload, which resulted in some decisions being given with a delay of ten years. Thus, while until 2007, the appeal only had to set out the facts and the legal grounds that alleged that a fundamental right had been violated, after the reform, that possible breach was no longer, in itself, enough, and it had to be justified by the special constitutional importance of the appeal. The Court will allow an appeal to be lodged if it is of special importance, all others being rejected *ad limine*. Article 50 of the LOTC lays down three criteria for the decision: 'its importance for the interpretation of the

Constitution, for its application or for its general efficiency and for the determination of its content and the scope of fundamental rights'. The plenary of the Constitutional Court set out in its judgment in 155/2009, 25 June, case *Vallejo Marchal,* the criteria in a catalogue of seven suppositions, although confirming that this was a first approach that could be changed in the future. Summarizing them, they are as follows: (1) that the appeal poses a problem on a fundamental right where there is no existing doctrine of the Constitutional Court; (2) that it gives the Court the opportunity to clarify or change its doctrine; (3) when the violation of a fundamental right appealed against comes from the law; (4) if the breach of the fundamental right results in a repeated jurisprudential interpretation of the law that the Court considers damages the fundamental right; (5) when the doctrine of the Constitutional Court on the fundamental right referred to in the appeal is repeatedly ignored by the ordinary jurisdiction; (6) in the case that judicial organ shows a manifest intention not to respect the doctrine of the Constitutional Court; (7) when the matter raised goes beyond the case in hand because it poses an important legal question with general social or economic repercussion or has general political consequences that might result in, mostly, though not exclusively, in specific electoral or parliamentary appeals.

Once the appeal has been accepted, the Constitutional Court may suspend the operation of the act appealed against to ensure the effectiveness of the appeal. Decisions granting it must set out three statements, which are normally cumulative: declaration of the nullity of the act appealed, recognition of the right asserted, and the restoration of the appellant to the full integrity of her/his right.

VIII. The Execution of the Judgments of the Constitutional Court

214. In 1979, the LOTC was approved with only a laconic provision on the execution of its rulings in which it limited itself to allowing the Court to establish who was to execute its rulings 'and, where appropriate, to resolve the incidents of the execution' (Article 92). That forecast seemed more than enough for the type of judicial resolutions that, by their very nature, are usually easy to execute: if the constitutionality of a norm, resolution, or act is declared, nothing should be done beyond its publication in the BOE, and if it is declared unconstitutional, it is enough for the public authorities to consider the norm, resolution, or act annulled to remove it from the order and to act accordingly. However, the confrontation between the Constitutional Court and the Supreme Court on the Statute of Limitations in penal matters led the legislator to introduce in 2007 a new paragraph in Article 92 of the LOTC to allow the Constitutional Court to declare the nullity of 'any resolutions that contravene those dictated in the exercise of its jurisdiction, on the occasion of their execution', a capacity the Constitutional Court has used on some occasions to annul sentences that did not respect previous judgments in the same case. Thus, for example, in its Court Order 186/2011, 22 December, it annulled the Judgment of the Supreme Court (Criminal Division) of 4 December 2009 because it returned to condemn a defendant who had already obtained the protection of the Constitutional Court in STC 195/2009, 28 September, and the Supreme Court did it without respecting the doctrine established in that Constitutional Court's ruling, according to which the mere presentation of a complaint does not suspend the prescription of a crime but rather that some action of the Administration of Justice is needed.

In 2015, Organic Law 15/2015, 16 October, on the reform of Organic Law 2/1979, 3 October, for the execution of Constitutional Court resolutions as a guarantee of the Rule of Law, completely modified Article 92 to strengthen the Court's capacity to execute its judgments, beginning with the vigorous reformulation of its first paragraph: 'The Constitutional Court will ensure effective compliance with its resolutions. It will be able to state in the sentence, or in the resolution, or in subsequent acts, who will execute it, the necessary execution measures and, where appropriate, resolve the incidents of the execution.' Amongst the specific measures that the Constitutional Court can adopt include: coercive fines (i.e., those imposed on a person for not having done what the court ordered and as a way to encourage him to do so), the suspension of the duties of the authorities responsible for the breach 'during the precise time to ensure the observance of the pronouncements of the court', and the substitute execution of the resolutions for 'what may require the cooperation of the Government of the Nation'. This organic law was motivated because the Generalitat did not accept the ban on holding the referendum on self-determination that had been convened for 9 November 2014 – euphemistically called process of citizen participation on the political future of Catalonia – which had been ordered by the Constitutional Court in its ruling of 4 November (then ratified in STC 138/2015, 11 June) and which nevertheless took place, although without any legal value. Organic Law 15/2015, promoted by the Government of the PP, did not have the support of the PSOE or, logically, of the Catalan and Basque nationalists who, by controlling their respective autonomous governments, were able to file separate appeals of unconstitutionality, rejected by the Constitutional Court because it considered that these measures did not distort the constitutional jurisdiction, nor modify the system of controls of the Autonomous Communities by the State, nor violate the principles of separation of powers and criminal legality (STC 185/2016, 3 November of 2016).

Chapter 6. Independent Organs

§1. Consultative Organs

I. The Council of State

215. Article 107 of the Constitution establishes the Council of State as the supreme consultative organ of the government, remitting its composition and function to be determined by an organic law. This constitutional definition does not make the Council of State, whose origin goes back to 1526 when it was created by Charles V, into an organ of the government 'but rather at the service of the conception of the state that the Constitution itself establishes' (SSTC 56/1990, 29 March, case *LOPJ-III,* and 204/1992, 26 November, case *Ley Orgánica del Consejo de Estado*). Thus, it exercises its consultative function with organic and functional autonomy. Its fundamental aim is to watch over the observance of the Constitution and the rest of the legal system, but without excluding other aspects such as the harmony of the system, the correctness of the normative technique, and 'the greater efficacy of the administration in the fulfilment of its purposes' (Article 2 LOCE). As we know, all these questions are not dealt with by the Constitutional Court, which is limited to judging the constitutionality of the norms.

216. The Council of State is formed by the President, the permanent Councillors, the elected councillors, and those who are so ex officio due to the post they occupy (the Director of the Royal Academy, the State Public Prosecutor, etc., up to a total of ten persons). Organic Law 3/2004, which reformed the LOCE, created the category of life appointment for the ex-presidents of the government, although until now, all of them have declined the position. The government appoints both the President and the other Councillors, but while the eight permanent members remain indefinitely, the ten who are elected are appointed for four years. The Council is organized into a plenary, the Permanent Commission, the Studies Commission, and eight specialized sectors according to the matters dealt with. The President of the Government and all the ministers, as well as the Presidents of the Autonomous Communities, have the right to consult the Council of State; private individuals can seek an audience when they are directly interested in the subject of the consultation. The LOCE requires the Council to be consulted in a series of important affairs: questions of international and European law, Legislative Decrees, parliamentary regulations that develop or carry out laws, conflicts of competences with the Autonomous Communities, claims of hereditary responsibilities, important administrative contracts, appeals of reviews, etc. (Articles 21 and 22 LOCE). Their reports are not binding, although the LOCE stipulates that the provisions and rulings informed by the Council shall express whether they are in accord with their report or 'the Council of State has been heard', the traditional formula used to express that it departed from the Council's opinion.

217. When the Constitution was drafted, many of the parliamentarians – practically all of them on the left – thought that the liberal economic model prevailing in Spain could be better developed with general economic planning by the State. As this view was not held by the right-wing parties, who feared that planning would lead to an intervened economy like the one existing in the USSR and Eastern Europe, there were long debates and intense negotiations to translate the two visions into the constitutional text. Thus, mandates were established to specify that Spain was part of the market economy (such as private property, Article 33, and freedom of enterprise, Article 38). However, Article 131 was also included to allow the economy to be planned by Law. Paradoxically, this much-debated article in the *Cortes Constituyentes* has never been developed, and not a single planning law has ever been passed, even though the State and the EU intervene in many ways in the economy. However, a law has been passed (with replicas in many Autonomous Communities) to create the body which, according to Article 131.2, should advise the government when drawing up planning projects: Law 21/1991, 17 June, creating the Economic and Social Council.

As it was already evident in 1991 that the chances of a general planning law being passed in Spain were not very high, if not nil, the functions attributed to the Council by Law 21/1001 do not revolve around planning (in fact, the Law omits to say that it is dictated as the development of Article 131.2 of the EC), but rather focus on its advisory nature to the government on socioeconomic matters. Thus, it prepares reports at the government's request – or on its own initiative – on economic matters, labour relations, employment, industry, consumption, regional development, etc. However, from the political point of view, its most important document is the annual report which it must present annually, setting out 'its considerations on the socio-economic and employment situation of the nation' (Article 7). As a consultative body, the Law grants it its own legal personality and guarantees its functional independence from the General State Administration. It is composed of 61 members, including its President, who is appointed by the government 'after consultation with the representative groups that make up the Council'. The first group represents the trade unions, the second the employers' organizations, and the third is subdivided into five sectors: three councillors from the agricultural sector, three from the maritime fishing sector, four from the social economy, four from consumers and users, and six experts, who – like the President – are appointed by the government.

§2. Organs of Control

I. The Court of Auditors

218. Although in the perfect scheme of the division of powers, only parliament would be in charge of controlling the power of expenditure, the truth is that in Spain – as in the great majority of the States of Law – the utility of creating an independent organ with external control of the State budget has been acknowledged. In 1828, the 'Principal Court of Auditors' was formed, which, under various names, has been maintained ever since in the catalogue of Spanish State institutions. Article 136 of the 1978 Constitution designed the Court of Auditors as a technical organ directly dependent on parliament which exercises its functions through delegation to it in the examination of the General Accounts of the State. Moreover, it maintains the traditional 'auditing jurisdiction' of the Court of Auditors, by which the 'accounts responsibility' of those who are in charge of managing public funds is decided. This jurisdictional function is exclusive to the court, while the function of controlling public financial activity may be shared with other similar organs of the Autonomous Communities, always providing that the Court of Auditors 'maintains its supremacy over other controlling organs' (STC 187/1988, 17 October, case *Sindicatura de Cuentas de Cataluña*). We must bear in mind that the statutory provisions on the relationship between these autonomous organs and the Court are not binding on the latter but only on those organs controlled by the Autonomous Communities (STC 31/2010, 28 June, case *Reforma del Estatuto de Autonomía para Cataluña*).

Organic Law 2/1982, on the Court of Auditors, sets its number of members at twelve Councillors, six chosen by the Congress of Deputies and six by the Senate, by a majority of three-fifths in each Chamber for a period of nine years. The twelve Councillors choose their President from amongst their number for a period of three years. The Court exercises its functions in full independence, and so it enjoys an autonomous internal regime, draws up its own budget, and the Councillors are independent and irremovable and subject to the same causes of incapacity, incompatibility, and prohibitions laid down for the judges in the LOPJ. Law 7/1988, on the operation of the Court of Auditors, is concerned with regulating, in detail, the proceedings by which the Court exercises its jurisdictional and controlling functions.

219. The main organs of the Court are the plenary, the Control section, and the Proceedings section. The plenary and Control sections have the duty of verifying the accounts of public service entities, consisting of the administration of the State, the Autonomous Communities, and the local corporations, as well as the autonomous bodies dependent on these administrations. In addition, the Court of Auditors controls subsidies, credits, guarantees, and other aid from the public sector received by physical or legal persons. It also controls the accounts of the political parties, as stipulated by the Organic Law, on the funding of Political Parties. It submits an Annual Report to parliament in which it analyses the General Accounts of the state and of the rest of the public services (Article 136.2 SC). The Proceedings section, organized in Courts, pronounces sentences in trials and other proceedings to determine the accounting liability of persons who manage or use public goods, funds or assets, always bearing in mind that if the activity to be tried is categorized as a crime, the Court of Auditors must remit the matters to the criminal courts.

II. The Ombudsman

220. Following what, with all respect, we can call the 'ombudsmania' of the last forty years or the worldwide expansion of 'Justitieombudsman' invented by the Swedish Constitution of 1809, Article 54 of the 1978 Spanish Constitution creates the office known as the Defender of the People or the High Commissioner of Parliament, to defend fundamental rights, with authority to supervise the activity of public administrations. Organic Law 3/1981, 6 April, which regulates the institution, states that he shall be jointly elected by Congress and the Senate, with a three-fifths majority needed in each Chamber, for a period of five years. The Law also creates two 'Assistants' to the Ombudsman for the express purpose of helping him in his tasks. In practice, the underlying function for which these assistants have been used is to facilitate agreement between the two main parties in the appointment of the Ombudsman: while they agree on one independent person to fill that office, the appointment of assistants is shared between them, a post to which party members have usually been appointed, although, at the moment of being chosen, they must resign their party membership since there is a strict regime of incompatibilities for the Ombudsman and his assistants. Equally, with the objective of guaranteeing their independence, they cannot receive instructions from any authority; they fulfil their roles with autonomy and enjoy inviolability and immunity during their period in office. Personally, I have my doubts about whether organic law can establish these two prerogatives of inviolability and immunity for the assistants, absolutely contingent organs, that the Constitution does not require since they are an exception to both the principle of equality as a legal responsibility, which may even cause an infraction of effective judicial protection for those who feel prejudiced by their actions.

221. The mission of the Ombudsman is the protection of the rights established in Title I of the Constitution for which purpose he/she can carry out, either ex officio or at the request of any party, any investigation of the acts and rulings of any administration, except the Administration of Justice since his competence extends to all the organs and authorities of the general administration of the State and of the administration of the Autonomous and local authorities. He must, however, suspend his investigation if the matter is sub judice. As a result of his investigation, the Ombudsman can make various rulings: suggestions, recommendations, reminders of legal duties, etc.; he/she can even present appeals of unconstitutionality and initiate the process of habeas corpus, but he/she himself/herself can never make an administrative resolution to restore a right to a citizen. He/she is a magistrate of persuasion who enjoys *auctoritas* but not *potestas*. As a general duty, he/she presents an Annual Report to parliament and has the legitimacy to appeal to the Constitutional Court laws that, in his/her opinion, have violated fundamental rights.

III. Other Organs in Defence of Fundamental Rights

222. With the aim to better guarantee respect for fundamental rights, several laws have created independent administrations, such as:

- Electoral Administration created by LOREG (*see* paragraph 120).
- The Data Protection Agency (Organic Laws 5/1992 and 15/1999).
- The Autonomous Commissions of Guarantees of Video Surveillance (Organic Law 4/1997).

§3. Economic Organs

223. The social and democratic State of Law entails constant intervention in economic activity by the public powers. Daily practice has shown how inadequate the traditional structure of public administration is for this intervention (bureaucracy, subordination to immediate political interests, etc.). For this reason, various organisms independent of political power have arisen in all democratic States, which only keep authority to appoint the members and indirect control over their decisions. The first Spanish independent administration was the Council of Nuclear Security, created by Law 15/1980. Various others have followed, particularly important being the Bank of Spain and the National Commission of the Markets and the Competence.[32] The Budget and other State laws permit the government to create organizations and public societies with full legal personality, although they do not reach the same level of independence as those first mentioned. Amongst the most important of these bodies representing functional decentralization is the State Agency of Tax Administration, the State Society of Industrial Participation, the National Institute of Social Security, and the National Institute of Health Management. Moreover, Law 13/1994 on the Autonomy of the Bank of Spain created this Bank as an entity of public law with a legal personality that acts independently of the general administration of the State in the fulfilment of its functions (which revolve around the effective operation of the financial system), subject to a private regulatory system except when it acts in the exercise of administrative powers conferred by law. The Bank of Spain is integrated into the European System of Central Banks (ESCB), which implies – according to Article 127 Treaty on the Functioning of the European Union (TFEU) – that in the exercise of its *European* functions (to participate in the government of the Central European Bank, to put money into circulation, etc.) neither the government nor any other national or community organ can give it instruction. The Governor of the Bank of Spain, who directs it, is appointed by the President of the Government for a period of six years without the possibility of renewal.

32. This macroregulator was created by Law 3/2013, 4 June, and united the six public organs like the National Commission of Competitivity, the National Commission of Energy, the Commission of the Telecommunications Market, and the National Commission of Market Values. On the constitutional problems that these organs pose for constitutional law, especially on the government's power of political direction, *see* Artemi Rallo Lombarte, *La constitucionalidad de las Administraciones Independientes* (Tecnos, 2002).

Part III. The State and its Subdivisions

Chapter 1. The Form of the State: The Autonomous State

§1. A Different Form of State: Neither Unitary nor Federal

224. When the constituent assembly chose on 15 June 1977 prepared to draw up a democratic Constitution for Spain, it found that many of the insuperable divisions that in the past had divided Spaniards into irreconcilable factions had either disappeared or could be overcome with the goodwill of all. Thus, it was relatively easy to reach an agreement to resolve matters as disruptive in the past as the Head of State (monarchy/republic), church/State relations and the economic model. However, it was much more difficult to achieve agreement on the territorial distribution of power on the *territorial Constitution*; while all political parties were in accord in rejecting the model of the unitary State prevailing under Franco, the proposals varied between the mere administrative decentralization of the unitary State put forward by Alianza Popular to confederation defended by the small parties on the extreme left.

225. The dilemma of the constituent assembly was truly difficult: the immense majority wanted a Constitution agreed upon by all political parties (a 'Consensus Constitution'), but their differences over the territorial distribution of political power prevented them from adopting a common model. The solution reached was what, in the terminology of Carl Schmitt, could be called an 'apocryphal agreement', an agreement to continue negotiating the form of the State in the future so that the Constitution established an open model that, as far as possible, included the three fundamental projects raised in the constituent process, leaving aside for a later moment its specific expression: the nationalist project that claimed substantial autonomy for certain parts of the territory (Convergencia i Unió of Catalonia and the Partido Nacionalista Vasco of the Basque Country), the federalist in favour of political decentralization for all the State (Partido Socialista, Partido Comunista, and certain sectors (basically the social democrats) of the UCD, and the decentralist (AP and the majority of the UCD). In spite of the efforts the parties made to reach a consensus on the *territorial Constitution*, it was not possible to integrate the Basque nationalists, who considered that the Constitution did not recognize the historical rights of the Basque Country. Therefore, the Basque minority absented itself in the final ballots on the draft Constitution, both in Congress and the Senate, and urged abstention in the referendum of 6 December 1978.

226. To achieve this open model of the form of the state, the constituent assembly started by establishing both 'national sovereignty' as well as the 'indissoluble unity of the Spanish nation, the common and indivisible homeland of all Spaniards' (Article 2) as the source of all powers (Article 1.2 SC) and thence to establish in the Constitution a series of procedures that would allow the 'nationalities and regions' to exercise 'their right to autonomy' and become Autonomous Communities (an expression employed to avoid 'Region', used in the 1931 Constitution and now considered to carry less political weight). Therefore, Autonomy Statutes had to be drawn up, texts which regulated both the institutions and the autonomous competences. As autonomy was conceived of as a 'right', the will of its holders acquired special importance, beginning with the very choice of the term 'nationality' or 'region', on which the Constitution does not expressly lay down any criteria for their use, and only gives a tenuous guideline to identify both types of collectivity: 'bordering provinces with common historical, cultural and economic characteristics, the island territories and the provinces with historical regional unity' (Article 143.1 SC).

227. Although what has come to be called the 'principle of willingness' or 'principle of disposition' could have resulted in the decentralization of just a part of the territory up to a large number of Autonomous Communities, it cannot be ignored that there was, implicit in the Constitution, a certain 'logic of duality' in the words of the ex-president of the Constitutional Court, Tomás y Valiente:[33] the distinction between 'nationalities' and 'regions', the two procedures for access to autonomy and the two levels of competences, made possible the creation of two types of Communities, some political, with their own legislative power, and others administrative, simply provincial communities. However, the growth of the Autonomous State in the period 1979–1982 was made not from logic but from equality, homogeneity, and the construction of seventeen political Communities, thanks mostly to the 'Autonomous Agreements' that the government (UCD) and PSOE signed on 31 July 1981. The difference between Communities was basically of degree, but no longer of *quality*: while the Communities of the 'first degree' (fundamentally the *historical* ones of the Basque Country, Catalonia, and Galicia, plus Andalusia) had a higher 'ceiling of competences' (Article 149 SC), those of the second degree were not seen as lesser (Article 148).

228. But as the Constitution itself made possible the expansion of the competences of these Communities (Article 148.2), new autonomous pacts in 1992 between the government (now PSOE) and PP enabled both degrees of Community to enjoy virtually the same competences, a reform carried out by modifying the Autonomy Statutes of the second degree during the period 1994–1999. At this point, it cannot be said that the development of the form of the State is over, not so much because the transfer of services and civil servants from the State to the Autonomous Communities has not yet been completed, but because in recent years, important political groups have demanded the reform of the autonomous State on crucial

33. Francisco Tomás y Valiente, '*Soberanía y Autonomía en las Constituciones de 1931 y 1978*', now in his *Obras completas*, vol. III, 2628 (Centro de Estudios Políticas y Constitucional 1997).

points such as the participation of the Communities in the EU, the financing system, the reform of the Senate and the attribution of more powers to the Communities.

This desire for change has brought with it a wave of reforms of the Autonomous Statutes which implies little less than a reformulation of the Autonomous State. For that reason, there is a certain feeling that the form of the state is somewhat provisional, that it is unlike other sections of the Constitution, such as fundamental rights or the Head of State. And there seems little possibility of reaching a point of equilibrium because the logic of duality has been substituted by a game of antagonistic logics: the logic of differentiation demanded by the peripheral nationalisms, in large measure with Catalonia as the driving force, of the new Autonomous State. The desire to match these changes exists in most of the representatives of the other Communities, as shown by the Parliament of Andalusia in copying the Catalan Statute when passing the proposed reform of its Statute in 2006. The same has happened to a greater or lesser extent with the reforms of the Statutes of the Balearic Islands, Aragon, and Castilla-León. The risk of this tension between asymmetry and equality activates a continuous upward spiral of demands from the Autonomies that fuels a dynamic centrifuge.

229. With things as they are, it is not easy to determine the form of State now prevailing in Spain. The Constitution maintains a careful silence on it, and the doctrine has called it by many different names: regional State, autonomous, autonomist, plural, complex, compound, federal-regional, unitary-federal, etc. Today, the name most used (even by the Constitutional Court) is 'autonomous state', although there is no agreement on whether we are talking of a type of State different from the federal state or one which is entirely comparable with it.

In my opinion, although it is true that the Autonomous State coincides in several essential points with the federal state (constitutional guarantee of autonomy, jurisdictional resolution of conflicts, etc.) and that the level of self-government of the Communities is very similar to that of many Member States of federations (for that it is enough to check the percentage of public expenditure they consume),[34] yet it seems to me that the legal differences are sufficiently relevant to make it feasible to distinguish them. But the fundamental characteristic is more political; that feeling of an unfinished model opens the continual change that prevails in Spanish politics with regard to the distribution of competences, and that does not correspond to Friedrich's theory of federalism as a process. In the strictly legal field, the following differences, amongst others, between the federal state and the autonomous should be highlighted:

(a) In the federal state, the autonomous bodies are either a legal reality foreseen in the Constitution or created at the same time since they are expressly included in

34. According to the OECD, Spain is one of the most decentralized States in the World. *See* OECD, *Fiscal Federalism 2022: Making Decentralisation Work* (OECD Publishing 2022) https://doi.org/10.1787/201c75b6-en. Spain also appears amongst the most decentralized States in the exhaustive comparative work of 185 sub-state entities Liesbet Hooghe et al., *Measuring Regional Authority: A Post-functionalist Theory of Governance* (Oxford University Press 2016).

that fundamental norm; on the contrary, in the Autonomous State, the autonomous bodies do not come into judicial existence until parliament has approved their Statute of Autonomy.

(b) The autonomous bodies of a federal state participate both in the approval of the Constitution and in its reform: in the autonomous, they do not take part in the drafting of the Constitution, and in its reform, they only play an indirect role through the autonomous senators (who are not subject to any instructions from their Communities), although they do have the power to initiate constitutional reform. The same lack of autonomous participation occurs in the ordinary legislative procedure. Thus, it is not surprising that many of the parties agree that the Senate should be reformed to make it a true 'Chamber of territorial representation', although until now, they have not agreed on how to do it.

(c) The autonomous bodies of a federal state have constitutional autonomy to draw up their own basic institutional text (normally denominated 'Constitution') without any form of intervention from the general organs of the State beyond the eventual control of constitutionality made by the courts; in Spain, on the contrary, the national parliament takes part in the drafting of the Statutes of Autonomy, even in the special proceedings of Article 151, which at best can be described – although many important authors do not agree – as a procedure between the representatives of a specific nationality and those of the Spanish nation.

(d) The willingness or disposition principle has important consequences for the system of competences in the Autonomous State, unknown in the federal state, as is the declaration of State law as supplementary to the autonomous. In this sense, a relevant difference is that the competences of the central State in a federation are set out in the Constitution itself and tend to be the same throughout the territory, while in the Autonomous State, those competences depend indirectly (via the supplementation clause) on what each Statute assigns to its Community, with the outcome that the state competences tend not to be identical throughout the national territory. This can even be considered a positive characteristic of the system insofar as it permits some Communities to have more competences than others (asymmetric federalism).

(e) The system of competences in the classic federal state turns on the concept of subject matter, and in the German model on that of function, distinguishing between legislation and implementation; for its part, the Autonomous State employs both these techniques but adds another that, although not unknown, has not previously been used with such enthusiasm: the distinction within the legislative function by differentiating between basic legislation (State competences) and complementary legislation (autonomous).

§2. The Neo-autonomous State

230. In February 2005, the Congress of Deputies rejected – by 313 votes against, 29 in favour, and 2 abstentions – the proposal to reform the Political Statute of the Community of Euskadi presented to it by the Parliament of the Basque Country. The main argument given by the two major parties to reject this reform was that it was a text incompatible with the Constitution, a thesis that had already led them to vote against it in the Basque Parliament. In November of the same year, the bill for reform of the Statute of Autonomy of Catalonia arrived at the Congress that entailed the rupture of the autonomous consensus between PSOE and PP: while the latter proposed that the same treatment should be given to it as to the proposal of the Basque parliament, PSOE considered that it was a text that should be transacted, although modifying many of its Articles. This was done without the postures of the parties being modified at the end of the process: the new Statute was approved in the spring of 2006 in Congress and in the Senate, with the PP voting against it, and it announced the presentation of an appeal of unconstitutionality. This appeal was decided by the Constitutional Court in June 2010. Thus, the third cycle of statutory reforms began very differently from the first deployment of the Autonomous State, which, as we know, was made with the consensus of the two major national parties of that era (the UCD and the PSOE), which managed to agree their first Statutes with the main Basque and Catalan nationalist forces. Therefore, the Constitutional Court found itself in the very difficult position of having to judge almost in its entirety a Statute, a quasi-constitutional text approved by the Catalan and Spanish Parliament, which also enjoyed the added legitimacy of having been endorsed by the Catalan people. The result was the very famous, much quoted, and discussed Sentence 31/2010, of 28 June, an interpretative sentence that brings the literal tenor of more than one hundred Statutory Articles to a meaning fully in accordance with the Constitution and declares a few Articles unconstitutional. The political lesson that can be drawn, and which the parties seem to have understood, is that no matter how much a Statute can be approved by an absolute majority in Congress, it is necessary for it to receive consensus support, a rule that has almost always been applied since the time of the Catalan Statute. Therefore, we shall have longer Statutes with a declaration of rights, lists of detailed powers, rules on external action, and instruments to strengthen the role of governments, such as the Decree-law, etc., as the STC 31/2010 highlights; none of this will change the nature of the territorial distribution of political power nor will it end with the dialectic differentiation-equality between territories, in such a way that we can call the particular form of the Spanish State a neo-autonomous State 2005.

Chapter 2. Autonomous Communities

§1. The Formation of the Autonomous Communities

231. The Spanish Constitution of 1978, following the precedent of 1931, did not draw a 'map' of the Autonomous Communities but remitted it to a later moment in which the nationalities and regions should exercise their right of autonomy. Therefore, the Constitution establishes two general procedures: one, ordinary (Article 143) and the other, extraordinary, more complicated but which permits a greater level of autonomy (Article 151). Moreover, the Constitution envisages special procedures for the African cities of Ceuta and Melilla and a closure clause by which, apart from the willingness principle, parliament could make them into an Autonomous Community. On the other hand, the First Additional Provision makes a reference to 'foral' rights, of which Navarre took advantage to accede to autonomy by a special procedure. We shall look at each of them briefly.

232. The sequence of the first autonomous procedure, the ordinary, is relatively simple and consists of three phases:

(1) The initiative, that is, the coming together of all the Provincial Governments of the interested provinces and two-thirds of the municipalities whose population corresponds to at least much of the electorate of each province or island.
(2) The drafting of the Statute by an assembly formed by the members of the Provincial Governments and the Members of Parliament (deputies and senators) elected in the territory.
(3) The processing of this bill as an organic law in the central parliament.

Eleven Autonomous Communities have been constituted by this route, whose Statutes were approved between 1982 and 1983, chronologically: Asturias, Cantabria, La Rioja, Murcia, Valencia, Aragon, Castile-La Mancha, Canary Islands, Extremadura, Balearic Islands, and Castile-Leon.

233. The extraordinary procedure is much more complicated than the former but, in return, allows the territory a greater participation in the drafting of its Statute and guarantees it a greater level of autonomy, 'the first degree':

(a) The initiative, that is, the coming together of the interested Provincial Governments plus three-quarters of the municipalities of each province who represent at least much of the electorate in each of them. The initiative must be ratified by a referendum with an absolute majority of the electors in each province. Only Andalusia dared to follow this procedure. The Basque Country, Catalonia, and Galicia were exempt because the second transitional provision of the Constitution validated the referendums that had been held to approve their respective Statutes in the 1930s during the Second Republic.

(b) The drafting of the Statute is made by an assembly formed exclusively of deputies and senators of the territory.
(c) For the processing of the bill in the central parliament, the Constitutional Commission of Congress and a delegation of the proposing assembly examine it, and the resulting text (which must receive the consent of the majority of the members of both sides) is put to a referendum of the citizens of the territory in question; if they approve it, Congress and the Senate submit it to a 'ratification vote'. Only four Statutes were approved under this procedure, albeit they were the first: the Basque Country and Catalonia, both in 1979, and Galicia and Andalusia in 1981.

234. Navarre, which during Franco's rule maintained an autonomous regime (although with all the limitations characteristic of a dictatorship), was constituted as a 'Foral Community' (i.e., based on its medieval status with a degree of fiscal and administrative self-government) through an agreement between the central government and the Foral Provincial Government of Navarre, under which it had some institutions and a level of autonomy similar to those of the first degree. That text called, using a historicist expression, 'Amejoramiento del Fuero de Navarra', was processed in parliament as a one-reading bill (meaning that the deputies could only vote for or against it, but not present amendments). It was slightly modified in 2001 by the same parliamentary process (LO 1/2001, 26 March). In spite of the official name of 'Foral Community', Navarre is an Autonomous Community similar to the other sixteen, as the Constitutional Court declared on an occasion when its government claimed the general rules of the Autonomous State were not applicable to it (STC 16/1984, 6 February, case *Investidura Presidente del Gobierno de Navarra*).

Article 144 of the Constitution provided that the central parliament could authorize a province that was not a historic regional entity to constitute itself into an Autonomous Community, and in this way, Organic Law 6/1982 authorized the Constitution of Madrid in accordance with the will of its Provincial Government. The Statute was drawn up the following year under the provisions of Article 143, so incorporating Madrid into the group of ordinary Communities.

235. The cities of Ceuta and Melilla in the north of Africa (and now claimed by Morocco as forming part of its territory) have enjoyed a Statute of Autonomy since 1995, although – due to the political concern of the major parties that the State would lose too much power in these territories –they were not approved following the procedure of the fifth transitory provision of the Constitution, especially designed for these historical places of sovereignty to become Autonomous Communities. Instead, the Statutes were approved using Article 144b), which, as the *Cortes* can approve them without any participation whatsoever by the territories involved, the Constitutional Court considers that they do not constitute an Autonomous Community. For this reason, the Court affirms that the legal nature of Ceuta and Melilla 'is that of municipal entities', which justifies the fact that their Statutes do not attribute legislative capacity to them, especially in the delicate area of town planning (STC 240/2006, of 20 July and, previously, AATC 201 and 202/2000 of 25 July). Consequently, the classification they receive in State legislation is that of 'autonomous cities'.

§2. The Distribution of Competences Between the State and the Autonomous Communities

I. Overview

236. The system of competences of the Autonomous State is technically one of the most complex in all comparative Law. In the first place, and as pointed out earlier, the Constitution assigns no competences to the Communities, a task mainly reserved to the Statutes. This technique implies that the national State competences are, in one sense, residual: at the first moment, it has universal competences in all matters, but as the Statutes of each territory are approved, the state loses the competences the Statute has taken from it. If there were no limits, the state would finally be left without any power. To avoid that result, Article 149.1 of the Constitution sets out the matters over which the State shall always be competent, and so this article is often called 'the ceiling of the Communities' competences' According to the 'logic of duality' (*see* paragraph 227) this article was only applicable to the first-degree Communities, given that the second has less capacity to assume competences (Article 148), but the article itself states that that limitation is only provisional, for five years; subsequently the Statutes of the Communities of the second degree have been reformed to endow them with all the competences permitted by Article 149.

The constitutional norms that assign competences and the Statutes of Autonomy are designated as the 'block of constitutionality', an expressive way to describe the set of norms that make up the system of competences in each territory. Strictly speaking, there are seventeen 'constitutional blocks' because there are seventeen Statutes, but here we must walk on tiptoes through the differences between Statutes. Also included in this 'block' are some norms that assign competences, such as the laws of transference and delegation of Article 150 (*see* paragraph 267).

237. From what has been said so far, it can be deduced that the system of competences of the Autonomous State is based on the technique of the division of the competences between the State and the autonomous bodies according to the subject matter in the classic federalist manner. However, if the list of thirty-two matters that Article 149 reserves to the State is read carefully, it will be seen that, under this common denominator of 'matters', this article includes concepts that are truly matters of the State (nationality, defence, administration of justice, etc.) and others that are no more than powers on a specific matter (labour legislation, civil law, etc.). In this way, our Constitution uses both the American technique of reserving the entirety of a matter to the State and the German one of sharing a matter, distinguishing between the legislation and its implementation. But, moreover, Article 149.1 of the Spanish Constitution employs another technique that had only been sporadically used in German: in several cases, only the 'basic legislation', the 'bases', and the 'basic norms' are reserved to the state, which means that not only a matter but also its legislation is shared in such a way that the division of competences between the State and the Communities is incorporated within the legislative power itself, giving the State the basic legislation and the Communities the complementary. Each of these three techniques of sharing has its own legal regime, which will now be set out, although without going into the peculiarities of certain specific Statutes.

II. Exclusive Competences on a Matter

238. When the Constitution assigns a 'set of activities, functions and legal institutions relating to a sector of social life' (i.e., a matter according to the definition of the Constitutional Court in STC 123/1984, 18 December, case *Centros de coordinación operativa*) to the exclusive competence of the State, it is using the simple legal regime of dual federalism: it makes a clear separation between the spheres of the State and the autonomy, conceding to the former all functions – both legislative and executive – and none to the latter. To this regime, Article 149.1 of the Constitution subjects the following matters:

- The regulation of the basic conditions that guarantee the equality of all Spaniards in the exercise of their rights and in the fulfilment of their constitutional duties.
- Nationality, immigration, emigration, aliens, and the right of asylum.
- International Relations.
- Defence and the Armed Forces.
- Administration of Justice.
- System of tariffs and customs; foreign trade.
- Monetary system: currency, exchange and convertibility.
- Determination of the official time.
- General finance and state debt.
- Exterior health.
- Maritime fishing.
- Regulation and concession of water resources and hydraulic schemes when the waters pass through more than one Autonomous Community, and the authorization of electricity installations when their use affects another Community or the transport of energy beyond its territory.
- Public works of general interest or whose realization affects more than one Community.
- System of production, sale, possession, and use of arms and explosives.
- Protection of Spanish cultural, artistic, and monumental heritage against exportation and exploitation, museums, libraries, and archives belonging to the State, without prejudice to their management by the Autonomous Communities.
- Public security, without prejudice to the possibility of creating police forces by the Autonomous Communities in the form established by their respective Statutes within the framework permitted by an organic law (*see* paragraph 253).
- Statistics for state purposes.
- Authorization for the calling of popular consultations by way of referendum.

Most of these titles can be greatly expanded (it is enough to ask oneself what law or administrative act does not in some way or another influence the exercise of a fundamental right), and so its interpretation must generally be strict, for otherwise, it would end by annulling all autonomous competences. It is also necessary to clarify that the existence of an exclusive State competence over a specific physical space does not preclude an autonomous one over the same space always, provided that its legal object is distinct. Thus, for example, the State competence of control over fishing vessels in inland waters is for the purposes of national defence, while the autonomous competence is limited to the technical inspection of the extraction of fishing resources (STC 113/1983, 6 December, case *Inspección pesquera*).

239. When the State assigns a matter in its entirety to an Autonomous Community, it alone has legislative and executive power in this matter, and the State can carry out no activity on it in the Community's territory. There are very few matters so regulated (basically only the self-governing institutions), not to say none since the State has almost always some right that permits it at least a minimum of activity in that sphere. So, for example, its competence over the general electoral regime allows it to regulate aspects of the autonomous elections, and equality in the law of property gives it a certain legislative capacity in matters of town planning, although this is the exclusive province of the Autonomous Communities, etc.

III. Competences of the State over Legislation and of the Autonomous Communities over Implementation

240. With this technique, the two spheres of political power – State and Autonomous Communities – share the same matter, the first having the legislative capacity, that is, the capacity of legal regulation in a matter and the second the executive function. According to the terms of Article 149.1, the following matters are subject to this technique:

- Mercantile, criminal, and prison legislation; legislation on procedure without prejudice to the necessary specialities which in this order may derive from the particularities of the substantive law of the Autonomous Communities.
- Labour legislation; without prejudice to its implementation by the organs of the Autonomous Communities.
- Civil legislation, without prejudice to the preservation, modification, and development by the Autonomous Communities of civil, special, or foral laws where they exist.
- Legislation on intellectual and industrial property.
- Legislation on weights and measures.
- Legislation on pharmaceutical products.
- Legislation on compulsory purchase.
- Legislation on water resources.

The legal problem posed by this distribution of legislation/implementation competences is to determine to whom the power to approve the regulations implementing the laws is attributed, whether to the central government or the autonomous regional governments. The 1931 Constitution expressly stated that this would correspond to the central government (Article 20), but the 1978 Constitution is silent on this point, as was the Bonn Basic Law of 1949. With formally impeccable legal criteria, the German Federal Constitutional Court has considered that regulations are included within the competence of execution and, therefore, correspond to the governments of the Länder. However, the Spanish Constitutional Court –perhaps inspired by the regulation of the integral State of the Republic – has preferred to use the material concept of legislation, which means that executive regulations or regulations for the development of laws correspond to the central government and not to the autonomous governments because in this way it is possible to ensure 'the aim of the constitutional precept of maintaining a uniformity in the legal ordering of matters that can only be achieved by collaboration between law and regulation or by a hypertrophy (undesirable from the point of view of legislative policy)' (STC 18/1982, 4 May, case *Registro de convenios colectivos*). This way of understanding the 'legislation' has been expressly recognized in the reform of some Statutes, so, for example, Article 12 of the Statute of the Region of Murcia (reformed by Organic Law 1/1998) reads, 'To the region of Murcia, in the terms established by the laws and the *regulatory norms* that in development of its legislation the state declares, is assigned the executive function in the following matters: … ' This was then followed in 2006 by Valencia and in 2007 by Castilla-León and the Balearic Islands. On the other hand, the new Catalan Autonomous Statute indicated that in the sphere of executive competences, the legislative power of the *Generalitat* included 'the passing of provisions for carrying out the norms of the State, as well as the executive function, which in every case includes the authority to organize its own administration and, in general, all those functions and activities that the legal system attributes to the Public Administration' (Article 112). As the first part of this definition is clearly contrary to constitutional jurisprudence, which excludes autonomous normative power over executive competences, the Constitutional Court's judgment 31/2010 has reinterpreted it, pointing out that it only means what is set out in the second half: that it deals only with the normative power of the internal organization. The Andalusian Statute of 2007 follows the Catalan in this point. However, in its passage through Congress, an enigmatic paragraph was added: 'when it occurs', which is a synonym for nothing, and which serves to save its constitutionality. Thus, in one way or another, the new Statutes of the twenty-first century maintain the same system of executive competences as before they were passed and that prevents them from legislating on matters included in this regime. Thus, the Constitutional Court has declared unconstitutional autonomous norms that seek to regulate these types of shared matters, such as, for example, a good part of the Law of Parliament of Cataluña 17/2015, 21 July, on equality between women and men, which encroached on the legislative competence of the State in employment matters (STC 159/2016, 22 September).

241. Therefore, the implementation by the autonomy of State legislation only includes administrative acts; however, this regional competence prevents the State from legislating by reserving general implementation powers in matters in which it does not have this competence (STC 39/2021, 18 February, case Estructura orgánica del Ministerio de Educación). Likewise, the Autonomous Community's regulatory power in matters whose legislation corresponds to the State is restricted to the sphere of organization of the autonomous community administration to the so-called *reflexive power*. In the use of this power, the Communities can create the organs they deem necessary to implement State legislation, relying on their exclusive competence in the organization of organs of self-government. The practical importance of this capacity is clearly shown by comparison: while the Autonomous Councils of Labour Relations are fully constitutional because they deal with a shared matter (STC 35/1982, 14 June, case *Consejo de Relaciones Laborales*), any similar organ referring to a matter within the exclusive competence of the State would be unconstitutional (e.g., a 'Council of Autonomous Military Defence').

242. Although the Spanish Constitution does not expressly provide the central State with the 'supervisory power' over the application of its legislation by the Communities, as does Article 84.3 of the Bonn Fundamental Law, the Law on Autonomous Procedure has expressly established the power of the State in its Article 3, 'The Government shall supervise the observance by the Autonomous Communities of the application of the state norms and it can formulate the appropriate requirements with the aim of rectifying any deficiencies when noticed.' The Constitutional Court has admitted this article conforms with the Constitution, although warning that those requirements are not binding nor entail a hierarchical relationship between the State and autonomous administrations because that would be incompatible 'with the principle of autonomy and the sphere of competences derived from it' (STC 76/1983, 5 August, case *LOAPA*). For their part, the first Statutes recognized the 'high inspection' of the State in certain matters, such as education and health (curiously, matters subject to the basic/development system and not legislation/execution). Some of the newest Statutes of the twenty-first century either do not expressly mention it (such as that of Aragon or the Balearic Islands) or direct it to other spheres (such as management of Social Security in the Catalan Statute).

IV. State Competences on Basic Legislation and Competences of the Autonomous Communities on Complementary Legislation and Implementation

243. With a frequency without precedent in Comparative Law, Article 149.1 of the Constitution uses the complex technique of distributing the same legislative competence on a specific matter between the State and the Autonomous Communities. Moreover, it does not always employ the same concept:

(a) Sometimes, it reserves the 'bases' of certain specific matters to the 'exclusive competence' of the State:
   - the ordering of credit, banking, and insurance sectors;
   - the general planning of economic activity;
   - health;
   - the legal regime of public administrations and the statutory regime of their civil servants;

- the system of mines and energy.

(b) In other sections, it reserves to the State the 'basic norms' of some matters:
- the regime of the press, radio, and television and, in general, all social communication media, without prejudice to the powers of the Autonomous Communities to develop and implement them;
- the development of Article 27 of the Constitution with the aim of guaranteeing the fulfilment of the obligations of public powers in this matter (education).

(c) Finally, a third group reserves the 'basic legislation' to the State:
- social security, without prejudice to the implementation of services by the Autonomous Communities;
- contracts and administrative concessions;
- the environment, without prejudice to the powers of the Autonomous Communities to establish additional norms of protection;
- woodlands, forestry and livestock trails.

244. The autonomous legislative competences of what, for the moment, we shall call the *non-basic*, the *rest* of the legislation have also not been clearly defined, and only in two cases are indications given: number 23 (Article 149. SC) mentions 'the additional norms of protection' that the Autonomous Communities can pass on the environment and number twenty-seven refers to the 'development' of the basic norms of the system of the media (social communication). Technically, it seems to me that the better term for this autonomous legislation is 'complementary legislation' such that under its cloak, legislative competences can be included, which in the Statutes are declared to be the exclusive competences of the Community 'without prejudice to the basic legislation on it' or 'in accord with the bases and the system of general economic action', or competences of 'legislative development'. This last description, habitual in the first Autonomous State, has, starting from the statutory reforms of 2006, been substituted by the expression 'shared competences' in an obvious attempt to highlight their political and legal importance. This name has been accepted by the Constitutional Court in its very famous judgment STC 31/2010. Beyond the specific name, the relevance of this autonomous legislation is that its constitutionality depends directly on its adaptation to State bases, which the State can modify as it deems fit, and so at any specific moment, an autonomous law that is constitutional can become unconstitutional if the State bases later change; for example, the Province of Extremadura passed Law 9/1995 on the public functions of the Community, which correctly developed the State law 30/1984 on measures for the Reform of Public Function. However, this became unconstitutional when Law 13/1996 modified public function in a sense incompatible with the Law of Extramadura (STC 1/2003, 16 January, case *Ley 5/1995 de la* Asamblea *de Extramadura).* In a similar sense, many Communities had implemented the 35-hour week for their civil servants until Law 2/2012, 29 June, of the State General Budgets ordered that the minimum weekly hours of all civil servants would be 37.5 hours. Therefore, from the entry into force of this new basic legislation, the previous autonomous norms that established a lower working day were without effect, while the later ones were directly unconstitutional because they invaded State competence, as occurred with the Castile-La Mancha Law 7/2015, 2 December, declared unconstitutional by the STC 158/2016, 22 September.

245. The legal system of the basic legislation and the basic norms are identical. That of the bases is slightly different from these two in its executive aspect: the implementation of the first two is wholly the responsibility of the Autonomous Communities as assigned by their Statutes, while in the case of the bases, the central Administration can, exceptionally, carry out executive acts (STC 1/1982, 28 January, case *Cajas de Ahorros* and 57/1983, 28 June, case *operaciones de crédito de las Corporaciones locales*).

To exercise its competence in the regulation of the bases of a matter, the Constitutional Court requires the State to pass a formal law or norm with the status of law that 'expressly designates its character as basic'. Exceptionally, the government can use its regulatory power to intervene in the regulation of bases, as long as it has 'legal authorization and that its regulatory rank is justified because it deals with matters whose nature requires a treatment for which the legal norms are inadequate by their very characteristics' (STC 213/2013, 19 December, which summarizes its previous jurisprudence). In addition to this formal requirement, the Constitutional Court demands a material requirement for which a law or regulation to qualify itself as 'basic' is not sufficient, but it must meet the material requirement of regulating only what was demanded, from the Court's first jurisprudence, a 'general criteria of regulation of a sector of the legal order or matter must be common throughout the state' (STC 25/1983, 7 April, case *Cuerpos nacionales de Administración local*). Article 111 of the Catalan Autonomous Statute seeks to take over this jurisprudence, establishing that when the *Generalitat* has shared competence, this refers to legislative and regulatory authority as well as the executive function within the framework of bases fixed by the State 'as a principle or minimum common normative in norms with the force of law except where they are determined by the Constitution and the present Statute'. But the whole of the subsection in inverted commas has been declared unconstitutional by the Constitutional Court in its judgment STC 31/2010, amongst other reasons, because to lay down exceptional suppositions in a Statute in which the bases cannot be contained in laws means that the bases will end by being different in every part of the territory and, furthermore, the procedural strictness of a Statute transforms it into 'a norm inappropriate to determine in detail the scope of the powers inherent in that legislation' (FJ 60). In any case, after that decision, the Constitutional Court has continued to maintain its doctrine of requiring the double requisite, both formal and material, that has to comply with the State bases. This, for example, has led it to declare unconstitutional a Resolution of a Secretary of State of Social Security because it lacked sufficient legal cover to have the character of a basic norm (STC 7/2016, 21 January) or to analyse whether a Decree-law had exceeded it when establishing the 'general regulation criteria' of autonomous civil servants when regulating their system of permissions and licences in much more detail than the previous legislation, concluding that it did not. In my opinion this was a rather lax view of what are some general criteria in a matter that has not exhausted its regulation and concedes a normative capacity to the Autonomous Communities (SSTC 156/2015, 9 July, case *Real Decreto-ley 20/2012 de medidas para garantizar la estabilidad presupuestaria*, and 9/2016, 21 January, case *Artículo 48 de la Ley del estatuto básico del empleado público*).

246. Summing up the Spanish system of competences, it can be said that when a matter has been wholly assigned to one or other of the spheres, either State or autonomous, this has the monopoly both of its normative regulation and its implementation, totally excluding the other from these functions. If the matter is autonomous, there is still always the possibility that the State has competence over it in other parts of the national territory because these matters are not regulated in the Constitution individually in each Statute. When the regime of competences is based on the sharing of the matter dealing with the distribution of legislation/implementation, the State has the competence of both drafting the laws and the parliamentary regulations of those laws and, moreover, has the supervisory power to ensure that the Autonomous Administrations carry out the State legislation correctly, while the Communities have competence to perform administrative acts and *reflexive* regulatory power to organize, as they think necessary, the Administration that must implement the State legislation and can even develop their own policy in the matter. Finally, when the legislation on a matter is shared on the bases/complementary legislation dichotomy, the State has the capacity to fix, by law, the general principles of the matter (exceptionally, this can also be done by administrative regulation), and the Autonomous Community has the 'shared competence' to legislate on other aspects of the normative regulation of that matter and is responsible for its ordinary implementation (again exceptionally, the State can do some executive acts when the block of Constitutionality reserves the bases to it). Evidently, the difficulty of applying these non-specific legal concepts to the case in hand has been one of the fundamental reasons for the conflict between the State and Autonomous Communities that has created the vast jurisprudence of the Constitutional Court on the order of competences and that, very briefly, will be explained in the following chapter.

V. Competences of the Autonomous Communities Ratione Materiae

A. *Introduction*

247. The block of constitutionality has undertaken the task of dividing the social reality into specific matters in great detail; both the twenty-two rules of Article 148.1 and the thirty-two of Article 149.1 of the Constitution have given rise to some 300 competences in the Statutes of Autonomy, which produce a great proliferation of matters and *sub-matters* of all types, generally based on the ideas of exclusivity and separation: the matters within the sphere of action of the central State cannot be in the competence of the Communities and vice versa. Therefore, the Constitutional Court has indicated that it is very important to clearly define the limits of each matter because 'as a legal concept relevant for the definitions of competences they have been set up as one of the principal lines of the system of competences' (STC 39/1982, 30 June, case *Información Comités de empresa sobre subvenciones autonómicas*).

B. Competences of Self-government and Public Corporations

248. The competence to regulate its own institutions is fundamental for any Autonomous Community. In the exercise of this competence, it must be borne in mind that the majority of the Statutes fix for themselves the basic features of the institutions of self-government (e.g., the maximum number of deputies, the duration of the legislature, electoral districts, etc.). Although the Statute does not mention it, each Autonomous Community can create the organs it deems necessary provided that they deal with matters of autonomous competence, even over matters in which it only has executive competences (the Councils of Labour Relations are a good example) or even outside its territory (thus autonomous delegations to the EC have been set up).

249. If it can generally be said that the Communities have exclusive competence to create the public organs they think necessary, that competence is complementary (i.e., an autonomous competence on complementary legislation and its implementation) in what concerns the legal system of those organisms in certain sub-matters at least we can be specific, namely the statutory regime of civil servants, contracts and administrative concessions, and the system of responsibility for the autonomous Administration (Article 149.1.18 SC and Article 47.2 EAA, for example).

250. The block of constitutionality distributes between the State and the Communities over various collectives, both those strictly public as well as private. Thus, the State fixes the bases of the local regime of the legal system of the public administration (Article 149.1.18), and the Communities approve the complementary legislation and its implementation (Article 10.4 EAPV and Article 160 EAC, Article 60 EAA, etc.); professional bodies, associations, and foundations have a similar regime. This shared or ‘double’ character of the legal regime of the local autonomies in the Autonomous State (STC 84/1982, 23 December, case *Presupuestos Generales del Estado 1982*) marks an important difference from the majority of federal states, where local corporations are considered a matter of the internal organization of autonomous bodies.

251. Without wishing to go into too much detail but bearing in mind the usual administrative assignment of this competence, the complementary autonomous competence over the regime of radio and television broadcasting can be included here. In the exercise of this competence, the Autonomous Communities are those empowered to grant broadcasting licenses for local radio and television stations. Some Communities, especially those that have their own language different from Spanish, have created public radio and television services (Basque Country, Catalonia, etc.), but there are now fourteen, all publicly funded, creating a political and social debate about their future.

C. Competences over Public Security and Justice

252. The most important competence in this section is the competence over public security, that – in the words of the Constitutional Court – is the 'activity directed towards the protection of persons and goods (security in the strict sense) and in the maintenance of calm and public order' (STC 33/1982, 8 June, case *Mejillones nocivos*). According to the Constitutional Court, autonomous competence includes the service available to guarantee security or *organic* aspect (the police force) but not the *legal* aspect (the regulation of security), which is exclusively held by the state (Article 149.1.29 SC). In this matter, there is an important difference between Communities since while some have their own autonomous police forces (Basque Country and Catalonia), the majority have not created one and have welcomed the possibility, established by Organic Law 2/1986 on Corps and Security Forces of the State, of attaching units of the national police force to the Communities, responsible only for the surveillance and protection of its buildings and facilities. All Communities do have the competence to coordinate local police forces. Precisely, Law 36/2015, 28 September, on National Security seeks to improve the use of all these police officers when there is a situation of 'interest for national security' declared by the President of the Government and binding on the Autonomous Communities and the Town Councils to place 'the necessary human and material resources' under the orders of an authority appointed by the government. The Constitutional Court has reinterpreted this obligation to maintain its constitutionality, ordering that this provision of resources must be understood as referring to those that are necessary during the said situation for the exercise of the powers of the Administration that must provide them, since 'Law 36/2015 configures the situation of interest for national security as a reinforced coordination mechanism in the performance by each Administration of its ordinary attributions, so it does not alter the competence framework' (STC 184/2016, 3 November, case *Ley 36/2015, de Seguridad Nacional*).

253. Civil protection can be considered, according to the Constitutional Court, a sub-matter of public security since it is an activity directed to the protection of persons and goods in situations of emergency, grave risk, or catastrophe. It is one of the few matters in which there is concurrent competence, and the criterion considered by the Constitutional Court in delimiting competences is the nature of the emergency situation, leaving to the Communities the competence to draw up plans and to direct its own services, taking into account that it is subordinate to the national interest in those cases in which this can come into play when the catastrophe is supra-territorial (STC 133/1990, 19 July, case *Ley de protección civil de 1985*). The most important state law in this area today is Law 17/2015, 9 July, on the National System, which, amongst other things, creates the National Civil Protection Council made up of representatives of the State, the Communities and the Spanish Federation of Municipalities and Provinces. It is also worth noting Organic Law 5/2005, 17 November, on National Defence, which – in line with the provisions of the 1985 Civil Defence Law on the participation of the Army in emergencies – attributes to the Armed Forces the 'mission' of 'preserving the security and well-being of citizens in the event of serious risk, catastrophe, calamity or other public needs'. And based on this law, in 2005, the Council of Ministers created the Military Emergency Unit, reporting directly to the President, in my opinion, to alleviate the poor regional management of civil protection.

254. Most Autonomous Communities have exclusive competence over both legislation and execution of public events, casinos, sports, and gambling. The Constitutional Court has specified that when the presence of the forces of order is normally required to control risk factors for the holding of a public event, then the competence is not that of public events but rather of public security in the strict sense so that the state can approve the norms dealing with it, even in those Communities with their own police force, and State legislation shall apply. Thus, the State was able to pass Law 10/1990, 15 October, on the Prevention of Violence at Sporting Performances and its parliamentary regulations to develop it (STC 148/2000, 1 June, case *Reglamento para la prevención de la violencia en los espectáculos deportivos*). The best-known and most controversial autonomous laws in this area are those relating to the protection of animals passed in the Canary Islands in 1991 and in Catalonia in 2010, prohibiting bullfighting. This latter law was appealed by the PP, and the Constitutional Court annulled it on the grounds that it would be an 'excess in the exercise of autonomous competences that would encroach on or undermine those that Article 149.2 SC endowed on the State' (STC 177/2016, 20 October, case *Prohibición de los toros en Cataluña*). Also, using this competence for entertainment –reinforced with that of consumer protection – the Communities have approved norms (sometimes laws, sometimes decrees) on the right of admission to shops and public premises. Thus, for example, Law 2/2011, 2 March, on access to public shows, recreational activities and public establishments in the Region of Murcia.

255. The Statutes of the first-degree Communities give them the powers that the Organic Law on Judicial Power reserves to the government of the State, a competence that all the others assumed in the reforms of their Statutes at the end of the 1990s. As a result, the phrase has been coined 'Administration of the Administration of Justice' (STC 56/1990, 29 March, case *LOPJ-III)*, denominating the aspects of the Administration of Justice that correspond to the executive power, such as the premises, financial management, and non-legal staff. It has already been mentioned that the new Autonomous Statutes establish an autonomous Council of Justice, which could be created if the LOPJ is modified (*see* paragraph 184).

Some Statutes (Basque Country, Catalonia, Galicia, Andalusia, and Navarre) also assign the management of penitentiary institutions to the respective Communities. However, until now, only the Autonomous Community of Catalonia (since 1983) and the Basque Country (2021) fully exercise this competence over prisons, as only the related services and staff have been transferred to them. The rest of the Communities do not claim in practice the transfer of these services, which are certainly not easy to manage.

D. Economic Competences

256. It is necessary to begin the study of these competences by stating that, beyond the description of exclusivity that many of them receive in the Statutes, practically all the powers of the Autonomous Communities are complementary (i.e., they can pass complementary legislation and are responsible for the ordinary implementation of the state bases) because the principle of economic unity – as the Constitutional Court has interpreted it – means that the State has reserved the legislation, via its right to competences over bases and coordination of the general planning of economic activity (Article 149.1.13 SC).

257. Almost all the Statutes begin the list of their economic competences by referring to that of the promotion and planning of economic activity and then continue with the complementary competence of the State bases for the regulation of credit, banking, and insurance (Article 149.1.11 SC). The Statutes have broken down the complementary competence of these bases into two areas: the competence 'exclusive without prejudice' on the public and territorial institutions of cooperative credit, the Savings Banks and Rural Savings Banks, and the competence 'of legislative development' of the regulation of credit, banking, and insurance. The State bases over the former (especially Law 31/1985, on Regulation of the Basic Norms on the Governing Organs of the Savings Banks) give the Autonomous Communities more leeway for intervention in these institutions than in the banks.

258. Competences over other matters connected with various sectors of economic activity and that, except where indicated to the contrary, maintain the same regime of complementary competences are:

(1) Competence over agriculture and livestock farming. Here can also be included competence over woodlands, livestock trails, marshes, lakes, pastures, and special projects for mountain areas.
(2) Competences over inland fishing, shell-fishing, and aquaculture (exclusive to the Communities). In the case of the open sea, the State has the competence over fishing and the Communities a complementary one over 'the regulation of the fishing sector'. This is an important distinction since it means that the Communities can develop both the State bases and those of EC Law and treaties, and so the Communities 'determine who may exercise the extractive activity, the conditions that the members of the fishing industry must comply with and the form of organization' (STC 56/1989, 16 March, case *pesca de coral*).
(3) Competences over industry and energy: facilities for production, distribution, and transport of energy 'when this transport does not go beyond the territory of the Community and its use does not affect other territories'; the system of mining and fuels and of industrial property; the Communities only have executive powers over this last, unlike the other two matters where they also hold complementary ones.
(4) Competences over tourism. The seventeen Statutes assign this matter exclusively to their respective Communities. In spite of this, the State is not totally

stripped of its powers because both the Constitution and the Statutes reserve to it the general direction of the economy and other competences that permit it to regulate activities connected to tourism, such as foreign trade (Article 149.1.10 SC), and so the State is in charge of promoting foreign tourism, or the granting of professional qualifications to those working in the industry (STC 75/1989, 24 April, case *turismo rural*).

(5) Competences over internal trade, consumer, and user protection, amongst which are included interior fairs and markets and the holding of international fairs within the Community's territory; the establishment and regulation of centres of contraction of goods and stocks in accordance with mercantile law.

(6) Other economic institutions over which the Communities hold complementary competences are the Chambers of Commerce, Industry and Navigation, Agrarian Associations (State law 18/2005 attributes their maintenance or abolition to the Communities), as well as the Councils responsible for regulating the quality control of goods (usually foods and wines) produced in designated areas, etc.

E. Competences over Transport and Public Works

259. Transport and public works have a common denominator in all the Statutes of Autonomy: for them to be the competence of the Autonomous Community, they have to be especially connected to the Community's territory and not of general interest to the State. Thus, the Communities are in charge of the public works that do not affect any other Community and 'always provided that they are not legally classified as of general interest to the state'. This also applies to ports, airports, and heliports that are not so classified as recreational ports and airports and generally those which do not carry on commercial activities. It also applies to railways, highways, and roads whose routes run completely within the Community's territory and, in the same terms, transport carried out by those means or by cable or rivers. Law 62/1997, 26 December, on Modification of the Law on State Ports of 1992, has allowed the Communities to participate in the management of State ports by the rather unorthodox expedient of giving them the right to nominate the majority of the members on the Councils of Administration of the Port Authorities.

The new Statutes lay down various formulae for participation in the State infrastructure. Thus, a prior report is required before declaring a specific part of the infrastructure as of general interest, with the possibility that its management is carried out by the Community and the participation of the relevant Community in the planning of infrastructure made in its territory that is of a wider, general interest 'in the terms determined by state law' (Article 140.4 EAC, Article 64.2 EAA) As in all these cases no obligation is imposed on the state, the Constitutional Court has held in its judgment 31/2010 that these cooperation techniques can never impose autonomous decisions on the State.

F. Competences in the Matter of Labour

260. These competences are solely executive, but in some way, it can be said that they are of secondary importance amongst the Community's powers, as shown by the fact that in nearly all cases, they have created Councils of Labour. Thus, the Autonomous Communities have competence over such relevant activities as active employment policies, mediation and arbitration between employers and workers, technical offices of hygiene, labour force adjustment plans, and the administrative records of Workers' Cooperatives. As the State wishes to keep executive competences over matters that affect employment (social security, immigration), Law 42/1997, 14 November, on Regulations on the Inspection of Labour and Social Security created in order to coordinate State and autonomous administrations, the Territorial Commissions of the Inspection of Labour and Social Security (presided over by a representative of the Community), whose system of operations and specific tasks are remitted to a bilateral agreement between the State and the respective Autonomous Community. The new Law 23/2015, 21 July, on Computer of the Labour and Social Security Inspection System maintains these Commissions, although it changes the name so that they are now called Autonomous Operating Commissions, and it considers them the basic pieces of a model of the organization of the shared inspection designed to avoid (according to its Preamble) 'duplicities, inefficiencies and extra costs and will serve as a framework for unified supervision of all social order regulations, fully compatible, therefore, with the principle of market unity advocated by the Constitution and the constitutional treaties of the European Union and that has been consolidated in the current legislature with the approval by Parliament of Law 20/2013, December 9, guarantee of the market unit'.

G. Competences over Health, Social Security, and Social Services

261. The State has the competence to regulate the bases of health care and coordinate with all the Communities (*see* paragraph 275). Amongst the most relevant laws regulating these bases are Law 14/1986, 25 April, on General Health; Law 41/2002, 14 November, on patient autonomy; and Law 16/2003, 28 May, on the cohesion and quality of the National Health System, which created the Interterritorial Council of the National Health System. This Council acquired great public notoriety with the COVID-19 pandemic declared in March 2020. For their part, the Autonomous Communities manage all public health facilities, previously in the hands of the State (which currently only operates those of Ceuta and Melilla plus two military hospitals) and the provincial councils. Thus, together with education, health care accounts for the bulk of the number of civil servants and regional public spending. In addition, state Law 16/1996, 25 April, attributed to all Autonomous Communities the planning of the number of pharmacies in their territory and the administrative authorization to open them.

Likewise, the Communities manage Social Security, although the State has reserved its economic regime (the 'single fund') to guarantee 'the unity and solidarity of the public Social Security system (SSTC 124/1989, of 7 July, and 133/2019, of 13 November). Because of this purpose of solidarity, the powers attributed by the Statutes to the Communities over the management of the economic regime cannot mean that the State is deprived of management functions but rather that the Communities will be responsible only for those functions that 'cannot compromise the unity of the system or disrupt its uniform economic functioning' (SSTC 124/1989 and 133/2019, 13 November), nor call into question the State's ownership of all Social Security resources or directly or indirectly engender inequalities between citizens as regards the satisfaction of their rights and the fulfilment of their social security obligations' (STC 36/2022, 10 March).

On the other hand, the Statutes attribute to the Communities exclusive competence over social assistance and services, public institutions for the protection and guardianship of minors and policies for the elderly. Furthermore, the Constitutional Court has specified that social assistance is to be understood as those activities of care for situations of personal need located 'outside' the Social Security system, that is to say, that they are financed 'outside any contributory obligation or prior financial collaboration of the recipients or beneficiaries' (STC 36/2012, 15 March).

H. Competences over Education, Research, Culture, and Sports

262. In contrast to the model of the Second Republic, which created two separate institutional networks, the State and the regional, the present block of constitutionality assigns the basic legislation on education to the State, with complementary competences to the Communities. This system has given rise to a high level of conflict that has caused the Constitutional Court to fix a casuistic method for distributing educational competences. This polemic on the boundary between the State and the Communities has not ended with the new century (often mixed with the different interpretations that the parties hold about the right to education), with the result that all the important educational laws passed by parliament have been appealed to the Constitutional Court. Thus, Organic Law 6/2001, of 21 December, on Universities and Organic Law 10/2002, of 23 December, on Quality in Education, initiatives of the PP that did not have the support of the PSOE, which modified them in the VIII Legislature of the *Cortes*. Following the same law of the pendulum, when the PP regained its absolute majority, it altered the socialist legislation through Organic Law 8/2013, of 9 December, for the improvement of the quality of education (LOMCE), which has again been modified by a left-wing majority through Organic Law 3/2020, of 29 December.

The Ley Orgánica 2/2006, de Educación (slightly modified on this point by LO 3/2020) includes the State's high inspection of the regional education systems in much greater detail than had previously been the case in all the Statutes. Although the Organic Law gives it many powers to supervise the adaptation of curricula to basic regulations, the activity of this high inspectorate (which is integrated into the Government Delegation in each Autonomous Community) seems to have focused more on administrative aspects (such as the recognition of equivalence of studies for employment purposes) and has avoided supervisory elements, not even when independent bodies had considered that some Communities were not teaching a subject adequately, as happened when the Royal Academy of History presented a highly critical report in 2000 on the history teaching texts used in several Communities.

For its part, the new Catalan Statute no longer contains this state reservation in educational matters, and those that have followed it subsequently follow its path, with some exceptions, such as the Valencian Statute, which still mentions it. The Andalusian Statute also includes it, but it refers to an inspection superior to the tutelage that the Junta exercises over educational establishments that are not its property (a conclusion deduced from Article 81.1 of the EAA since it does not exercise any tutelage over its own establishments, but only a power of direction). As this is a State competence, these statutory omissions do not imply the disappearance of the High Inspectorate of Education. However, the State must regulate this supervisory body while respecting the competences of the Autonomous Communities, something which the LOMCE did not do when it allowed the High Inspectorate to replace the Autonomous Communities in taking decisions on the schooling in Spanish of pupils in bilingual areas because, while it is true that 'it is the State's responsibility to ensure respect for linguistic rights in the education system, but also that such a function must be deployed without going beyond the competences constitutionally reserved to it' (STC 14/2018, 20 February, LOMCE-1 case).

This implies that, for example, although the Statute of Autonomy declares that the Autonomous Community has exclusive competence 'in matters of knowledge, conservation, research, training, promotion and dissemination of flamenco' (Article 68.1 EAA), the State can also develop actions to promote this musical genre. To put it in the words of the Constitutional Court itself: the declarations of exclusive competence in cultural matters in the Statutes 'do not affect the concurrent competences of the State within the subject of culture itself, as a consequence of the provisions of Art. 149.2 CE, nor do they question the impact that other competences different from those of the State provided for in Art. 149.1 CE may have' (STC 31/1010, 28 June).

263. Autonomous activities in the field of culture are very wide, and the Communities enjoy an exclusive competence that goes from the 'promotion and encouragement (of culture) in all its manifestations and expressions' to archives, museums and libraries 'that do not belong to the state' and conservatories and academies with their main offices in the Community. Furthermore, the Statutes assign to their Communities management of museums, archives, and libraries belonging to the State and the complementary competence over historical, artistic, monumental, archaeological, and scientific heritage. Remembering that Article 149.2 SC assigns a general competence to the State in cultural matters, it can only be assumed that both spheres have competence in this area.

264. The first Autonomous Statutes reserved to their Communities exclusive competence over sports, a matter not referred to in Article 149.1 of the Constitution (so in Article 10 EAPV, Article 9 EAC, Article 27 EAG, etc.) For this reason, all the Communities have passed laws on sports regulating autonomous sporting organizations, federations, and regional sports clubs, measures for promoting sports, etc. In a couple of them (specifically in the Basque Law 14/1998 and Catalan Law 9/1999), there are articles which have brought them into conflict with the State: the provisions dealing with autonomous sports teams and their participation in international competitions. This was rejected by the State in Law 10/1990, which establishes a monopoly according to which only national organizations can participate in international federations and only national teams can take part in international competitions in which other national teams compete. However, autonomous teams may participate in international matches provided that, first, Spain is not doing so and, second, the match is only friendly. The Constitutional Court has saved the constitutionality of the Basque and Catalan laws by means of a conforming interpretation: the regional federations may associate directly with the international federations 'whenever it is a case of sports in which there are no Spanish federations and which, under no circumstances are the competences of the State of coordination and international representation of Spanish sport, prevented or disturbed'.[35]

I. Competences over Territorial Planning Policy and the Environment

265. The competences of territorial planning policy include the regulation of land use in the territory and on the coast, as well as town planning and housing. The Judgment in STC 61/1997, 20 March, case *Ley de suelo*, was of great importance in this matter as it held that the block of constitutionality deprived the State of most of its powers that historically it had exercised, reducing it to establishing the basic conditions for the exercise of the right of ownership of land. Thus, it annulled a good number of the articles of state law because the State lacked the competence to pass them and did not even have a right supplementary to the autonomous legislation.

One subject, halfway between territorial policy and the environment, which has its own importance, is water or, to give it its more technical name, hydraulic resources. Bearing in mind its great political, economic, and social importance, it leads to 'water wars' which, like summer storms, occur periodically amongst the Communities, particularly over the rivers Ebro and Tajo. Article 149.1.22 reserves to the state, legislation on water resources and their management when the 'waters run through more than one Autonomous Community', which the Law on Water of 1985, with the backing of STC 227/1988, 29 November, defined as the concept of a water basin or territory in which the waters 'flow to the sea through a network of secondary rivers that converge into one single main river'. That is why the first Autonomous Statutes reserved to their Communities the exclusive competence over – to quote the first Statute, the others are in similar terms – 'the use of hydraulic sources, canals and waters for irrigation when the waters run entirely within the Basque Country' (Article 10.11 EAPV).

The new Statutes of the twenty-first century are, as in other matters, extremely thorough, and some of them have introduced certain specifics which have led to

35. STC 80/2012, 18 April, FJ 11, case *Ley vasca del deporte*. The CC repeats the same argument in the STC 110/2012, 23 May, case *Ley catalana del deporte*. This jurisprudence had already been advanced by the CC when it judged the constitutionality of the Statute of Catalonia, which contains similar provisions on international sports relation: the norms do not attribute to these Communities the capacity to affiliate with any international sporting organizations that they think fit, participating in their competitions but rather of mandates that permit them to participate when the State decides, so 'regulating their scope and modalities' (STC 31/2010, (FJ 80)).

controversies on their constitutionality. In this sense, the most legally arguable provision is Article 51 of the Andalusian Statute that attributes to Andalusia the complementary competence ('exclusive without prejudice' is the literal wording of the Statute) on 'the waters of the Guadalquivir Basin that runs through its territory and does not affect any other Autonomous Community'. The Council of Extremadura appealed to the Constitutional Court against this article in 2007, and the Court, in its STC 20/2011, 16 March, upheld the appeal and declared the clause null and void since it is undeniable that the Guadalquivir basin extends not only through Andalusia but also through Extremadura, Castile-La Mancha and Murcia. The Court, in a similar sense, has also declared unconstitutional and void Article 75.1 of Organic Law 14/2007, 30 November, on the reform of the Autonomous Statute of Castille-León, which attributed competences of legislative and executive development over the Duero Basin to the Council of Castilla-León (STC /2011, 17 March). However, the Constitutional Court admits that the Statutes reserve the flow of inter-community rivers for the exclusive use of the citizens of one Community but interprets it that it is a form of participation in the State competence of planning and not a binding provision for the State as does the new Aragonese Statute with the Ebro (STC 110/2011, 22 June). In my opinion, in this way, the constitutionality of the provision of the Aragonese Statute on the Ebro is saved in a similar way to how many Catalan Articles had been saved in STC 31/2010: it is deprived of normative value, converting it in a political mandate, without a doubt very relevant in the area concerned, but without legal force properly speaking.

266. The role of the Constitutional Court in the sharing of competences between the State and the Communities in the matter of the environment has been particularly relevant and has turned from a vision favourable to the State to one more autonomist. So, the Decision 102/1995, 26 June, case *Ley de los espacios naturales* rectified an earlier precedent, which had considered that in this matter, the 'basic legislation, without prejudice to the powers of the Self-governing Communities to take additional protective measures, could be extended to aspects that it could not in other areas, thereby restricting autonomous competences. By virtue of this new doctrine, it declared that the provisions of Law 4/1989 giving the management of the national parks to the State were not basic. As a result, the Autonomous Communities had to participate in the management of the parks. This line of interpretation was subsequently reinforced by holding that the 'transversal' competence of the state in the environment must be '*de minimis*', limited to regulating those activities directly aimed at the preservation, conservation, or improvement of natural resources (STC 306/2000, 12 December, case *Picos de Europa*); or with the declaration of unconstitutionality of various Articles of Law 11/2013 *de Evaluación Ambiental* by not demanding a prior report from the Community of Aragon to make diversions in the Tajo-Segura basin (STC 13/2015, 5 February) and another Article that declared as basic norms for proceeding with environmental impact reports (STC 53/2017, 11 May).

VI. The Extension of Competences by State Delegation or Transfer

267. As has already been mentioned in the analysis of the constitutional blocks (see paragraph 236), the attribution of powers to the Autonomous Communities can not only be made in their respective statutes, but the Constitution also provides in Article 150 that the State may delegate or transfer powers to 'all or some of the Communities' employing organic laws, i.e., laws originating exclusively from the will of the State legislative power, which means that they do not have the special procedure of being drafted with the participation of the Autonomous Communities. In the constituent *Cortes*, this Article 150 was very controversial because some political and academic sectors feared that essential State powers could be transferred in this way. However, the subsequent development has not been so much to increase the competences of the historical Communities (whose Statutes were already quite advanced) as to increase the competences of some second-degree Communities (the Canary Islands and Valencia, whose competences were practically equal to those of the first-degree Communities thanks to two transfer laws of 1982). They have also been used to give a certain homogeneity to the autonomous system, delegating powers that some Communities lacked and others already had. Thus, for example, Organic Law 16/1995, 27 December, on the transfer of powers to Galicia and Organic Law 9/1992, 23 December, on the transfer of powers to the Communities that acceded to autonomy under Article 143. Organic Law, 6/1997 on the transfer of executive powers in traffic matters to Catalonia, was used – as its name indicates – to increase the powers of one Community, differentiating it from the others. However, it is necessary to clarify that this law put Catalonia on par with the Basque Country, whose Statute attributed these powers to it.

Curiously, all these delegation laws have been passed using the authorization of Article 150.2 of the Constitution, which, as it allows the transfer of 'powers corresponding to matters of state ownership' without mentioning whether it includes legislative power, was initially thought to be designed to transfer executive powers. By contrast, Article 150.1, which does expressly mention the power to enact 'legislative norms', has never been used. Possibly because the constitutional article then adds: 'within the framework of the basic principles and guidelines established by state law'. Of course, our legislators have not lacked imagination when deploying the autonomous State: in addition to the transfer of competences via organic laws under Article 150.2, simple ordinary laws have also been used, not provided for in any constitutional article. For example, the State Ports Act of 1996 allowed the Autonomous Communities to designate the governing bodies of the Port Authorities. Also, Law 41/1997, which modifies Law 4/1989 on the Conservation of Natural Spaces, establishes that the Aigües Tortes National Park is part of the network of National Parks but adds that, instead of being governed by State legislation like all other national parks, it will maintain 'however, the current management and organization regime in the terms established by the autonomous community regulations'.

§3. Collaboration Between the State and the Autonomous Communities: Prevention and Resolution of Conflicts

I. The Principle of Collaboration

268. From its first judgments, the Constitutional Court has pointed out that for the 'good functioning of the Autonomous State', collaboration between the two powers is necessary 'regardless of the distribution of competences'. Moreover, it considers that mutual help and collaboration between distinct administrations are 'a duty related to the principle of coordination, and that for reasons of security and urgency, it is even capable of altering the normal order of competences in case of urgency and necessity when the actions of the usually competent authorities cannot be waited for' (STC 95/1984, 18 October, case *Reestructuración órganos de la Administración central*).

269. Basically, two types of collaboration can be distinguished, coordination and cooperation. While the first is aimed at allowing a certain simplification and unity in a system, the second is a relationship between powers to achieve ends satisfactory to both. The essential difference between them turns on the position of the parties: in coordination, the coordinating body has a certain position of pre-eminence, a 'power of direction', as against the coordinated entity. This said, it must be admitted that coordination and cooperation are usually used almost as synonyms by the doctrine and the Constitutional Court. Therefore, here the techniques of relations between State and Communities are not going to be grouped according to hierarchy but according to the form that collaboration takes whether or not representatives of the State and the Communities are integrated into the same organ. In the first case, it is an 'organic' or 'intra-organic' collaboration, while in the second, it is 'functional' or 'inter-organic'.

II. Techniques of Functional Collaboration: Cooperation Agreements and Conventions

270. The first consequence of the principle of cooperation in the administrative sphere is the duty of reciprocal information of the State and autonomous administrations (STC 76/1983, 5 August, case *LOAPA*). Moreover, the Constitution itself recognizes a multiplicity of techniques of functional collaboration, from the assigning of a legislative initiative to the Communities (Article 87.2 SC) to the carrying out of joint activities, by way of the delegation of competences (Article 150.2 SC),[36] without forgetting the conventions between Communities (Article 145 SC). To these techniques, we can add others used in different laws: the making of prior reports by one administration when the decision has to be taken by the other, joint

36. A good example is Organic Law 4/1981, 1 June, on the States of Alarm, Emergency and Siege, where it establishes in its Art. 7: 'In case of a state of alarm the competent authority shall be the government or, at its delegation, the President of the Autonomous Community when the declaration exclusively affects all or part of the territory of a Community' (*see* para. 448).

making of plans, etc. Possibly, Law 1/2002, 21 February, *de Coordinación de las Competencias del Estado y las Comunidades Autónomas en materia de Defensa de la Competencia* (on Coordination of the Competences of the State and the Autonomous Communities in matters of defence of Competences) offers the most carefully drafted of these techniques of functional collaboration (and another we could say on the organic laws, also very relevant in that law).

271. Conventions are a formula much used in comparative law because, without altering the constitutional system of competences, they permit two Administrations to collaborate on terms of equality to resolve common problems. In Spanish practice, the conventions most used are the 'vertical', between the State and one or more Communities, curiously a type of convention not expressly referred to in the Constitution, although it does mention the 'horizontal', which is much less used. Article 145.2 SC determines that the Autonomous Communities if their Statutes so permit, can conclude conventions inter se for the management and provision of services. A limit is put to this technique of collaboration in that a federation of Communities 'will in no case be permitted' and the authorization of cooperation agreements is reserved to parliament 'in other cases'; this provision was included due to a certain fear on the part of the constituent assembly that the Catalan-speaking territories (Catalonia-Balearics-Valencia) might form such a confederation. Cooperation agreements between the State and the Communities are currently regulated by Law 40/2015, 1 October, on the Legal Regime of the Public Sector (LRJSP), which sets out the requirements they must meet. It is worth noting that in many of these agreements (especially in the areas of social assistance, infrastructure and the environment), the State makes financial commitments so that the central government uses them – in the application of the old saying, he who pays the piper calls the tune – to encourage the Communities to carry out the policies it deems appropriate.

The Statutes of Autonomy, when regulating the conventions, have, following Article 145.2 of the Constitution, distinguished between those for the management and provision of services and the politically more important cooperation agreements. Therefore, agreements always need parliamentary authorization, while for the legal validity of conventions, a simple notification before coming into force is enough, although parliament can make objections within the period of thirty days. If it does so, the convention is processed as a cooperation agreement. In practice, conventions are used quite often, while agreements are virtually unknown. The new Catalan Autonomous Statute regulates these agreements in greater detail and stipulates that both the conventions and agreements be published in the Official Gazette of the Generalitat within a maximum period (forty-five days for the conventions) after signing, without doubt, a requirement that strengthens legal certainty and the control of public institutions compared to the practice of many autonomous Executives who fail to publish the conventions or who do so only after much delay.

272. The Constitutional Court has clarified that conventions cannot assign competences as this is a function of the Statutes of Autonomy and to the rest of the block of constitutionality. Thus, the ordinary courts exercise legal control over the carrying out of a convention that, although not granting competences, does generate rights and duties for both parties. For twenty years, no law expressly established this judicial competence, a lacuna now filled by Law 29/1998 on Regulator of Contentious-Administrative Jurisdiction. As with other norms, that a specific convention could be the object of a conflict of competences before the Constitutional Court cannot be ruled out if the State or a Community consider that the parties to it do not have competence or are breaking that of the challenging institution.

III. Techniques of Organic Collaboration

273. The first institution that is designed in the *Lex legum* as the centre of these techniques of organic collaboration is the Senate, defined in Article 69 as the 'Chamber of territorial representation'. However, its constitutional form does not permit it to play that role because its composition is far from meeting that definition, with little more than one-fifth of its members' representatives of the Autonomous Communities and its clearly subordinate position to Congress in the exercise of its parliamentary functions. This is so even in questions markedly autonomous in nature, such as the drafting and reform of the Statutes, particularly those drafted by the procedure of Article 151.2 SC, the authorization of inter-Community agreements (Article 145.2 SC), and the drafting of the Law on the Interterritorial Compensation Fund (Article 158.2 SC).

274. There are two provisions (Articles 150.3 and 155 SC) in which the role of the Senate is truly decisive in relation to the Autonomous Communities; however, these two cases are so exceptional that the first has never occurred and the second only once, in October 2017:

(1) In the event of the need to promulgate laws to harmonize the normative provisions of the Communities, the Senate, as with Congress, must approve them by an absolute majority (*see* paragraph 277).
(2) Only the Senate can authorize the government to adopt the measures necessary to oblige the Communities to fulfil their constitutional and legal obligations (*see* paragraph 278).

275. A very common coordination technique in federal states, normally without express support in the Constitution, is the periodic meeting of those responsible for the same matter in the central State and the autonomous bodies to exchange opinions and agree on standards. Article 4.1 of the Law on Autonomous Procedure has introduced this technique in Spain under the generic name of 'Sectorial Conferences of the Councils of the different Autonomous Communities and of the Ministry or Ministries in the matter' which, according to the Constitutional Court, can only make agreements binding on the public powers when they originate in the express attribution to the State of 'coordination' in a specific sphere, as happens with economic planning and health (Article 149.1.13 and 15 SC). In other cases, the Conferences cannot substitute for the organs of the Communities, having only the character of 'meeting groups for the examination of common problems and for the discussion of appropriate lines of action' (STC 76/1983, 5 August, case *LOAPA).*

State legislation has created a good number, almost forty, of these organs: the Council of Fiscal and Financial Policy (Article 3 LOFCA), the Commission on the Coordination of Public Function (Law 30/1984, 2 August, on Measures for the Reform of Public Function), the National Commission on Civil Protection (Law 2/1985, 21 January, on Civil Protection), the Conference on matters related to the European Communities (Law 2/1997, 13 March), etc. In general, they were regulated for the first time in 1992 by the Law de *Régimen Jurídico de las Administraciones Públicas*, substituted in 2015 by *Ley de Régimen Jurídico del Sector Público* (LRJSP), which determines that the sectorial conferences are instruments of voluntary cooperation convened by the corresponding minister who makes agreements, whose nature is that of 'recommendations' that only bind the members who have voted in favour of them. In spite of this, if the State exercises its competence to coordinate a specific subject, then the agreements of a conference will be binding. The LRJSP attributes a new function to these conferences, which, on paper, can be useful for increasing coordination amongst institutions: that of being informed about bills and the draft regulations of the government of the nation or of the Governing

Councils of the Autonomous Communities, when they directly affect the scope of competence of the other Public Administrations or when so envisaged in the applicable sectorial regulations.

Following the example of other composite states, most notably Canada, in 2004, the Socialist Government set up a Conference of Presidents made up of the President of the Government, the seventeen Presidents of the Autonomous Communities, plus those of the Autonomous Cities of Ceuta and Melilla, to meet once a year and reach agreements for the better functioning of the Autonomous State. The LRJSP gave legal support to this political initiative, although it was limited itself to defining it and establishing that its purpose was to deliberate on matters and adopt agreements of interest to the State and the Autonomous Communities, but without attributing specific functions to it or establishing norms for its convening. The conference itself subsequently specified these issues by approving a set of regulations.[37]

IV. Extraordinary Instruments of State for the Resolution of Conflicts

276. The Constitution provides two extraordinary techniques to resolve conflicts between the state and the Autonomous Communities, one legislative and the other executive: the law of harmonization and State coercion. It must be pointed out that, fortunately, State coercion has still not been used, and only once, in November

37. The current operating regulations were approved at the Twenty-Sixth Conference of Presidents held on the island of La Palma on 13 Mar. 2022. At present, the various conferences number some thirty and their results can be consulted at http://www.mptfp.es/portal/politica-territorial/autonomica/coop_autonomica/Confer_Presidentes.html. For the doctrine, *see* Raúl Bocanegra Sierra & Alejandro Huergo Lora, *La Conferencia de Presidentes* (Iustel 2005).

1983, has a Law on Harmonization been passed, the Organic Law on the Harmonization of the Autonomous Process. This did not come into force because a preliminary appeal of unconstitutionality was lodged against it, and the Constitutional Court, in its Judgment 76/1983, denied its character as a law of harmonization and declared a good number of its articles unconstitutional.

A. *Laws of Harmonization*

277. The final paragraph of Article 150, inspired by Article 19 of the 1931 Constitution, declares that: 'The State may enact laws establishing the principles necessary for harmonizing the rule-making provisions of the Autonomous Communities, even in the case of matters over which jurisdiction has been conferred upon the latter when this is necessary for the general interest. It is incumbent upon the Cortes Generales, by an absolute majority of the members of each House, to evaluate this necessity'.

According to the Constitutional Court, the law of harmonization can only be used when the State legislator has no other instruments available to guarantee the harmony demanded by the general interest in a given matter (STC 76/1983, 5 August, case *LOAPA*). In practice, this residual conception of the *last resort* of the law of harmonization means that its use will be minimal, not to say non-existent, because a specific State competence will nearly always be found that will allow it to legislate in any matter, as proved by the fact that no new harmonization law has been passed to date.

B. *State Coercion*

278. Article 155 of the Constitution establishes that when an Autonomous Community 'does not comply with the law and the Constitution and other laws imposed on it', the state can adopt 'the necessary measures' for which the government needs the authorization of the Senate by an absolute majority and previously to address the President of the affected Community to ask him to fulfil his obligations. Although some authors of note have sought to 'de-dramatize' this article, trying to include it in the State's power of supervision, the truth is that the idea has become stronger, and so it can only be used in extreme situations. This happened at the end of 2017 when the approval in the parliament of Catalonia of two laws to organize a referendum of self-determination and the transition to an independent State was followed by the holding of the referendum and a bizarre proclamation of the Republic of Catalonia. Then the Spanish Government used this article to dismiss the President of the Generalitat and all its Government Councils and, at the same time, called for regional elections. For its part, the Organic Law 2/2012, 27 April, of Budgetary Stability and Financial Sustainability (dictated by mandate of the reformed Article 135 SC) establishes that the government must request the Senate for authorization to adopt measures 'of forced compliance' against an Autonomous Community that does not comply with its deficit limit and does not follow the indications of the financial, economic plan that must be drafted to comply with it.

V. The Ordinary Resolution of Conflicts: The Constitutional Court

279. In the purest federal style, the Spanish Constitution conceived a legal solution for the conflicts that inevitably arise between the State and the Autonomous Communities, entrusting the resolution of controversies between both powers to the Constitutional Court, for which the Constitution establishes two specific procedures: the conflicts of competences (*see* paragraph 204) and the challenging of provisions without the force of law and resolutions of the Autonomous Communities (*see* paragraph 205). To these must be added the appeal against unconstitutionality because although its scope of action is not limited to State–Community conflicts, it is the correct procedure when an institution considers that the law approved by another has encroached upon its sphere of competences (*see* paragraph 201).

280. Generally speaking, the Constitutional Court has successfully fulfilled its role as the impartial judge it was designed to be, despite the frequency with which appeals have been made to it, unusual in the majority of compound States. Its doctrine – far from unbreakable rigidity – is widely accepted by the jurists, conferring on it an undeniable *auctoritas,* which perhaps now has been damaged by the controversy arising from the judgment 31/2010 on the Catalan Autonomous Statute, adopted with great internal divisions (of the ten judges participating in the decision, five delivered minority judgments). However, in the political field, the nationalist parties have criticized its decisions, even reaching the point of an overall condemnation in the *Declaración de Barcelona* made in 1998. While it is not possible to agree with the Declaration's vision of a clearly 'centralist' jurisprudence, there is, perhaps, some justification when it claims that its composition could be improved: the nationalist parties argue that the Autonomous Communities should be able to nominate some magistrates directly since their participation is now very indirect, through the Senate that chooses four magistrates (four are chosen by Congress, two by the government and two by the GCJP), which in practice has been a decision taken by agreement between the two main parties PP and PSOE, with very little possibility for the other parties to choose. For this reason, and as we have already seen, the LOTC was changed to enable the Autonomous assemblies to propose two candidates amongst which the Senate would choose (*see* paragraph 195). However, the practice observed in 2010 to select these judges shows that the change has been merely formal: renewal has only occurred when the State leadership of the two main parties have agreed, not permitting the real participation of other parties but simply the autonomous organs of their own parties.

§4. The Financing of the Autonomous Communities

I. Introduction

281. As in the other aspects of the Autonomous State, in financial matters, the Constitution limits itself to laying down some general principles that subsequently have to be made specific by-laws that develop them. So, in Article 156.1, the financial autonomy of the Communities is established based on the principles of coordination with the Ministry of Finance and solidarity amongst the people of Spain. However, while the autonomous competences are generally determined by the Autonomy Statute, Article 157.3 SC sets out a specific regime for finance, stating that 'the exercise of the financial competences enumerated in the preceding paragraph 1, the norms to resolve conflicts that may arise and the possible forms of financial cooperation between the Autonomous Communities and the state shall be regulated by means of an organic law'. Thus, the Organic Law 8/1980, 22 September, on Financing the Autonomous Communities (LOFCA) appears as a 'point of reference to determine the extension and limits of the financial autonomy of the Communities' (STC 179/1987, 12 November, case *Avales de la Comunidad Autónoma de las Islas Baleares*). LOFCA has been modified on seven occasions – 1989, 1996, 1998, 2001, 2009, 2015 and 2022 – adapting to the progressive expansion of the Autonomous State.

282. Financial autonomy has two aspects, referred to respectively as revenue and expenditure. The autonomy of expenditure, which is given specific legal expression in the Budget, is guaranteed both by LOFCA and the Autonomy Statutes. The former endows the Community budgets with the principles of universality, regularity (annual), and unity that Article 134 establishes for the central government. For their part, the Autonomy Statutes reserve the drafting and implementation of the Community budget to the respective Governing Councils while assigning to parliament 'its examination, amendment, approval and control' (Articles 212 EAC, 53 EAG, 190 EAA, etc.)

283. The capacity of the Autonomous Communities to carry out their budgets is not only subject to their Statutes and the mandates of LOFCA but must also consider Organic Law 2/2012, 27 April, of Budgetary Stability and Financial Sustainability, which develops the reformed Article 135 of the Constitution. The Law establishes the principles applicable to the budgets of all public administrations, amongst which budgetary stability stands out; this is achieved when an administration does not incur a structural deficit (i.e., when the expenditure of an administration exceeds its revenue in a permanent situation and not just in a single year). The other important principle is sustainability, which is defined as the ability 'to finance current and future expenditure commitments within the limits of deficit, public debt and delays in paying commercial debt in accordance with the provisions of this Law, the regulations on delays in payment and European regulations' (Article 4). Another important mandate of this law is the expenditure rule, according to which the public administrations' expenditure may not increase above the reference growth rate (fixed by the government) of the Gross Domestic Product of Spain.

284. To achieve autonomy of revenue, essential for the Communities to be able to express their power of self-government freely, comparative law shows that a great number of models are possible, ranging from full authority to levy taxes to simply sharing in the income of the State, but without normative authority. Strangely, the original draft of LOFCA was going to establish both, so establishing two models of financing: the ordinary regime focused on the participation in State taxes and with a much reduced normative authority for the Communities, and the very different system designed for the Basque Country and Navarre. Here, the competent institutions of both Communities (the three Basque Provincial governments and the parliament of Navarre) determined the tax rates and other normative elements of taxation with a fair degree of autonomy: that regulation imposed a global (but not a tax by tax) burden equivalent to the rest of the State. Moreover, while in the early days of the ordinary regime, the bulk of tax collecting was done by the State, which then distributed it amongst the Communities according to their legal entitlement, in the Basque Country and Navarre, it was these Communities which collected most of the taxes, and it was they who handed over a 'share' or 'quota' for the common services carried out by the State.[38]

285. The subsequent reforms of the ordinary system have patently increased the normative competences of the Autonomous Communities in the standard regime, although not to the extent of matching the financial autonomy enjoyed by the Basque Country and Navarre. Without doubt, this development corresponds to the natural logic of a compound state that not only guarantees full financial autonomy of expenditure, since – in the words of the Constitutional Court – 'the material support of financial autonomy is revenue', but also inevitably means that the Communities must have authority to decide on their income (STC 135/1992, 5 October, case *Ley de intermediarios financieros*). Referring to the original provisions of LOFCA in 1981 and the subsequent reforms mentioned above, there are five historical periods during which the Autonomous State expanded in financial matters:

(1) The transitional period from 1981 to 1986 based on the 'effective cost' of the transferred services. The main idea in this period was to permit the Communities to supply the services transferred to them by the State while maintaining the same level of quality so that when the State handed over employees, premises, and all the necessary assets, new funding was calculated according to that cost, which was fundamentally met by the granting of State revenues made by Law 30/1983 and an annual percentage of each Community's participation in State income (PSI).
(2) The ten-year period from 1987 to 1997 that established a system based on participation in State revenues. To ensure that no Community would lose financially under the new system, a fixed percentage of PSI was calculated for the entire five-year period starting from socioeconomic and geographical variables: coefficient of the population (the most important with a weighting of approximately 95%), income level, size of territory, etc.
(3) The period from 1997 to 2001: a new method of financing based on joint fiscal responsibility. Part of the TIPP was granted to the Communities that

38. Law 12/2002, 23 May, passed the Economic Agreement, establishing that every five years a law approving a five-year plan would be passed. The law now in force is Law 1/2022, 8 February, amending Law 12/2002, 23 May. Navarra is governed by Law 28/1990, 26 December, approving the Economic Agreement between the State and the Foral Community of Navarra, a law amended several times, the last by Law 14/2015, 24 June.

accepted the new system (all except Andalusia, Castilla-la Mancha, and Extremadura, which kept the system of the previous five years), giving some normative power over this stage to the Communities. Normative power over the taxes surrendered, albeit with many conditions, was also assigned.

(4) The period 2001–2009: In July 2001, the Council of Fiscal and Financial Policy reached an agreement to adjust the system of joint fiscal responsibility, increasing the normative powers of the Communities. The system that arose from the desire to put an end to five-yearly reviews rapidly acquired a provisional character in practice since the Catalan Autonomous Statute of 2006 contained provisions contrary to it, as did that of Andalusia and the others passed later.

(5) In July 2009, the Council for Fiscal and Financial Policy agreed on a new system of financing to remain in force indefinitely, with three great aims: to improve the provision of autonomous services, mostly those relating to the welfare state, to reduce the differences in financing amongst the Autonomous Communities and to increase the financial autonomy of the Communities. This new system is the most complex in Spanish democracy, so much so that the Minister of the Economy, during its drafting, compared it to Sudoku because its very varied political and technical matters had to be compatible *inter se*.[39] This system will be briefly explained in the following section, not without first indicating that, at present, practically all the Autonomous Communities have asked for its reform.

II. The Financial Resources of the Autonomous Communities in Common Regime

286. Article 157 of the Constitution lists the resources of the Autonomous Communities, which are then specified in the LOFCA. On our account, we can classify them by distinguishing between ordinary resources and extraordinary or, better, supportive resources:

1. Ordinary Resources
   1.1. From the state
      1.1.1. Surrendered state taxes
      1.1.2. Shares in State revenues through the funds and mechanisms established by law.
   1.2. Own Resources
      1.2.1. Taxation: Community taxes plus surcharges on state taxes
      1.2.2. Public prices
      1.2.3. Fines and sanction fees

39. *See* Carlos Monasterio Escudero, *El laberinto de la hacienda autonómica* (Civitas 2010). The specific figures of the financing system for each year and each Community can be consulted on the website of the Secretary of State for Territorial Administrations: https://www.hacienda.gob.es/es-ES/Areas%20Tematicas/Financiacion%20Autonomica/Paginas/DatosFinanciacionCCAA.aspx.

1.2.4. Private rights: profits on assets, income from private rights, legacies, donations and subsidies,
1.2.5. Resources resulting from the issuing of debt and credit operations

2. Solidarity Resources
   2.1. The Fund to Guarantee Basic Public Services.
   2.2. The Overall Sufficiency Fund.
   2.3. The Funds for Autonomous Convergence: The Fund for Competitivity and the Fund for Cooperation.
   2.4. Participation in Interterritorial Compensation Funds: Compensation Fund and Complementary Fund.
   2.5. Transfers from the European Union.

A. *The Ordinary Resources Received from the State*

287. The taxes ceded are those that belong to the State and which it has the capacity to regulate, while their product belongs to the Communities. Until 1996, the Autonomous Communities only had executive competences over the taxes ceded, but the reform of LOFCA of that year established a 'fiscal co-responsibility' that attributed normative competences over secondary aspects of the taxes ceded; in the agreements of 2001 and 2009 between the state and the Communities that co-responsibility was again widened, now having undoubted monetary repercussions, as can be appreciated by reading Law 22/2009 which regulates the system of financing the Autonomous Communities under the common regime and the Cities with an Autonomous Statute. Thus, the Communities can modify the taxes to be paid on gambling, pass an autonomous scale of income tax, modify the personal minimums and deductions, fix the minimum free from wealth/property tax, reduce death duties (even eliminate them), etc. In July 2010, parliament passed fifteen individual laws for each Autonomous Community on State taxes (from Law 16/2010 for Catalonia to 30/2010 for Castilla-León in strict protocol order). In spite of this individual formula, the content of each was practically identical. Each one listed the taxes ceded, and the scope and conditions of the concession were remitted to Law 22/2009. With these tax assignments, Spain became one of the most decentralized OECD states not only in terms of the administration of public expenditure but also in terms of revenue (*see* paragraph 229). The taxes ceded, with the latest reform in 2022, are the following:

(a) Personal Income Tax, on a partial basis with a maximum limit of 50%.
(b) Wealth Tax.
(c) Transfer Tax and Stamp Duty.
(d) Inheritance and Gift Tax.
(e) Value Added Tax, partially with a maximum limit of 50%.
(f) Special Manufacturing Taxes, partially, up to a maximum limit of 58% of each of them, except for the Electricity Tax and the Tax on Hydrocarbons.
(g) The Tax on Electricity.
(h) The Special Tax on Certain Means of Transport.

(i) Taxes on Gambling.
(j) The Tax on Hydrocarbons, partially with a maximum limit of 58% for the general state rate and in its entirety for the special state rate and the Autonomous Community rate.
(k) Tax on the deposit of waste in landfills, incineration, and co-incineration of waste.

B. The Autonomous Community's Own Resources

288. Article 133.1 of the Constitution provides that the original power to establish taxes belongs exclusively to the State, only to add immediately afterwards that the Autonomous Communities are authorized to 'establish and levy taxes in accordance with the Constitution and the laws'. However, LOFCA forbids those taxes to be levied on sources of taxable income taxed by the State or by local bodies. Thus, a great effort of the imagination is needed to find something taxable that is not already taxed; however, in the field of environment, there were possibilities: cleansing, waste, hunting, polluting emissions, large commercial establishments, etc. On the other hand, the Community's authority to impose surcharges on State taxes is practically unknown, possibly because the autonomous governments have preferred to sidestep such a clearly unpopular measure.

For these reasons, the Communities' own resources play a secondary role in their finances. And an even lesser part, virtually anecdotal, is played by the private sector, which year after year contributes little more than 2% of total revenue. The same cannot be said of credit operations (Article 14 LOFCA) which are an important source of income, particularly the issuing of public debt. This source of finance started to grow from 1987 onwards to finance new investment expenditure; in 1992, the State and the Communities were obliged to make a pact, 'Scenarios of Budgetary Consolidation' within the Council of Fiscal and Financial Policy, fixing the maximum deficit and debt for each one of the Communities as a way of complying with the requirements of budgetary discipline envisaged in the European Union Treaty (EUT), which demands that the total volume of indebtedness of Public Administrations shall not exceed 60% of GNP. This Accord was renewed in 1997, with the commitment of all the Administrations to reduce their level of debt. For their part, the Laws on Budgetary Stability limit the debt of the Communities, even permitting the state not to authorize the issuing of debt or credit operations by those Communities that have failed to comply with the aim of budgetary stability fixed annually by the Council of Fiscal Policy.

C. Resources Received as Solidarity Payments

289. Article 158 of the Constitution lays down two exceptional sources of finance for the Communities: an Interterritorial Compensation Fund directed toward investment expenditure for the purpose of correcting the 'territorial imbalances and implementing the principle of solidarity' and the allocations 'to provide a minimum level of basic public services'. In the last reform of LOFCA, this minimum level of fundamental services, which the law itself specifies in three sections: education, health, and essential social services, are guaranteed by the Fund to Guarantee Basic Social Services, which is made up of 75% of the taxes collected by the Autonomous Communities plus 5% of that amount contributed by the State. It is shared annually amongst the Communities so that each obtains the same amount for each inhabitant 'adjusted according to their different needs' (Article 15 LOFCA). To determine those needs, a series of criteria are applied, the weightiest of which are population (30%), population under 16 years of age (20%), over 65 years of age (8.5%), etc.

To guarantee the financing of the other competences transferred or non-basic public services, the 2009 reform of LOFCA created the Overall Sufficiency Fund. The purpose of the Fund is to ensure that all the Communities maintain the same quantity of resources in 2011 as they received under the previous system, so this is called a guarantee of the *status quo*.

Law 22/2009 also created two new funds for autonomous convergence and an economic contribution from the State according to what is foreseen in the annual budget:

(a) the Fund for Competitivity to reduce the differences in per capita financing amongst the Autonomous Communities;
(b) the Fund for Cooperation, with the aim of facilitating convergence in the level of life for citizens independently of their place of residence. To do this, the resources of the Autonomous Communities with the lowest per capita income and that have an especially negative population growth that could compromise their future development are increased.

Law 22/2001, 27 December, on the Regulation of Interterritorial Compensation Funds, created two Funds: the Compensation Fund and the Complementary Fund, with the aim of financing not only investments but also current expenditure associated with that investment and establishing the criteria of the division amongst the Communities set out each year in the General Budget of the State, selecting the Communities with least income and the Cities of Ceuta and Melilla.

§5. The Internal Structure of the Autonomous Communities

I. General View

290. The dualistic logic of the Autonomous State in the Spanish Constitution (*see* paragraph 227) leads it to guarantee the power to pass legislation only to the Communities of the first degree, as well as designing a parliamentary system for them (Article 152 SC) while remaining silent about the institutions for those of the second degree. However, when their Statutes were drafted, the same model was adopted so that today all seventeen Communities enjoy a very similar parliamentary system, within what the doctrine has called a 'rationalized parliamentarianism', with a one-chamber parliament representing the people of the Community and exercising legislative power, and a president and Governing Council who holds the executive power.

Ignoring the terminological differences used to designate these institutions (some Statutes employ the term parliament, others Legislative Assembly, etc.), the most relevant distinction in the relationship between the powers is that only some autonomous Presidents (those of the Basque Country, Catalonia, Galicia, and Andalusia) have the authority to dissolve their parliament and call elections in their Autonomy before the end of the four-year period for which the deputies are elected, while the others must hold the autonomous elections every four years at the same time as the local elections on a predetermined date, the fourth Sunday in May.[40] However, this important difference is in the course of disappearing in the second Autonomous State now being designed since it seems that most of the statutory reforms give the President the power of dissolution. This is the position in the Organic Law 1/2006, the reform of the Valencian Autonomous Statute and the new Statutes for the Balearic Islands, Aragon, and Castile-León.

The Autonomous Communities do not have their own judicial power, although they all have competences over the management of the 'Administration of the Administration of Justice' (*see* paragraph 255). In addition, the new Statutes – such as the Catalan, provide for Autonomous Councils of Justice, pending the time when they are ordered by the LOPJ.

II. The Autonomous Parliament

A. Composition and Electoral System

291. All the Autonomous Parliaments are made up of members chosen directly by the citizens for a legislature that, in principle, lasts four years. The number varies according to the population of each Community, from 33 in La Rioja, the least populated, to 135 in Catalonia. In most Communities, the province itself is the electoral district, although in the island Communities (Balearics and Canaries), the island is the district, and in some Communities with only one province (such as Asturias and Murcia), it is divided into smaller constituencies. The seats are shared out amongst the constituencies in proportion to the population, except in the Basque Country, where twenty-five deputies are allotted to each 'historical territory' (the provinces of Álava, Guipúzcoa, and Vizcaya). Most Statutes and autonomous electoral laws contain provisions to moderate the weight of the most populated constituencies; for example, the Andalusian Statute forbids any province from having

40. In the reforms at the end of the 1990s all the Statutes assigned to their respective autonomous Presidents the power to dissolve the Legislative Assembly but with a series of restrictions that make it practically inoperative: the Chamber cannot be dissolved during the first session of the legislature nor when there remains less than a year before its end and in any case the new Chamber so chosen 'will have a limited mandate for the natural term of the original legislature' (Art. 25 EA, Asturias and the others in similar terms; except for Castilla-León, which does allow for total dissolution). Automatic dissolution also occurs when no candidate is chosen within the period of two months from the first ballot, but here too this new legislature finishes when the previous one should have done so.

more than twice as many as any other, although the most populated province has four times the number of inhabitants as the least. In some cases, as in the 1999 and 2003 Catalan elections, these limitations have resulted in the party winning the most votes in the Community elections gaining fewer seats than the second party, which was in the majority in the districts with fewer inhabitants.

In all cases, the elections are held under the system of proportional representation designed by D'Hondt, so that it is the same as the one for Congress; moreover, most Communities have established an electoral barrier per district (3% in Andalusia, 5% in Valencia, etc.). This barrier is so low that it is hardly a curb on obtaining parliamentary seats, except in the Canary Islands. Here, the smaller parties need to obtain 6% in the territory or 20% in each island in order to gain a share of the seats, a barrier that does not defeat the proportionality of the electoral system (STC 225/1988, 25 November, case *Reforma de 1996 del Estatuto de Canarias*) nor violates the electoral rights guaranteed by the ECHR (Decision ECtHR 7 June 2001, case *Federación Nacionalista Canaria v. Spain*, in which the claim was declared inadmissible).

292. The electoral procedure is not the exclusive competence of the Communities since the state also intervenes under the provisions of Article 81 of the Constitution, which stipulates that the general electoral system shall be regulated by an organic law and Article 149.1.1 that gives the state exclusive competence on the conditions of equality of all Spaniards in the exercise of rights. Thus, LOREG regulates that the national regime is also applicable to autonomous elections: active and passive suffrage from the age of eighteen, organization and control of the electoral process, arrangements for and financing of electoral campaigns, and prevention of electoral irregularities.

293. The prerogatives of the Autonomous Parliaments are those characteristics of a State of Law: governmental, budgetary, and regulatory autonomy (the regulations must be approved by an absolute majority of the members of the parliament) and to these is added the inviolability of the parliamentary seat, a prerogative little known in comparative law and which all the Statutes have copied word for word from Article 66.3 of the Constitution. The most important legal consequence of this prerogative is the specific legal protection of the Autonomous Parliaments in the Criminal Code, equivalent to those of the general parliament (crimes of rebellion, invasion of parliamentary premises, etc.) and Organic Law 4/2015, on the protection of public safety categorized as a serious administrative fault due to the disturbance of public order in front of its buildings).

294. The prerogatives of individual autonomous members are:

(1) Inviolability, that is, non-responsibility for opinions voiced during parliamentary acts and votes cast in the exercise of office, even after leaving it. This prerogative is exactly the same as that enjoyed by members of the State parliament (*see* paragraph 128).
(2) Semi-immunity, which means that during the term of office, deputies can be neither arrested nor detained for criminal acts committed within the territory

of the Community. Unlike the situation with members of the State parliament, the authorization of the Chamber (the *suplicatorio*) is not needed to bring charges against an autonomous deputy.

(3) The special protection by which members will be judged by the High Court of their Community when they are on trial for offences alleged to have been committed in their territory and by the Supreme Court for crimes outside it. In recent years, there has been a movement to abolish this prerogative because if in the past it was necessary to guarantee the function of parliamentarians, today it is 'considered by the society we represent as a privilege and not as a right' (from the Preamble of the Organic Law 1/2021, on the amendment of the Statute of Autonomy of the Region of Murcia. In similar terms, LLOO 2/2021 and 1/2022 on the amendment of the Statutes of Cantabria and the Balearic Islands).

In addition to these prerogatives, the members have the classic rights of any Member of parliament in order to exercise her/his functions: to attend parliamentary sessions with voice and vote, to be a member of at least one committee, to receive the documentation necessary to carry out her/his work, salary, etc. It is interesting to note that most of the Statutes of the second degree originally prohibited the payment of a salary to the deputies, but this has disappeared during the various reforms.

B. *Internal Organization and Operation*

295. The seventeen Autonomous Parliaments, broadly speaking, follow the organization and operation of Congress, and so all have plenary sessions and committees, and the governing organs are the President, the Bureau, and the Board of Party Spokespersons. Equally, the Autonomy Statutes have established a Permanent Deputation to watch over parliamentary powers when its mandate has expired or it is not in session. As mentioned earlier, the legislature lasts for four years, though it can be shorter if the President uses the power of dissolution (*see* paragraph 290).

C. *Parliament's Functions*

296. The Autonomy Statutes include a long list of functions that fall into four main groups:

(a) The representative function of representing the people of the Community.
(b) The legislative function. Here it should be pointed out that in almost all the Communities this function can be delegated to the respective government to pass Legislative Decrees. The processing of legislation in the Autonomous Parliaments is very similar to that of Congress, with the three phases of initiative, deliberation, and publication. In the initiative phase – in practice almost

monopolized by the government – it must be pointed out that in some Statutes (such as those of Andalusia, Navarre, etc.), the legislative initiative is with the Town and City Councils.

(c) The functions of creating, maintaining, and controlling the Governing Council.

(d) Other functions:

- The appointment of the members of the autonomous institutions dependant on parliament, such as the Ombudsman, the Chamber of Auditors, etc.
- The appointment of the autonomous senators, bearing in mind the criteria of proportional representation of the various political forces in the Chamber.
- The remitting of bills to Congress.
- The lodging of appeals of unconstitutionality 'against the normative provisions with the force of law that can affect the scope of the autonomy of the Community' (Article 32.2 of LOTC). Most Parliamentary Regulations have laid down that an absolute majority is needed to lodge an appeal, so distinguishing the situation from that of the national parliament where a proportion of it (fifty deputies or fifty senators) can do so.
- The proposal of two jurists to the Senate so that it may choose the four judges of the Constitutional Court (*see* paragraph 195).
- The Autonomous Parliament's final relevant function concerned with other State organs is the approval of the conventions and cooperation agreements with other Autonomous Communities, whose projects are drafted by the Governing Council.

III. The Executive

A. *The Pre-eminence of the President*

297. The Autonomy Statutes have designed the President of the Community as the most important figure of the executive since he is 'responsible for directing the Governing Council, the supreme representation of the respective Community as well as the State's ordinary representation in the latter' (Article 152 SC) and only he is directly chosen by parliament (investiture). The quorum for this election is, in every case, the absolute majority of the deputies in the first ballot and a simple one in the second. If the candidate does not gain this, in all of the Communities, parliament is dissolved, with the single exception of Castile-La Mancha, where after two months, there is an automatic election of the candidate of the party which had won the most seats.[41]

41. In the first autonomous State this was the habitual formula, which the EAA created, and which was followed by all the rest, only to be abandoned thereafter. The proposed reformed Statute of Castile-La Mancha (presented in Parliament and subsequently withdrawn in May 2010) also abandoned this formula of automatic appointment, so unusual in comparative parliamentarism. The brief Organic Law 2/2014, 21 May, *de reforma del Estatuto de Autonomía de Castilla-La Mancha* did not change this system of investiture because it was limited to modifying the number of deputies for each constituency.

The cessation of the President also results in the cessation of the rest of the executive and is caused by the election of a new parliament, resignation, death, or incapacity of the President, approval of a motion of censure, or the rejection of a question of confidence.

B. Functions of the President

298. All the Statutes endow the President with a triple status: President of the Governing Council, the supreme representative of the Community and the ordinary representative of the State in the Autonomous Community:

(a) Beginning with this last, it should be explained that the representative function is in the sense of representing the unity of the State as a legal order (most Presidents promulgate autonomous laws 'in the name of the king'), but the President does not represent the central institutions of the State, a function carried out by the Government Delegate (Article 154).
(b) The President of the Community is the 'supreme representative of the Autonomous Community'. However, this representation is not political but symbolic and legal: he represents the unity of the autonomous legal order of the Autonomous Community as a legal person. Thus, he represents the Community in relations with other State institutions, signs conventions and cooperation agreements with other Autonomous Communities, convokes autonomous elections, etc.
(c) The different laws governing the Communities have set out the functions of the Autonomous Presidents as Presidents of the Governing Council. In general, it can be said that they reinforce the leadership role of the President: he fixes the general guidelines of the government's policy, freely appoints and dismisses the councillors (regional ministers), organizes the internal work of the Council (convokes its meetings, decides the agenda, gives the casting vote when needed, etc.); he signs the Decrees agreed by the Governing Council, ensures the fulfilment of its agreements, and poses questions of confidence, etc.

C. The Governing Council

299. The autonomous governments who exercise the executive and administrative functions on behalf of their Communities consist of the President of the Community and the Councillors he freely appoints. Most of the Laws on Government permit him to appoint vice presidents, but in practice, little use is made of this possibility, being almost solely limited to coalition governments. The Laws on Government fix the number of Councillors but, in general, allow the President to vary it. They are fewer than in the central government and usually number between nine and fourteen, depending both on the level of competences and the agreements of the government in each case.

300. The different functions assigned to the Governing Councils can be grouped as follows:

(a) Those related to parliament: to approve bills, draft the budget and the conventions and cooperation agreements with other Communities, etc. Moreover, almost all the Statutes permit it to issue Legislative Decrees and, from 2006, Decree-laws (*see* paragraph 77). The Council also deliberates on the presentation of a question of confidence, although in this case, the final decision is the exclusive responsibility of the President.
(b) Those related to other State institutions: to agree to lodge appeals of unconstitutionality and conflicts of competence; to designate the Community's representatives to the Sectorial Conferences and other State organs, etc.
(c) Those related to the directing of the autonomous administration: all the Communities have created an organization similar to that of the State, with central services and peripheral administrations. As with the state, autonomous organizations are proliferating as Agencies (Environment) and Institutes (Youth, Women, etc.). The Governing Council has an important group of functions in these affairs: to approve the Parliamentary Regulations for the development and implementation of the laws, determine the resources granted to them, approve the structure of the Councils, appoint, and dismiss the senior administrative officers, authorize expenditure, etc.

D. *Political Control over the Executive*

301. All Autonomous Parliaments have established the ordinary controls of Spanish parliamentary law, questions, interpellations, and investigating Commissions:

(a) Questions are put by Members of parliament individually and can only be rejected by the Parliamentary Committee if they are of exclusively personal interest or of a strictly legal nature. They can be presented to be answered either in writing or orally and, in the latter case, to the committee or plenary.
(b) Interpellations are qualified questions since they must deal with the reasons or proposals of the executive on questions of general policy, either of the Governing Council or of any ministry. Unlike questions, interpellations – which both deputies or parliamentary groups can present – are always dealt with in the plenary and give rise to a debate in which all parliamentary groups take part, and if the group presenting the interpellation deem appropriate, it can lead to a motion; if this is approved by the plenary, it is a mandate to the Council, so transforming an instrument of control into a way of initiating the executive's actions.
(c) The investigating committees are created to investigate a specific case; therefore, they are a powerful means of controlling the executive. However, all the Parliamentary Regulations demand that these committees are created by an absolute majority and that their composition maintains the same proportions between the parliamentary groups as in the plenary, resulting in their playing,

until now, a marginal role. As happens with Congress and Senate Investigating Committees, their conclusions are not binding on the Courts.

302. The Extraordinary controls, as we have said, are used to demand accountability of the Council and, if successful, can lead to the downfall of the government. All the Statutes have adopted the two typical forms of political responsibility: directly, through the motion of censure or indirectly, through the vote of confidence. In general, either in their Statutes or in the Laws on Government, all the Communities have a 'constructive' motion of censure, following the German model, which demands that the motion contain an alternative candidate and must be approved by the absolute majority of the Chamber. The various autonomous legal orders have taken the regulation of the question of confidence from Article 112 of the Constitution: the President of the Community can, after deliberation by the Council, present it on his programme or on a declaration of general policy. The vote in favour of the majority of the deputies is sufficient.

IV. Other Autonomous Institutions

303. In addition to parliament, the President, and the Governing Council, the Autonomous Communities have been endowed with several institutions of self-government, amongst which should be mentioned: the Ombudsman, the Consultative Council, the Auditors Chamber, and the Economic and Social Council, to a large extent, have been designed along the lines of the State models. Thus, the Autonomous Ombudsmen (they have been set up in thirteen Communities at present) are Parliamentary Commissioners for the protection of the rights and liberties of Title I of the Constitution. The Consultative Councils serve the function of giving legal advice to their governments, while the Auditors Chambers control the economic activity of the autonomous business institutions. From the point of view of the State, the main problem of these institutions lies, precisely, in the delimitation of their competences with those of similar state entities; to overcome this, various State laws have been passed, such as Law 36/1985, 6 November, which regulates the relation between the Institution of the Ombudsman and similar figures in the different Autonomous Communities, and Law 7/1988, 5 April, on the Operation of the Court of Auditors, where various mechanisms of coordination between institutions are established. Moreover, several judgments of the Constitutional Court have detailed some aspects of these relations, particularly STC 31/2010, 28 June, case *Reforma del Estatuto de Autonomía para Cataluña* (*see* paragraphs 213 and 217).

Chapter 3. Local Authorities

§1. General View

I. A Brief History

304. As in most of Europe, Spain has a strong municipal tradition that can be traced back to the Middle Ages, when the towns were an oasis of liberty compared with the feudal estates, as the old Spanish saying reminds us: 'The air of the city makes one free.' As Emperor Carlos V had occasion to discover with the rebellion of the 'Comuneros' – led by the cities – these towns enjoyed considerable power in the political and administrative organization of the State, with universal competences: health, public order, taxes, charitable establishments, etc. After the defeat of the Comuneros at the beginning of the sixteenth century, the absolute State succeeded in controlling the municipalities through the technique of imposing a 'Magistrate' or 'Mayor' who faithfully carried out the king's will, which was nothing other than to transfer all possible competences to central government and to convert the Town and City Councils into tools for implementing the state's will. Liberalism, without breaking the centralizing tendency that operated to the prejudice of Spain's different kingdoms and regions, wanted both to rationalize the territorial structure of the State and to return autonomy to the municipalities. Therefore, in the 1812 Constitution, all the national territory was divided into provinces, generalization and equality of the town Councils were proclaimed, and they were granted a system of a democratic election in two degrees. So determined was it that its Article 312 should signal the end of the old absolutist system, it set out that 'The Mayors, Aldermen and Legal Trustees shall be elected by the citizens, the position of Aldermen and other perpetual offices of the Town Council, whatever their title and denomination being abolished'.

305. The regulation of the local government system was by no means peaceful in the liberal Spanish State since the composition and election of the Town Councils was one of the great political disputes in the nineteenth century. Although all the Constitutions of that century referred to the elective nature of the local authorities, the progressives held the idea that the municipalities had their own interests and place in the democratic system, while the moderates argued that they were organs of state, subject to the central power. Thus, while some advocated the extension of suffrage, others sought a strictly limited electorate. By an irony of fate, the local government system, with technically the best quality and with almost acceptable democratic participation, was approved during the dictatorship of Primo de Rivera in 1924. More specifically, when he tried to organize the return to the liberal system of the 1876 Constitution, he began by calling municipal elections, held on 12 April 1931, which, far from achieving the aim with which the government had convoked them, resulted in the fall of the monarchy (*see* paragraph 14).

306. The 1931 Constitution signified, in local government, as in so many other matters, the triumph of the democratic concept. And there is no better or simpler proof than its Article 9, the clear forerunner of Article 140 of the present Constitution, 'The Constitution guarantees the autonomy of the municipalities in the matters over which they have competence and shall elect the Town Council by universal equal, direct and secret suffrage, except when functioning under the system of Open Council. The Mayors shall always be chosen by direct vote of the residents or the councillors.' To develop this constitutional mandate, the Municipal Law of 1935 was passed, though it was short-lived since the military coup of General Franco meant the return to the despotic system of the appointment of the mayors by the central power and the exclusion of democracy from all institutions.

II. Constitutional Principles of Local Government

307. The 1978 Constituent Assembly had no great difficulty in reaching a *consensus* on the local government bodies, which it conceived of as democratically elected, representative corporations that, nevertheless, had administrative functions. The Constitution made no reference to them in the Preliminary Title, although it did to nationalities and regions, but in Article 137, it proclaimed that the state 'is organized territorially in municipalities, provinces and the Autonomous Communities that may be constituted. All these entities enjoy autonomy in the management of their respective interests'. However, the development made in the articles following this affirmation shows that there is a substantial difference between the autonomy of the local bodies and that of the Autonomous Communities since the latter enjoy legislative and governmental powers that endow them with political autonomy superior to that of the local bodies, as they are granted 'political and administrative power over the municipalities and provinces included in their territory' (STC 84/1982, 23 December, case *Presupuestos Generales del Estado 1982*).

308. The scope of action of the Autonomous Communities is determined by the Constitution and the Autonomy Statutes. However, that of the local government is laid down in the ordinary legislation of both the State and the Autonomous Communities, for this is a shared matter or – to use the description of the Constitutional Court – 'double' (*see* paragraph 250), over which both legislative agencies have competence according to the model of State bases and autonomous complementary legislation. The state decides the principles or basic criteria of the organization and competences generally applicable throughout the State, although not to the extent of establishing 'a uniform regime for all the local entities of all the State as it must permit various options for the normative power of the Autonomous Communities, which is not in these cases regulatory' (STC 84/1982, 23 December, case *Presupuestos Generales del Estado 1982*).

Law 7/1985, 2 April, LBRL, modified more than twenty times, has come to establish these principles of organization and competence for all Spanish local government bodies. Thus, LBRL is integrated into the block of constitutionality that the Autonomous Communities must respect when passing their own legislation on local government (STC 159/2001, 7 June, case *Participación local en los tributos estatales*). LOREG is also very important in shaping these local entities as it regulates their composition and the method of electing their members.

309. The Constitution establishes an *institutional guarantee* in favour of the Town Councils, Provincial Governments and those of the Basque Provinces, which must be respected by the State and the Communities alike since local autonomy demands its own bundle of competences to be able to develop its specific interests (Articles 137, 140 and 141). According to the Constitutional Court, that institutional guarantee means that the Constitution's remitting to ordinary legislation the power to establish the complete form of local corporations is not without conditions since there exists an irreducible core composed of the essential elements that make an institution recognizable as such by the citizens according to the social conscience in every time and place. When the state or autonomous legislator regulates the institution in such a way as to break that commonly accepted image, there is a violation of that institutional guarantee. An example would be if it is so limited 'that it practically deprives it of its possibilities of real existence as an institution so as to make it nothing more than a name' (STC 32/1981, 28 July, case *Diputaciones Catalanas*).

310. Local autonomy precludes the State and the Autonomous Communities from establishing – as did the legislation in Franco's time – general and indeterminate controls that subordinate the local government to the other public powers. Thus, the legislator can establish legal controls but not 'merely opportunistic' as the Constitutional Court declared in one of its first judgments (STC 4/1981, 2 February, case *Ley de Bases de Régimen Local de 1953*). The general system established by LBRL is that of legal control of the acts or agreements of local bodies. Exceptionally, the Government Delegate in each Autonomous Community can suspend these acts and agreements when 'they seriously attack Spain's general interests' (Article 67), but this suspension is purely provisional while the Contentious-Administrative Courts decide on the legality of the act. Much more exceptional – to the extent that it has been used only once[42] – is that the Council of Ministers, with the prior authorization of the Senate and the knowledge of the Governing Council of the Autonomous Community in question, can agree to the dissolution of a local organ 'in the event of an action seriously prejudicial to the general interest that would result from non-compliance with its constitutional obligations' (Article 61).

311. The financial autonomy of local government demands that sufficient funds are available to enable them to carry out their competences, although this does not mean that all the money comes from their own sources as it can be transferred to them from other public powers. The State determines the basic elements of local tax revenue, while 'financial protection' is a power assigned to the Autonomous Communities in all the Autonomy Statutes. The reserve of tax matters to law reserved in Articles 31.3 and 133 SC implies that the law must fix the essential elements of local authority taxes, but, by virtue of the recognition of local taxes in the Constitution itself (Articles 133.2 and 140), the law has to allow some leeway for local authorities to make decisions to complement their regulation, always bearing in mind that the legislation cannot 'be limited to a mere formal mediation, authorizing the Town Council to settle the taxes, without any predetermination, given that the reserve of

42. Royal Decree 421/2006, 7 April, providing for the dissolution of the Town Council of Marbella.

revenue law in the local sphere is grounded on the preservation of the unity of the legal order and on basic equality in the position of the taxpayers' (STC 233/1999, 16 December, case *Ley de Haciendas Locales*). In the same sense of applying the general tax principles of Article 31 of the Constitution to the local regime, the Constitutional Court has declared that the system that the law, used by local tax offices to calculate the tax on the increase of the value of urban land (popularly known as *plusvalia*, surplus value), was unconstitutional in that it was not linked to the existence of a real increase in the value of the property 'but to the mere ownership of the land for a period of time', which meant violating the principle of economic capacity (STC 37/2017, 1 March) and caused the town Councils to impute that tax on sales of houses in which the owner sold the property at a lower price than the one he bought it at, a situation that is habitual since the economic crisis that began in 2007.

312. During the early days of the 1978 Constitution, the main political concern about the structure of the State was how to achieve its transformation from a centralist State to an autonomous one. Therefore, the local bodies remained in the background from which little by little they had been emerging until the *Local Pact* agreed between the principal political parties in 1997 to reform the local government system. This was incorporated in a set of laws enacted by parliament in April 1999, designed to increase the role of local bodies in the Spanish institutional structure in line with the Charter of Local Autonomy, adopted in Strasbourg on 15 October 1985 and ratified by Spain on 20 January 1988: to increase their competences, give them legitimacy to appeal laws to the Constitutional Court, enhance their authority for action by assigning greater powers to the mayors, etc. In 2003 this line of reinforcing local power continued with Law 57/2003, 16 December, on measures for the modernization of local government. The crisis of 2007 gave rise to several rules intended to help solve the financial problems of local bodies (such as Royal Decree-law 13/2009, 26 October, setting up the State Fund for employment and local sustainability) and the much-discussed Law 27/2013, 27 December, on the rationalization and sustainability of the Local Administration (so much so that the Constitutional Court has already passed more than ten judgments on it in which it has cancelled or reinterpreted a good number of articles). This law was approved with the objectives – according to its Preamble – of clarifying the municipal competences to avoid duplication with the competences of other administrations; rationalizing the organizational structure of the local administration in accordance with the principles of efficiency, stability, and financial sustainability; guaranteeing a more rigorous financial and budgetary control; and favouring private economic initiative avoiding disproportionate administrative interventions.

§2. The Municipalities

I. Introduction

313. The *Arreglo Provisional de los Ayuntamientos del Reino* (The Provisional Arrangement of the Town Councils of the Kingdom) of 23 July 1835 drew the Spanish municipal map that, however unlikely it may seem, is still in its broad lines maintained today. In the 1960s, as in many other European States, there was an impetus in Spain for a policy of merging municipalities which was not maintained with the coming of democracy; on the contrary, since 1978, the secessionist demands from some nuclei of the population have continually increased. However, the idea (as in Germany, France and other European States) is becoming increasingly widespread, so a substantial reduction in their number is necessary in order to manage public funds more efficiently. The official data show the problem: as on 1 January 2022, Spain has 8,131 municipalities, with a very unequal distribution, both in territorial size and number of inhabitants. No fewer than 4,991 municipalities (61.38%) have a population below 1,000, while only 64 (0.79%) have a population above 100,000, but in them live 18,926,803 persons, 39.9% of the Spanish population. Although the municipal legislation has sought formulae to encourage the merger of municipalities (especially Law 27/2013), the truth is that that aim is far from being achieved: 2006 (the date of the publication of the first edition of this book) to the present day not only has the total number of municipalities not diminished but has in fact increased by more than thirty.

II. Local Institutions

314. The institution of government and administration of the municipalities is the Town Council, made up of the mayor and the councillors. Article 140 of the Constitution States that the councillors shall be chosen by the residents of the municipality by equal, free, direct, secret, and universal suffrage, but it remits to law the regulations both for the electoral system and the method of choosing the mayor 'by residents or by the councillors'. LOREG maintained the pre-constitutional system established by Law 39/1878, 17 July. This system applied to municipalities of more than 250 inhabitants, the system of proportional representation chosen for Congress, with some slight modifications. The following are the most important features:

- The whole municipality makes up one electoral district with the number of councillors determined by the number on the electoral roll, starting with 5 councillors for municipalities with fewer than 250 inhabitants and ending with the 55 of Madrid and the 41 of Barcelona, the two great Spanish municipalities. Regardless of the size of their population, the Autonomous Cities of Ceuta and Melilla each choose an assembly of 25 members.
- The D'Hondt formula as a variant of proportional representation has been adopted, with closed, blocked lists.
- The electoral barrier is 5% for municipalities of more than 20,000 inhabitants, where a minimum of 21 councillors is chosen.
- For municipalities of fewer than 250 inhabitants, a majority system with restricted votes is applied (4 candidates are chosen for 5 seats).
- As in the case of general elections, all citizens 18 years of age or over with full capacity to use her/his political rights are entitled to vote. In addition, the citizens of the EU have been able to participate since the local elections of 1999, both as candidates (right of passive suffrage) and as voters (right of active suffrage), as

guaranteed by Article 20 of the Union Treaty. Citizens of other states that have a reciprocal arrangement with Spain, as in the case of Norway, also enjoy these rights.

- In every case, the legislature is fixed for a four-year period and cannot be dissolved by the mayor. The elections are held on the fourth Sunday in May of the relevant year (the last two were in 2011 and 2015), coinciding with the autonomous elections in the Communities with the ordinary regime (all except Basque Country, Catalonia, Galicia, and Andalusia).

315. The mayor is chosen by absolute majority of the councillors in the same constitutive assembly of the new Town Council. LOREG specifies that in the closed list system, only those who head the list can be put forward as candidates, but in the open list system (municipalities with fewer than 250 inhabitants), all councillors are eligible. If an absolute majority is not obtained, the councillor who heads the list most voted for by the residents or, in the case of open list municipalities, the councillor who won the most popular votes is proclaimed mayor.

The term of office of the mayor is, in principle, for the whole legislature. However, the mayor can be dismissed by a motion of censure that has to be presented by an absolute majority of the councillors legally composing the Town Council and must include the name of a candidate as mayor. The motion succeeds if the absolute majority of the councillors vote in favour of it. However, Organic Law 2/2011 modified the LOREG to make it more difficult to prevent transfuguism (*see* paragraph 406): when the motion of censure is signed by one or more councillors who have formed part of the municipal group to which the mayor belongs, the absolute majority required will be increased by the same number of councillors who are in such circumstances. The mayor is also automatically dismissed if he puts a motion of confidence to the plenary and he loses. This motion was introduced by the LOREG in 1999 with the aim of giving the mayor an instrument to win the support of his councillors when approving matters of great importance: the annual budget, the organic regulation, fiscal by-laws, and general town planning policies.

316. In addition to these systems for electing councillors, there is another rather unusual method of government and administration called the regime of 'Open Council', which operates in villages with fewer than one hundred inhabitants as well as those that, by tradition or municipal decision – and with the consent of the Autonomous Community – adopt this regime. In this case, there are no councillors since all the residents meet together in a 'Neighbourhood Assembly' and themselves directly choose the mayor. The same assembly can dismiss the mayor if the absolute majority of the residents present a motion of censure, which must also include the name of an alternative mayor.

317. The Town Councils are ruled by a parliamentary system of government in which the plenary has normative, budgetary, and planning competences and approves the most important actions, while the mayor holds executive and representative functions. The mayor appoints the traditionally named Governing Commission (since 2003, it has come to be called the Council of Local Government), which cannot exceed one-third of the councillors (Article 23.1 LBRL). But this same article permits the mayor to appoint the Councillor-Delegates that he deems pertinent: in practice, the mayor names as many Delegates as councillors that support him, having the perverse effect that the *government* of the Town Council is chosen not so much on the criteria of efficiency and the fulfilment of the political programme as for purely opportunistic reasons. It was precisely to achieve greater efficiency in the Town Councils and their better adaptation to the model of *rationalized parliamentarianism* of the State and the Autonomous Communities that, in 1999, LBRL was modified by reinforcing the powers of the mayor (even granting the authority to present questions to him) and limiting the plenary to the role of a normative and controlling body. In 2003 the Law on Modernization Measures of Local Government took this development of the local regime towards a parliamentary system to its highest point, allowing – amongst other matters – the mayors of cities with more than 250,000 inhabitants to choose the Members of the 'Council of Local Government' freely without being constrained to form it only from elected councillors. For its part, Law 27/2013, *de racionalización de la Administración Local* (mentioned previously) limited both the number of exclusive public offices for the local authorities as well as limiting the salary of the councillors, creating salary scales according to the number of inhabitants of each municipality.

III. Municipal Competences

318. LBRL distinguishes between the local authority's own competences and those assigned to it by delegation. The former are exercised with autonomy and can only be established by law, while the latter are exercised according to the terms of the delegation, which can establish 'techniques of direction and control of opportunity' (Article 7 as set out in its new wording by Law 27/2013). The state, and especially the Autonomous Communities, can intervene by co-coordinating the competences belonging to the local bodies when a series of requisites are met: the local services go beyond their own interests, are concurrent or complementary with those of other administrations, etc.

319. LBRL does not so much directly determine the competences of the municipalities as set out an extensive list of matters (Article 25.2) in which 'in every case' they shall have competence, remitting the question of their concrete expression to the corresponding – state or autonomous – law: town planning, security in public places, traffic control, civil protection, parks and gardens, street paving, culture, tourism, sport, etc.

This formula has the advantage of fixing the minimum content of local autonomy, permitting the state or Autonomous Community – according to the division of the matter between them – to decide exactly the extent of the municipal competences. When doing so, both normative powers must bear in mind the conception of local autonomy, not merely as the link to a block of 'local competences' but rather as the right: 'of the local community to participate, through their own bodies, in the government and administration of those matters that concern them, regulating the degree of this participation according to the relation between local and supra-local interests in such affairs or matters' (STC 32/1981, 28 July, case *Diputaciones Catalanas*).

320. In any event, LBRL determines the services that the Town Council must offer residents. Four situations can be distinguished according to the number of inhabitants:

(a) All municipalities must provide the minimum services of street lighting, cleansing, drainage and paving, a cemetery, waste collection, supply of domestic drinking water, access to the villages, and control of food and drink.
(b) Municipalities with a population of over 5,000 people must additionally provide public parks, public libraries, markets, and waste treatment.
(c) Municipalities with a population of more than 20,000 have to supply further: civil protection, social services, prevention and extinction of fires, and sports facilities for public use.
(d) Finally, in municipalities with a population exceeding 50,000, collective public passenger transport and environmental protection must also be supplied.

§3. The Provinces

I. Introduction

321. The division into provinces (known in Spanish as *Diputaciones*) now existing in Spain dates from the nineteenth century (1883), with a slight modification in 1927 to divide the Canary Islands into two provinces. At present, there are fifty provinces, which the Constitution simultaneously forms as local entities with their own legal personality, made up of a group of municipalities, and as territorial divisions for carrying out the State's activities (Article 141). Amongst these activities, the Constitution highlights the province's function as an electoral district for both the Congress and Senate elections. The provincial boundaries can only be modified by an organic law, something that happens very rarely and only with the aim of including a municipality in a different province of the same Community, as with Organic Law 15/1995, 27 December, on Alteration of Provincial Limits, which transferred the municipality of Gátova from Castellón to Valencia.

322. Since the 1812 Constitution, the provinces as local bodies have been governed and administered by Provincial Councils. In the Autonomous State, seven Communities consisting of only one province do not have such Councils, their self-governing organs having assumed these competences and civil servants. The Councils also do not exist in the Canary Islands, substituted by the 'Cabildos', a Council directly elected by the voters of each island (*see* paragraph 329). As administrative providers of services, the Provincial Councils have been losing competences, and their percentage of total public spending has reduced in practically all the Autonomous Communities (the most important exception being the Basque Provincial Councils) because the autonomous and local laws dealing with matters have been transferred to the autonomous administration. Thus, the design set out in a report of a group of experts on autonomies (the *Enterría* Report, so named after its President), prepared in 1981, and which served as the bases of the Accords signed by UCD and PSOE that year, on the development of the Autonomous State was abandoned. In that report, it was argued that because the Communities had no peripheral administration, this function should be carried out by the Provincial Councils, as it was considered undesirable that there should be more than one administrative level between the State and the locality. Therefore, what, from the strictly technical point of view, may have been more correct and improved the administrative structure would have proposed their integration into the Autonomous Communities, although reasons legal (the Constitution guarantees their existence), political (the parties did not want to renounce a source of power), and social (in some regions there is a strong provincial sentiment) have prevented this for the moment.

II. The Provincial Institutions

323. LOREG lays down that the Provincial Council shall consist of a number of deputies varying from 25 in the provinces with fewer than 500,000 residents to 53 in those with more than 5,000,000 (only Barcelona). The number of deputies is shared amongst the local legal administrative areas (*see* paragraph 179) of the province in proportion to the number of residents, considering that there must always be a minimum of one deputy and no area can have more than three-fifths of the total number of provincial deputies. As the province does not form the electoral district and as the seats are not shared out in strict accordance with the number of inhabitants, the paradoxical result can be that the party most voted for at the provincial level obtains fewer deputies, as has happened in some cases, the last being in Malaga in the May 2003 elections.

324. The system for electing deputies in each area is indirect and takes place in two stages:

(1) The Electoral Board for the Zone shares the seats between the political parties and electoral groups applying the D'Hondt proportional system to the number of popular votes that each one has obtained in the local area, always provided that there is a least one councillor.
(2) Once the allocation of deputies has taken place, the same Electoral Board assembles the councillors of each political group separately for them to choose from amongst their number those who shall be proclaimed provincial deputies. LOREG states that in this election, the lists of successful candidates must be voted for by at least one-third of the total of their group. From this, it follows that more than one list per group can be presented, which has been upheld by the constitutional jurisprudence (STC 174/1991, 16 December, case *Diputados provinciales de Almería*). However, the usual practice is for each party or electoral coalition to present only one list.

325. The three Basque Provincial Councils of Álava, Guipúzcoa, and Vizcaya have a special regime based on their historical traditions, recognized by the Constitution: LOREG (Article 209) and LBRL (Additional Provision 2a). EAPV stipulates that the Basque Parliament regulates these elections heeding the criteria of free, direct, secret, and universal suffrage and proportional representation, using electoral districts that ensure an adequate representation of all the zones of the territory. This direct legitimacy of the Basque Councils is the basis of their normative authority, especially in revenue matters (*see* paragraph 284), such that the Organic Law of the Constitutional Court was equivalent to the autonomous laws in the sense that the *foral* revenue norms could only be appealed to the Constitutional Court when there was doubt as to whether they fitted into the Block of Constitutionality. The President of the Provincial Council is chosen by the provincial deputies in the same constituent session of the Council. The candidate must obtain an absolute majority in the first ballot and a simple one in the second. With express reference to the norms applicable to mayors, LOREG lays down that the President of the Provincial Council may be dismissed through a constructive censure motion and also if he loses a question of confidence, which must be connected with approval or amendment of the annual budget, the organic regulatory system and the provincial plan of cooperation in works and services under municipal competence.

326. LBRL authorizes the President to appoint vice presidents and a Governing Commission formed exclusively by provincial deputies. As with the Town Councils, greater powers were assigned to the President in 1999 by this Act, although the parliamentary system of government was maintained: the plenary of the Provincial Council was responsible for passing provincial norms, the budgets, plans of public works, and other important matters while the President and the Commission of Government exercised executive functions.

III. Provincial Competences

327. The basic function of the Provincial Councils is to assist and cooperate with the municipalities, particularly those with fewer economic and management resources, so as to guarantee the provision of obligatory minimum services imposed by the Law on Municipalities as well as a general function of promoting and administrating the particular interests of the province (Article 36 LBRL). In general, the tendency of many Communities (headed by Catalonia and Andalusia) has been to deprive the Provincial Councils of a good number of their traditional competences in the economy, agriculture, public works, transport, health, and social services, so converting them into little more than advisory institutions for the small towns, with unimportant powers over environment, culture, tourism, and sport. On the contrary, State Law 27/2013, on rationalization of the local administration, reinforces the role of the Provincial Councils by attributing to them the coordination of certain services in municipalities with a population of less than 20,000 inhabitants and the attribution of new functions, such as provision of tax collection services, electronic administration, or centralized contracting in municipalities with a population of less than 20,000 inhabitants.

328. The most important competence of the Provincial Councils is the provincial planning of cooperation in municipal works and services; however, this is not a full competence since it is subject to the 'coordination' of the Autonomous Community. Moreover, both the Community and the state can submit the subsidies for these plans to specific criteria and conditions in their utilization or employment (Article 36.2 LBRL).

§4. Other Local Government Bodies

329. Article 141.4 of the Constitution stipulates that the Islands shall have their own administration. The respective Autonomy Statutes have regulated seven 'Cabildos Insulares', that is, a form of Provincial Council in the Canary Islands (El Hierro, Fueteventura, Gran Canaria, La Gomera; Lanzarote, la Palma, and Tenerife) and four Insular Councils in the Balearics (Mallorca, Menorca, Ibiza and Formentera). The Councillors of the Cabildos are directly chosen by the citizens, the president being the first candidate on the most voted for list on each island. The Insular Councillors of the Balearics, after the reform of its Statute in 2007, are directly chosen by the citizens from whom the President of the Council is chosen.

330. Article 141.3 of the Constitution authorizes the creation of groups of several municipalities of the province. For its part, Article 152.3 permits the Autonomy Statutes to establish their own territorial electoral districts. With the support of these provisions, most of the Statutes have established zones (*comarcas*) as their own territorial organization of the Autonomous Community, remitting specific regulation to the autonomous laws (Articles 83.2 EAC, 40 EAG, 97 EAA, etc.). The autonomous legislators have acted very differently when exercising this competence since while some have legislated intensely on the zones, extending them throughout their territory (Catalonia and Aragón, for example), others have not created even one (Galicia and Andalusia). Very sensibly, some Communities have created *comarcas* to recognize the distinctive features of an area, such as the Valley of Arán in Catalonia and the Comarca del Bierzo in Castile-Leon.

331. LBRL permits the formation of other groupings of municipalities, such as Metropolitan Areas (created by autonomous Law) and Municipal Associations as voluntary groups of municipalities for the provision of services. While Metropolitan Areas (only Barcelona is recorded in the register of local entities in 2017) are still practically unknown, the Municipal Associations are spreading rapidly throughout the national territory (976) because the grouping together of small and medium-sized municipalities enables them to improve the quality and management of many of the services they have to offer (water supply and purification, waste collection, etc.).

332. LBRL also allows the creation of local entities smaller than the municipality for the decentralized administration of separated nuclei of the population. As on 1 January 2022, there existed in Spain 3,680 villages whose legal regime has to be established by the Autonomous Communities: in default, LOREG sets out that the residents shall directly elect the district mayor, who forms the Neighbourhood Council, together with two or four representatives (according to whether or not the village has 250 people). The Town Council (of which the nucleus is part) appoints these representatives according to the electoral results of each party in this nucleus.

Part IV. Citizenship and Fundamental Rights

Chapter 1. Spanish Nationality

§1. Constitutional Provisions on Nationality

333. As is the general rule in comparative law and historically in our Constitutions, Article 11 SC establishes that Spanish nationality is acquired, preserved, and lost in accordance with the law, although it specifies that no one of Spanish birth may be deprived of his nationality. Thus, at a stroke, one of the favourite instruments of dictators to punish disloyal subjects was abolished. A democracy cannot do this since it considers nationality as a basic quality of Spaniards, which citizens may renounce but which the State cannot take away. It is precisely to facilitate the preservation of Spanish nationality that the Constitution authorizes the state to make dual nationality treaties with Latin American countries or others with which that may have had or may have a special bond with Spain. Spaniards may become naturalized in those countries without losing their original nationality, even when a reciprocal right is not recognized.

§2. The Legal Regulation of Spanish Nationality

I. The Acquisition of Nationality

334. The law that traditionally regulates nationality is the Civil Code, whose Title 1, 'On Spaniards and Aliens' has been modified on a good number of occasions from its original wording in 1885 to adapt its provisions to accord with social reality. The last of these modifications were made by Law 12/2015, which facilitated the acquisition of nationality by Jews of Spanish descent (Sephardi Jews) without having to renounce their nationality of origin. Spanish nationality can be obtained in three ways: by origin, by choice, or by naturalization. Exceptionally, it may be acquired in a fourth way, by naturalization granted by the government when the person concerned has 'exceptional circumstances'. The 1812 Constitution, the first law regulating nationality, declared that 'all men born and brought up in Spain and its dominions and their children' were Spanish. This duality of methods to obtain Spanish nationality (either by birth on Spanish soil or by being a child of Spanish parents) was retained in the Civil Code until 1957, when preference was given to the *ius sanguini,* according to which only persons born of a Spanish parent had Spanish nationality. From then on, the *ius soli* only operated in certain situations:

- For the second generation, Article 17 CC establishes that persons born in Spain of foreign parents will be Spanish if at least one of them was born in Spain.
- Foreign Parents of those born in Spain where neither of them had a nationality (stateless) or if the legislation of either did not attribute nationality to the child, which, as can easily be imagined, is a fairly unusual situation.
- Those born in Spain whose connections/particulars are unknown.

Another circumstance in which a nationality of origin may be acquired is adoption by a Spaniard, provided that the adoptee is always a minor.

335. Certain persons have the possibility of obtaining Spanish nationality of their own free will if they:

(a) are or have been subject to the *patria potestas* of a Spaniard;
(b) have a father or mother who was originally Spanish and born in Spain;
(c) are the children of Spanish parents when the connection is discovered after the age of 18;
(d) are adopted and over the age of 18 after living for two years in Spain.

336. Aliens living legally in Spain can be naturalized after the following periods of time, which must be continuous and must immediately precede the application:

- after ten years: general cases;
- after five years: political refugees;
- after two years: nationals of Latin American countries, Andorra, Philippines, Equatorial Guinea, Portugal, or who are Sephardim;
- after one year: exceptional cases, such as birth in Spanish territory, spouse of a Spaniard, born outside Spain but of a father, mother, grandfather, or grandmother who was originally Spanish. This last case was modified by Law 36/2002 to facilitate the granting of nationality to the grandchildren of Spanish emigrants.

In this regulation of the acquisition of nationality by residence, what I think catches the attention is that the citizens of the majority of the other EU Member States are not treated, at least, as generously as the Portuguese and Latin Americans and are subject to a general regime of ten years' residence and have to renounce their nationality of origin.

II. The Loss of Spanish Nationality

337. Spaniards of origin can only lose their nationality by renouncing it. The CC sets out that this occurs in the case of those born abroad to a Spanish mother or father, also born abroad when the laws of that country assign its nationality to the child born there unless the person so born declares the wish to retain Spanish nationality before an official of the Civil Registry within three years of reaching the majority age or emancipation. However, this tacit renunciation does not apply to those who acquire the nationality of any country of Latin America, Andorra, Philippines, Equatorial Guinea, Portugal, or who are Sephardim. One of the penalties foreseen by Spanish legislation for Spaniards who are not so by origin is the loss of nationality, but this was resolved in the new Criminal Code of 1995. As a result, Spaniards not so by origin may only lose their nationality as well as by a judicial decision declaring that it was obtained fraudulently, in two eventualities:

(1) When, for a period of three years, they exclusively use the nationality that they had renounced on acquiring Spanish nationality.
(2) When they willingly enter the armed services or a political office of a foreign state against the express prohibition of the government.

§3. The Relevance of Spanish Nationality

I. The Constitutional Position of Spaniards and Aliens

338. In Spanish constitutional history, nationality was decisive in order to be the holder of the rights recognized in the Constitution, leaving the regulation of the legal status of aliens completely to the will of the legislator. Article 13.1 of the Constitution could have been interpreted in that traditional sense as it stipulates that aliens 'enjoy in Spain the public freedoms guaranteed in the present Title in the terms established by the Treaties and the Law'. However, the Constitutional Court rejected that interpretation and deemed that the Constitution itself recognize a good number of rights belonging to all persons who find themselves under Spanish jurisdiction and which cannot be arbitrarily restricted by the legislator. Thus, 'all' have the right to life and the exercise of the rights inherent in human dignity, such as personal freedom; the same applies to effective legal protection, where the Constitution admits no differences. At the other extreme, the Constitution lays down a second group of rights that only Spaniards may enjoy, such as the rights of political participation and access to public offices and positions. Between these two groups lies a third in which the situation of Spaniards and aliens is not identical, and laws and treaties may introduce differences between them, provided that they are not always irreconcilable with the law, for it is one thing for Article 13 to authorize distinct treatment between Spaniards and foreigners 'and another to understand that authorization as a possibility of legislating without taking into consideration constitutional mandates' (STC 115/1987, 7 July, case *Ley de Extranjería*). Therefore, the legislator cannot remove, for example, the rights of assembly and association from aliens by submitting their exercise to express governmental consent. The status of aliens will be discussed further at the end of this section, in Chapter 7.

II. The European Citizenship

339. The Treaty on European Union (TEU) created European citizenship as a series of rights for the holders who are all the nationals of the Member States of the Union. The Lisbon Treaty has strengthened it, giving binding force to the European Charter on Fundamental Rights (ECFR), which sets out, in detail, the rights that make up European citizenship. These rights are, according to the literal tenor of Chapter V of the Charter, five: (1) the rights of active and passive suffrage to the European Parliament and in the local elections of the area where they reside, (2) the right to good administration, (3) the right of petition, (4) the liberties of free movement and residence within the Union, and (5) the diplomatic and consular protection of any of the Member States in third countries. To these rights must be added the clauses of direct and indirect equality of the Constitutive Treaties (such as the prohibition of discrimination amongst workers of different nationalities), which the CJEU has interpreted to ensure its maximum effectiveness, including restricting the differences that the Treaties themselves admit. So, for example, the reservation of employment to nationals set out in Article 48.4 of the TEU was considered applicable only to public posts in which 'they take part in the exercise of public powers' (JCJEC 17 December 1980, case *Commission v. Belgium*).

Despite these provisions, the citizens of other states of the EU are not Spanish. Therefore, the Constitutional Court declared that to consider them as Spaniards as the only effect of granting the right of passive suffrage, as the government intended in 1992, is a fragmentation or manipulation of nationality forbidden by the Constitution (*see* paragraph 66). However, the fact that other Europeans are not Spanish does not mean that their status in Spain is equivalent to that of other aliens. On the contrary, if their legal status is compared carefully, it will be seen that it is closer to that of Spaniards than to other aliens. Moreover, in the present state of development of European integration, it seems more logical to think that the traditional contradistinction between Spaniards/aliens from which the Constitution began in 1978 has been overcome and has been substituted by a threefold division into Spaniards/European citizens/aliens.

III. The Paradox of Spanish Nationality

340. As in Spain, most democratic states are reducing the differences between nationals and aliens, a tendency reinforced by the effects of the UDHR and the closely woven network of international treaties and conventions in defence of fundamental rights. Thus, it does not seem far-fetched to think that the basic status of rights inherent in everyone will continue to grow to the point that the distinction between a foreigner and a national will become irrelevant. Until that moment arrives, what can be called the paradox of Spanish nationality must be borne in mind: while it has lost relevance from the viewpoint of Spanish domestic law, as the position of aliens in general and Europeans, in particular, it is now not so different as it was in the past, internationally, it has become more important; all Spaniards enjoy European citizenship with all the many rights that that status implies in international and European law and the domestic law of other European States.

Chapter 2. The General Regime of Fundamental Rights

§1. The Concept of Fundamental Rights

I. Definition

341. Since the time of John Locke and the later theoreticians of the social pact, the constitutional movement has always considered that citizens have certain inalienable rights that the state must respect, so much so that the instruments creating new rights are concerned to reflect in their terminology that these rights existed previously, albeit subjugated or omitted, for example, the 1776 Declaration of Rights of Virginia, the 1789 Declaration of the Rights of Man and of the Citizen, etc. The UDHR has come to endorse this idea that public powers, including the legislative power, must respect certain inherent rights to those persons who are the basis of the state itself. Article 10 of the Spanish Constitution puts it elegantly: 'the dignity of the person, the inviolable rights that are inherent, the free development of the personality, respect for the law and the rights of others are the foundation of the political order and social peace'. Specifically, both texts allow us to distinguish between human rights and fundamental rights: while the former are the rights which, from a moral point of view, society recognizes that each and every one of its components possesses (to the point of recognizing them in the UDHR), fundamental rights are the crystallization of those human rights in a particular Constitution.

II. Sources

342. In the nineteenth-century system of international relations, with the preeminence of the concept of the independent sovereign State, the only source of fundamental rights was the State's Constitution and, starting from that, the respective laws that developed it. However, after the Second World War, and in harmony with the creation of the United Nations Organisation (UNO) and other multilateral organisms, a good number of international conventions were approved, which, when ratified and published in Spain, have been fully incorporated into the Spanish legal system, such as the International Covenant on Civil and Political Rights (ICCPR), the International Covenant on Economic, Social and Cultural Rights of 1966 (ICESCR), the European Social Charter of 1961, etc. Of all these, the 1950 European Convention for the Protection of Human Rights and Fundamental Freedoms is outstanding. At the first moment, it laid down a brief statement of rights, forming what has been called a minimum standard for fundamental rights in all the Member States of the Council of Europe, subsequently going further until it has now established a broad catalogue, guaranteed by a specific supra-State instrument, the ECtHR (*see* paragraph 357). In the EU, its Charter of Fundamental Rights sets out the rights of European citizens against the Union's public powers and against national public powers when applying European law. The Constitutional Court considers that this Charter was incorporated together with treaties which, according to Article 10.2 SC, are instruments of interpretation of fundamental rights, a provision that Organic Law 1/2008, 30 July, also established, authorizing the ratification of the Lisbon Treaty.

III. Classification of the Rights in Title I

343. The specialists have classified rights in many distinct ways and according to a wide variety of criteria. Possibly, the most popular is the one made by Karel Vasak, a French jurist of Czech origin, in 1974, parallel to the slogan of the French Revolution (*liberté, égalité, fraternité*) and in the spirit of the historical moment of its diffusion, and which refers to three generations of rights: the first generation includes the rights of freedom, public freedoms or civil rights, the second those of political rights or equality and the third the rights of solidarity or economic, social and cultural rights.[43] We can roughly apply this classification to Title I of the Spanish Constitution when it distinguishes between the 'Rights and Freedoms' of Chapter II (in turn subdivided into sections) and the 'Guiding Principles of social and economic policy' of Chapter III. However, the soundest criterion for classifying the rights of Spanish fundamental law is that derived from Article 53, which establishes the guarantees of rights:

(a) Rights which enjoy special protection: the rights set out in Section I of Chapter II (Articles 14–29). These are fundamental rights in the strict sense, in that the Constitution assigns them a special legal regime, as now set out: the right to life and physical and moral integrity; freedom of ideology, religion, and cult; freedom and safety; the right of honour, privacy, and identity; free choice of residence and to travel in the national territory; freedom of expression and information; the rights of assembly association and participation; guardianship, the right to judicial protection; the right to education and the freedom of instruction; the right to form trade unions and the right to strike and to petition.
(b) Rights with ordinary protection: second section of Chapter II (Articles 30–38) brings together the 'Rights and Duties of Citizens'. The Constitution guarantees their essential content and direct effect, as developed by ordinary law. They are the right and duty to defend Spain, the right to marry to hold private property, the right to create foundations, the right to work and of free election of career, the right to collective labour negotiation, and to establish businesses.
(c) Guiding Principles of public authorities: 'Rights' of Chapter III (Articles 39–52), which, although established as such in that chapter ('right' to health, culture, environment, housing) are not designed as subjective rights directly

43. Karel Vasak *Le droit international des droits de l'homme*, 140 Recueil des cours de l'Académie de Droit international de La Haye 133–415 (1974 333-415). The first generation of civil rights are characterized by being negative, in the sense that public authorities can respect them by not interfering in the lives of citizens; the political rights of the second generation require action by the public powers so that they can be carried out (organization of elections, for example); and the third generation of social rights require much more action by these powers, hence they are also called benefit rights.

enforceable before the Courts. On the contrary, their role is to 'guide' the legislation and the actions of the public authorities, but before the Courts, they can only be argued (Article 53.3 SC) 'through the procedures established in the laws affecting them'.

344. In addition to the rights set out in Title I, the Constitution recognizes other rights in other constitutional Titles. Doubtless, the constituent assembly designed it in this way to systemize it and, for the most part, to shape it as orders to the legislator; moreover, almost all of them are specific instances of the fundamental rights already recognized in Title I. They are as follows:

- The right to autonomy of the nationalities and regions as set out in Article 2 and expanded in Article 143 and following (*see* paragraph 226).
- The right to use Castilian (Article 3).
- The right to create political parties (Article 6).
- The right to vote for Spaniards who are outside the territory of Spain (Article 68.5).
- The right of civil servants to form trade unions (Article 103.3).
- The right of audience in the process of elaborating administrative decisions and accessing administrative archives and registers (Article 105).
- The right of private individuals to be indemnified for any harm suffered when such harm is the result of the functioning of the public services (Article 106.2), even when caused by judicial error or from the abnormal functioning of the Administration of Justice (Article 121).
- The right to exercise popular action and participate in the Administration of Justice through the institution of the Jury (Article 125).
- The right to participate in social security, in public agencies and private enterprises (Article 129).

§2. Fundamental Rights: Past and Present

I. Direct Efficacy and the Double Dimension of Fundamental Rights

345. Traditionally constitutional rights are considered in the liberal European State to be those rights proclaimed in the Constitution but whose implementation and efficacy depended on the laws that developed them. Only when those laws regulated them did they become citizens' legal rights, limiting the actions of the public authorities and protecting by jurisdictional instruments against possible interference by the State in the sphere of their liberties (subjective public rights). The 1978 Constitution did not remit the efficacy of fundamental rights to the law, but itself fixed its 'essential content', so converting these rights into genuine constitutional mandates capable of restricting the legislator and of being implemented directly. In the words of the Constitutional Court, fundamental rights 'bind all public authorities and are the immediate origin of rights and obligations, and not mere programmatic principles' (STC, 21/1981, 14 July, case *Pitarch*). Article 7 of the LOPJ has laid down this constitutional mandate ordering that 'fundamental rights and public liberties bind, in their totality, all judges and courts ... they will be recognized, in every case, according to their content constitutionally declared, and judicial decisions cannot restrict, lessen or fail to apply such content'.

The Constitution also shapes fundamental rights as subjective rights and as fully operative rights for individuals; it endows them with a new objective dimension since 'at the right time, they are essential elements of an objective legal system of the national community and are formed as the framework of a just and peaceful human conscience, historically embodied in the social and democratic state of Law' (STC 25/1981, 14 July, case *Legislación antiterrorista I*). The consequences of this double dimension are manifold, from the correct interpretation of each one of the fundamental rights from the intervention of the Prosecutor General of the State in the legal proceedings in defence of these rights, through to their inspirational role throughout the legal system. This is the reason why Article 10 of the Constitution proclaims that 'the dignity of the person, the inviolable rights which are inherent, the free development of the personality, respect for law and the rights of others are the foundation of political order and social peace'.

II. Entitlement to Constitutional Rights

346. This same classic vision of fundamental rights confers them on Spanish citizens. The 1978 Constitution confers on them a wide network of rights as laid down in Title I, hence the importance of clearly determining the bases of citizenship such as the majority of age (fixed at 18 years old by Article 12 SC) and nationality. But as we have already seen, aliens, too, have certain fundamental rights (*see* paragraph 338). In the same way, minors are holders of rights as implicitly deduced from the Constitution when it uses 'all' or 'no one' as the subject of some fundamental rights (arts. 15, 17, 25, 27) and expressly recognized by the Convention on the Rights of the Child of 20 November 1989 and Organic Law 1/1996, of 15 January, on the legal protection of minors (LOPJM). To summarize this law telegraphically, it can be said that they enjoy personal rights (life, liberty), intellectual freedoms (ideological, religious, educational freedom, etc.) and some specific political rights such as the rights of association and assembly. The Constitutional Court has had to specify that the enjoyment of these rights may depend on the degree of maturity of the minor, which allows the public authorities to intervene to protect the minor's right in a way that would not be admissible in the case of an adult. For example, judicial intervention to authorize a blood transfusion to a minor who refuses it by exercising their constitutional right to religious freedom (STC 154/2002, 18 July, case *Alegre Tomás*). But as this maturity depends on each minor with a name and surname, a generic prohibition on the use of a right that minors are entitled to be not constitutional, as the Constitutional Court ruled when analysing the requirement of the age of majority for a change of sex established by Law 3/2007, of 15 March, regulating the registry rectification of the mention of a person's sex: it is a disproportionate restriction for minors with 'sufficient maturity' and who are in a 'stable situation of transsexuality', which entails a violation of the right to privacy and the free development of the personality of these minors (STC

99/2019, 18 July, case *Ley 3/2007, reguladora de la rectificación registral relativa al sexo*). In any case, the Constitutional Court has held that those with personality can only enjoy constitutional rights, so neither the unborn nor the deceased person is entitled to constitutional rights (SSTC 53/1985, 11 April, case *Despenalización del Aborto* and 231/1988, 2 December, case *Pantoja-Paquirri*). The Civil code establishes that personality is obtained at the moment of birth with life, once produced with 'the complete separation from the mother' (Article 30[44]) and is extinguished on death (Article 32).

Things being so, it is not surprising that in one of its first judgments, the Constitutional Court denied that the entitlement to rights could be determined 'in relation to each and every one of them' (STC 19/1983, 14 March, case *despido en la Diputación Foral de Navarra*). In the casuistic analysis of this entitlement, the most complicated matter is to determine who is a legal person since, in our Constitution, there is no general reference to it as in German and Portuguese. The Constitutional Court has, however, declared that fundamental rights 'also govern national legal persons as far as is applicable, according to their nature' (STC, 23/1989, 2 February, case *Quiosco de prensa*). Thus, it is clear that while they are excluded from a group of rights (the personal ones such as physical integrity, personal liberty, etc.), others are recognized (the collective: freedom of association, religious belief, membership of a trade union, etc.) and a third group of rights whose ownership is doubtful. In general, it can be said that constitutional jurisprudence tends to consider that legal persons are holders of most of these arguable rights: inviolability of the home, privacy of communications, freedom of expression and even the right to reputation. Within the concept of legal persons, public authorities are also exceptionally the holders of certain rights, such as guardianship, because although this right protects – in the words of the Constitutional Court – 'before anything else, individuals in the face of power', public persons can also be the holders of effective judicial protection in those disputes in which 'they do not enjoy procedural privileges and their position is equivalent to that of private persons' (STC 11/2008, 21 January, case *Menores acogidas en un centro de la Junta de Andalucía*) because although this right protects – in the words of the Constitutional Court – 'before anything else individuals in the face of power', public persons can also be the holders of effective judicial protection in those disputes in which 'they do not enjoy procedural privileges and their position is equivalent to that of private persons'. This requirement entails, in my opinion, that the litigation in which the administrations can allege the violation of judicial protection – and therefore can file an appeal for constitutional protection of fundamental rights – will be those processed by the civil and social orders, while that equality will rarely occur between the administration and those administered in the contentious-order. This right even includes the Public Prosecutor in its condition as a procedural party (STC 17/2006, 30 January, case *Indefensión del Ministerio Fiscal en exploración de menores*).

44. In the wording of Law 20/2011, 21 July, *del Registro Civil*, which intends to fix personality according to the criterion of the Convention on the Rights of the Child of 20 Nov. 1989. Until then, Art. 30 of the Civil Code established that 'only the foetus born in human form who lives for twenty-four hours independently of the mother' will be considered born.

III. Consequences of Fundamental Rights Between Private Persons

347. Traditionally, fundamental rights have been considered as asserted against the State. However, the strict terms of Article 9 of the Constitution – stipulating that this article binds citizens – means that this opinion can no longer be held, and that forces us to think that fundamental rights also affect the relationship between individuals, with 'horizontal' effects or, according to the German word used, *Drittwirkung*. Nevertheless, the entitlement to all rights cannot be treated in the same way, nor does each and every right has the same efficacy between individuals as it does between an individual and a public authority. Let us look first at its structure: while there are rights that can be exercised against public authorities (the right to participate in public affairs, the right to petition and political rights in general), others normally protect citizens from other citizens (the right to reputation, for example). The Constitutional Court has decided casuistically how certain interpersonal rights shall function: while it does not admit substantial differences in most of them (freedom to form a trade union, prohibition of discriminatory treatment within a business, etc.), some can be restricted by virtue of these relations, for example, the ideology of an educational centre means that the scope for academic freedom is not as wide in a business of this type as in a State school (*see* paragraph 388); freedom of contract gives a greater margin to businesses to contract employees than the public authorities have in selecting civil servants, etc. Some sectoral laws have expressly pointed out the linkage of fundamental rights between private individuals. For example, Law 3/1991 on Unfair Competition considers that 'Discriminatory treatment of consumers in terms of prices and other conditions of sale shall be considered unfair unless there is a justified cause'; the General Law for the Defence of Consumers of 2007 prohibits the refusal to satisfy consumers' demands for goods and services for discriminatory reasons; the Statute of Workers of 2015 considers that dismissal in violation of fundamental rights shall be null and void, etc.

§3. Guarantees of Fundamental Rights

348. Section 1 of Chapter II of Title I, called 'Basic Rights and Public Liberties' (Articles 15–29), lays down fundamental rights in the strict sense of the term, technical and constitutional or 'nominally and substantially fundamental', since it is only for those that the Constitution creates total protection, both in its normative regulations and in the jurisdictional guarantees to ensure their enforcement by the courts. From the point of view of the general theory of law, and in accordance with the spirit of the UDHR and ECHR, the content of Chapter II (Articles 30–38) can also be thought of as fundamental rights; but if we want these classifications to help us understand the legal reality, a wider sense has to be added, since although they have that capacity to be regulated by law, which must respect their essential content (Article 53.1 SC), they do not have the other characteristics of the rights of the first Section which we now shall seek to explain.

I. Normative Guarantees of Fundamental Rights

A. The Essential Content

349. The Constitution does not expressly determine the elements that form the essential content of fundamental rights. Therefore, legal operators must specify the essential content of each right. According to the Constitutional Court, this is a casuistic task for which it gives two cumulative criteria (STC 11/1981, 8 April, case *Decreto-ley de huelga*): first, the essential content of a right is formed by those features that make it recognizable to society (e.g., no one would say that there is a right to strike where workers who strike are punished) and, second, what are the elements that serve to protect the interests that the fundamental right protects (In our example, a law would be unconstitutional that ordered that strikes could only be carried out on holidays because that would be removing the strike as an instrument to defend the interests of workers). The essential content of fundamental rights is fixed by the Constitution, which has at least two far-reaching consequences:

- That essential content is the basis on which the legislator must construct the legal regime. If the legislator fails to give it a specific form (as until now has happened with the right to strike), it does not, for that reason, cease to be a true subjective right that citizens can exercise and can demand that the courts protect since the Constitution grants direct enforcement of fundamental rights. What is more, the absence of a developing law can in itself be a violation of a fundamental right, since in no case can the public authorities restrict them, as shown in the case STC 31/1994, 31 January, case *TV por cable*, which annulled the closure of a local television station (*see* paragraph 43). Other cases in which the Court recognized direct enforceability in spite of the lack of *interpositio legislatoris* have been the immediate application of conscientious objection, involving the deferment on incorporation in the army for anyone who requested it until the development law was passed (STC 15/1982, 23 April, case *Recurso contra acuerdo Junta de Clasificación del Estrecho*), and the right of access to computerized administrative records (STC 254/1993, 20 July, case *Olaverri Zazpe*).
- The legislator must respect the essential content of fundamental rights so that laws that violate them can be challenged in the Constitutional Court, either by appeal or by alleging unconstitutionality (*see* paragraph 194). Logically, it is no easy task to determine the essential content of each right or whether it has not been respected by the legislator. According to the Constitutional Court, it is a question of a casuistic task with two cumulative criteria (STC 11/1981, 8 April, case *Decreto-ley de huelga*): in the first place, the essential content of law has certain characteristics which make it recognizable in society (e.g., nobody would say that there is a right to strike if the workers who called it were sanctioned) and, in the second place, it is made up of those elements that serve to protect the interests that the fundamental right supports (in our example, a law would be unconstitutional if it stipulated that strikes could only be held on public holidays because that would take from the strike its character of defending the workers' interests).

B. *The Extraordinary Reform Procedure*

350. Articles 15–29 can only be reformed under the special procedure laid down in Article 168. Although this serves as a maximum guarantee for fundamental rights, the formula employed has the inconvenience of making it difficult to modify certain secondary aspects of these rights that have remained regulated by those articles protected by the *extraordinary* procedure (*see* paragraph 54).

C. *The Reservation to Organic Law*

351. The legal regulation of fundamental rights must be by organic law, a law thought up by the constituent assembly to maintain the political *consensus* in the development of the essential aspects of the Constitution. This reservation to organic law only covers the direct development of constitutional precept, the right in the abstract, so that ordinary state and autonomous laws can influence fundamental rights provided that the aim is to regulate a matter in which the State or the Autonomous Communities have competences, and they do not directly regulate a fundamental right (*see* paragraph 67).

II. Jurisdictional Guarantees of Fundamental Rights

A. *The Appeal Process Before the Ordinary Courts*

352. Fundamental rights can be invoked in every type of judicial process; even so, the Constitution stipulates that citizens may assert their claim to the protection of the rights and liberties recognized in Article 14 and Section I of Chapter II before the ordinary courts under a procedure based on the principles of preference and speed. Parliament, which initially passed a law regulating this procedure in the various legal systems,[45] has subsequently incorporated new, specific procedural laws with the general aim of introducing as few changes as possible, so trying to avoid the procedural distortions that the practical implementation of Law 62/1978 had revealed. For this reason, there are, at present, five different forms of procedure to protect fundamental rights, one for each of the orders into which the Spanish legal system is divided and which are regulated as follows:

- Civil Law: Ley 1/2000, 7 January, *de Enjuiciamiento Civil.* (Civil procedure).
- Criminal Law: Law 38/2002, 24 October, (Partial Reform of the Law of Criminal Procedure).

45. Law 62/1978, 26 December, Legal Protection of the Fundamental Rights of the Person, which was extended to all fundamental rights by the second transitional provision of LOTC. Law 62/1978 is still formally in force since it has not been expressly repealed by Parliament; however, each and every one of its fifteen articles has been repealed by subsequent laws, leaving only its final, transitory, and repealing provisions in force, so that it now has no legal effect.

- Contentious-Administrative law: Law 29/1998, 13 July, Regulation of Contentious-Administrative law.
- Social/Employment Law: Law 36/2011, 10 October, regulating the Employment Courts.
- Military Law: Organic Law 2/1989, 13 April, on Military Procedure (modified several times, the last occasion by the Organic Law 14/2015, 14 October).

353. The common features of these five processes of legal protection of fundamental rights are:

(1) Their urgent and preferential nature with shorter time limits than in ordinary procedures.
(2) The limited subject of the process, which can only deal with the violation of a fundamental right; this has the effect of limiting both the method of proof and the content of the judgment, which can only refer to the breach of the fundamental right alleged. However, in the contentious-administrative sphere, the LRJCA reformulated the subject of this appeal, broadening it so that it provided a remedy for breach of those rights capable of appeal to ensure that the administration's action was in conformity with the legal system. This means that the decision will grant the appeal when the provision, conduct, or act 'results in any infraction of the legal system, including the incorrect use of power, and as a consequence violates a right that can be appealed' (Article 121 LJCA).
(3) In accordance with the limitation of the aim of the procedural process, the effect of the fact judged in the decisions of these procedures only extends to the constitutional aspects judged but does not affect the legal aspects between the parties. Therefore, a new judgment can be given in an ordinary trial on those aspects that have not been determined in the appeal proceedings. Let us imagine, for example, a civil servant who has been sanctioned for distributing union propaganda at his workplace and for repeatedly arriving late. In the preferential process, only the possible infringement of freedom of association will be discussed, but not the lack of punctuality, which is a problem of legality (determining whether or not it is true that he was late).

354. Starting from these common features, these five procedures have their own characteristics and, in some cases, are subdivided into other special procedures, as in the specific procedure for processing appeals for breach of the right of assembly in the contentious system (*see* paragraph 405). Of the distinct features of each one, it is worth mentioning those relating to allegations of sex discrimination or any other fundamental right. When these are supported by prima facie evidence of their infringement – 'credible or prima facie evidence', says the Constitutional Court – the defendant is required to give an 'objective and reasonable justification, adequately proved, of the methods adopted and of their proportionality'. The grounds for this partial reversal of the burden of proof are, in the words of the Constitutional Court, 'in the special difficulty in revealing in legal proceedings the constitutional harm, hidden behind the apparent legality of the employer's acts' (STC 90/1997, 6 May, case *Resolución de* contrato *laboral en Pryca*).

B. *The Appeal for Constitutional Protection of Fundamental Rights Before the Constitutional Court*

355. As was seen when explaining the competences of the Constitutional Court, Article 53 of the Constitution designed the appeal on the grounds of unconstitutionality as an appeal subsidiary to the ordinary jurisdictional instruments, whose practical effect has been to integrate fundamental rights into the daily activity of judges and courts. There, too, the characteristics of this procedure were set out so that there is no need to repeat them here (*see* paragraph 213). However, the relationship between the ordinary and the constitutional jurisdictions should be explained here. The situation is not a happy one since all decisions that have exhausted ordinary legal methods can be appealed. This results in a good number of decisions being appealed to the Constitutional Court from the lower ones without the intervention of the Supreme Court. Hence, many specialists have proposed some type of appeal to the Supreme Court, which would have the double effect of giving it the opportunity of remedying the breach of a right committed by the ordinary courts as well as reducing the workload of the Constitutional Court.

C. *International Guarantees, in Particular, the Appeal to the ECtHR*

356. The UDHR, proclaimed by the UNO, was the first text that aspired to universality. Its value was symbolic, moral, and political, but it imposed no binding legal obligation on the States. Subsequently, UNO has approved a long list of legally binding texts in defence of human rights which the States have to ratify expressly, as with any other international treaty. The most important are: (1) the previously mentioned (ICCPR), (2) the ICESCR, (3) the 1965 Convention on the Elimination of All Forms of Racial Discrimination, (4) the Convention on the Elimination of All Forms of Discrimination against Women, (5) the 1985 Convention against Torture, (6) the 1989 Convention on the Rights of the Child, (7) and the 1990 Convention on the Protection of the Rights of All Migrant Workers and their families; apart from this list, which came into force in July 2003, Spain has ratified all the rest.

Each of these international conventions establishes a committee to ensure the observance of its provisions. Logically, the most relevant is the Human Rights Committee, composed of eighteen specialists, to whom any citizen of a Member State that has recognized the competence of the committee can appeal after all domestic remedies have been exhausted. The committee does not make decisions, only 'reports' (as set out in paragraphs 407 and 427 of this monograph), which cannot annul the resolutions that the State has adopted in the particular case being litigated because; although the committee considers the State has infringed the fundamental rights of the 'author', which is the official name given to the appellant, its functioning Protocol is limited to establishing that the committee will present its observations to the 'interested State Party and to the individual'. However, in some cases, the Supreme Court has treated these reports in a way that, although it is not that of a mandatory sentence for the Spanish State, it is very similar to it in that it allows the State's patrimonial liability claim for abnormal functioning of the Administration of Justice. Thus, for example, it ruled that a woman was entitled to compensation of EUR 600,000 because the CEDAW Committee (Convention on the Elimination of All Forms of Discrimination Against Women) considered that the Spanish State had infringed the rights of the claimant and her deceased daughter by not protecting them correctly against the aggressor father who murdered the daughter (STS (3) 2747/2018, 7 July).

Furthermore, in 1947 the Commission on Human Rights was created in Geneva and elevated in April 2006 to the category of Human Rights Council, which is more political than the Committee in that it is made up of representatives of the States and not by specialists.

357. The most effective international instrument in defence of human rights that has been created until now is the ECtHR which, with its seat in Strasbourg, ensures the observance of the ECHR. It is composed of one judge from each European State that has ratified the Convention (forty-seven at the present time) chosen for a period of nine years, and they act with total independence. Because of this great number of members, the ECtHR judges sit either in Chambers of seven members or in the 'Grand Chamber' of seventeen. Any High Contracting Party (state suitor) or person who claims to be the victim of a violation of the Convention (individual suitor) can petition the ECtHR directly. The individual appeal must be made after all domestic remedies have been exhausted and presented within a period of six months. If the ECtHR accepts the application, it tries to achieve a friendly settlement between the parties, and only if this is not possible will it make a finding. If the appeal is allowed, the sentence can order the state to either change its laws or adopt other measures necessary to comply with the ECHR, as well as awarding damages (just satisfaction) to the victim. However, the Convention does not provide that the decisions of the ECtHR have a direct effect on the domestic legal system; thus, they do not, in themselves, annul previous decisions that failed to repair the breach, leaving this aspect to be decided by the legislation of each state. For many years in Spain, there has been no express regulation on this matter, and so, generally, judgments condemning Spain only have the effect of declaring that there has been a violation of a right. However, the Constitutional Court held that in some circumstances, these declarative decisions could have a domestic effect, creating a new judicial activity in Spain; thus, for example, it can be the grounds for a motion to review a prison sentence in a trial in which, according to the ECtHR, a fundamental right has been violated (STC 245/1991, 14 November, case *Bultó-II*). Organic Law 7/2015 has brought together this doctrine, creating a new Article 5*bis* of the LOPJ that grants the appeal of review before the Supreme Court in all jurisdictional orders when the ECtHR has declared that a judicial ruling has violated the ECHR 'provided that the violation, by its nature and seriousness, entails effects that persist and cannot cease in any other way than through this review'. For its part, Law 41/2015, 5 October 2015, introduces these judgments in the LECrim amongst the grounds of appeal for criminal review.

In any case, some of the more than one hundred judgments that have condemned Spain since joining the ECHR in October 1979 have had a great impact on our legal system. For example, the ECtHR judgments of 6 December 1988 and 19 June 1989, case *Barberá* and *Sanders*, respectively, forced an amendment to the Spanish procedural laws to reinforce the guarantees of the accused. For its part, the Judgment of the European Court of Human Rights (JECtHR) 9 December 1994, case *López Ostra*, led to the reinterpretation of a fundamental right such as the inviolability of the home. And of course, JECtHR 21 November 2013, case *Del Rio Prada*, resulted in the annulment of the Parot doctrine on the calculation of time in prison for violation of the right to criminal legality enshrined in Article 7.1 of the Convention.

III. Institutional Guarantees

358. The Spanish Constitution created the Ombudsman as the 'Parliamentary High Commissioner' for the defence of the rights set out in Title I. For reasons of organization, this was studied in the chapter dedicated to the organs independent of the State (*see* paragraph 215), as were the other state organs in defence of fundamental rights (*see* paragraph 217) and the Autonomous Parliamentary Commissioners with similar functions to the Ombudsman (*see* paragraph 296).

Article 124.1 of the Constitution includes amongst the functions of the office of the Public Prosecutor that of defending the 'rights of citizens', whose first specific incorporation is in Article 162 of the Constitution itself, which gives the right to lodge an appeal on the ground of unconstitutionality as long as there is a legitimate interest, with a similar right given to the Ombudsman. The LOPJ determines its participation in all such appeals (*see* paragraph 213).

IV. Restrictions on Rights

359. The well-known philosophical maxim of the Enlightenment, 'my freedom ends where that of the others begins', is reflected in Article 10 of the Spanish Constitution, which lays down amongst the basic rights of the political order, 'respect for the law and the rights of others'. This formula is incorporated in the legal system in the general form of *'abuse de rights'* (expressly prohibited in Spanish law and especially in the ECHR)[46] and in the specific limitations put on certain rights. Thus, the Spanish Constitution itself establishes that:

- freedom of ideology, religion and cult is limited only by the need for the 'maintenance of public order protected by law' (Article 16.1);
- the inviolability of the home implies that to enter the home, either the consent of the owner or legal authority is required 'except in the case of *flagrante delicto*' (Article 18.2);

46. 'Article 17. Prohibition of abuse of rights Nothing in this Convention may be interpreted as implying for any State, group or person any right to engage in any activity or perform any act aimed at the destruction of any of the rights and freedoms set forth herein or at their limitation to a greater extent than is provided for in the Convention.' A similar provision is contained in Art. 30 of the UDHR. In the Spanish legal system, the abuse of rights is prohibited in Art. 7.2 of the CC and in Art. 11.2 of the LOPJ.

- freedom of expression, artistic creation, academic freedom, and of information find 'their limitation in the respect for the rights recognized in this Title, in the precepts of the laws which develop it and, especially, in the right to honour, privacy, personal identity and protection of youth and childhood' (Article 20.4).
- the 'social function' of the rights to private property and inheritance 'shall determine the limits of their content in accordance with the law' (Article 33.2).

Moreover, as we shall see later, the Constitution permits certain fundamental rights to be restricted when, due to exceptional circumstances, states of alarm are declared (*see* paragraph 440), such that an organic law regulates the form in which rights relating to preventative detention, the inviolability of the home, and secrecy of communications can be suspended for persons accused of terrorism (*see* paragraph 445).

360. The ECHR also permits the exceptional restriction of rights in situations of crisis (Article 15) so that, ordinarily, the legislator can limit certain rights. Thus, Articles 8 (privacy), 9 (freedom of thought), 10 (freedom of expression), and 11 (freedom of peaceful assembly) admit – with slight changes in wording legislative restrictions of these rights 'that are necessary in a democratic society in the interests of national security or public safety, for the prevention of disorder or crime, for the protection of health or morals, or for the protection of the rights and freedoms of others' (Article 11). The ECtHR has drawn up a precise jurisprudence on these restrictions of rights in which it details these three requisites of legislative predetermination, the aim specified in the Convention, and the necessity in a democratic society. Due to its uncertainty, the latter is the most relevant since the Court controls it through the 'test of proportionality', which the Spanish Constitutional Court has followed to a great extent. For example, the prohibition of strikes by Spanish police officers established by Organic Law 2/1986 on Security Forces and Bodies meets these three requirements because: first, it is a mandate established in law; second, its purpose is to guarantee public safety; third, it is a restriction that, by affecting only the armed bodies and not all civil servants, 'does not go beyond what is necessary in a democratic society' (JECtHR 21 April 2015, case *Junta Rectora del Ertzainen Nazional Elkartasuna v. Spain*).

361. Although neither the ECHR nor the Spanish Constitution has a general clause restricting fundamental rights, as other Declarations do,[47] there is a jurisprudential tendency to admit this type of legal restriction to all fundamental rights, considering that certain limits are implicit in the Constitution to which the legislator can give specific expression. The complex and nuanced jurisprudence of the Constitutional Court in this matter can be summarized telegraphically as follows:

(a) Fundamental rights can only yield to the limits that the Constitution itself expressly imposes when defining each right or to those that are indirectly

47. For example, the 1982 Canadian Charter: 'The Canadian Charter of Rights and Freedoms guarantees the rights and freedoms set out in it subject only to such reasonable limits prescribed by law as can be demonstrably justified in a free and democratic society.'

'inferred by being justified by the need to preserve other rights' (STC 18/1999, 22 February, case Unconditional imprisonment without informing of the reasons).

(b) These limitations must be established in the laws (formal requirement), which must regulate them in a clear and foreseeable manner (material requirement) because if the wording of the law generates indeterminacy as to the cases in which it should be applied, then 'it no longer fulfils its function of guaranteeing the fundamental right that it restricts, as it simply leaves it to the will of the person who has to apply it' (STC 76/2019, 22 May, case *Article 58bis of the LOREG*).

(c) When a public authority has to adopt a measure restricting a fundamental right that is provided for in law, it must take into account that it cannot obstruct the right beyond what is reasonable 'so that any act or resolution limiting fundamental rights must ensure that the limiting measures are necessary to achieve the end pursued and must take into account the proportionality between the sacrifice of the right and the situation of the person on whom it is imposed and, in any case, respecting its essential content' (STC 120/1990, of 27 June, case Huelga de hambre preso de Grupo). Thus, and as we shall see when studying privacy, a police body search contemplated in legislation (LECrim, LOPSC and Leo Organic General Penitentiary) is a restriction that, if carried out by the police without any grounds, would be an excessive intrusion into privacy. Yet, at the same time, in certain justified cases, it would be entirely constitutional.

§4. The Interpretation of Fundamental Rights

362. We have already seen that the objective dimension of fundamental rights establishes them as structural elements of the legal system (*see* paragraph 338). Therefore, the interpretation of this system is now added here, including the regulation of the rights. This must be done in such a way as to permit citizens to exercise them; in particular, when various interpretations of a legal text are possible, the one which is 'most favourable to the widest meaning of the fundamental right' (STC 153/2003, 17 July 2003, case *Candidatura Independientes de Pontedeva*) must be chosen. The reverse of this rule is the restrictive interpretation of the norms that limit fundamental rights, which in case of doubt, must be resolved by applying the rule *in dubio pro libertate* (STC 98/2002, 29 April, case *Marquina Lorenzo*). In this way, if the judge is not clear which rule should apply in a particular case, that rule requires the 'election and application of that which is the least restrictive of freedom' (STC 217/2015, 22 October, case *Rodríguez Rivera*, in which the Court rejected that the provisional prison extension of LECrim can be applied to a person with mental problems in preference to the precautionary internment of the LEC).

363. Article 10.2 of the Constitution orders that the norms relative to basic rights recognized in it 'shall be interpreted in conformity with the UDHR and the international treaties and agreements on those matters ratified by Spain'. The Constitutional Court has ruled that the rights recognized in those treaties but not in the

Spanish Constitution shall, in that way, acquire the character of Spanish fundamental rights. These rights are incorporated in our legal system under the plan of legality under Article 96 of the Constitution. Therefore, human rights treaties are not an autonomous canon of constitutionality but rather play a complementary role to the constitutional text; they are 'an interpretative source that contributes to the better identification of the content of the rights but without being able to claim that a relevant legal precept automatically infringes Constitutional Article 10.2 SC' (STC 80/2010, 26 October, case *Article 153.1 CP*). Hence, the most important practical effect of Article 10.2 is in the frequent use made of the jurisprudence of the ECHR, both by the Constitutional Court and by the other constitutional interpreters when settling the content of constitutional rights, although, in view of what is happening in the other European States, it is most probable that European jurisprudence would have played a very similar part in Spain even if Article 10.2 SC did not exist.

Organic Law, 1/2008, 30 July, authorizing the ratification of the Lisbon Treaty laid down in its second article that the constitutional norms shall also be interpreted in accordance with the Charter of Fundamental Rights. Leaving, for now, on one side, the doubtful constitutionality of including an article whose only purpose is to interpret the Constitution (*see* paragraph 60) in a formal law; the truth is that the Constitutional Court has been citing it since 2000, even while warning of its normative defect. After it entered into force in December 2009, the Constitutional Court incorporated it as a further instrument of interpretation of fundamental rights.[48]

48. The first judgment of the Constitution Court citing the ECFR is 292/2000, 30 Nov. 2000, case *LOPD*. Other judgments are 53/2002, 27 February, case *Modificación de la Ley de Asilo*, 163/2009, 29 June, case *Régimen de visitas paternas* and (already with the Charter in force) STC 41/2013, 14 February, case *Ley 40/2007 de medidas en materia de Seguridad Social*.

Chapter 3. The Principle of Equality

§1. Aims of the Principle of Equality

364. The principle of equality was one of the great engines of the French Revolution and the other European liberal movements against the *Ancién Regime*, laden with privileges for the Estates of the Nobles and the Clergy. Hence, in Article 1 of the 1789 French Declaration of the Rights of Man and the Citizen, it was proclaimed that 'Men are born free and equal under the law. Social distinctions can only be founded on common utility' and Article 6 ordered that the law 'must be the same for all, whether it protects or punishes'. These provisions and many other similar ones of the founding norms of the liberal States (e.g., Article 248 of the Cadiz Constitution that established the unity of laws 'for every class of persons') had the clear objective of putting an end to legally guaranteed privileges, which had gone so far as to create distinct legal systems for each Estate. Almost 200 years later, in 1978, and still maintaining the same will to achieve a more just society, the perspective of the Spanish Constituent Assembly was completely different because now there were no generally privileged Estates, although certain groups (the military, the clergy) enjoyed some sectorial privileges in specific matters. However, what did exist, the legacy of Franco's regime, were many situations of legal and social discrimination. To combat these, the Constitution in Article 1 established a 'social and democratic state of law' and proclaimed equality as one of the superior values of its legal order. Article 9 gave the public powers the task of promoting the conditions in which liberty and equality of the individual and the groups he joins be real and effective.

365. If in a liberal state, the function of equality before the law was to put an end to every type of privilege of the dominant Estates, in the social State, it is conceived of to prevent discrimination. Thus, in Article 14 of the SC, it affirms that 'Spaniards are equal before the law, without any discrimination for reasons of birth, race, sex, religion, opinion, or any other personal or social condition or circumstance.' The constituent assembly was not satisfied in setting out this solemn declaration as the first article of the chapter devoted to 'Rights and Freedoms' and returned to it to include references to equality in the regulation of different rights. Perhaps, technically, it is a little superfluous, but at the time it was approved, it was very necessary since it demonstrated the will to prevent legally tangible discrimination, so well-known to the Spaniards of the 1970s. Thus, the Constitution bestowed the right to accede, in conditions of equality to public functions and positions (Article 23.2), equality and progressive taxation of the tax system (Article 31), legal equality in marriage (Article 32), the prohibition of discrimination in employment for reasons of sex (Article 35), and the responsibility of parents for their children, whether born in or out of wedlock (Article 39.3).

§2. The Principle of Equality as a Mandate of the Public Powers

I. Equality in Law

366. The equality value of Article 1 of the Constitution is developed in Article 14 in such a way that it is a limit on the state's normative power since both the laws and the regulations forbid different treatment of persons in the same situation but do not forbid different treatment for persons who are in different situations. The application of the principle of equality in the legislative sphere in the liberal State leads to the law being a general and abstract norm directed to all citizens. In the social State, the norm does not lose this characteristic of binding everyone but does allow that, in certain situations, norms with a specific addressee can be passed, those known as 'made-to-measure laws' or 'unique case' laws (*see* paragraph 63) because the constitutional function of the public powers is to promote real equality, removing 'those obstacles that impede or make difficult their full implementation' (Article 9). This requires these powers to take into legal account social differences and to regulate them distinctly so as to seek real equality. This enables them to carry out positive discrimination policies for disadvantaged groups. Of course, for this, there must be a substantial difference so that the legislator cannot give legal importance to circumstances that are either expressly forbidden in the Constitution itself or are 'artificial or arbitrary distinctions between situations whose real differences, in fact, if they exist at all, lack relevance from the point of view of the *raison d'être* discernible in the norm' (STC 83/1984, 24 July, case *Ley de Bases de la Sanidad Nacional*). Of the many laws designed to achieve this aim, it seems to me worth mentioning three that have been specially approved to achieve equality between men and women: Law 33/2006, 30 October, on equality between women and men on the order of succession of titles of the nobility; Organic Law 3/2007, 22 March, for the effective equality of women and men, some of whose provisions are dealt with when studying the institutions affected by this principle (elections, government, etc.) and Royal Decree-Law 6/2019, 1 March, on urgent measures to guarantee equal treatment and opportunities between women and men in employment and occupation. About such a historically forgotten group as people with disabilities, protected by Article 49 of the Constitution, it is worth recalling Royal Legislative Decree 1/2013, 29 November, approving the Consolidated Text of the General Law on the Rights of Persons with Disabilities and their Social Inclusion.

This policy of positive action in favour of disadvantaged groups does not allow the public authorities to specify any collective and carry out for it any policy they deem appropriate. To begin with, they must start from a substantial difference, without the legislator being able to give legal transcendence to circumstances that are either expressly prohibited in the Constitution itself or that are 'artificial or arbitrary distinctions between factual situations whose real differences, if they exist, lack relevance from the point of view of the reason for being discernible in the standard' (STC 83/1984, 24 July, case *Ley de Bases de la Sanidad Nacional*).

367. To distinguish an arbitrary normative difference, prohibited by the Constitution, from one which is admissible, the Constitutional Court holds a *trial of equality* employing various criteria that can be summed up in three steps: that there is an objective and justifiable reason to introduce, directly or indirectly, a difference of treatment amongst persons; that the regulation adopted is proportional; and that the means adopted are suitable to achieve the ends desired. Applying these criteria, the Constitutional Court has held – amongst other assumptions – that the following norms were not discriminatory: a State Decree granting an unemployment subsidy for agricultural workers in Andalusia and Extremadura (STC 90/1989, 11 May), a law of expropriation of the Grupo Rumasa (STC 6/1991, 15 January), a law on pensions for Republican disabled and ex-combatants (STC 158/1993, 6 May), 'the law on civil responsibility and insurance in the circulation of motor vehicles that established different compensation for death in road traffic accidents according to whether there are one or various persons harmed or beneficiaries' (STC 105/2004, 28 June) and the Statute of Workers, which establishes a shorter period of paternity leave than maternity leave (STC 111/2018, 17 October).

On the contrary, it has held that the 1974 Law of Social Security violated the right to equality in establishing a more favourable system of pensions for widows (STC 103/1983, 22 November), as well as another giving pensions exclusively to daughters and sisters which, far from being a positive action, had the effect of reinforcing the historical discrimination against women (STC 3/1993, 14 January); the Law on military service for the volunteers in Morocco of 1932 that demanded good conduct from these soldiers if they were to have the right to a pension, a requirement that did not correspond to any constitutional aim to establish this difference for other soldiers (STC 114/1987, 6 July); the 1978 law on income tax that established the accumulation of spouses' incomes in order to establish an unreasonable differentiation with single people with identical incomes (STC 45/1989 20 February); the Third Additional Provision to Law 40/2007, 4 December, of measures in matters of Social Security that ordered that the widow's pension could only be received if the deceased and the beneficiary had had children in common (STC 41/2013, 14 February), etc.

II. Equality Before the Law

368. The equality of all citizens before the law obliges the public powers to apply the norms uniformly for all those in the same situation, where there is no difference between the persons concerned or in the circumstances not specified in the law. The unequal application of the norms by the public administrations can be appealed and indemnified before the courts. While the principle of hierarchy compels all the organs of each administration with its own legal personality to apply a norm with the same criteria, in the sphere of Judicial power, the principle of independence of the courts limits this uniform application to each jurisdictional organ. However, this principle of equality does not mean that a judge or court is bound by its precedents but only that it cannot depart from them without reason. As the Constitutional Court has said, equality before the law is not violated only because a jurisdictional organ dictates a resolution different from a previous one but also necessary is the 'absence of any motivation that justifies in general terms the change of criterion, whether it is to separate it from a previous and consolidated doctrinal line, whether it breaks with an immediate antecedent in time and exactly the same' (STC

13/2011, 28 February, case *Torregrosa*). Amongst those reasons that allow the change of criteria, the Constitutional Court itself has cited that the social reality in which the rules have been applied has changed (Article 3.1 CC) and that 'it is considered necessary to correct erroneous interpretations of precedents'.[49]

§3. THE RIGHT TO EQUALITY

369. The right to equality is differentiated from the other fundamental rights in that it is not an autonomous subjective right with its own content, but rather it is a connected, comparative, or 'relational' right since its content is always established with regard to specific legal relationships. For this reason, it can be the subject of appeal 'to the extent that the question is whether the right has been breached in a specific legal relationship and, on the contrary, it cannot be the subject of a regulation or general normative development' (STC 76/1983, case *LOAPA*).

This comparative character has important consequences for the efficacy of the right of equality; this element of comparison is vital since the claimant who alleges such a violation must show it at the beginning, the *tertius comparationis;* it must be appropriate, and it cannot be based on similar conduct which was illegal and had no legal repercussions since – in the powerful formula of the Constitutional Court – 'a right to equality in illegality' does not exist, nor are generic references to former cases adequate. To enable the person or body dealing with the matter to hold 'the hearing of equality and to reason about the possible violation of the right to equality a sufficient term of comparison must be adduced, without which such operation cannot be carried out' (STC 262/1993, 20 July, case *Mutua General de Seguros*). However, when the petitioner shows that comparative element and indications of inequality can be deduced from it, it is then for the defendant to prove that the difference has an objective and reasonable basis, with a constitutional end and that the measure is proportional to that end (*see* paragraph 354). This disparity of criteria – contrary to the principle of legal certainty – in such similar cases in which the plaintiff is the same has even been committed by the Supreme Court, which, in five appeals lodged by the same company in the municipal expropriation of five plots of land, admitted three and rejected two. Surprisingly, the Constitutional Court did not consider this a matter of particular constitutional importance. Still, it did lead to a ruling by the ECtHR condemning Spain for violating the company's right to a fair trial, as provided for in Article 6 of the ECHR (JECtHR 14 September 2021, case *Inmovilizados y Gestiones*).

---

49. STC 200/1989, 30 November, case *Aviaco*. Thomas Hobbes has already used this idea of correcting erroneous interpretations to deny the binding force of precedents: 'Therefore all the Sentences of precedent Judges that have ever been, cannot all together make a Law contrary to natural Equity: Nor any Examples of former Judges, can warrant an unreasonable Sentence, or discharge the present Judge of the trouble of studying what is Equity (in the case he is to Judge,) from the principles of his own natural reason.' *Thomas Hobbes, Leviathan (1651)* 242 (A.P. Martinich & Brian Battiste ed by, Broadview 2011) 242.

Chapter 4. Civil and Political Rights

§1. Personal Rights

I. The Right to Life and Personal Integrity

370. Article 15 of the Spanish Constitution commences with the enumeration of the fundamental rights by declaring that 'everyone has the right to life', which is conceived in such absolute terms that it prohibits the death penalty 'except in those cases which may be established by military penal law in times of war'. This exception itself disappeared with Organic Law 11/1995, abolishing the death penalty, repealing all Articles of the Military Penal Code of 1985 that established the death penalty in times of war. In addition, Spain ratified Protocol 13 to the ECHR in 2009, which establishes the abolition of the death penalty in all circumstances. Therefore, and with good judgment, Amnesty International has called for the Constitution to be reformed on that point, but this does not seem likely considering how complicated the extraordinary reform procedure is. In any case, the new Organic Law 14/2015, 14 October, of the Military Penal Code, makes no mention whatever of the death penalty.

Although in the past Spanish public powers violated this right on many occasions, at present, the greater risk comes from private individuals, and the traditional form that the legal system takes to prevent this is by classifying in the Criminal Code as a crime unlawful conduct against the right to life: murder, manslaughter, assisting suicide, etc. The Spanish State has reacted to the new possibilities of acting against human life offered by scientific advances by punishing genetic manipulation (Articles 159–162 Criminal Code) and by ratifying various international Conventions, such as the European Convention for the Protection of Human Rights and the Dignity of the Human Being in the Applications of Biology and Medicine of 4 April 1997 and its Additional Protocol of 12 January 1998, under which the cloning of human beings was prohibited. Article 3.2 of the ECFR expressly stipulates that physical integrity implies that practices that – amongst others – seek selection of persons, traffic of human organs and cloning of human beings are prohibited.

It is precisely in the classification as crimes of some of these alleged attacks on life that legal controversies on the extent of Article 15 of the Constitution have arisen, such as the criminalization of abortion and active euthanasia. The former was completely prohibited during Franco's regime, but in 1985 it was decriminalized in three circumstances: when the foetus was gravely defective (eugenic abortion), when there was a serious risk to the mother's life (therapeutic), and when the pregnancy was the result of rape (criminological). The Constitutional Court, in determining a preliminary appeal of unconstitutionality brought by the PP in 1985, held that 'everyone', with which Article 15 begins, does not include a foetus or the future issue of a marriage since it is not a person and only persons are holders of fundamental rights (*see* paragraph 346). This, however, did not prevent it from being a legal good which should be protected, even by the criminal law, although the three cases of decriminalization were constitutional on finding the reasons for them were justified (STC 53/1985, 11 April, case *Despenalización del Aborto*).

Organic Law 2/2010, 3 March, on sexual and reproductive health and the voluntary interruption of pregnancy, changed the consideration of abortion as a crime that is not penalized in specific cases to consider it a woman's right to terminate her pregnancy within the first fourteen weeks of gestation, for which only two requirements must be met: (a) the pregnant woman must be given information on rights and public benefits to support motherhood, and (b) three days must be allowed from the time the information was given until the intervention is carried out. This system of time limits with informed consent is in force in most EU states and is recommended by Resolution 607/2008 of 16 April 2008 of the Parliamentary Assembly of the Council of Europe. Even beyond the fourteen-week time limit, the Organic Law admits that abortions can be carried out for four medical reasons (such as grave risk to the health of the pregnant woman) and only criminalizes abortion in extraordinary cases (new wording of Articles 145 and 145*bis* of the Criminal Code). Both PP and the government of Navarra appealed this law, finding much support in STC 53/1985 for their objections. Surprisingly, PP did not change the law after its electoral victory in November 2011, and neither did it withdraw its appeal that was waiting to be decided in the Constitutional Court. Undoubtedly the judgment of the Constitutional Court will not be unanimous and will be very controversial, as happened in 1985. This can be seen in the decision of the Constitutional Court 90/2010 of 14 July, in which the Court refused to provisionally suspend several articles in this Organic Law 2/2010 by seven votes to four.

371. At the other extreme, the end of life, the constitutional problems that have arisen have turned on the possibility of voluntarily terminating one's own life. The Constitutional Court has considered that Article 15 does not have a negative aspect which includes a hypothetical right to one's own death; therefore, although personal freedom means that a person who puts an end to her/his own life will not be penalized, there is no right to demand that the authorities shall collaborate in this end; what is more, in the extreme case of a prisoner on hunger strike who loses consciousness the General Penitentiary Law establishes the obligation on the administration to force-feed her/him, an order that is totally in agreement with the right to life and the liberty of the citizens.[50] Equally, the judicial authorization to carry out a blood transfusion to a minor against his will and that of his parents is constitutional, even though they claim their right to religious freedom (STC 154/2002, 18 July, case *Alegre Tomás*).

Our legislation does, however, recognize the right of patients, or when appropriate, their families, to refuse medical treatment when they consider it unnecessary because the situation is irreversible (Article 10 of Ley 14/1986, General de Sanidad, General Law on Health), and they can even request the disconnection of any machine keeping them alive. To facilitate this right, Law 41/2002, *de autonomía del*

50. STC 120/1990, 27 June, case *Hunger strike prisoner of Grapo*. In the same line of considering that the State has a special duty to prevent the death of persons subject to a regime of special subjection, the ECtHR has condemned Portugal for violation of the right to life because it did not take the necessary measures to prevent a person admitted in a psychiatric institution committing suicide (JECtHR 7 Mar. 2017, case *Fernandes de Oliveira*).

paciente (on the Autonomy of the Patient), established a 'National Register of Previous Instructions (Living Wills)' in which persons can register their living will. In the absence of this, the ECtHR has considered that it is enough with the statement of witnesses to corroborate the previous will of the person who is in the irreversible grave state that prevents him from expressing his opinion (JECtHR 5 June 2015, case *Lambert v. France*). For their part, some of the new Autonomous Statutes have come to recognize 'the right to receive adequate pain treatment and integral palliative care and the right to die in dignity' (Article 20 EAC, Article 25 EAA, etc.) This right is totally constitutional, provided that it is given the same scope as Article 15 of the Constitution 'without it necessarily implying the right to assisted suicide or euthanasia' (STC 31/2010, 26 July, case *Reforma del Estatuto de Autonomía para Cataluña).* The Andalusian parliament was the first to develop the mandate of its Statute with its Law 2/2010, 8 April, on Rights and Guarantees of the Dignity of Persons in Process of Dying, and after it, other parliaments have passed similar laws: Canary Law 1/2015, 9 February, on rights and guarantees of the dignity of the person before the final process of his life; Basque Law 11/2016, 8 July, of guarantee of the rights and dignity of people in the final process of their lives; Navarre Law 4/2017, 9 March on Rights and Guarantees of Persons in the Process of Dying, etc.

Historically, Spanish legislation did not allow a third party to administer substances to a patient to end their life, nor any other form of active euthanasia, which was always punishable as cooperation with suicide, although with a lesser penalty if the express request of an incurable patient with severe suffering was on record (Article 143.4 CP). However, Organic Law 3/2021, of 24 March, on the regulation of euthanasia changed the prohibition into a right to benefit, as it admits the right to euthanasia or assisted suicide for those who suffer a 'serious, chronic and incapacitating suffering' or 'a serious and incurable illness' and establishes a procedure for people who meet one of these requirements to 'request the benefit of assistance in dying', which is included in the standard portfolio of services of the National Health System and is financed with public resources. The holders of this right are Spaniards of legal age and foreigners legally resident in Spain or who have a certificate of census registration that 'accredits a period of residence in the Spanish territory of more than twelve months', a requirement designed to avoid 'suicide tourism', while at the same time consolidating registration in the municipal registers as a way of normalizing foreigners who do not enjoy the right of residence. The request for help must be made 'autonomously, consciously, informed' and without pressure from third parties and must be repeated at least fifteen days later. The process is reviewed by a 'Guarantee and Evaluation Commission' of the Autonomous Community, which will decide on the benefit. The Law also regulates the right to conscientious objection of health professionals who do not wish to assist applicants to die.

Organic Law 3/2021 has been one of the laws with the most votes in favour of those passed in recent years in Spain, with 198 votes in favour in Congress. However, the opposing parties, PP and Vox, considered that it violated the Constitution and filed appeals of unconstitutionality, which are currently pending before the Constitutional Court. In my opinion, if the Constitution does not guarantee a right to euthanasia, neither do I believe that it prevents a decision by the democratic legislator to establish, with due judicial control, its decriminalization as a manifestation of individual freedom and the prohibition of inhuman and degrading treatment, as is increasingly happening in some States such as Holland, Belgium, Switzerland, Oregon, etc.[51] That said, the Law may violate the Constitution on some specific points, such as the requirement to register for health professionals to exercise the right to conscientious objection.

372. Article 15 of the Constitution also guarantees the right to physical and moral integrity, prohibiting torture and inhuman and degrading treatment. All of these, distinguished *inter se* by the degree of suffering of the person on whom it is inflicted, are punished by the Criminal Code (Articles 173–176). The Constitutional Court has had to specify these concepts in various cases in relation to prison administration, starting by indicating that a punishment is not in itself degrading and only reaches that category if it causes especially intense suffering or provokes a humiliation 'that reaches a distinct and higher level than that usually entailed in the imposition of the sentence' (STC 65/1986, 22 May, case *Condena por malversación de caudales públicos*). For this reason, the aggravating factor of recidivism is completely constitutional (STC 150/1991, 14 July), as is the force-feeding of a prisoner on hunger strike (STC 120/1990, 27 June), and penitentiary punishments such as the prohibition of having a television in the cell and special communications (STC 119/1996, 8 July, case *Presos clasificados en primer grado de tratamiento*). Nor is sterilization of mental defectives, at the request of their legal guardian with previous judicial authorization, considered to be degrading treatment, and is permitted by Article 156 of the Criminal Code (STC 215/1994, 14 July, case *Esterilización deficiente*). The ECtHR has specified that a State not only violates the physical integrity of a person when one of its officials submits a prisoner to torture but also does so when it does not sufficiently investigate a complaint of this type that has a certain plausibility, especially if the police have held the complainant incommunicado because it is a 'situation of vulnerability' that forces the judges to 'a thorough and effective investigation into the alleged allegations of the plaintiff' (JECtHR 5 May 2015, case *Arratibel v. Spain*).

II. Personal Liberty

373. Liberty is – in the concise definition of the dictionary – the natural faculty of a person freely to determine her/his acts. As a fundamental right, this implies the prohibition of taking arbitrary and illegal measures 'that restrict or threaten the liberty of any person to organize his individual and social life in accordance with his convictions at any moment and place in the national territory' (STC 15/1986, 31 January, case *Arenas*). The legal regime of the right to liberty is similar to the right to live in that it is protected by sanctions in the penal law for any violations (crimes of illegal detention, kidnap, threats, and duress). However, unlike that right, the public powers can deprive citizens of this fundamental right, although only 'in those cases and in the form prescribed by law' (Article 17.1 SC).

51. In this line of admitting euthanasia in the world, one of the most spectacular pronouncements has been the Sentence 6 of February of 2015 of the Canadian Supreme Court that, unanimously, considers the penalty of assisted suicide unconstitutional: http://canlii.ca/t/gg5z4.

A. Detention

374. The first form of deprivation of liberty set out in the Constitution itself is 'preventive arrest', normally carried out by the police – and exceptionally by private individuals – for the time strictly necessary for the investigation into the alleged crimes, within a maximum period of seventy-two hours, which can be extended a further three times in cases of terrorism. At the end of that time, 'the person detained must be freed or placed at the disposition of the judicial authority' (Article 17.2 SC). In addition to this government detention, judges can also order arrests. In this judicial detention, the deadline for the judge to issue a new order ordering the release or provisional detention is also seventy-two hours because this is what is prescribed in Article 497 of the LECrim. This develops Article 17.1 of the Constitution and not 17.2, designed only for government detention. Logically, those seventy-two hours of deprivation of liberty must begin to be computed from when the person is arrested by the police and not – as in an interpretation against defendants maintained by some judges – from the moment in which the police take the detainee before the judge (STC 179/2011, 21 November, case *Tomás Olivo*). As well as the purpose and maximum duration of the governmental and judicial detention, Article 17 of the Constitution enumerates other guarantees for persons detained:

(a) To be informed immediately, and in a way that is understandable to him, of his rights and the reason for his arrest.
(b) Not to be forced to make a statement.
(c) To be accompanied by a defence lawyer during police and judicial proceedings. In general, persons detained have the right to appoint their own lawyer, except where the prisoner is held incommunicado, where the lawyer will be appointed by the College of Lawyers ('de oficio' or duty lawyer, Article 527 LECrim). The Constitutional Court has specified that this right to defence is violated if the police do not provide the lawyer with the 'atestado policial' (police report, document explaining how a crime took place and the detention of the suspect), a widespread practice in Spanish police stations (STC 21/2018, 5 March, case *Atestado policial*).
(d) To have the right for the legality of his arrest determined by a judge through the rapid procedure regulated by the Organic Law 6/1984 of habeas corpus. Through this procedure – whose roots go back to the English Magna Charta of 1215 and the Fuero (law) of Aragon of 1428 – any person who finds herself/himself detained can apply immediately (either he/she himself/herself, her/his family or the Public prosecutor and the ombudsman) to be brought before the judge to review the legality of her/his detention. It should be noted that it is not her/his innocence or guilt that is judged but simply to decide if the legal grounds for keeping her/him in custody are satisfied. They are not satisfied, for example, if a person is detained for painting on a wall and is accused of a misdemeanour (which does not carry a prison sentence), or he/she is not informed of the reasons for her/his arrest, or the maximum period of detention is exceeded, etc.

(STC 29/2006, 30 January, case *Detenido acusado de una falta).* The Constitutional Court has held that a judge who limits herself/himself to simply rejecting the appeal *ad limine* but without studying the reasons alleged by the appellant is herself/himself violating the liberty of the person detained (STC 172/2008, 18 December, case *Internos del Centro El Matorral de Fuerteventura).*

B. Provisional Custody

375. The principle of the presumption of innocence implies the general rule that no one can be held in prison until a court has established guilt. However, the Constitution permits provisional imprisonment remitting its regulation to law to fix the maximum period (Article 17.4). The democratic legislature has modified Articles 503 and 504 of the Law on Criminal Procedure no less than five times, the last by Organic Law 13/2015, 5 October, to adopt the demands that the Constitutional Court has imposed to ensure that this institution respects the rights of liberty and the presumption of innocence. Thus, provisional imprisonment can only be an exceptional and proportional measure adopted by the judge at the request of the prosecutor or the accusing parties and after there has been a hearing. This request will only be granted to avoid any of the following risks: that the accused will not present herself/himself for trial, that evidence can be hidden or destroyed; or that there is a real risk of the accused re-offending. In short, its duration will be only for the 'indispensable time' to meet these aims with maximum time limits according to the length of penalty for the crime of which he is accused (STC 47/2000, 17 February, case *Castillo Lomas*). Very foresightedly, the Organic Law of the Judiciary regulated the possibility of financially compensating acquitted defendants who had been 'harmed' by having been held in provisional ('preventive', prefers Article 294 of the LOPJ, departing from the expression of Article 17.4 CE) imprisonment. However, it did so by limiting compensation to those who had been declared innocent 'due to the non-existence of the act charged', which implied a difference between innocent people depending on the reason for their acquittal, reasoning incompatible with the equality of citizens and the right to the presumption of innocence, which led the Constitutional Court to declare this clause unconstitutional, adding that this did not imply an unconditional right to compensation for all those acquitted who had suffered pretrial detention, but that the prejudices should be verified in each 'specific case' (STC 85/2019, 19 June, case *Compensacion por prisión preventiva*).

C. Penalty: The Right to Penal Legality

376. The normal way in which a state deprives its citizens of liberty and other fundamental rights is by a sentence passed in a trial in which the accused's guilt is proven according to law. The Spanish Constitution elevates this rule – traditionally considered a principle of the legal system – to the category of a fundamental right, including not only punishments but also administrative sanctions: 'No one may be convicted or sentenced for actions or omissions which when committed did not constitute a crime, misdemeanour or administrative infringement, established by legislation in force at that moment' (Article 25 SC). In constitutional jurisprudence, this right is given concrete form through various guarantees, which with the traditional Latin expressions, are as follows:

(a) *Lex scripta*: The law is the only source of a system of punishment, distinguishing between Organic Law for the regulation of crimes and misdemeanours and the ordinary law (including the autonomous and other norms with the force of law) for administrative breaches and their sanctions.
(b) *Lex certa*: The law must stipulate with precision and certainty the presuppositions and the consequences of specific conduct so that open, vague, and imprecisely formulated laws are not admissible. This requirement of certainty prevents the courts from using analogy and interpretation that weigh against the accused, as can be done in other sectors of the legal system.
(c) *Lex previa*: The law that permits punishment of conduct must precede that conduct; this is a specific example of the general principle of the non-retroactivity of 'punitive provisions which are most favourable to, or which restrict individual rights' (Article 9.3 SC). According to the Constitutional Court, retroactivity *in bonam partem* is included in this Article 9 and not in Article 25, because it is not a fundamental right that can be sued directly to the court.
(d) *Non bis in idem*: The same facts cannot be the subject of two convictions nor of a criminal conviction and an administrative sanction.

III. Privacy

A. *Rights to Honour, Privacy and Identity*

377. In the country of Don Quijote, the Mayor of Zalamea, and so many other literary characters obsessed with their honour, it was inevitable that the Constitution would devote a group of rights to protecting private and family life (Article 18), although they are not commonly found in Constitutions in comparative law and are absent from the ECHR.[52] Equally inevitable were the great jurisdictional disputes that they have originated, giving rise to a casuistic jurisprudence so that the person or body deciding the matter has to make a fine judgment between the right to honour and the right to information or the freedom of speech.

The Constitutional Court has avoided abstract definitions of honour beyond understanding it as fame, social reputation, and good name, which both natural persons – even after death (Article 6.1 of LO 1/1982 and STC 51/2008, 14 April) – and

52. Article 8 ECHR, which bears the title 'Right to Respect for Private and Family Life', is limited to stating that 'Everyone has the right to respect for his private and family life, his home and his correspondence'. For its part, Art. 12 of the UDHR does make express reference to honour but does not put it as a principle, as does Art. 18.1 SC: 'The right of honour, personal and family privacy and identity is guaranteed', and in the other sub articles, home, family, correspondence, honour and privacy are also guaranteed.

private legal entities have, but not public ones (STC 139/1995, 26 September). On the contrary, it has been considered that it is necessary to analyse each specific case in which its violation is discussed, starting from the norms protecting this right (basically the Criminal Code and Organic Law 1/1982, *de protección civil del derecho al honor, a la intimidad familiar y a la propia imagen*; on civil protection of the right to honour family privacy and personal identity) to the ideas and values prevailing in society at any given moment. The right to privacy is only breached if, after careful analysis, the conclusion is reached that the defendant has sought to bring the complainant into disrepute in consideration of third parties 'as a consequence of expressions uttered in contempt, or to the discredit of someone, or were held by public opinion to be insulting' (STC 223/1992, 14 December, case *Moner Codina*).

378. The right to personal and family privacy, which according to the Constitutional Court is directly connected to human dignity, is the right to maintain one's personal life protected from the curiosity of others; it is the right – to put it bluntly – to be left in peace, not to be interfered with. For this reason, any illegal interference in the private sphere is a violation of this right without requiring malice on the part of the defendant. However, the State can affect privacy without violating it when there is some other constitutional aim that justifies it. So, for example, the just distribution of the maintenance of public expenditure justifies the investigation of a private individual's bank accounts (STC 110/1984, 26 November, case *Garrido Falla*) and social interest and public order justify the investigation of paternity (STC 95/1999, 31 May, case *Prueba biológica de paternidad*). On the other hand, forcing a prisoner to submit to a strip search before and after an intimate relationship with a visitor from outside without any valid reason is a violation of this right (STC 57/1994, 28 February, case *Cacheo integral preso Nanclares de Oca*).

379. Image rights are the expression of a personality in the public domain. So, they protect persons from the diffusion without their consent of pictures showing their physical appearance since this constitutes their 'first shaping element of privacy and the basic element of the external projection and essential for their very recognition as an individual' (STC 81/2001, 26 March, case *Emilio Aragón*). However, images can be diffused without the consent of the persons shown in them when the circumstances in which they were taken – public acts and places – justify the limitation of the right to protection of identity in favour of the right to information of the rest of the citizens. But, what a means of communication cannot do is reproduce a photograph from a social network without the owner's consent, not even to illustrate news protected by the right to information and even though it is a public profile accessible by anyone, because the person who voluntarily uploads his photographs to the Internet is not granting any implicit right to others to use them without his permission (STS (1) 91/2017, 15 February and STC 27/2020, 24 February). On the other hand, in this time of audiovisual media, the image can be exploited economically, as shown by the multimillion contracts that famous people make (rights of image). This financial aspect/property right is not covered by the fundamental right, as it is a civil contract protected by ordinary legal proceedings and not by way of appeal to the Constitutional Court (STC 231/1988, 2 December, case *Pantoja-Paquirri*).

380. Until now, we have dealt rather superficially with what may be called the general theory of the rights to honour, privacy, and identity; we must now go into the matter a little deeper, referring to a special category of persons in which these three rights have a more limited scope than for the general public: public persons, understanding by that phrase not only persons who have institutional positions but also those who make their professional activity from the public use of their image. As compared with private individuals, public ones have more restricted rights because of the public's right to information. The Constitutional Court has developed – inspired by the ECHR – a broad theory on the respective weight to be given to both rights, which can be summed up telegraphically in the idea that there is no illegitimate interference in the privacy of a public person when the information refers to conducts linked to their public activity or can influence it; the facts published must be true, and no offensive expressions should be used in the journalistic style, which does not bear the 'least relation to the formation of a free public opinion', nor does the Constitution guarantee a hypothetical 'right to insult' (STC 105/1990, 6 June 1990, case *José María García*). Equally, there is no public interest or social criticism in publishing a manipulated photograph of the face of an artist on a semi-naked body; on the contrary, it was deemed to be a violation of the person's image since the intention of the review was merely to 'mock, with a markedly sexist slant, her persona, exclusively her physical appearance and so obtain a financial benefit' (STC 23/2010, 27 April 2010, case *Fotomontaje de Isabel Iglesias).*

381. Now, within the class of public figures, we can still say that politicians are a special category whose rights to honour, privacy, and self-image are rather more limited than the rest of the population because in weighing judgment between those rights and freedoms of opinion, the judge must take into account that they have a preferential position when dealing with matters of public interest because the freedoms of information and opinion are essential to achieving a free public opinion (*see* paragraph 393). Therefore, the Constitutional Court has considered that a series of insults broadcast in a radio programme against some politicians and their party (saying 'terrorist', 'Roviretxe', 'ERC is always violent, always making coups', etc.) are 'protected by the freedom of expression, inasmuch as they are framed in a clearly public debate and of notorious interest, were uttered by a journalist and referred to the activity of political leaders as such, which extends the limits of permissible criticism' (STC 79/2014, 29 May, case *Puigcercós y Carod-Rovira v. Jiménez Losantos*). However, our courts have not always been able to protect freedom of criticism correctly; for example, this same journalist Jiménez Losantos was sentenced to pay a fine of EUR 36,000 for insulting the mayor of Madrid by calling him 'a complete traitor to the substance and the forms of your party', 'you are a nuisance, you are a calamity', etc. As the Constitutional Court did not accept his appeal, he turned to Strasbourg, which ruled that Spain had violated the journalist's freedom of expression because this also includes the possible use of 'a certain amount of exaggeration, indeed, of provocation' (JECtHR 14 June 2016).

B. *Rights Instrumental in the Protection of Privacy: The Inviolability of the Home and Secrecy of Communications*

382. Article 18.2 SC prohibits entry into the home without the consent of the owner, legal authority or in case of *flagrante delicto*. To these three cases in which there is no violation of this right must be added force majeure (fire, flood, etc.) as set out in the Criminal Code.

The inviolability of the home is designed as an instrument of protection for personal privacy so that it protects not only the legal domicile but also any physical space in which a person can develop his private life without submission to social uses: a holiday home, a hotel room, a cabin, even a room in a military barracks (STC 189/2004, 2 November, case *Barrios Espinosa*). For this reason, the Constitutional Court declared Article 557 of LECrim unconstitutional, as it did not treat hotels as the domicile of persons who 'were there or lived there accidentally or temporally' (STC 10/2002, 17 of January, case *Article 557 LECrim*). In the other direction, places open to the public – bars, offices, etc. – are not protected by this fundamental right.

Although the traditional way of breaching this inviolability was through physical entrance, at the present time, the Constitutional Court has held that penetrating the home by technical means (such as electronic listening devices) is also an infringement. Following the ECHR, it has even held that acoustic pollution violates the right to private life and the enjoyment of the home (STC 119/2001, 24 May, case *Moreno Gómez*[53]).

It should be clear that judicial decisions authorizing entry are not only issued – as we tend to think intuitively – by criminal investigating judges in search of persons or evidence as permitted by the LECrim. It is also possible for entry orders to be issued by other judges to protect other legal assets. These are the cases envisaged in ordinary legislation:

(1) Criminal: the investigating judge may order entry into a home when 'there are indications that there could be the defendant or effects or instruments of the crime, or books, papers or other objects that may serve for their discovery and verification' (Article 545 LECrim).
(2) Civil: the civil judge may order entry into a home to execute a judicial decision in two cases. The first is when the house must be handed over to its owner and is occupied by another person, a provision used in eviction cases (Article 704 LEC). The second case is the entry for enforcing measures to protect minors (Article 778).
(3) Contentious-administrative: the contentious judge can order entry into the home to comply with administrative resolutions; for example, if urgent repair

53. However, the plenary of the Constitutional Court (with two dissenting opinions) did not grant relief in this particular case since it considered that the appellant must have 'understood the level of noise within her dwelling'. Ms Moreno Gómez applied to the ECtHR which considered 'that it would be unduly formalistic to require such evidence in the instant case, as the City authorities have already designated the area in which the applicant lives an acoustically saturated zone' and 'the fact that the maximum permitted noise levels have been exceeded has been confirmed on a number of occasions by council staff' (JECtHR 16 Nov. 2004).

work must be carried out on a building or the demolition of an illegal construction site and the resident refuses to facilitate entry (Article 100.3 LPACAP). Likewise, the General Tax Law empowers these contentious judges to allow tax inspectors to enter the homes of 'taxpayers'.

However, in all these cases, the judge may only authorize entry 'after weighing up the different rights and interests that may be affected and adopting the necessary precautions to ensure that the limitation of the fundamental right involved is carried out in the least restrictive way possible' (STC 139/2004, 13 September, case *Mora Rincón*).

383. Secrecy of communications protects physical and legal persons, both from the interception of messages (the misappropriation of others' letters) as the knowledge of their contents (simply reading them) since it is a formal right, protecting communications independently of content, which can only be lifted with judicial authorization or by consent of any of the parties to the communication. Not even when one of the parties reveals its content against the will of the others is this right violated, since to force someone to keep it secret then would be contradictory 'to the very possibility of the processes of free human communication' (STC 56/2003, 24 March, case *Almedia Cardoso*). It also protects the identity of the communicants themselves, which cannot be obtained even indirectly by knowing the telephone numbers to which they have called, information that the telephone companies can only give to the police under judicial order (STC 123/2002, 20 May, case *Jiménez Escobedo*). However, the fact that no rights are violated when someone reveals what another has communicated does not prevent privacy from being violated when a person receives an intimate image of another and then disseminates it with the intention of harming her/him. Therefore, the penalty for 'sexting' that was introduced by Organic Law 1/2015 in the Criminal Code seems completely constitutional: 'He will be punished with a prison sentence of three months to a year or a fine of six to twelve months, who without authorization from the affected person, disseminates, discloses or transfers to third parties audiovisual images or recordings of that which he obtained with his consent in a domicile or in any other place beyond the reach of the gaze of third parties when the disclosure seriously undermines the personal privacy of that affected person' (Article 197.7 CP).

384. The broad scope of Article 18.3 of the Constitution, which guarantees 'secrecy of communications, particularly postal, telephonic and telegraphic', has made it possible to extend this right to new means of communication, such as electronic mail. In its practical application, the inviolability of communications has had its greatest importance in relation to the validity of evidence in judicial trials obtained through the interception of a communication, in which Constitutional and Supreme Courts have been rigorous. Hence, in the first few years of its existence, the former held that a recording obtained in breach of secrecy of communications or, in general, of any other fundamental right, could not be used in a judicial trial

(STC 114/1984, 29 November, case *Poveda Navarro*).[54] This doctrine was reflected when in the following year, the LOPJ established in its Article 11 that 'Evidence obtained, directly or indirectly, in breach of fundamental rights and liberties shall be of no legal effect'. For its part, the Supreme Court did not admit evidence obtained by a telephone recording, judicially authorized, but to investigate a person other than the accused for a different crime (Court Order 18 June 1992 Criminal Chamber of SC, case *Naseiro*). Logically, this doctrine is applicable to new technologies, as held by the Criminal Chamber of the Supreme Court in its Judgment 51/2010, 5 February, in which it annulled the conviction that the Provincial Court of Valencia had imposed on an alleged drug trafficker to three years of prison because the Civil Guard had used as proof of the charge the messages the accused kept on his mobile phone, which the Civil Guard accessed without judicial authorization. Finally, Organic Law 13/2015, 5 October, modification of the Criminal Procedure Law for the strengthening of procedural guarantees and the regulation of technological research measures, takes into account all this jurisprudence to regulate modern interception of communications with judicial authorization: new technological research techniques are included, such as the remote search of computers, which should always aim at clarifying a specific punishable act; only the judges may authorize the police to carry out these investigations, clearly specifying both the objective and the subjective scope of the persons to whom this restriction of their right to secrecy of communications applies. The maximum period of this investigation is established as three months, subject to judicial extension, etc. (Articles 579 and 588*bis* and ss.). In addition, Law 25/2007, 18 October, on the preservation of data relating to electronic communications and public communications networks (which transposes Directive 2006/24/EC of the European Parliament and the Council) establishes two guarantees intended to respect the secrecy of communications: first, it orders that the data that companies have an obligation to keep will be the data exclusively linked to the communication, either by telephone or by Internet, but in no case revealing its content; and, second, that the cession of such data that affect a specific communication can only be made through prior judicial authorization.

C. Computer Freedom/Data Protection

385. In 1978, the computer was beginning to enter the lives of Spaniards, and the Constituents took the precaution of ordering that 'The law shall limit the use of information to guarantee personal and family honour, the privacy of citizens, and

54. In this judgment, with express citation of American case law, the theory of the American Supreme Court of 'The fruit of the poisonous tree' is applied in Spain, whereby not only evidence obtained in violation of fundamental rights cannot be assessed, but also any other evidence derived from it. However, the Constitutional Court has subsequently qualified this doctrine by admitting that, exceptionally, such derived evidence will be assessed when it 'can be considered legally independent' (SSTC 81/1998, 2 April, case *Domínguez Durán*; 171/1999, 27 September, case *Italo Nelli*, etc.). The SC has considered that evidence obtained by a private individual without judicial authorization does not automatically become prohibited evidence under Art. 11 of the LOPJ in such a way that the data collected in a Swiss bank by Hervé Falciani can be used to convict for tax crimes [STS (3) 116/2017, 23 February, confirmed by STC 97/2019, 23 February].

the full exercise of their rights' (Article 18.4). The Constitutional Court, in its settled jurisprudence, has considered that the basic nucleus of computer freedom consists of the right to control the use of the data included in a computer programme (habeas data) and includes, amongst other aspects, the opposition of the citizen to certain personal data being used for purposes other than the legitimate one that justified obtaining them (STC 96/2012, 7 May, case *Cesión de ficheros del BBVA*). Organic Law 3/2018, 5 December, on the Protection of Personal Data and Guarantee of Digital Rights, complies with this constitutional mandate, in addition to complementing Regulation 2016/679 of the European Parliament and of the Council, 27 April 2016 (which is directly applicable in Spain), on the protection of natural persons concerning the processing of their data and the free movement of such data. According to the Preamble of the Organic Law, the main difference between the new data protection regulation and the old one (EU Directive 95/46 and LO 15/1999) is that it has moved from a model based on the control of compliance with the legislation to another based on the principle of active responsibility, which requires a prior assessment by the file owners of the risk that could be generated by the processing of the personal data in those files to adopt, based on this assessment, the appropriate measures. For this reason, the Organic Law now establishes a set of strict requirements for the use of data files held by both public authorities and private individuals (they may only be used for the purpose that justifies them, they are governed by the criteria of confidentiality, truthfulness, rectification, prohibition of transfer without the data subject's consent, access by the data subject to the files, etc.); moreover, it expressly prohibits files created to collect ideology, religion, beliefs and other personal characteristics. As this prohibition is a direct result of multiple constitutional rights and is binding on all persons, natural and legal, the Constitutional Court annulled – on appeal by the Ombudsman – the article of the LOREG that allowed parties to collect personal data relating to the political opinions of citizens (STC 76/2019, 22 May, case *Artículo 58 bis de la LOREG*).

In terms of citizens' rights, the Organic Law includes the various rights that guarantee our freedoms in the digital environment, such as the neutrality of the Internet network and its universal access, the right to be forgotten, freedom of expression and the right to clarify information in digital media, etc. It even recognizes the right to digital disconnection in the workplace. In addition, the Organic Law creates (or, to be exact, maintains the one already created by LO 5/1992) an independent authority to ensure compliance with its articles and protect citizens' rights, the Spanish Data Protection Agency.

IV. Freedom of Residence and Movement

386. Article 19 of the Constitution establishes the right for Spaniards of residence and movement within the national territory, so excluding aliens who, in this matter, are governed by international treaties and the Organic Law on Rights and Freedoms of Aliens, with a clear tendency to a regime equivalent to that for Spaniards (*see* paragraph 334). The same article of the Constitution specifies that Spaniards have the right to enter and leave Spain freely under the conditions established by law. This right cannot be restricted 'because of political or ideological motives'.

This is perhaps a trifle superfluous, bearing in mind the great number of articles that would be infringed by law with this aim, commencing with Article 1.1 laying down the superior values of liberty, justice, equality, and political pluralism; Article 14 forbidding discrimination on the grounds of opinion; Article 16 guaranteeing freedom of ideology; etc. Without a doubt, the constituent assembly wanted to mark a clear distance from the Franco dictatorship when entering and leaving Spain was restricted on political grounds. At present, as is appropriate to a democratic country, the only limitations apart from the purely formal (the need to identify oneself at the borders, authorization from the father or mother for minors travelling alone) are strictly legal: when a judge prohibits someone who could thereby avoid justice by leaving Spain. Furthermore, the TEU states that the Union shall offer its citizens 'an area of freedom, security and justice without internal frontiers, in which the free movement of persons is ensured' (Article 3.2). This mandate has been developed by Directive 2004/38/EC of the European Parliament and of the Council of 29 April 2004 on the right of citizens of the Union and their family members to move and reside freely within the territory of the Member States, which Royal Decree 240/2007 of 16 February 2007 has fully incorporated into Spanish legislation. Therefore, EU citizens can enter the territory of all Member States without needing a visa and live in that territory 'for a maximum period of three months without being subject to conditions or formalities'.

387. The freedom to reside and to move anywhere in Spain not only means that physical and legal Spanish persons can establish their home in any part of the Spanish territory but also implies a correlative obligation on the part of the public powers 'to not adopt measures that restrict and hinder this fundamental right' (STC 28/1999, 8 March, case *Comunidad de propietarios de Valladolid*). As for the rest, Article 139.2 expressly sets out this right, a clarification without a doubt necessary in a compound State in which, by definition, the legal position of the citizens is not exactly the same in all the Autonomous Communities. Nevertheless, freedom of residence can be limited by the public powers in several circumstances: in case of proclamation of a State of emergency (*see* paragraph 452), and in individual cases by means of a criminal sentence or order of expulsion from the house or where it is justified by general interest, such as the construction of a reservoir (STC 160/1991, 18 July, case *Embalse Riaño*) or when the law imposes on civil servants the obligation to reside in a specific municipality (STC 308/1994, 21 November 1994, case *Aprovechamiento de montes comunales*), etc.

V. The Right to Contract Matrimony

388. Following the 1931 Constitution, the first Spanish constitutional text to make reference to what until then was purely a private contract governed by the Civil Code, the 1978 Constitution declared the right of both man and woman to contract matrimony 'with full legal equality', although this constitutional right is found in Article 32, thus, making it the only personal right not included in section 1 of Chapter II, with the difference in legal regime that this implies and, in particular, the exclusion of its regulation by Organic Law and the impossibility of protecting it by means of an appeal for constitutional protection of fundamental rights (*see* paragraphs 341 et seq.). The Constitution remits its total regulation to law and stipulates that it includes 'the rights and duties of the spouses, causes for separation and dissolution and their effects'. From this, it can clearly be appreciated that the aims of the 1978 Constituent Assembly (as with those of 1931) in transforming matrimony into a right of liberty were those of guaranteeing the full equality of the spouses and the possibility of divorce, two aspects that were not present in the legislation of the Franco dictatorship. To achieve these objectives, no few normative modifications were required, beginning with the Concordat between the Spanish state and the Holy See on legal matters dated 3 January 1979, to substitute the preferential regime that until then had been given to marriage in the Roman Catholic Church, and Law 30/1981, 1 July, modifying the regulation of the causes of nullity, separation, and divorce. In spite of the concern of the democratic legislature, the Constitutional Court has had to intervene to declare other provisions contrary to Article 32, such as the suspension of a contract of employment for women workers after contracting matrimony (STC 7/1983, 14 February, case *Trabajadoras de Telefónica*) and the rule that established that where the spouses did not share a common legal system their relationship would be governed by the national law of the husband (STC 39/2002, 14 February, case *Antiguo Article 9.2 CC*), etc.

389. The new legal controversies arising from Article 32 have turned on its relationship with other forms of cohabitation. Hence, the Constitutional Court has held that this Article does not protect common-law marriages since 'marriage and cohabitation are not in all respects equivalent realities' (STC 184/1990, 15 November, case *Article 160 de la Ley General de Seguridad Social*). However, this does not mean that any legal differences whatever between marriage and cohabitation are permissible since the protection of the family (Article 39) and the general clause of equality (Article 14) prohibit normative differences that result in manifest injustice, such as in the case of tenancies, allowing only the spouse to take over the tenancy after the death of the original tenant and excluding a person who had cohabited with the late tenant in a stable relationship as if they were married (STC 222/1992, 11 December, case *Artículo 58 de la LAU*). In the opposite sense, the Law infringes Articles 14, 31, and 39 of the Constitution if it establishes a tax regime that bears more heavily on married couples than on those who are living together without contracting matrimony (STC 45/1989, 20 February, case *Tributación conjunta del IRPF*). In recent years, the social extension of unmarried couples has led the legislature to attribute specific legal effects to these couples, which must be registered in a register of unmarried couples. Thus, the Law on Urban Leases recognizes that if a renter dies, their unmarried partner can be subrogated to the rent; and the Social Security Law stipulates that the surviving partner is entitled to a pension, etc. There is no specific law in Spain for these couples, but there it is in a good number of Autonomous Communities, amongst which Catalonia stands out because it has regulated the inheritance rights of unmarried couples, equating them to the inheritance rights originated by marriage. Equally, and despite fierce opposition from the PP, the Catholic Church and other groups, Law 13/2005, 1 July, was passed, so modifying the Civil Code on the right to contract matrimony to permit marriage between persons of the same sex, which has now been put on equal footing with heterosexual marriage, including the right to adopt. The Constitutional Court considered this regulation was in accord with the Constitution (STC 198/2012, 6 November), arguing that the law made an evolving interpretation of the Constitution. For its part, the ECtHR decided in 2015 that the States parties had an obligation to legally protect the cohabitation of persons of the same sex, at least offering them the possibility of contracting a civil union, since not doing so would breach Article 8 ECHR that establishes the right to a private and family life (ECtHR 21 July 2015, case *Oliari v. Italia*).

§2. Intellectual Freedoms

I. Ideological Freedom

390. There is an old Spanish saying, 'under my cloak I kill the king' as a way of pointing out the radical freedom of thought of the human being. However, under the *Ancién Régime,* it was a liberty that came not from law but from nature since authority could not discover what was in the minds of its subjects. It was precisely to legally guarantee, to a great extent, freedom of thought that the Rule of Law was created. Article 16.1 of the 1978 Spanish Constitution sought a wider, more modern formula than the traditional freedom of thought and conscience (set out in Article 18 of UDHR), 'ideological freedom', which consists of the intellectual position that a person adopts towards life. The Constitutional Court considers it to be of such importance that without it, the other superior values of our legal system, established in Article 1.1 of the Constitution, would not be possible. This right is considered to be autonomous and broader than freedom of expression, and through it, opinions contrary to the Constitution itself can be maintained and disseminated (though not by violence), so demanding a 'restrictive interpretation of the limitations on ideological freedom and the right of expression, without which it would lack all effectiveness' (STC 20/1990, 15 February, case *Mundiales del 82 e injurias al Rey*).

To reinforce this liberty and that of religion, Article 16.2 specifies that nobody can be forced to disclose his ideology, religion, and beliefs. Logically, this stipulation must be interpreted systematically: this prohibition is not violated if a party or association demands that a proposed member accepts the ideology of the group, while it would be unconstitutional to require an ideological declaration in order to work in the administration or in a private business; equally, swearing the oath to respect the Constitution does not mean that one forswears any ideology that could be counter to it (let us say, for example, republicanism) but rather one simply swears to respect the Constitutional channels to make that ideology effective (*see* paragraph 122).

II. Religious Freedom

391. We do not have to go back to the terrible religious wars that ravaged Europe in the sixteenth century nor to the century-long wave of terror of the Inquisition in Spain to realize the enormous social benefit from admitting that religion is a private matter that must be kept apart from the State. It is enough just to look around our world as it is now. Aware of this, the Spanish Constituent Assembly established religious freedom and the secular State, although it added that the public powers must bear in mind the religious beliefs of Spanish society and maintain the consequent relationship of cooperation with the Catholic Church and other faiths (Article 16.3). This formula entailed a rupture with the Catholic faith of the Franco period and had immediate and direct consequences on the legal system, such as no longer recognizing canonical decrees of nullity of marriage, which would only have civil legality if they satisfied Spanish law (STC 1/1981, 26 January, case *Ejecución de sentencia de tribunal eclesiástico*) or with the obligatory attendance of members of the Armed Forces and security corps at religious services (STC 101/2004, 2 June, case *Procesión de Jesús el rico*).

Religious freedom, regulated by Organic Law 7/1980, 5 July, guaranteed a field of action for individuals and groups totally independent of the State and other citizens, including the right to profess no religion. In addition to this internal aspect, this liberty had an external side that permitted citizens to act in accordance with their convictions and to carry out activities evidencing their beliefs (acts of worship, religious teaching, meetings, etc.), with no other limitations than those necessary to keep the peace as protected by law. This, for example, does not mean that religious freedom protects such a dangerous and harmful practice as female genital mutilation; but it does protect an adult Jehovah's Witness who opposes a blood transfusion; it even protects parents of the same religion who refuse to convince their minor son to accept a transfusion necessary to save his life and were convicted of manslaughter by omission (STC 154/2002, 18 July, case *Alegre Tomás*).

392. The relationship of cooperation between the State and religious faiths referred to in Article 16.3 does not grant them a fundamental right but rather an obligation on the part of the state that establishes a triple legal regime for religious associations: (a) that of the Catholic Church, expressly recognized in the Constitution; (b) the faiths that for 'their scope and number of believers have become deeply rooted in Spain' (Article 7 LOLR); and (c) the other minority faiths registered in the register of religious associations. The State only has an obligation to cooperate with the Catholic Church and the deeply rooted faiths. This obligation at present it fulfils – quite generously, I think – in a series of accords, which began in 1979 with the Catholic Church, with four Accords on legal and economic matters, teaching and the attendance of the Armed Forces at religious ceremonies (modified later in 1988 and 2006). In 1992 similar cooperation accords were signed with the Protestant, Jewish, and Islamic faiths that were embodied in Laws 24, 25, and 26 of 1992. Amongst the most important aspects of these accords was the State's commitment to support religious teaching in compulsory education – to the extent that the public authorities pay the salaries of teachers of religion – who are proposed by the religious authorities. This capacity to make proposals has given rise to a good number of legal conflicts because the bishops refuse to appoint teachers who have not respected religious precepts (such as divorce) in their private life. The Constitutional Court has considered that this legal regime of freedom for religious denominations to decide the suitability of the persons in charge of imparting their creed does not violate the Constitution, although this does not mean that this religious decision cannot be controlled by 'the judicial organs and, where appropriate, this Constitutional Court, which will have to find practicable criteria to reconcile in the concrete case the requirements of religious freedom (individual and collective) and the principle of religious neutrality of the State with the jurisdictional protection of fundamental rights and of teachers' (STC 38/2007, 15 February, case *Sistema de contratación del profesado de religión católico).* The ECtHR has also considered that this legal regime is compatible with the ECHR (JECtHR 12 June 2014, case *Fernández Martínez*). In the field of financing, the State gives citizens the option of dedicating a percentage of 0.7% of their total income tax to the Catholic Church (Law 42/2006, 28 December, of General State Budgets for the year 2007), which, predictably, other confessions will be allowed in the future through a legislative change. The government refused, in 2015, to do it itself by adding a box for other confessions in the IRPF declaration model, as requested by the Federation of Evangelical Religious Entities of Spain (FEDERE), without its reasoned refusal to consider that inclusion cannot make it a regulation that can be considered a violation of Articles 14 and 16 of the Constitution (STS (3)2612/2016, 14 December). There is, of course, equality between the Catholic Church and the other three confessions that have an agreement with the State on the tax exemptions they enjoy: none pay local taxes for their buildings destined for worship or education, nor the property transfer tax for the acquisition of goods destined for worship and enjoy the other tax benefits of non-profit organizations, etc. The CJEU has ruled that these exemptions are compatible with European Law whenever they occur on goods and activities that have a strictly religious purpose but not when they are intended for economic activities because this would mean a 'competitive advantage' over companies that do pay these taxes, stating that it has this economic character of non-subsidized education, while it lacks subsidized education (Judgment of the Court of Justice of European Union (JCJEU) (Grand Chamber) 27 June 2017, case *Congregación de Escuelas Pías Provincia Betania*).

III. Freedom of Opinion

393. From Aristotle's classical definition of man as a social animal, we know that communication is a determining feature in rational life. The possibility of communicating freely is one of the essential features of the Rule of Law, so much so that the more or less hidden tyrannies that still exist in the world seek one hundred and one subterfuges to prevent the traditional 'freedom of the press'. They do it not only to eliminate a fundamental right but also to inhibit criticism of their political regime, which is the first step to dismantling it. Our Constitutional Court, in one of its first judgments, put it bluntly: without free public communication, 'the other rights established by the Constitution would be emptied of real content, representative institutions reduced to sterile formulas and the principle of democratic legitimacy set out in Article 1.2 de la Constitution made absolutely false' (STC 6/1981, 16 March, case *Medios de Comunicación Social del Estado*). For this reason, the Spanish Constitutional Court has followed in the footsteps of the US Supreme Court and of the ECtHR and held that freedom of opinion has a preferential position against other rights in so far as it contributes to the formation of free public opinion. And to achieve it is essential for opinions to be confronted, which requires admitting as part of the debate expressions that 'offend, disquiet or disturb the State or any sector of public opinion'. Therefore, to qualify the president of a democratic government as 'immoral', 'unworthy' and to use the 'vilest opportunism' in an opinion article is protected by freedom of expression (JECtHR 8 July 1986, case *Lingens v. Austria*). Moreover, ECtHR considered that Spain violated freedom of expression when the Supreme Court (with the confirmation of the Constitutional Court) sentenced a Basque independence leader to one year in prison for calling the king 'chief of the torturers' (JECtHR 15 March 2011, case *Otegi Mondragón*). In short, this freedom even protects those who deny it and attack the democratic system. It does not protect, however, those who maintain 'hate speech' because they violate equality and human dignity. The Constitutional Court defines – following the ECtHR – this speech as 'that developed in terms that suppose a direct incitement to violence against citizens in general or against certain races or beliefs in particular'. Therefore, it is not unconstitutional that our Criminal Code sanctions those who disseminate ideas that justify genocide (STC 237/2007, 8 November, case *Article 607.2 CP*).

Article 20 of the Constitution deals with freedom of communication in four aspects that we shall now examine, but not before pointing out, as laid down in Article 20.1.4, that this liberty is, on the one hand, limited by other rights, especially those of privacy (*see* paragraphs 352, 370–380) while on the other hand, it is protected by two guarantees referred specifically in Article 20: no type of prior censorship can be established (Article 20.2 SC), and the seizure of publications, recordings, and other means of information can only be determined by judicial resolution (Article 20.5 SC). This type of judicial decision has rarely occurred during the democracy; what is more, with the new means of communication, especially the Internet, it has proved, in practice, inefficient in protecting the privacy of the plaintiff. Moreover, the seizure of the publication would give added publicity that it could not have obtained otherwise. This was demonstrated in 2007 when a judge of the National High Court ordered the seizure of a humorous magazine accused of insulting the Prince of Asturias, the heir to the throne: the dissemination of the physical review could be halted but not its reproduction on hundreds of web pages. This Internet phenomenon is known as the Streisand effect because, in 2003, the actress Barbra Streisand sued a website for refusing to remove a photograph of her house. The result was that hundreds of web pages replicated the photograph, giving her a great deal of free advertising that would not have occurred if she had not filed her lawsuit.

A. *Freedom of Expression*

394. Article 20.1a of the Constitution protects the dissemination of thoughts, ideas, and opinions by whatever means (words, writings, pictures, internet, etc.). That is to say, that a person or group's particular vision of the world, the opinions of the public authorities or members of the Community, in general, can be disseminated since, logically, freedom of opinion includes the right to criticize. As befits value judgments, a direct connection between reality and the opinion expressed is not necessary, and so this right protects equally a well-documented article on global warming or a pamphlet on the imminent arrival of the Antichrist. Evidently, freedom of expression will not support the attribution to someone of actions that he/she has not committed (to do so may even be a misdemeanour of defamation) or a series of insulting opinions that violate the honour of the person criticized and do not contribute to the formation of a free public opinion (*see* paragraph 380). In a controversial decision, the plenary of the Constitutional Court considered that freedom of expression (or ideological freedom) does not protect anyone who burns, in public, photographs of the King because it is not conducted 'from which a politically articulated censorship or opposition can be inferred against the monarchy', and 'it is not only an offensive act but also an incitement to hatred, insofar as the cremation of its physical image expresses, in a way that is difficult to surpass, that they are worthy of exclusion and hatred' (STC 177/2015, 22 July, case *Quema de fotos de los reyes*). In a diametrically opposed sense, the ECtHR considered that this action was protected by freedom of expression because it could not be qualified as a hate crime and, actually, it was 'one of those provocative events which were increasingly used to attract media attention' (JECtHR 13 March 2018, case *Stern Taulats and Roura Capellera v. Spain*). With that reasoning, the ECtHR condemned Spain for restricting freedom of expression to criticize the King, similarly as it did in 2011 for the Otegi case (*see* paragraph 393).

Finally, the law may establish narrower limits to certain groups' freedom of expression, justified by protecting other constitutional rights. For example, Organic Law 9/2011, 27 July, on the rights and duties of members of the Armed Forces, recognizes that members of the military have the right to freedom of expression and to freely communicate and receive information, but adds that there may be limits for national security, prohibits them from speaking publicly about political parties and establishes that in 'matters strictly related to service in the Armed Forces, members of the military in the exercise of freedom of expression shall be subject to the limits derived from discipline' (Article 12). In practice, and to cite a specific case, this limitation on freedom of expression means that while an individual can criticize in the press the state of military equipment, say the Super Puma maritime rescue helicopters, if a lieutenant who flies them does so, he can be sanctioned by his superiors for giving opinions contrary to discipline (STS (5) 1859/2019, 6 June).

B. *Freedom of Artistic and Scientific Creation*

395. Historically, freedom of expression has protected intellectuals' and artists' freedom of creation; however, the Spanish Constituent Assembly preferred to guarantee it specifically by recognizing the right to literary, artistic, scientific, and technical production and creation in Article 20.1b. In daily practice, the courts have scarcely used this right and have almost always refused to apply it to the case in hand, as has occurred in various criminal and civil trials on intellectual property in which one of the parties has cited it in their favour or in proceedings against the public authorities' technical specifications for the making of particular products. Thus, for example, the Supreme Court has held that government regulation of the way in which the magisterial formulae of specific pharmaceutical products shall be made is not a breach of this right for 'it is one thing for pharmacists and doctors investigate medicinal substances that can be included in the formulas and preparations, which is a truly scientific creation, and something else entirely the composition of a formula that cannot be controlled so that it is fit to be dispensed to the public' (STS (3) 2455/2003, 8 April). For its part, the Constitutional Court has held that the scientific freedom of the historian as against the right to reputation of the protagonists of history and their successors offers a wider-than-usual field of action for freedom of expression and information of present-day facts; to do otherwise, given that historical research is always controversial, would prevent 'the formation of a historic conscience worthy of the dignity of the citizens of a free and democratic society' (STC 43/2004, 23 March, case *Documental 'Sumaríssim 477' de TV3*). In a similar sense, it has been considered that the honour of a deceased person is not violated if he appears as a character in a novel with negative characteristics because literary freedom 'protects the creation of a fictional universe' without it being possible to 'resort to criteria of veracity to limit a creative work'; so that in the specific case of this literary work 'the disputed fragment cannot be considered vexatious in itself' (STC 51/2008, 14 April, case *Novela 'Jardín de Villa Valeria'*).

C. Academic Freedom

396. Just as the State of Law has no official religion, neither has it an official science. But in addition to not passing judgment on the truth or otherwise of scientific theories, the best way of stimulating scientific and technical progress is to guarantee freedom of expression, specifically in the sphere in which traditionally science has flourished: in the heart of the universities. Thus, academic freedom has historically been deemed to be the freedom of university professors to develop their teaching and research without interference from public powers. With the 1978 Constitution, this liberty was extended to all educational levels, although with limited content at the lower reaches since the educational authorities can determine with greater precision than in the university their study plans and 'the range of teaching methods amongst which the teacher may choose' (STC 5/1981, 13 February, case *Estatuto de Centros*).

Academic freedom is a guarantee that teachers can develop their teaching without external interference, always bearing in mind that the State's ideological neutrality prevents teachers in state schools from being propagandists for specific ideologies (STC 77/1985, 27 June, case *LODE*). However, the Constitution itself recognizes the right of physical and legal persons to set up teaching centres (Article 27.6 SC), which do not have to observe this neutrality but, on the contrary, can have their own ideology, and this inevitably influences the academic freedom of their teachers: although they are not obliged to disseminate the centre's ideology, they are not free to attack it, and so they must do their work as they think fit but always taking into account, following serious and objective criteria, that it must not be contrary to that ideology. As a consequence of this, a teacher's disagreement with the ideology of the centre in which he/she is working 'cannot be grounds for dismissal if it has not been made public in any of the centre's activities and is so proved' (STC 47/1985, 27 March, case *Sala v. Colegio Lestomac*).

D. *Freedom of Information*

397. Article 20.1d recognizes the right to communicate and receive truthful information freely by any method of dissemination. The main legal problem with these rights is determining when information that is relevant to the public is true and its author is protected by this right, normally against other persons who claim the protection of their right to reputation or other rights of privacy (*see* paragraph 380). The truth that, wisely, the Constitutional Court demands is not that it should be 100% objective, showing total correspondence between the facts described and reality, since if this were so, most news would be nothing but court reports. On the contrary, the truth demanded is subjective, that is, when the journalist or author has adequately checked the information with various sources. This duty of care does not have to be as exhaustive as a judicial enquiry since it is 'that wide space that lies between strict and exhaustive verification of a fact and the transmission of suppositions, simple rumours, mere inventions, insidious insinuations and gratuitous and unfounded news' (STC 61/2004, 19 April, case *El Mundo de Valladolid*). Another constitutional dilemma that has sometimes arisen in practice is whether, by making information public, journalists may have committed a crime of disclosure of secrets (to cite real cases: because they have published a politician's bank account statement or a WhatsApp conversation). In this case, the Constitutional Court does not focus on how the information was obtained (which could be a crime for other people), but on whether the information is truthful and of public relevance, without revealing irrelevant or gratuitous information. If this is the case, the news passes the 'judgment of necessity', and freedom of information will prevail (STC 24/2019, 25 February, case *Leonnoticias*). To encourage this type of leak to the press by civil servants or company employees, the EU has approved a Directive on whistleblowers, Directive 2019/1937 of the European Parliament and of the Council of 23 October 2019, on the protection of persons who report breaches of Union law. In order to comply with the obligation of the States to transpose this directive, in September 2022, the government presented a Draft Law that regulates the protection of persons who report infringements that violate European and national law, which is being processed in the Spanish Parliament at the time of writing this book. Precisely so that the public can check that veracity and as a means of protecting the honour of persons affected by a news item, Organic Law 2/1984 establishes the right of correction, through which every person can give her/his own particular version of the facts referred to, by whatever method it was made public and the publisher has the obligation to publish it, without insisting in turn that the complainant prove what is stated (STC 168/1986, 22 December, case *Ediciones Tiempo*), even though it includes value judgments and personal opinions, provided that its relevance in the totality of the rectification is slight and has a direct relationship with the facts (STS (1) 376/2017, 14 June).

398. As additional guarantees of freedom, Article 20.1d establishes that the law shall regulate the right to protection of the clause on conscience and professional secrecy; until now, this has only been expressly complied with in respect of the former by Organic Law 2/1997, 19 June, on the conscience clause for information professionals, in which it is laid down that reporters may rescind their contract of employment and receive compensation when the information medium in which they worked had substantially changed its ideological orientation. The conscience clause also covers the motivated denial of journalists to 'the production of information contrary to the ethical principles of information' (Article 3 Organic Law 2/1997). Professional secrecy is understood as the right of journalists not to disclose their 'sources' (i.e., the people or documents on which they base their information) that – as most of the collective agreements of the media companies of Spanish communication – have a double dimension: against third parties – for example, a public power – but also against the journalist's own company itself. The Constitutional Court has not had to rule directly on any case in which professional secrecy was considered to be violated.[55] On the contrary, it has heard cases in which a person alleged a violation of the right to honour by a journalist, and he/she used professional secrecy to refuse to disclose the origin of their information. In these cases, the Constitutional Court has granted protection of the constitutional fundamental right to the claimants of the right to honour because 'the duty of diligence in the reasonable verification of the veracity of the information is not satisfied with the pure and generic referral to indeterminate sources, which, under no circumstances, free the author of the information from compliance with that duty' (STC 21/2000, 31 January, case *Blasco Parras*, who had been accused by a journalist from the daily newspaper *El Mundo* of having paid millions in commissions to senior officials of the Ministry of Defence).

Equally, the freedom to create means of communication and the right of access to the public media granted to social and political groups can be considered to be guarantees of the freedom of information and, more widely, of expression; under Article 20.3 SC, this is regulated by law. In the case of radio and television, this freedom to create is mediated by certain technical requirements that justify a normative regulation and action of the government to authorize broadcasting, but the lack of such action does not mean prohibition (SSTC 31/1994, 31 January, case *TV por cable* and 88/1995, 6 June, case *TV por ondas*).[56] In my opinion, the legislative gap in the professional secrecy of journalists can be filled – until the *Cortes* comply with the constitutional mandate – with an analogical application to the journalists of Article 417

---

55. Indirectly, it had done so in STC 30/2022, 7 March, case *Filtraciones a la prensa de documentos judiciales* in which it granted protection to two journalists for violation of effective judicial protection when an investigating judge ordered the police to seize their mobile phones to find out where leaks about a case he was investigating had come from. The TC considers that this decision (which was endorsed by the Provincial Court of Palma) affected 'directly the right to professional secrecy of journalists and could have a dissuasive effect on the collaboration of citizens with the media'. For this reason, 'limitations on the confidentiality of journalistic sources must be subject to a stricter control of proportionality than any other means of investigation'.

56. There are, however, significant differences between these two cases: while in the former and others similar dealing with cable TV (SSTC 47/1994, 240/1994 and 307/1994) it was upheld, in the latter

of the LECrim, which exempts priests and civil servants from testifying when they are unable to do so 'without violating the secrecy that they are obliged to maintain because of their positions'.

IV. The Right to Education and Freedom of Teaching

399. It was explained previously that in the drafting of the 1978 Constitution, the right to education did not so much reflect an agreement on its essential elements as an accumulation of proposals from the drafters, to some extent contradictory, resulting in a long and paradoxically ambiguous Article 27. In my opinion, if that consensus solution allowed one of the most delicate problems of the drafting process (so much so that the socialist Professor Peces-Barba walked out of the session over disagreement with the initial text) to be solved, subsequently, it has enabled almost all the laws passed by Parliament to be appealed to the Constitutional Court by the minority (sometimes of the left, others of the right), since arguments can always be found in the text of Article 27 to support their reasoning, normally reinforced by appeals to the distribution of territorial competences (*see* paragraph 256). Fortunately, the Constitutional Court knows where to draw the line between constitutional and ordinary policy, reminding the parties that within the Constitution, various educational models can be fitted and that the complete development of the personality should be promoted in accordance with democratic principles of coexistence and fundamental rights and liberties (Article 27.2 SC), while at the same time expelling from the legal system several articles of the different laws on education that were contrary to the terms of the Constitution. Of course, the party that wins the elections has legitimacy to establish the educational model that it deems fit within the terms of the Constitution, but this does not mean that it would not be better to achieve an 'educational agreement' amongst the principal political forces that would give stability and continuity to the system.

400. The most striking characteristic of the form that Article 27 gives to the right to education for Spaniards and foreigners in Spain, even those without administrative authorization, lies in the fact that the State's obligation in the matter does not end with its normative regulation, as is generally the case with public freedoms. In addition, it has to play an important executive role since the Constitution stipulates that basic education is compulsory and free (Article 27.4), while at the same time, it makes the public authorities guarantors of 'the right of all to education through a general educational programme, with the effective participation of all the sectors affected and the creation of educational centres' (Article 27.5). Thus, the right to education is both a right of liberty and a right to provision: public authorities are compelled to provide basic education for all, and the holders of this right can, when necessary, demand this right directly before the courts since it is included in Section

---

it was refused (with two dissenting votes), arguing that given the complexity of airwave TV broadcasting, granting this would be a 'precondition, the undeniable sphere of the freedom of configuration of the legislator'. Cf. Artemi Rallo Lombarte, *Pluralismo informativo y Constitución* (Tirant Lo Blanch 2000).

1 of Chapter II of Title I and is a genuine subjective right (STC 86/1985, 10 July, case *Subvenciones a Centros privados*). The length of basic compulsory education is remitted to law (which is currently Organic Law 2/2006 on Education), and it is at present from 6 years to 16 years of age. Free education for children is from 3 to 6 years, although this is not obligatory.

401. Freedom of teaching consists, basically, in the classic right of physical and legal persons to found educational institutions with their own 'ideology' or 'own character', with the limit that they respect constitutional principles (Article 27.6 SC) and 'the demands of science and other aims of education, mentioned in Article 27.2 SC and in Article 13.1 of ICESCR' (STC 5/1981, 13 February, case *Estatuto de Centros*). Moreover, the distinctive ideology of the educational centre does not imply the elimination of the academic freedom of the teaching staff (*see* paragraph 383). According to the Spanish tradition, reinforced by protection of free enterprise (Article 38 SC), the owners of the centres can seek and earn profits and not only, as still occurs in some countries, foundations and other charitable bodies.

The Constitution imposes on the public authorities the obligation to help teaching centres that meet the requirements established by law (Article 27.9 SC), which has given rise to a legal regime of agreements under which those private schools who so wish can receive public funding in return for fulfilling the requisites set out in the legislation. Amongst the most important of these are admission criteria equal to those of the state schools and an internal organization in which teachers, parents, and students participate in the control and management of the centres (Article 27.7 SC), but these legal requisites cannot be taken to the point where the owners are deprived of the power of the centre's direction (STC 77/1985, 27 June, case *LODE*). For their part, private schools that do not wish to be state aided have more freedom to organize themselves, fix their own admission criteria, and require fees from their pupils. They remain, however, subject to administrative supervision since the Constitution lays down that the public authorities shall inspect and standardize the educational system so as to guarantee compliance with the laws (Article 27.8 SC). Perhaps the most relevant of these public functions over private schools is that of permitting their opening, which, at primary and secondary levels, takes the form of an administrative authorization that confirms compliance with the objective requirements laid down in the Organic Law on the right to education, while a law of the state or Autonomous Community is demanded for the establishment of a private university.

402. The Constitution guarantees the right of parents to choose the type of education that they want for their children, also recognized in Article 13.3. of PIDESC, which is given concrete expression in the possibility of selecting educational centres other than public ones (JECtHR 23 July 1968, case *Laws on the use of languages in education in Belgium*) and in the right of parents for their children to receive the religious and moral teaching that is in accord with their own convictions.[57] The Constitutional Court has pointed out that that right set out in Article 27.3 of the Constitution does not directly include the right to educate one's children at home, although it does not 'exclude other legislative options that incorporate a certain flexibility in the educational system and in particular in elementary education' (STC 133/2010, 2 December, case *Educación en casa*), which means that in future the law could recognize this type of education but always with some type of public control because elementary education is compulsory under the Constitution (Article 27.4 SC). In practice, the Autonomous Communities – responsible for the management of Education – often distinguish teaching at home (sometimes called homeschooling) and absenteeism, sanctioning only the latter. It is less clear to determine whether the constitutional right of parents to educate their children according to their convictions also includes receiving education in the language of their choice in the Autonomous Communities that have two official languages: at first, the Constitutional Court considered that they did not, in such a way that 'the right to choose Centres of compulsory education in a certain language is a right of legal configuration' (SSTC 195/1989, 27 November case *Censal School of Castellón-I* and 19/1990, 12 February, case *Census School of Castellón-II*). Later this doctrine became somewhat ambiguous in its reasoning because it stated that 'it is legitimate for Catalan, in view of the objective of linguistic normalization in Catalonia, to be the centre of gravity of this model of bilingualism, provided that this does not result in the exclusion of Castilian (Spanish) as a teaching language'. This led it to admit the model of 'integral bilingualism or linguistic conjunction' established in Law 7/1983, of the Parliament of Catalonia, on linguistic normalization in Catalonia (STC 337/1994, 23 December), a model that, in practice, had led to a system of immersion, a reality that the Constitutional Court did not consider advisable to take into account for its legal analysis Finally, in its Judgment 31/2010 the Court repeats that idea that Catalan may be the 'centre of gravity' of the educational system of Catalonia, but now it explains the position of Castilian in more detail: 'Catalan must, therefore, be the vehicle and learning language in education, but not the only one that enjoys such a condition, a characteristic that also shares Castilian as an official language in Catalonia. [... Therefore,] Castilian cannot cease to be also a vehicular language and of learning in teaching', an approach that led it to reinterpret various Articles of the Estatut that only referred to the right to study in Catalan. For its part, Organic Law 8/2013, 9 December, for the Improvement of Educational Quality (LOMCE), ordered: 'Parents, mothers or legal guardians shall have the right to have their children or pupils receive education in Spanish, within the framework of educational programming', and this law regulated two complex systems so that the Autonomous Communities with their own language comply with this right.

---

57. Article 27 SC requires public authorities to guarantee this right (which is at present observed), by, on one hand permitting educational centres to have their own ideology and, on the other, by establishing religious teaching in compulsory education. The inclusion of religion as a school subject in the curriculum – resulting from the 1979 Accord with the Holy See – has given rise to a long political and legal controversy that is still far from being resolved. This situation continues because LOMCE of December 2013 made a regulation that the subject of religion (it has again full academic validity) which was only supported by PP but not by PSOE and the other opposition parties. *See La enseñanza de la religión en la escuela pública* (Isabel Cano Ruiz ed., Comares 2014).

Organic Law 3/2020 repealed this LOMCE in its entirety. Thus, at present, state legislation does not allow parents to choose the language of instruction for their children. The Organic Law on Education limits itself to establishing a somewhat obscure mandate: 'Educational administrations shall guarantee the right of students to receive education in Castilian and the other co-official languages in their respective territories, per the Spanish Constitution, the Statutes of Autonomy and the applicable regulations'. As the autonomous 'applicable regulations' in Catalonia only require Spanish in the subject of Spanish Language, some individuals have appealed to the courts so that their children could be taught in Spanish. The High Court of Justice of Catalonia, first, and the Supreme Court, later, have set a minimum of 25% of teaching hours in Spanish (SSTS 1668/2015, 23 April and 1670/2015, 28 April). However, this percentage has been left without effect as it is not required in the controversial Catalan Law 8/2022, 9 June, on the use and learning of official languages in non-university education, which has been appealed before the Constitutional Court.

V. The Universities' Right to Autonomy

403. The text of Article 27.10 of the Constitution reads as follows: 'The autonomy of the universities is recognized under the terms established by law', from which the majority of the scholars who commented on this article in the first years of the Constitution had deduced that this was an institutional guarantee for the universities, similar to that established for local corporations in Title VIII (*see* paragraph 303). However, the Constitutional Court, in its first judgment on the matter, considered that for both the literal wording of Article 27.10 (is recognized) as for its position in the system (Title I) and its aim (to protect academic freedom), it was a genuine fundamental right of the University community, made up of the members of the institution who carry out research, study, and teach there (STC 26/1987, 27 February, case *LRU*). There are two practical consequences of this characterization as a right: on the one hand, the legislator must respect the essential content of the right (which is wider than that of an institutional guarantee), and on the other hand, the universities can defend their fundamental right in court both in the appeal process before the ordinary courts as in the appeal for constitutional protection of fundamental rights.

§3. Political Rights

I. The Right of Assembly

404. Article 21 of the Constitution recognizes the right to peaceful, unarmed assembly, which is now classified as a hybrid of the rights of ideological freedom and of association: 'it is a collective demonstration of the freedom of expression exercised through a temporary association' (STC 85/1988, 28 April, case *Mesas petitorias*). As it is a right of political participation, only some meetings are protected by this right: those with a political purpose, in its broadest sense: 'it is a collective manifestation of freedom of expression exercised through a temporary association of persons that operates as an instrumental technique at the service of the exchange or presentation of ideas, the defence of interests or the publicizing of problems or demands' (STC 42/2000, 14 February, case *Galafate Parra*). For this reason, concerts or parties are not protected by the right of assembly. The holders of this right are natural persons, including minors, as expressly recognized by the LOPJM (*see* paragraph 346). Moreover, it is a right held by both Spanish and foreign persons, regardless of their administrative status in Spain (*see* paragraph 338). Although the military, judges and prosecutors are restricted in their specific legislation as a way of reinforcing the neutrality of the public authorities (LO 9/2011 on the rights and duties of members of the Armed Forces, LOPJ and Law 50/1981, on the Organic Statute of the Public Prosecutor's Office, respectively). Organic Law 9/1983, 15 July, regulating the right of assembly, defines an assembly as the temporary meeting of more than twenty persons by prior arrangement for a specific purpose. To this, we would add that in present-day society, it is normally an instrumental right: it is usually used for or against a government measure (therefore, as an expression of the right to political participation), to support an industrial dispute (right of collective negotiation) and is, for some social groups 'one of the few means at their disposal to express their ideas and demands publicly' (STC 66/1995, 8 May, case *FEBASO-UGT*).

The right of assembly in a closed space needs no administrative approval, while the Constitution demands that demonstrations and those meetings that occur in places of public transit must give prior notice to 'the authority, which can only forbid them when there are reasons based on disturbances of public order, with danger for persons or property'. In this way, the *Lex legum* turned the regulations under Franco's dictatorship on their head, where demonstrations were always prohibited except with prior permission. To comply with the constitutional mandate, the Organic Law establishes a period of ten days, which for reasons of urgency can be reduced to twenty-four hours, so that the organizers of an assembly or demonstration shall inform the delegate or sub-delegate of the government (or, in the case of a Community with competence in matters of security to the Councillor responsible) of the day and duration of the act, the proposed route and the means of security envisaged or requested. This lengthy period is justified to help the organizers themselves: in the first place, so that the forces of public order can prepare themselves as well as to protect the act and adopt the traffic measures necessary for it to be held; in the second place, if the governing authority, through a resolution moved within seventy-two hours, forbids it or suggests an alternative route, that decision can be legally appealed and a judicial order obtained before the date of the demonstration (Article 122 LJCA). The only express reason given in the Constitution for forbidding a demonstration is the disturbance of public order, and so the possible interference with other rights cannot be put forward, such as free movement of traffic, unless the demonstration would cause a total obstruction of the roads so that certain areas were cut off and essential services, such as ambulances, fire engines, etc., could not be provided. Thus, a person who blocks the traffic for forty-five minutes during the time and on the route agreed cannot be sanctioned (STC 42/2000, 14 February, case *Galafate Parra*). It is constitutionally permissible to prohibit a demonstration if, due to an epidemic, the health of the demonstrators and, indirectly, of society as a whole is put at risk (ATC 40/2020, 30 April). Likewise, if the purpose of a demonstration is to commit a crime, such as the exaltation of terrorism, which happens when acts of homage to convicted members of the terrorist group ETA are called.

Particularly controversial was its EUR 600,000 sanction for severe disruption of public safety occurring during demonstrations in front of the seats of the Congress of Deputies, the Senate and the legislative assemblies of the autonomous communities. In addition, the same sanction can be applied to demonstrations that are not communicated or prohibited in and around basic infrastructures for the community. The PSOE appealed against both provisions, which the Constitutional Court did not consider contrary to Article 21 (STC 172/2020, 19 November). As is well known, the constitutionality of a law does not mean that it is the only possible regulation; however, to date, the new PSOE-UP majority that emerged from the November 2019 elections has not changed these provisions.

II. The Right of Association

405. The liberal State's mistrust of associations during its early years, as it feared they could revive the guilds and other intermediate bodies, was overcome in Spain in the 1869 Constitution, and not even the conservative Constitution of 1876 or the progressive one of 1931 hesitated in recognizing this right. Equally, that of 1978 recognized it in Article 22, setting out that associations that pursued purposes or methods classified as crimes were illegal and directly forbidding secret and paramilitary associations.[58] Furthermore, Article 22 creates a register of associations 'for purposes of public information only' and sets out the guarantee that they can only be dissolved or suspended by judicial order.

The legislation took its time to pass in passing the law to develop Article 22, so much so that it had to wait for the Organic Law of 1/2002, 22 March, Regulator of the Right of Associations (LODA) to enjoy post-constitutional regulation and expressly repeal the 1964 Law of Associations. The delay had the advantage that LODA incorporated both the jurisprudence of the Constitutional Court and the practice of those years, distinguishing between the essential content of the right and those elements that, according to the Constitutional Court, can be developed by the

58. Article 515 of the Criminal Code states:

> Illegal associations are punishable, being those that:
>
> 1. Have as their aim the commission of a crime, or after their formation, promote it.
> 2. Are armed bands, organizations, and terrorist groups.
> 3. Although having an illicit objective, employ violent means or alteration or control of personality.
> 4. Paramilitary organizations.

Autonomous Communities (STC 173/1998, 23 July, case *Ley vasca de asociaciones*). Equally, the specific legislation on regulation of special associations was remitted, and so LODA has only a supplementary application in the following: political parties, trade unions, business organizations, churches, sports federations, consumers' and users' associations, or any others regulated by special laws. Amongst these, we must remember that the Constitution has regulated, in Articles 6 and 7, those associations that are for the liberal State historically most conflictive, political parties (*see* paragraph 97) and the trade unions (*see* paragraph 103).

406. Curiously, the most arduous problems of interpretation of Article 22 have arisen not from the so-called 'right of association' (widely recognized entitlement, almost automatic inscription on the register, legal demand for structure and democratic functioning, rights of members, etc.) but from the right not to belong, or the negative aspect of Article 22, since in the Spanish legal system, there are many instances when membership in an association is compulsory in order to carry out certain activities. The Constitutional Court has considered that obligatory membership, an exception to the principle of freedom, can only be permitted under Article 22 of the Constitution if sufficient justification can be found in constitutional provisions or if it is in the public interest and would be difficult to obtain 'without forced membership of a corporative body' (STC 132/1989, 18 July, case *Cámaras agrarias*). In general, the CC has been strict when judging these requirements, which has led it to declare unconstitutional various cases of compulsory membership of professional organizations without considering whether, under Article 52 of the Constitution, remitting the matter to the law regulating professional organizations would be sufficient. This occurred, for example, with membership of the agrarian, urban, and commerce Chambers regulated by the pre-constitutional law of 1911 but, surprisingly, not with obligatory membership of the Chambers of commerce demanded by the 1993 law (STC 107/1996, 12 June, case *Cámaras de Comercio-II*). Wisely, the Court has also held that the power to remit matters to the law regulating the 'peculiarities of the legal governance of the Professional Colleges' as given by Article 36 of the Constitution, does not justify in every case the compulsory membership in those Colleges, as it will only be compatible with the freedom of association if it is justified that it affects 'in a serious and direct manner, matters of special public interest, such as the protection of health and physical integrity or the personal or legal security of natural persons, and membership proves to be an efficient instrument of control of professional practice for the better defence of the recipients of the services' (STC 3/2013, 17 January, case *Artículo 30.2 de la Ley del Parlamento de Andalucía 15/2001*).

Incidentally, the decision to declare compulsory membership – even for health professionals who only practise their profession in the public administrations – is the exclusive responsibility of the State law, without the Autonomous Communities being able to vary this regime, which has led to the declaration of unconstitutionality of a large number of regional laws (a broad summary of these rulings can be found in STC 82/2018, 16 July, case *Artículo 17.2 de la Ley 1/2001 de colegios profesionales de Cantabria*).

III. The Right to Participate in Public Affairs

A. *The Right to Political Participation Directly or Through Representatives*

407. The proclamation of the social and democratic Rule of Law made in Article 1.1 of the Constitution has one of its most logical expressions in Article 23, which states that citizens have the right to participate in public affairs, directly or through representatives, freely elected in periodic elections by universal suffrage. From the literal wording of this proclamation, there appear to be two exclusions from this right: (i) it applies exclusively to Spaniards and not to foreigners (although they can vote in local elections as permitted by Article 13.2 SC), nor to legal persons (STC /1984, 25 April, case *Sindicato de Farmacéuticos de Valencia*); and (ii) that it relates exclusively to the political and not to other social spheres that the Constitution deals within other articles that require citizens' participation, as, for example, Article 9.2 on economic, cultural and social life, but that does not have the special protection of this fundamental right (STC 212/1993, 28 June, case *Elecciones Junta de Facultad*). Specific expression of this right to direct political participation found in the Constitution is the legislative popular initiative, the various types of referendum and the popular local consultations (*see* paragraph 104), as well as the open Municipal Council (*see* paragraph 317). Most new Statutes of Autonomy have regulated autonomous consultations (*see* paragraph 106). Indirect political participation is the right to vote (or not vote) in the 'periodic elections', national, autonomous, and local, enjoyed by Spaniards who have attained the age of majority and have the full use of their capacity to act.[59] By including the negative aspect of not voting, it is not possible to establish compulsory voting in Spain or to sanction abstention, as happens in other European States, where the vote is considered a right and duty.

According to the Constitutional Court, Article 23.1 includes the right of the electors that elected persons only lose their representation by popular will or by legal causes justifiable constitutionally (resignation, condemnation, etc.). For this reason, expulsion from a party does not entail the loss of the position of councillor, as provided for by Law 38/1978 on local elections (STC 5/1983, 4 February, case *Cese concejal de Andújar*). The experience of more than forty years of local elections has shown that in most cases where a councillor is expelled from the party and maintains the seat, what is undermined is the right of the person who chose him from a closed, blocked list, trusting more in the Party than in its members, since the councillor almost always breaks the party discipline to negotiate, with other parties, his/her inclusion in the municipal government (turncoats). As a result, various legal mechanisms have been sought to fight turncoat politics, such as the new system used to calculate the number of members of a city council who must sign the motion of censure, which is increased if the motion involves turncoats who belong to the same list as the mayor (*see* paragraph 315).

59. Article 3.1 of LOREG states that the right to vote is denied to those condemned by a final legal sentence to the penalty of deprivation of the right of suffrage, those declared incapable by a final legal sentence and those interned in a psychiatric hospital provided the detention is under legal authorization. Cf. Pablo Santolaya Machetti, *Procedimientos y garantías electorales* (Civitas 2013).

B. The Right of Access to Representative Public Office

408. Article 23.2 lays down that citizens have the right to access, under conditions of equality, to public functions and positions, in accordance with the requirements established by law. This reference to the law implies that this right has a legal form, which is shown not only at the moment of access – the possibility of presenting oneself to election by universal suffrage (the passive right of suffrage) – but also to permanence (as stated in the case just mentioned, STC 5/1983) and in the exercise of the office. As in the case of active suffrage, aliens also have the right to be elected in local elections and in the elections to the European Parliament (*see* paragraph 340). The Constitution itself is concerned to guarantee equality of opportunity to candidates by setting out the precise *causes de ineligibility* (Article 70) in LOREG, the Autonomy Statutes and in autonomous electoral laws. This right of access is not breached by the fact that those elected have to comply with certain formal requisites established by the legislation, including swearing the oath to respect the fundamental Norm, in order to fully exercise their function, nor does the electoral legislation demand a certain number of votes – the electoral barrier – to obtain a seat.

409. The right to exercise office, or *ius in officium,* means that the representative can carry out his/her functions in accordance with the applicable legislation – including parliamentary Standing Orders – without the law controlling the exercise in such a way that it 'is emptied of the function he has to play, or that it is hindered by artificial obstacles' (STC 32/1985, 6 March, case *Ayuntamiento de La Guardia*). Not only can the normative regulations be contrary to Article 23.2, but the decisions of the parliamentary bodies responsible for applying them also violate the 'essential nucleus of the representative function', such as, according to the Constitutional Court, the right to information, to ask questions, to process proposals, etc. To ensure this violation does not occur, the Constitutional Court has been exercising, using the Amparo appeal, a jurisdictional control over a field traditionally exempt from it, such as the internal decisions of the legislative powers, the *interna corporis acta*. Its rulings have been increasing over the years, especially when, in 2015–2017, the Catalan pro-independence forces began to adopt resolutions and laws in parliament to achieve independence for Catalonia (*see* paragraphs 103bis and 136.2).

C. The Right of Access to Public Employment

410. While the historical Spanish Constitutions did not recognize the right of access to public office, the position was different with access to public employment, traditional since the 1837 Constitution declared, 'all Spaniards are admissible to public employment and positions, according to their merit and capacity'. Article 23.2 of the Constitution maintained this tradition, although, for a purely grammatical reason (to include in the same phrase the right of access to public employment and representative office), it says nothing of merit and capacity, set out now in Article 103. However, they are integrated into the fundamental right of Article 23.2, and so the law cannot demand access to public employment 'any requisite or condition that does not relate to the indicated concepts of merit and capacity' (STC 50/1986, 23 April case *Medrano Autor v. Diputación Foral de Navarra*), although it can – by virtue of Article 9.2 and other constitutional mandates – establish a percentage of places for disadvantaged groups. In its abundant jurisprudence on the matter, the CC has had occasion to lay down the criteria to be included in the concepts of merit and capacity and to point out what violates them. Thus, knowledge of a language other than Spanish, or even in certain circumstances to demand it, services provided, and seniority are criteria of merit; on the contrary, the residence and the centre where they obtained their qualifications and age of candidates are discriminatory, unless the age requirement is reasonable for the characteristics of the position to be filled (STC 37/2004, 11 March, case *Artículo 135B del RDL 781/1986, sobre régimen local*). In any case, the norms of access to public employment must be general and abstract, and the merits demanded must correspond to the work which the person chosen is going to carry out (STC 148/1986, 25 November, case *Profesor Agregado de Universidad*). The way in which the selection bodies apply these norms are rarely reviewed by the courts, given their technical discretion, which the judges cannot substitute, except where there is a very obvious arbitrariness (STC 219/2004, 29 November, case *Oposiciones a Inspector-jefe del Cuerpo Nacional de Policía*). The protection of Article 23.2 is not limited to access to public employment since – as in the case of representative office – it also guarantees permanence in the position, and so it grants protection from discriminatory promotion, arbitrary dismissal or suspension, unjustified transfers, etc.

IV. The Right of Petition

411. The old medieval right of petition – which in Spain never achieved the importance it had in England in the struggle against absolute power – has survived in Spanish Constitutions since it was first introduced in 1837. Article 29 of the 1978 Constitution deals with it succinctly since it limits itself to stating that Spaniards have the right of 'individual and collective petition, in writing, in the form and with the effects that the law determines', specifying that the military can only exercise it individually 'and in accordance with the terms set out in its specific legislation'. For its part, Article 77 – rather repetitively – specifies that Congress and the Senate can receive individual and collective petitions, forbidding them from being presented by demonstrations, that the Chambers can remit them to the government demanding that it 'explain itself over the content'.

As Law 92/1960 (technically well-drafted as was customary during the rule of Franco when regulating *peripheral* institutions of human rights) served as a channel for this right, which is merely residual in a democracy, the constitutional law to develop it was not passed until 2001. Organic Law 4/2001, 12 November, regulator of the Right of Petition (LODP) followed the line established by the Constitutional Court's scant jurisprudence on this right and, after extending it also to aliens, shaped it as a right only designed for initiatives that had no other specific way since it excludes from its application requests, complaints, and suggestions for which the legal system establishes a particular procedure for their satisfaction, whether parliamentary, administrative, or judicial. LODP even specifies that petitions will not be admitted on 'whose object a parliamentary, administrative or judicial process already exists and where agreement has not been reached or a judgment finalized'. If these criteria are applied to the letter of the law, the right of petition, rather than a residual right – as the CC and LODP call it – should have been named a rare right since it can seldom be invoked successfully. Fortunately, there is no lack of citizens' groups who, ignoring the literal wording of the law, enrich political life by demanding this or that action from the public authorities (the passing of concrete measures against some social blemish, the dismissal of a public official whose conduct is considered blameworthy, etc.) knowing that its greatest strength is publicity – now reinforced thanks to the Internet – which will achieve its object. In short, it is self-evident that the right to petition does not impose any obligation on the public authorities to grant what is requested, but they must acknowledge receipt of it and inform 'the interested party of the resolution adopted' (STC 243/1993, 14 July de 1993, case *Llarena González v. Parlamento de Canarias*). Therefore, the Supreme Court has held that the government does not violate this right – or any other – when it justifies its refusal to include a box on the income tax declaration to finance a religious faith (*see* paragraph 392) or when it rejects the request to remove Franco's body from the *Valle de los Caídos* (Valley of the Fallen), despite the fact that in this case, the government's response was later than the three-month deadline set by the LODP (STS (3) 910/2017, 13 March). In 2019, the government (but with a socialist president) took on its initiative the decision to exhume the body of the dictator and transfer it to the cemetery of El Pardo without the family's judicial appeals being able to prevent it (STS (3) 2824/2019, 30 September, and ATC 119/2019, 17 October).

§4. Procedural Rights

I. Effective Judicial Protection

412. Article 24 of the Constitution brings together a group of procedural rights and guarantees that are known generically as effective judicial protection. Even more than with the right to education, the right to effective judicial protection demands of the State not only laws to develop it but also an organization capable of applying that legislation, which in this case is the judicial power. Thus, the Constitutional Court has reiterated that the nature of this right is not a right of liberty that can be exercised directly from the Constitution, 'but rather that of a right to a service, that can only be exercised through the channels established by the legislator or, to put it another way, it is a right of legal configuration' (STC 99/1985, 30 September, case *Bowitz*). Evidently, the Court does not think that judicial protection lacks essential content (as is the case with the rights in Chapter III) but that the law is of great relevance in outlining its boundaries. To be precise, to this, ideas must be added, as in the case of the American *due process of law,* with which it is frequently compared, that to a great extent, judicial protection is a right shaped by jurisprudence in that the Constitutional Court has developed it greatly in its extensive jurisprudence on Article 24, which year after year is the rightmost put forward in appeals alleging the violation of constitutional rights (to the extent that they make up more than 75% of the appeals that the Court receives). This jurisprudence normally follows the lines laid down by the ECtHR in its application of Articles 6 and 13 of the European Charter of Human Rights, producing a number of confrontations with the Supreme Court, which on some occasions has considered that the CC has exceeded its functions (*see* paragraph 213). Overall, the most relevant feature of the CC's jurisprudence has been its break with the courts' traditionally literal interpretation of procedural laws, excessively formalizing procedure to the point that it refused to admit claims for lack of requisites that could easily be put right, such as the omission of the signature of the lawyer who drafted the document. Time and again, the Constitutional Court has insisted that procedural norms are instruments to grant legal remedies and not ends in themselves, and so the court must seek the interpretation of the norms that most favour the effectiveness of the fundamental right and that when the non-compliance or omission of a procedural requisite is noticed, the consequence should be proportionate to the fault (STC 43/1985, 22 March, case *Ajuria*).

A. The Right of Access to the Courts

413. If there is no access to the judges and courts, then, logically, an effective judicial protection cannot exist; so true is this that the Constitutional Court considers the 'nucleus of the fundamental right to an effective judicial protection in access to the jurisdiction' (STC 223/2001, 5 November, case *Segura Gubern*). For this reason, any requisite that prevents a natural or legal person, including the public administration (STC 173/2002, 9 October, case *Martínez Calderón v. la Generalidad de Cataluña*), from being a party to legal proceedings and promoting jurisdictional acts must be considered with the utmost care. In particular, the service of a summons by putting it on the door of the court as permitted by the rules of procedure, which was completely logical in the agrarian society of the nineteenth century, is only admitted by the Constitutional Court when the party's address is not known and the judicial office has exhausted all normal means within its possibilities to discover his whereabouts (that doctrine began in STC 9/1981, 31 March, case *Coto Minero Merladet* and after many other judgments the parliament take it in Act 19/2015). Equally, the costs of the proceedings cannot be an obstacle to one who pleads for justice, nor for aliens illegally in Spain (STC 95/2003, 22 May, case *Justicia gratuita de extranjeros ilegales*). Article 119 of the Constitution declares that justice will be free for those who have insufficient means to litigate, a provision developed by Law 1/1996, 10 January, on free legal aid (widely modified in subsequent years, especially by Laws 42/2015 and 2/2017), which recognize this right for all natural persons, although foreigners without legal residence who are not citizens of the Union only have it in criminal matters and in contentious litigation when they demand the right of asylum. The Law does not recognize the benefit of legal aid for profit-making companies, but it does recognize it for foundations and associations that justify their lack of economic resources for litigation. The Constitutional Court has considered that this difference between legal entities does not violate either the right to judicial protection or the right to equality because it is not an artificial difference; rather, it is objectively justified (some are for profit, and others are not), overcoming the judgement of proportionality both between the measure adopted and the result produced and with the purpose intended by the legislator in establishing the difference (STC 117/1998, 2 June). Finally, the Catholic Church has the benefit of gratuity by virtue of the Agreement with the Holy See on juridical matters of 3 January 1979.

B. The Right to a Judgment Founded on Law

414. Effective judicial protection includes the right to judicial decision that, evidentially, does not have to be in favour of the plaintiff. The determining factor of the judicial decision is that it must be motivated by reason. This is stipulated by Article 120.3 of the Constitution, which is integrated into the essential content of Article 24 for the right to obtain a judgment founded on law, 'which directly connects with the principle of the democratic state of law' (STC 169/2004, 6 October, case *Macia Vega*). Reasonability is logically deduced from that same motivation (an unreasonable decision is not one that is motivated or founded on law) and the prohibition of arbitrariness of public authorities established by Article 9.3 of the Constitution. Moreover, judicial protection is not satisfied by using general and stereotypical reasons but by reasoning applicable to the case at hand (STC 223/2003, 15 December, case *Leal Fernández*). However, from the point of view of the function of the Constitutional Court, it has repeatedly considered that it can only review the selection, interpretation, and application of a legal precept made by an ordinary court if the reasoning on which it is based occurs 'in such a degree of arbitrariness, unreasonableness or error that, due to its evidence and content, it is so manifest and serious that it is obvious to any observer that the resolution, in fact, lacks any motivation' (for all these cases, STC 30/2006, 30 January, case *Entrega de española en virtud de una euroorden*). It is, without doubt, a logical doctrine to prevent the subsidiary remedy of the Constitutional protection of fundamental rights from becoming an appeal similar to the ordinary appeal of cassation. An important example of this doctrine on effective judicial protection is STC 232/2015, 5 November, which annuls a judgment of the High Court of Madrid because it was arbitrary in that it did not apply a European Directive that had already been previously interpreted in a similar case by the CJEU, which was an obvious violation of the principle of primacy of European Law. Also, by controlling the selection of the applicable norms by the courts, the Constitutional Court may resolve the antinomies between international treaties and domestic legislation, a function which, in principle, corresponds to the ordinary jurisdiction (*see* paragraph 64).

415. To guarantee that this decision founded in law is reached, the procedural laws may establish appeals; this does not come directly from Article 24 of the Constitution, except in the case of criminal proceedings, where the interpretation of

Article 14.5 of the ICCPR[60] requires a superior court to review the finding of guilt and the sentence or, more precisely, demands a double trial/appeal because if a person is found not guilty in the first trial but convicted in the second, he has no right to a third, as can be understood from a literal reading of the Covenant (STC 60/2008, 26 May, case *Intelhorce*). However, while the legislator is free to establish or not those appeals that he thinks fit, including fixing certain guarantees in order to appeal (such as depositing a quantity of money), once created, the appeal process forms part of the right to judicial protection, and its requisites of admission must be interpreted with the same tone of anti-formalism and proportionality appropriate to judicial protection in such a way that a formal interpretation of those legal requirements that impede access to the remedy would be unconstitutional. An example would be to deny a civil appeal based on a restrictive interpretation of the LOPJ rules that regulate a financial deposit for the parties to be able to lodge an appeal against a judgment (STC 129/2012, 18 June, case *Construcciones Conde*). That said, the Constitutional Court has also specified that the review that it itself makes on the correct application by the courts of the rules on lodging appeals cannot be as rigorous as in the case of access to the jurisdiction because it is directly integrated into the essential core of Article 24 SC, while appeals do not (STC 252/2004, 20 December, case *Doucet Dejoie*). For this reason, the Constitutional Court will only review cases of inadmissibility of appeals when it is declared to be based on a legally non-existent case or through an 'arbitrary, unreasonable or based on factually patent error' (for all these cases, STC 55/2008, 14 April, case *Gironés Nebot*).

C. The Right to Execution of Legal Decisions

416. The judicial protection would have little effect if, once having obtained a favourable judgment, the party could not execute it in accordance with its terms and the principle of the finality of legal decisions. This situation was not uncommon in the past in the Contentious-Administrative Jurisdiction when it was the very same administration that had been condemned that was required to execute the sentence. As the legal system had no express provision against non-execution, the courts had no means of ensuring compliance with their judgments. Against these acts, the Constitutional Court created a vigorous jurisprudence holding that a court that could not

60. 'Every person found guilty of a crime has the right to have the declaration of guilt and the sentence examined by a superior jurisdiction in accordance with law.' The UN Committee on Human Rights has held on three occasions (Decisions dated 20 Jul. 2000, 5 Nov. 2002, and 30 Jul. 2003) that the Spanish legal regulation of 'appeal to a higher criminal court' (which the CC has held to be an effective legal remedy) does not meet the requirements of Art. 14.5 of ICCPR. The CC has not followed the Committee's criteria (whose decisions are not legally binding) and continues to argue that the Spanish right of appeal does meet the requirements of double process (cf. SSTC 70/2002, 3 April, case *Pichardo Miranda* and 26/2006, 30 January, case *Pizarro Dual*). In any case Organic Law 19/2003, 23 December, *de modificación de la LOPJ*, generalized the second Criminal Court to assign the hearing of appeals of appellation to Higher Courts of Justice against resolutions dictated in the first instance by Provincial Courts (Art. 73) and created the Chamber of Appeal in the National High Court (Art. 64*bis*).

solve the problem of non-execution of its sentences was violating the right of effective judicial protection (STC 119/1988, 20 June, case *Boyero Vicente*). Exceptionally, it can be declared that a sentence will not be enforced, but this can only be done for legal cause and a reasoned judicial order to avoid any arbitrary act by the public authorities (STC 33/1987, 12 March, case *Martiañez*). Equally, the principle of the finality of sentences is not violated if, as Article 267.2 de la LOPJ permits, a declaration is made to clarify a sentence to correct a patent disparity between the reasoning and the finding or any other material error 'that can be deduced with total certainty from the text itself of the judicial sentence' (STC 140/2001, 18 June, case *Labat de la Plaza*). In 1988 the law of Contentious-Administrative Jurisdiction, applying this precedent, regulated in detail the execution of judgments, specifying the grounds on which they need not be executed and could be substituted by a financial indemnification, as well as with several measures that the Contentious-Administrative courts can adopt in the event of non-execution of their decisions (Articles 103–113). The Constitutional Court has had occasion to specify that those legal reasons must be strictly interpreted, and amongst them, it does not include the mere expectation of a future change in the law. Thus, the Supreme Court cannot fail to execute a judgment requiring the demolition of a property because the municipal Council concerned intended to change the General Town Planning Plan to legalize the building whose demolition it had ordered (STC 22/20009, 26 January, case *Petición del Ayuntamiento de Síero de suspender una demolición*).

II. The Right to a Defence

417. Defencelessness is the situation of a defendant in any of the phases of the proceedings when, due to an incorrect act by a judicial body, he/she is deprived of her/his means of defence or the principles of cross-examination and equality of the parties are breached to the extent that real prejudice is caused to the party's rights and interests; this is an essential feature because not every infraction of procedural norms produces this situation but only one that results in 'a deprivation or a limitation of the right defence recognized in Article 24 SC' (STC 40/2002, 14 February, case *Comercial Caroe*). Examples of depriving a defendant of this right include not appointing an interpreter for a defendant who does not know Spanish, not assisting a deaf-mute, or not admitting a tax document in evidence because the amount due on it has not been paid. In particular, to avoid violation of this right, the judicial decision must be in accord with the parties' requests, without comments on aspects not raised during the proceedings on which there has not been the necessary cross-examination or preventing a party from replying to essential questions put by them (STC 39/2003, 27 February, case *Moreno Noguera*). This situation is also produced when the legal position of one of the parties worsens only as a result of an appeal/motion he/she himself/herself has made (STC 250/2004, 20 December, case *Reformation in peius del BBVA*).

III. Procedural Guarantees of Article 24.2

A. *The Right to Appear Before the Ordinary Judge Predetermined by Law*

418. Article 24.2 of the Constitution begins its long recital of procedural guarantees by stipulating that all persons have the right to be tried by the ordinary judge predetermined by law, a right that is fulfilled not only when the body judging the matter was created by law before the commission of the acts giving rise to the trial but also when in the specific case 'the procedure legally established for the appointment of the members who must make up the corresponding organ has been followed' (STC 69/2001, 17 March, case *Rafael Vera*). The legal and political debate on Article 24 has centred on whether the ordinary judge required must always be determined by the sole criterion of the place where the alleged offence has been committed, that is to say, judge of the place (sometimes called the natural judge), or if the law can set up courts with territorial jurisdiction superimposed on those judges and whose competence is determined according to the nature of the alleged crimes. This debate has great practical consequences because the National High Court is an organ with jurisdiction throughout Spain and competent to judge certain, especially complex, crimes (terrorism, drug-trafficking, etc.), which, in this way, are removed from those judges with limited territorial jurisdiction. The Constitutional Court has not hesitated to concede its constitutionality, given that the aim of Article 24 is impartiality of the judicial organ, which is achieved through the creation of general courts created by law. These do not violate the desired impartiality because the legislator determines these competences of the courts not only by the criterion of territoriality but also by taking into consideration other criteria such as the nature of the acts, the extent of the territory in which they occurred, and 'their importance for society as a whole' (STC 199/1987, 16 December, case *Ley antiterrorista II*).

B. *The Right to Public Trial Without Undue Delay*

419. We saw that publicity is the first technique to control political power (*see* paragraph 137), and it is also an essential instrument to avoid the arbitrariness of judicial power, present in our constitutionalism since the Magna Carta of 1812. The 1978 Constitution established publicity of trials both in the organic aspect, the functioning of the courts (Article 120.1 SC), as well as in the dogmatic, where it acts as a guarantee for the parties in any trial and very especially for those accused of a crime (Article 24.2 SC). Therefore, the Constitutional Court has stated that public process has two aims: that of protecting the parties from a Justice removed from public control and that of maintaining public confidence in the judges and the courts (STC 96/1987, 10 June, case *Juicio de Herrera de la Mancha*). Exceptionally, the ECHR's Article 6.1 – which has been incorporated in Article 232 LOPJ – prohibits the access of the press and the public to a trial when it is in the interest 'of morality, public order or national security in a democratic society'.

420. In addition to being public, the proceedings cannot be subject to undue delay, an uncertain legal concept that is not violated every time a judge does not respect a procedural time limit but only when there is excessive delay in pronouncing a sentence according to various criteria, amongst which, the Constitutional Court (according to its jurisprudence that follows that of the ECHR) emphasizes: (1) the circumstances of the trial; (2) its objective complexity; (3) the duration of other similar trials; (4) the performance of the judicial organs and the means available; (5) the conduct of the appellant who is demanding due procedural diligence, as well as 'the prior complaint to the judicial organ of the unjustified delay' (STC 22/1997, 11 February, case *Calero Baena*). A reason that does not avoid delay is one alleged with a certain frequency in the courts: the fact that the delay is due to structural reasons and to the workload of the judicial organ 'although it could exclude responsibility of the people intervening in the procedure, this in no way alters the unjustified nature of the delay' (STC 63/2016, 11 April, case Lapo Estrada). For this reason and to compensate in some way for the damage that defendants suffer from these delays, the Criminal Code includes, since 2010, the mitigate criminal accountability of 'Extraordinary or undue drawing out of the formalities of the proceedings, as long as this is not due to the convict, such prolongation being disproportionate to the complexity of the cause'. In any case, the difficulty of applying these criteria in each specific case has given rise to several instances in which the Court in Strasbourg has held that there has been undue delay although the Constitutional Court had held that there was not (e.g., JECtHR 11 November 2001, case *Díaz Aparicio* and JECtHR 15 March 2016, case *Menéndez García*).

C. The Guarantees of the Accused in Criminal Proceedings

421. Article 24.2 includes a set of guarantees especially designed for criminal proceedings:

(a) The right to defence and to the assistance of counsel: the accused in a criminal trial (and in general any party in any proceedings) always has the right freely to appoint counsel of his choice, and if he does not do so, the court will appoint one for him. This right to defence includes the right to speak last in the trial, which the LECrim expressly recognizes. The right to the last word is unconditional, and the court cannot circumvent it by requiring that what the accused has to say is of such relevance that it could lead to 'the issuing of a different ruling' (STC 35/2021, 18 February).
(b) The right to be informed of the accusation: in contrast to the inquisitorial proceedings of the absolute state, modern criminal trials are governed by the accusatory principle, which demands the defendant be told both the facts alleged against him/her and the legal category into which they fall (STC 56/1994, 24 February, case *Juicio de faltas*). Moreover, according to the European Convention, that information must be in a language he/she understands, so that this right carries with it for anyone who does not know the language used by the court, 'the right to be helped by an interpreter, free of charge whose fees cannot subsequently be reclaimed' (JECtHR 26 April 1979, case *Luedicke*).
(c) The right to use the evidence pertinent for his defence: to be able to defend their position, the parties in a trial have the right to put forward the proof they deem

necessary, which the judge can admit or reject, in a separate hearing on its relevance, if he/she does not consider it useful, legal, or appropriate (STC 43/2003, 3 March, case *Chuliá Rebolleda*).

(d) The right to refrain from incriminating oneself and pleading guilty: the duty of collaborating with the courts, established in the Constitution (Article 118), does not apply to the accused, who can remain silent about the facts imputed against them or even purely and simply lie in their own statements to avoid conviction (STC 153/1997, 29 September, case *Torrecilla Gómez*). Equally, Article 24.2 envisages a law to regulate those cases in which, for reasons of family relationships or professional secrecy, collaboration is not demanded. This stipulation is developed by Article 416 of LECrim.

(e) The right to the presumption of innocence: to convict a defendant, evidence is required to displace the presumption of innocence since the accused comes to court as innocent and 'can only leave it as guilty if that first state of innocence is totally nullified by the evidence brought forward in support of the charges' (STC 124/2001, 4 June, case *José María Sala*). The principle of free assessment of the evidence (Article 741 LECrim) permits the court to consider when the defendant can be convicted beyond all reasonable doubt, always bearing in mind that the proof to be assessed must be given in oral proceedings and without using evidence forbidden or obtained in violation of fundamental rights as expressly mandated by Article 11 of the LOPJ (*see* paragraph 384).

Chapter 5. Economic, Social and Cultural Rights

§1. Constitutional Rights

I. Property Rights

A. *The Right to Private Property and Inheritance*

422. Far from the controversies of the first half of the twentieth century, private property has become consolidated throughout the world as a right of persons, and there is no political democratic force that does not accept it. The 1978 Spanish Constitution does so in Article 33; however, this does not have the quality of a fundamental right since it is set out in Section 2 of Chapter II, and so its legal regime is neither regulated by organic law nor is it protected by an appeal for constitutional protection of fundamental rights. This does not mean a return to the eighteenth-century individualistic concept of private property but rather that the Constitution is very conscious of society's general interests, and so it orders that 'the social function' of these rights 'shall determine the limits of their content, in accordance with the law' (Article 33.2); furthermore, it permits expropriation only for justified cause of public utility or social interest, after proper indemnification in accordance with the provisions of law (Article 33.3). Although, by its very nature, expropriation is an administrative act, and the Constitutional Court has accepted legislative expropriations by single laws: in the first case, it did so considering that Article 33 of the Constitution was not violated provided that there was an exceptional situation that justified not using the ordinary process but rather the exceptional way of such a State law (STC 6/1991, 15 January, case *Ley de expropiación del Grupo Rumasa*) or an autonomous law (STC 73/2000, 14 March, case *Ley Foral 9/1996, de Espacios Naturales Protegidos de Navarra*). Subsequently, placing more emphasis on effective judicial protection (which weakens when those expropriated *ex lege* cannot go to the Contentious-Administrative courts) has also demanded, moreover, that those laws of a single case are not discriminatory and do not prevent the exercise of fundamental rights (*see* paragraph 68). It is precisely the lack of justification of this exceptional situation that has led the Court to the only declaration of unconstitutionality, which it has made until now for the breach of the right of property: against the Law passed by the Parliament of the Canary Islands 2/1992, 26 June, that expropriated certain buildings contiguous to its parliament without justifying why those were chosen and not others equally contiguous (STC 48/2015, 5 March). On the contrary, the Constitutional Court denied that the right to property is affected by a legislative expropriation when the Courts approve a law that lowers the retirement age, thus, causing officials to retire earlier than they thought when they agreed to their places or when, by law, it is established that pensions will not be revalued the following year, because in both cases it is about expectations of rights and not of real rights and 'only the deprivation of property and rights can be expropriated and, therefore, compensable. And even legitimate patrimonial interests not yet guaranteed as subjective rights (for example, precarious situations); but in no case are they expectations' (SSTCC 108/1986, 29 July, case *LOPJ-II* and 49/2015, 5 March, case

108/1986, 29 July, case *LOPJ-II* and 49/2015, 5 March, case *Real Decreto-ley 28/2012, de medidas de consolidación y garantía del sistema de la Seguridad Social*).

For this social function, the Spanish legal system does not include a unifying property statute, but the legislator can establish a number of types of property according to the various types of goods that can be subject to ownership. Moreover, private property is not merely a bundle of rights over things but also 'a set of rights and duties established, in accordance with the law, paying attention to the values and interests of community' (STC 37/1987, 26 March, case *Ley andaluza de reforma agraria*).

This capacity of the law to include social interest when defining the content of property has special relevance when applied to urban property, where the State can employ legal concepts for this type of property very different from those regulated by the Civil Code to the extent of dissociating ownership of land from the right to build, which is subject to considerable public intervention (STC 164/2001, 11 July, case *Ley sobre régimen del suelo y valoraciones*).

B. The Right to Create a Foundation

423. Article 34 of the Constitution recognizes, for the first time in a constitutional text, the right to create a foundation 'for purposes of general interest, in accordance with law'. In the first draft of the text, this right was regulated in the same article as the right to association, Article 22, but the Senate wisely moved it to follow the article on the right to property since, historically, it has always been linked to it, as the Constitutional Court has recognized on one of the few occasions when it has had cause to refer to it: 'it is another example of the autonomy of will with respect to goods, by virtue of which a person can dispose of his property freely, within limits and in the conditions established by law' (STC 48/1988, 14 July, case *CEMSATSE*). On the other hand, by situating definitively the right to create foundations in Article 34 and not in Article 22, the constituent body shaped it as an ordinary constitutional right without the regime of fundamental rights in the strict sense (*see* paragraph 321). By this move, two of the characteristics of Article 22 were maintained: the prohibition of foundations that pursue criminal aims or use such methods and the guarantee that they can only be dissolved or suspended by virtue of a reasoned judicial resolution.

Law 50/2002 on Foundations establishes a common regime for all Spanish foundations and regulates those under State competence, while Autonomous Communities have the competence to regulate those that carry out their activity within the Community territory. Amongst these common conditions, the traditional public protectorate over foundations catches attention, a control that the law seeks to justify by 'the proper exercise' of this right; a very weak argument if understood literally and which must be understood more broadly because both the social aims and the tax incentives enjoyed by foundations authorize a public control over these 'non-profit making organizations, that by the will of their creators, have so greatly affected their property by carrying out work of general interest' (Article 1).

C. Free Enterprise

424. The old freedom of industry, whose promotion was one of the powers of parliament, according to the meritorious Constitution of 1812, appears in its modern counterpart as a free enterprise that Article 38 recognizes 'in the framework of a market economy', ordering the public authorities to guarantee it 'in accordance with the demands of the general economy, and as the case may be in keeping with planning'. The guarantee of free enterprise by the public authorities and the proclamation of the market economy justify the many norms dedicated to supervising competition so that it is not a restriction on economic liberty but rather a way of 'avoiding practices that could seriously affect or damage an element so decisive in the economy of the market as competition amongst businesses' (STC 208/1999, 11 November, case *Ley 16/1989 de Defensa de la Competencia*). Evidently, Article 38 is an essential piece of the economic Constitution, the constitutional norms that lay down the field of action of the public authorities in this area and that, logically, centre on the market as the basic system to produce and distribute goods and services, a system that was reinforced with Spain's entry into the EC in 1986, whose economic principles are established precisely to achieve a broad market governed by the four liberties of free circulation of persons, goods, services, and capital.

Article 38 does not proscribe all public intervention that does not fall within the supervision of competition since the demands of the general economy permit the State and the Communities to intervene in many varied situations; to require special conditions in the setting-up of certain businesses (such as banks), to regulate trading hours, to impose certain requisites for the production of some types of goods, etc. However, it must not be forgotten that free enterprise, and especially the power of management enjoyed by businesses, must be exercised in such a way that the dignity of the workers is respected and their fundamental rights are not violated (STC 98/2000, 10 April, case *Casino de la Toja*).

II. Employment Rights

A. The Right to Work and the Free Choice of Occupation

425. Article 35 establishes 'the duty to work and the right to work', a right that, although does not create a corresponding obligation on the public authorities to provide a job for everyone who wants to exercise that right, does carry with it the obligation to establish an economic policy that makes its exercise feasible, as shown expressly by Article 40 which states that the public authorities shall realize a policy aimed at full employment. For this reason, the Constitutional Court has referred to the double aspect, individual and collective, of the right to work. The first is given expression in the equal right of all to a particular post if they fulfil the necessary requirements and qualifications and in the right to continuity and stability of employment, that is, not to be unfairly dismissed; the collective aspect of the right to work 'implies an order to the public authorities to carry out a policy of full employment, since otherwise the exercise of the right to work by one part of the population necessarily brings with it the denial of that same right to the other part' (STC 22/1981, 2 July, case *Estatuto de los Trabajadores-I*).

As an element of the freedom to work, Article 35 itself recognizes the free choice of profession or occupation, which is not the right to perform whatever economic activity that a person desires but rather that of freely choosing one's occupation, provided that it is always in accord with the normative demands applicable to that activity, since to protect the general interest, the public authorities 'can intervene in the exercise of certain professional activities, requiring that an authorization or administrative license be first obtained or aptitude tests passed' (STC 122/1989, 6 July, case *Exámenes para guías en Cantabria*). Moreover, the unusual Article 36 of the Constitution (without precedent in Comparative Constitutional Law) orders the legislator to regulate the legal system of the professional associations and the exercise of graduate professions, so giving the legislator special power to regulate certain professions, even to the extent of permitting restrictions in the fundamental law of associations since compulsory membership of a professional association can be required when it is necessary to regulate a specific profession (*see* paragraph 406).

B. The Fundamental Right to found Trade Unions and Collective Negotiation

426. Maintaining the system of the Constitution, which cites trade unions in the preliminary title, we have already had occasion to speak of freedom of association in dealing with the relevant actors of the social and democratic State of Law, parties, trade unions, and associations of entrepreneurs (*see* paragraph 102). Let us now add some notes from the individual perspective, beginning by specifying that it is a right that can be exercised by all employees, including civil servants, although Article 28.1 of the *Lex Legum* allows the law to limit or exempt members of the Armed Forces and other bodies subject to military discipline, as is currently the case. Article 127.1 SC prohibits it to judges, although it recognizes the right of professional associations. Organic Law 11/1985 on Freedom of Association (LOLS) specifies that self-employed workers, the unemployed, and pensioners do not have the right to form unions for the protection of their particular interests, but they can join the unions already constituted as well as have the right of association. Therefore, the most representative organization of the self-employed is not a union but an association, the Association of Autonomous Workers, which has managed to become a regular interlocutor of the government and participate both in the State Council of Autonomous Workers and in the Economic and Social Councils. The same LOLS specifies that its content includes the right to form trade unions, the right to join the trade union one wishes, the right of members to elect their leaders, and the right to trade union activity, which the Constitutional Court has had the opportunity to protect in a diversity of assumptions, from the crudest dismissals for belonging to a union to the most sophisticated ones, such as the prohibition of using corporate email to disseminate information amongst union members (STC 281/2005, 7 November, case *CCOO v. BBVA*). We have already had occasion to point out that, procedurally, the simple indications are sufficient to consider the violation of freedom of association has occurred, the defendants having the burden of proving that their apparently anti-union acts had another justification (*see* paragraph 354).

427. Free enterprise and the right to work converge in Article 37 of the Constitution in recognizing the right of workers and employers to collective negotiation, guaranteeing the binding force of the agreement reached in such negotiations. The Law of the Statute of Workers gives concrete expression to the regime of collective negotiations and collective agreements, a text that was approved for the first time in 1980 (Law 8/1980, 10 March), but since then, there has not been a year in which no modifications have been made, up to the point that there have already been two consolidated texts, one in 1995 and another, the current one, in 2015, Royal Legislative Decree 2/2015, 23 October, approving the revised text of Law of the Statute of Workers. Next came Act 3/2012, 6 July, on urgent measures for the reform of the labour market, which profoundly changed the system of collective bargaining, which was appealed by the opposition parties, but held to be constitutional by the highest interpreter of the Constitution (STC 8/2015, 22 January, case *Ley 3/2012, de medidas urgentes para la reforma del mercado laboral*). As in the case of education legislation, each change of political majority in parliament means changes in labour legislation, which in one way or another end up before the Constitutional Court. Thus, Law 3/2012, with a PP majority, has been amended by Royal Decree-Law 32/2021, of 28 December, on urgent measures for labour reform, guaranteeing employment stability and the transformation of the labour market, with a PSOE-UP majority. Perhaps one day, the parties will achieve a stable framework for labour relations in which ideological differences are less marked.

The incorporation of labour agreements in the system of sources does not mean that the whole of a sector of such importance as labour relations is left to self-regulation regardless of what is established by law since this, a manifestation of popular will, is hierarchically superior to agreements. In consequence, it can 'deploy a limiting potential over collective negotiations and can equally, in exceptional circumstances reserve to itself certain matters that are, therefore, excluded from collective contracts' (STC 58/1985, 30 April, case *Estatuto de los trabajadores-II*). Therefore, 'by virtue of the principle of normative hierarchy, it is the collective agreement that must respect and submit not only to the formal law but, more generically, to the norms of greater hierarchical rank and not the other way around' (ATC 85/2011, 7 June, citing many previous rulings such as the SSTC 210/1990, 92/1994 and 62/2001). This doctrine has been applied on several occasions by ordinary courts. One of the most spectacular judgments on this matter is the Judgment of the Social Chamber of the High Court 47/2010, 10 May, which endorsed the constitutionality of Law 9/2010, 14 April, which regulates the provision of air traffic services and sets certain working conditions for civil air traffic controllers. This had the effect of modifying the Collective Agreement subscribed by AENA and the air traffic controllers once the negotiations for its renovation had failed.

C. *The Right to Adopt Measures in Collective Conflicts and the Fundamental Right to Strike*

428. Subsection (2) of Article 37 recognizes the right of workers and employers to adopt measures dealing with collective conflicts, remitting to law the exercise of this right, including precise guarantees to ensure the functioning of the essential services of the community. However, one of the measures that logically can be thought of in this context, the strike, is expressly recognized in Article 28, along with the right to form trade unions, so designating it as a true fundamental right (*see* paragraph 269). Therefore, the Constitutional Court has indicated that there is no equality of arms (*Kampfparität*) between employers and workers from the point of view of the Constitution since the latter has a fundamental right that the former lack, perhaps – I would add – as a means of compensating for the superiority of weapons that employers have in daily life. The Court itself has explained the practical differences between this lack of equivalence between the employers' power of the lockout and the strike: the lockout 'is not a strike of employers, because it is a defence, not a claim. A lockout is not legal when it is used to prevent or punish a strike, that is, when it destroys the content of the fundamental right to strike, or when it acts as a barrier to prevent it. Furthermore, the burden of proof of the existence of the real elements of an abusive strike lies on the employer' (STC 226/1988 28 November, case *Montefibre Hispania*).

A striking feature of the Spanish legal system is the lack of the organic law demanded by Article 28.2 to develop the right to strike. In 1992, the parliament was about to pass one, with the approval of the main trade unions, but its early dissolution prevented it, and no political party has since proposed its regulation. That is why the provisions of the pre-Constitutional Decree-law 17/1977, 4 March, on Labour Relations have been completed largely by the jurisprudence that both the Constitutional Court (starting with its STC 11/1981, which annulled several Articles of that Decree-law) and the jurisdiction has dealt casuistically with the polemical concepts of this right: the fixing of the essential services of the community referred to in Article 28.2,[61] the definition of abusive strike, the administration's power to determine the minimum services that must be provided, etc. Perhaps the most interesting precedent that the Constitutional Court has created on the right to strike has concerned the concept of 'workers' interests' that Article 28.2 of the Constitution requires for a strike to be legal. According to the Court, this is not limited to the interests of the strikers resulting from specific collective negotiations but has to be interpreted in a broad sense, namely, the interests of 'the category of workers'. This makes a general strike rejecting a government decision totally constitutional even when it has been adopted by law or norms with the force of law as Royal Decree-law (RDL); for example, the strike called on 20 June 2002 against RDL of 24 May for urgent measures for the reform of benefits for the unemployed and improvement

61. This fixing of minimum services 'by companies responsible for the provision of any kind of public services or of recognized and unavoidable necessity' (Art. 10 RDL 17/1977) is the most problematic aspect of strikes, where unions often consider that the governmental authority sets excessively high percentages and appeals to the courts. *See* Francisco Javier Gárate Castro, *Derecho de huelga* (Bomarzo 2013).

of training for employment (STC 183/2006, 20 July, case *Servicios mínimos en RTVE).* The same applies to the general strike of 29 September 2010 against the reform of employment law set out in Law 35/2010, 17 September.

§2. Guiding Principles of Social and Economic Policy

I. The Legal Value of the Guiding Principles

429. Chapter III of Title I of the Constitution, an inevitable result of the shaping of Spain as a social and democratic State of Law, includes under the rubric 'guiding principles of social and economic policy' 14 Articles (39–52), where various types of norms are brought together under the legal regime framed in Article 53.3, which is substantially distinct from the one that previously protected fundamental rights: 'recognition, respect and protection of the principles recognized in the Third Chapter shall guide positive legislation, judicial practice and the actions of public authorities. They may also be argued before ordinary jurisdiction through procedures established in the laws affecting them'. For this reason, not only are Articles 39–52 excluded from the appeal for constitutional protection of fundamental rights, but the petitions based directly on the articles in Chapter III to the ordinary courts cannot succeed, not even on the few occasions in which the word 'right' is used: as the Constitutional Court has pointed out, these are, basically, commands and authorizations to the legislator, not subjective public rights that can be directly argued before the courts but only in accordance with the laws that develop them. Moreover, in this *interpositio legislatoris* the legislator's freedom to shape the law is greater than in the case of fundamental rights since only they have their essential content guaranteed. Even the development of programmatic norms is not reserved exclusively for formal law (STC 19/1982, 5 May, case *Jon Carbonell v. INSS*).

But the fact that the programmatic norms of Chapter III do not give subjective rights does not mean that they are empty and rhetorical, *ad pompam obstentationem*. In the first place, by their inclusion in the Constitution, they serve to control legislative action, both by limiting it and by influencing its design. Thus, for example, the Constitution demands a public pension system without prejudice to enhancing the 'constitutional guaranteed minimum' by a private system (STC 113/1989, 22 June, case *Article 22 de la Ley General de la Seguridad Social*). In the second place, because the guiding principles direct judicial practice and the actions of the public authorities, legal bodies and persons are obliged to interpret the law in force in accordance with the Constitution, *secundum Constitutionem*, while not forgetting the guiding principles of economic and social policy (STC 95/2000, 10 April, case *Roig Broz*).

430. In short, the legal and political role of these constitutional rights must be considered not only for grounding the actions of the public authorities but also to support the claims of specific social groups who can demand certain conduct from the State based on these rights.

II. Classification of Guiding Principles

A. *Social Rights*

431. Various articles of Chapter III set out social rights, although, as already seen, it is a question of legally configured rights. They are as follows:

(a) Article 43 recognizes the right to health protection, authorizing the public authorities to organize a public health system. These authorities are the States responsible for basic legislation such as Law 14/1986, 25 April, General Health, and the Autonomous Communities responsible for providing medical services. Using this basic competence, the government approved Decree-Law 7/2018, 27 July, on universal access to the National Health System, by which the health coverage traditionally offered to Spaniards and resident foreigners was extended to foreigners who, being in Spain, did not have their legal residence in Spanish territory, the *illegals* in popular parlance (*see* paragraph 445).
(b) The right to 'access to culture' (Article 44 SC), which completes cultural freedom guaranteed by Article 20 (*see* paragraph 305), with a mandate to the public authorities to promote culture, science, and scientific and technical research. Both the State and the Autonomous Communities pursue a very active policy (perhaps, at times, too interventionist) in the cultural sphere with a vast number of tax incentives, subsidies, prizes and organization and sponsorship of cultural events of all types.
(c) The conservationist concerns of the constituent body caused them to follow the line of the latest Constitutions approved at that time – such as the Greek in 1975 and the Portuguese in 1976 – and to recognize the right to enjoy the environment 'for the development of the person'. The Constitutional Court has underlined this aim of Article 45 and does not intend to renounce economic growth and the exploitation of natural resources but to propose sustainable development (to use the fashionable phrase of the *Brundtland Report*), which does not have only the single aim of 'the maximum exploitation of natural resources, the increase of production at all cost, but rather of harmonizing the 'rational use' of these resources with the protection of nature, all for the better development of the person and ensuring a better quality of life' (STC 64/1982, 4 November, case *Ley catalana de espacios de especial interés natural afectados por actividades extractivas*).
(d) Article 47 recognizes the right of all Spaniards 'to decent and adequate housing', for which it orders the public authorities to promote the conditions necessary to make this right effective by 'regulating the use of land in accordance with the general interest to prevent speculation'. Based on that mandate, or perhaps in an interventionist tradition, both the State and the Autonomous Communities have passed several laws to regulate land and encourage the building of affordable housing (*see* paragraph 422). Examples are the Royal Decree-Law 7/2019, 1 March, on urgent housing and rental measures (partially declared unconstitutional by STC 14/2020, 28 January, due to insufficient justification of the enabling budget), the Foral Law of Navarra 10/2010, 10 May, on the Right to Housing in Navarra, and Law 1/2010, 8 March, Regulating the Right to

Housing in Andalusia, the latter backed by Article 25 of the new Andalusian Autonomous Statute of 2007 which recognizes the right to decent housing and stipulates that this right should be guaranteed for persons with insufficient resources. The local authorities also have competences for town planning and execution, and so they play a very active role both in the marketing of local building sites and in the construction of buildings. The economic crisis of 2008 led to a new wave of laws that sought to realize the right to decent housing by protecting homeowners against their expulsion for non-payment of their mortgage. Thus, the State Law 1/2013, 14 May, sets out measures to strengthen the protection of mortgage debtors, restructuring of debt and social rent; the Andalusian Decree-law 6/2013, 9 April, of measures to ensure compliance with the Social Function of Housing; the Basque Law 3/2015, 18 June, of Housing, etc. The always difficult articulation between the basic state legislation and the autonomous one of development – even more so when the ideologies of the governing parties do not coincide – has given rise to appeals before the Constitutional Court that have originated the declaration of unconstitutionality of some provisions of these autonomous norms due to invasion of the sphere reserved to the State, such as SSTC 93/2015, 14 May and 37/2022, 10 March. The former declared unconstitutional and null several articles of Andalusian Decree-Law 6/2013 because they defined the essential content of the right to property and regulated the expropriation of uninhabited dwellings, both of which are matters that correspond exclusively to the State. In contrast, the second annulled several articles of the Law of the Parliament of Catalonia 18/2017 because they affected the principle of free determination of the rent established by the State legislator.

B. *Mandates to Protect Specific Social Groups*

432. It has already been repeatedly pointed out that the social and democratic State of Law does not have the strict liberal view of society as a set of individuals, free citizens, equal before the law and the public authorities, whose integration into intermediate groups – that had served so well in the absolute State to permit inequalities and privileges – was a hindrance to progress that had to be combated (*see* paragraph 22). The social State recognizes the existence of social groups who deserve to be treated differently, precisely, so that freedom and equality 'are real and effective' (Article 9.1 SC). The consequences for the constitutional system are far-reaching in all spheres: from the admission of particular *laws* in the system of sources to a new interpretation of the principle of equality, without forgetting the differentiated application of certain fundamental rights, such as the right to public position (*see* paragraph 410). Logically, Chapter III of Title I is the right place to enumerate those collectives whose interests must be safeguarded by the social state:

(a) The family: Article 39 orders the public authorities to ensure the social, economic, and legal protection of the family.

(b) The workers: full employment is an objective of the public authorities, who must also guarantee professional training, safety, and hygiene at work, as necessary rest through the restriction on working days and paid holidays (Article 40). There are innumerable State and autonomous norms to achieve these ends, although the economic crisis that began in 2007 has resulted in a situation far from full employment.

(c) The State shall especially safeguard the rights of Spanish workers overseas (Article 42). Whether for the success of the measures adopted by the State to comply with this principle or for more complex economic development reasons, the fact was that of some 3 million Spaniards abroad in 1978, in 2010, the figure had lowered by half, only – because of the economic crisis of 2007 – to go back up to almost 2.5 million in 2017. At present, the most relevant rule in this matter is Law 40/2006,14 December, *del Estatuto de la ciudadanía española en el exterior* (on the Statute of Spanish citizenship abroad) that sets the legal framework that guarantees Spaniards abroad the exercise of their constitutional rights and duties in terms of equality with Spaniards residing in Spain. In addition, this Statute sets the forms of collaboration between the State and the Autonomous Communities, both in support of Spaniards abroad and those who decide to return.

(d) Young People: the public authorities shall promote the conditions for the 'free and effective participation' of young people in political, social, economic, and cultural development (Article 48). The law specifically developing this Article is Law 18/1983, 16 November, *de Creación del Organismo Autónomo Consejo de la Juventud de España* (Creation of Body of Autonomous Council of Spanish Youth).

(e) Disabled people: the public authorities shall not only implement a policy that meets their needs (for medical treatment, care, etc.) but shall also ensure that they can enjoy all the rights that the first Title attributes to citizens (Article 49). This mandate has been the basis for a good deal of legislation for social integration and positive discrimination measures, such as those set out in Law 53/2003 on public employment for the handicapped and in the Royal Legislative Decree 1/2013 approving the Consolidated Text of the General Law on the rights of persons with disabilities and their social inclusion. This last norm largely transposes in Spain the International Convention on the Rights of Persons with Disabilities, adopted by the UN General Assembly on 13 December 2006.

(f) Old People: the public authorities shall establish 'adequate and periodically updated pensions' and a system of social services to take care of 'the specific problems' of elderly people (Article 50). In 1995 Congress approved a report on the structural problems of the Social Security system and the main reforms to be undertaken, which is known as the 'Toledo Pact' due to the place where the major parties agreed on this document. The main objective of this pact was to reduce the pressure to which the Social Security budget was subject. Since then, different reforms have been carried out in this line, the last one of which has been for the moment – and with great controversy – the Decree-law 28/2012, 30 November, *de medidas de consolidación y garantía del sistema de la Seguridad Social* (on consolidation measures and guarantee for Social Security), which was appealed before the Constitutional Court by the PSOE, although the Constitutional Court rejected its appeal (STC 49/2015, 5 March). With the accession of the PSOE government in 2018, this reform was partially amended by Royal Decree-Law 1/2020, 14 January, which establishes the revaluation and maintenance of pensions and public benefits of the Social Security system.

(g) Consumers: the public authorities shall guarantee health, safety, and economic interests of consumers (Article 51). The bulk of the rights of consumers, which logically is to say everyone, are laid down in Royal Legislative Decree 1/2007, 16 November, which approved the Consolidated revised text of the General Law for the defence of consumers and users, modified several times to adapt it to the directives of the EU and to strengthen the protection of consumers. Thus, for example, by Royal Decree-Laws 9/2017, 26 May and 7/2021, 27 April, transposing EU directives; by Law 4/2018, 11 June (approved by the Spanish Parliament at the initiative of the Parliament of Navarre) to prevent discrimination against AIDS patients, especially in the field of insurance; by Law 4/2022, 25 February, on the protection of consumers and users in situations of social and economic vulnerability, etc.

C. *Other Objectives of Public Policies*

433. As well as laying down social rights and protection of specific groups who need the special care of the social State, Chapter III contains other mandates that the public authorities must pursue, such as:

(a) A more equitable distribution of regional and personal income (Article 40). This mandate still needs to be achieved as the 1978 distribution of personal and regional income remains unchanged in the 2020s if it has not increased.[62]

(b) The maintenance and services of a public system of social security for all citizens that will guarantee social assistance sufficient in case of need, especially in cases of unemployment (Article 41). The Constitutional Court has clarified that that public regime does not require 'necessarily and in every case a system of direct public management' (STC 84/2015, 30 April, case *Ley 8/2012, de medidas fiscales y administrativas de la Comunidad de Madrid*). To this must now be added the creation in 2020 of the Minimum Living Income as a non-contributory economic benefit within the protective action of the Social Security system (Royal Decree-Law 20/2020, 29 May).

(c) The protection of the national heritage, which stipulates that any actions against it shall be treated as crimes (Article 46), which is an unusual clause to find in a constitutional text. Following this mandate, the Criminal Code categorized crimes against the national Heritage in Articles 321–324.

62. *See* Fundación FOESSA, *VIII Informe sobre exclusión y desarrollo social en España* (Cáritas Española Editores 2019).

§3. Protection of Minorities

434. As we have just seen, the Spanish Constitution sets out norms to protect various groups, such as children, young people, the elderly, and the disabled but does not establish any specific care for what in Comparative law – with Article 27 of ICCPR at its head – are known as minorities, groups identified by race, religion, or language; in fact, it does not even use the term 'minority' in this sense.[63] It does, however, have an impressive number of provisions to give effect to the right of autonomy of the 'nationalities and regions', a form of protection for minorities settled in a territory. From the general perspective of the collective of persons distributed throughout the territory of Spain, the Magna Carta contains many provisions that play a major role in defending these minorities, beginning with the superior values of the legal system proclaimed in Article 1.1 and in the right to equality of Article 14. Liberty of ideology, religion, and worship are also norms that protect minorities. Moreover, most fundamental rights act to protect them by setting out and defending their interests (freedom of expression, association, meeting, etc.). There is no need to go back to the expulsion of the Jews in 1492 or to the Moors in 1609 to understand the importance of the right of equality for the protection of minorities, understood as the right not to be discriminated against on the grounds of birth, race, sex, religion, opinion, or any other personal or social condition or circumstance. It is enough to recall the legal system of Franco that contained discriminatory norms against the Roma people, the most numerous minority throughout Spain.[64] In contrast, Article 9.3 commands the public authorities to promote conditions so that liberty and equality of the individual and the groups to which he/she belongs shall be real and effective; facilitate a specific policy – including positive discrimination for this minority by the State and the Autonomous Communities (such as Andalusia, where the greatest number of Spanish Roma reside, has been doing for years), which has its principal institutional expression in the State Council for the Roma People – *Consejo Estatal del Pueblo Gitano* – created by Real Decree 891/2005, 22 July. At the autonomous level, the statutory reforms of the twenty-first century have taken this minority into account. Thus Article 42 of the Catalan Statute orders the public authorities to guarantee the recognition of the rights of the Roma people 'as a safeguard of the historical reality of this people'. Equally, Article 9 of the Andalusian Statute places amongst the aims of the Autonomous Community (where the greatest number of Spanish Roma live) the promotion

63. The word 'minority' and the word 'minor' appear only twice in the SC, referring to persons under the age of majority: in Art. 39, stating, 'parents must provide their children, born in or out of wedlock, with assistance of every kind during the time they are minors', and in Art. 59, establishing the Regency 'during the King's minority'. Art. 27 of the ICCPR has been developed by the Declaration on the rights of persons belonging to national or ethnic, religious or linguistic minorities, approved by Resolution 47/135 of the General Assembly of UNO, 18 Dec. 1992. For Europe, *see* the European Charter on Regional and Minority Languages, signed in Strasburg on 5 Nov. 1992 and the Framework Convention for the Protection of National Minorities (No. 157 of the Council of Europe), Signed in Strasburg on 1 Feb. 1995. Spain has ratified both international instruments for the protection of minorities.

64. For example, Arts 4–6 of the Regulations of the Guardia Civil of 1943, which required special vigilance over the Roma population, remained in force until 1978 when a Roma deputy proposed its repeal.

of the 'conditions necessary for the full integration of minorities, and especially that of the Roma, for its complete social integration'.

435. For its part, the Constitutional Court has had several appeals alleging a breach of constitutional rights in which belonging to a minority was a crucial factor in determining a possible violation of a fundamental right. An example is STC 214/1991, 11 November, case *Violeta Friedman v. León Degrelle,* where the Court held that the defendant had violated the plaintiff's right to honour in his declarations in which he doubted the existence of the gas chambers and made offensive comments about the Jews. However, the Court rejected the appeal of a black woman against a police officer who demanded her identification in a railway station, even though she was the only person whom he asked to identify herself (STC 214/2001, 29 January, *Williams Lecraft)* However, the UN Committee on Human Rights considered that the action of the Spanish police officer was contrary to Articles 2.3 and 26 of ICCPR because he differentiated the appellant without using any objective criteria, and, moreover, the Spanish State had 'offered her no satisfaction, such as an apology by way of compensation' (Decision approved 27 July 2009 in case 1493/2006, *Williams Lecraft v. Spain*). The ECtHR has also had occasion to correct a similar decision of the Spanish Constitutional Court, STC 69/2007, 16 April, when the court in Strasburg gave its Judgment of 8 December 2009, holding that Spain had discriminated against Mrs Muñoz Diaz in not recognizing the evidentiary value of her Roma marriage in 1971 for a widow's pension although it had previously accepted it for other legal acts such as the family book and social security card.

436. A group that in recent years has been receiving special protection in advanced States is that of Lesbian, gay, bisexual, transgender and intersex (LGBTI) people, especially since a group of jurists meeting in the Indonesian city of Yogyakarta in 2007 approved the Yogyakarta 'Principles on the Application of International Human Rights Law in relation to Sexual Orientation and Gender Identity', which, although logically they do not have normative value, are a source of inspiration. As we have already studied, Spain was one of the first States to regulate same-sex marriage, with its inclusion in the Civil Code in 2005 and STC 198/2012, considering it not only compatible with the Constitution but protected by Article 32 (*see* paragraph 389). In recent years, various parliamentary groups have submitted bills 'on social equality for lesbian, gay, bisexual, transgender and intersex people' (UP in 2017, in similar terms Ciudadanos in 2020). However, they were not taken into consideration by the Plenary of Congress. For its part, the government approved in 2022 a Draft Bill for the real and effective equality of trans people and the guarantee of the rights of LGTBI people; therefore, by one means or another, it is foreseeable that Spain will not take long to have a law protecting this group. There is already one in different Autonomous Communities, from the pioneering Galician Law 2/2014, 14 April, for equal treatment and non-discrimination of lesbians, gays, bisexuals, transgender and intersex people in Galicia (with a similar name in Catalonia, Extremadura, Murcia, La Rioja, etc.).

Chapter 6. Constitutional Duties

§1. Overall View

437. The constitutionalist movement has always maintained in its conception of citizenship that people are not only holders of 'inalienable and sacred' rights – in the phrase used in the French Declaration of 1789 – but also subject to duties towards others and to society in general. The first and most elemental is, logically, respect for the legal system, as the 1812 Constitution demanded (every Spaniard 'is obliged to be loyal to the Constitution, to obey the laws and respect the established authorities'), while Article 9 of the present one reads: 'The citizens and public powers are subject to the Constitution and the rest of the legal system.' Derived from this submission to the legal system and the very conception of fundamental rights arises the duty to respect the rights of others, as required by Article 4 of the French Declaration of 1789 and set out in Article 10.1 of our Constitution. In my opinion, this is the latent idea behind the obligation to 'be just and charitable' laid down in the 1812 Constitution, a peculiar and simple transposition of the three *iuris praecepta* of Roman law (to live honestly, to harm no one, and to give each his due).

438. But as well as these generic duties, the historic texts bring together the two basic duties of collaborating with society: the duty to make an economic contribution to the expenses of the State and that of defending 'the Fatherland' by arms, duties that the 1978 Constitution updated in modern terminology, at the same time as it introduced a whole raft of duties unknown in our constitutional history. Inevitably, the Constitution does not go into detail to spell out the specific content of each duty, the procedures for their enforcement or the sanctions in case of non-compliance. Thus, none of them can be directly demanded by the citizen; it is rather a question of legal duties. This is markedly different from fundamental rights, which are directly and immediately effective, since, thanks to the essential content of the Magna Carta, they can be exercised and, where appropriate, claimed against the public powers without intermediate legislation. This *Lex interposita* which develops constitutional duties imposing specific determined obligations will normally be 'law' in the strict sense of the word, above all, if it establishes sanctions in the event of non-compliance, as demanded by the principle of penal legality punishment set out in Article 25 of the Constitution. This law will also be a State law, as Article 149.1 specifies that the State shall regulate the basic conditions that guarantee equality in fulfilling constitutional duties (*see* paragraph 238).

§2. Classification

I. The Duty to Defend Spain

A. *Military Obligations*

439. Since the 1812 Constitution established the duty to 'defend the fatherland by arms' (Article 9) and ordered that 'no Spaniard will be excused from military service when and in the form, he is called by law' (Article 361), all historical Constitutions have recognized this duty in similar wording. In the 1978 Constitution, this became the 'right and the duty to defend Spain' (Article 30.1 SC) and was given expression in obligatory military service; although conscientious objectors were exempted from this duty, although the obligation to perform substitute social service was demanded (Article 30.2 SC). As at the time the Constitution was approved, this objection was not recognized and the obligation to join 'the ranks' still existed, the immediate problem that presented itself was the way in which conscientious objection could be exercised, solved by the Constitutional Court through the device of delaying enlistment until the legislator passed the necessary law. In 1984 such a law was approved, establishing a system of compulsory military service and a substitute civil social service for objectors. However, Law 17/1999, 18 May, on the Personal Regime of the Armed Forces, created, with the support of all the major parties, an exclusively professional army, functioning since January 2002, and logically suspended compulsory military service. In my opinion, this law entailed a change in Article 30.2 of the Constitution since although this does not literally set out that military service is obligatory, its terms leave little room for doubt: by ordering that a law should regulate 'with all due guarantees, conscientious objection, as well as other causes for exemption from compulsory military service' it is clear what this presupposes; otherwise it would have specified that conscientious objection would be regulated in the event that the law established compulsory military service. Now Article 30.2 can be interpreted differently from when it was passed in 1978: it is not so much a mandate to the legislator to regulate conscientious objection as a power to the legislator ('the Law shall fix the military obligations of Spaniards' it states at the beginning) to establish if it deems necessary, compulsory military service and, if it does so, it will also have to regulate the cases in which conscientious objection is permissible. Law 32/2002 supports this reinterpretation of military service that the constituent assembly had in mind as being obligatory for Spaniards by permitting foreigners to join the army and navy.

B. The Duties of Civil Protection

440. Within that same Article 30 of the Constitution, there are two subsections that empower the legislator to establish obligations for Spaniards that can be considered as derived from the duty to 'defend Spain' in Article 30.1: a civilian service may be established for the accomplishment of objectives of general interest (Article 30.3) as well as 'the duties of citizens in cases of serious risk, catastrophe or public calamity' (Article 30.4). Knowing that the legislator has abolished compulsory military service, it is not hard to understand why no use has been made of this constitutional power to establish an obligatory civilian service. It has used the constitutional permission to establish duties to approve Law 17/2015, 9 July, on the National Civil Protection System, whose Article 7*bis* establishes for all citizens and legal persons 'the duty to collaborate, personally or materially, in civil protection, in the event of a request from the competent authority per the provisions of Article 30.4 of the Constitution'. In the event of an emergency, this obligation is extended to any person (therefore also foreigners, including tourists) from the age of majority, who will be obliged to carry out the personal services required by the competent authorities in matters of civil protection without the right to compensation. It should be recalled that according to the system of distribution of competences, these authorities can be either State or regional, depending on the case (*see* paragraph 253).

II. Financial Duties

441. Maintaining a tradition that goes back to Article 8 of the Cadiz Constitution, Article 31 of 1978 orders that 'all' – Spaniards and foreigners, physical and legal persons – shall contribute to the sustenance of public expenditures according to their economic capacity. But the present *Lex legum* does not stop there and specifies that that contribution shall be made through a 'just tax system' based on the principles of equality and progressive taxation, which in no case shall be of a 'confiscatory scope' (Article 31.1). It establishes the principle of programming public expenditure according to criteria of efficiency and economy (Article 31.2) and creates a legal reservation that personal or property contributions may only be made in accordance with law (Articles 31.3 and 133.1). This does not mean that all regulation of taxes has to be found in the law, but only its essential elements (STC 108/2004, 30 June, case Real Decree-law 12/1996, *de medidas tributarias urgentes*, where the jurisprudence on the relative character of this legal reservation on tax law is summarized). This 'just tax system' is made up of a great number of laws, amongst which some of the most relevant are Law 58/2003, 17 December, General Tributaria (General Taxes); Law 37/1992, 28 December, *del Impuesto sobre el Valor Añadido* (Value Added Tax); Law 35/2006, 28 November, *del Impuesto sobre la Renta de las Personas Físicas* (Law on Taxes on Personal Income), and Law 27/2014, 27 November, *del Impuesto sobre Sociedades* (Corporation Tax).

442. Article 31.1 of the Constitution not only establishes the duty of taxpayers to contribute to the sustenance of public expenditure according to their economic capacity but also, by establishing the principles of generality, capacity, equality, and progressive taxation, it shapes a mandate that binds the public powers, obliging them to 'demand that contribution from all taxpayers whose situation shows an economic capacity capable of being taxed' (STC 96/2002, 25 April, case *Incentivos fiscales a los residentes en el resto de la Unión Europea*). Because of the dual nature, as a duty for citizens and a mandate for public authorities, there are some Constitutional Court judgments in which Article 31.1 is used to justify a specific power of the administration, such as its capacity to investigate the wealth of a citizen without violating his privacy in so doing (*see* paragraph 378), but there are many more decisions in which the limits of State's powers of taxation are fixed according to the principles of the tax system imposed by the Constitution. To briefly summarize some of its most important judgments in the matter:

(a) The principles of generality and economic capacity compel the legislator to design taxes for 'all', not only for Spaniards, and to classify as taxable all acts that show economic capacity. But this is an obligation not only to raise money since it can also be done for an economic policy (e.g., to protect the environment), provided that the principles of Article 31.1 of the Constitution are always respected, especially 'economic capacity or, what is the same thing, the taxable action has to constitute a demonstration of wealth' (STC 276/2000, 16 November, case *Article 61.2 LGT-II*). Logically, these extra-fiscal aims can also justify non-discriminatory tax allowances. However, they do not empower the legislator to tax the same economic resources (e.g., irregular income subject to income tax) more onerously for persons who have no other income and more generously for those who do (in this case those with regular incomes) because this would impose greater fiscal pressure on those least able to pay (STC 46/2000, 17 February, case *Article 84.1 LIRPF*).

(b) The principles of equality and progressive taxation require the legislator to establish an equal taxation system for equal economic situations, which can result in greater fiscal pressure for certain persons whenever the degree of progression is determined 'according to the taxable base, not taking into account the taxpayer's situation' (STC 214/1994, 14 July, case *Ley 18/1991 del IRPF*). As we have already seen, joint taxation of married couples originally established by *Ley del Impuesto de la Renta de las Personas Físicas* (Taxation Law on Income of Physical Persons) violated – according to STC 45/1989 – the principle of equality by increasing the tax payable by couples over that due from them individually, and so the law was discriminating against married persons in comparison with other couples who had not formalized their union (*see* paragraph 366). Following that reasoning on equality of spouses with other taxpayers, the Constitutional Court subsequently held that it was unconstitutional that a member of a family could not deduct in his/ her income tax return the salaries paid to other members of the family, but only 'the average annual cost of a member of the staff, if there were any, or in other cases, the amount of the interprofessional minimum salary' (STC 146/1994, 12 May, case *Ley 20/1989 de Adaptación del IRPF*); already, in the twenty-first century, it has considered that equality of taxation has been violated by treating differently families who make a joint tax declaration by permitting a variable deduction only when the taxpayer's income comes from external sources but not when it comes from another family member, as in the case – which the Court was dealing with – of a dentist who employed his wife (STC 255/2004, 23 December, case *Article 19.2b de la LIRPF*).

(c) Until now, the Constitutional Court has only considered one norm to be confiscatory: the objective system for calculating the capital gains tax on land and buildings was unconstitutional when the amount to be paid by the taxpayer was higher than the gain obtained from the sale (STC 126/2019, 31 October). Except for this obvious case, the Court has never considered that any of the norms it has had to pass judgment on were confiscatory. Wisely, and after putting forward clear examples of confiscatory norms (100% tax on income, an accumulation of various taxes that deprived the taxpayer of his income and properties), it has held that the legislator has a wide margin to determine the limits of fiscal pressure since there is 'difficulty in drawing the line, with technically operative criteria, where progressive taxation or, perhaps better, just taxation, degenerates into confiscatory' (STC 150/1990, 4 October, case *Recargo del tres por ciento*).

III. Other Constitutional Duties

443. In addition to the basic duties to defend Spain and to contribute to its economic upkeep of Articles 30 and 31, the Constitution utilizes the concept of 'duty' in other articles, briefly listed below in their order of appearance in the Magna Carta:

(a) The duty to know Castilian (Article 3.1): a duty that creates a presumption that all Spaniards know it and that justifies Castilian being the language of communication with the public powers of the State, but the right given in Article 24.1 that no one shall be undefended means that Spaniards who show that they do not understand Castilian – contrary to the literal tenor of LECrim – shall be attended by an interpreter in police enquiries (STC 74/1987, 25 May, case *Article 520.2e de la LECrim*).
(b) Family Duties: Article 32 determines that the law shall regulate the rights and duties of spouses, a logical consequence of any contract, and Article 39 orders that parents shall aid their children 'born in or out of wedlock, during the time they are minors and in other cases where it is legally proper'. The Civil Code gives concrete expression to these various family obligations.
(c) The duty to work: The constituent assembly included the duty to work in Article 35, possibly for reasons that were more pedagogical and exemplary than legal. Nevertheless, it seems to me that it can serve as a constitutional foundation for certain norms, such as the special obligation to collaborate in civilian protection activities for the unemployed who are receiving economic help, established in the repealed Law 2/1985 on Civil Protection (not maintained in the current law of 2015). It is also a basis for the requirement to prove availability to 'actively seek employment' and other similar obligations that the unemployed must fulfil if they wish to receive unemployment benefits (Law 45/2002, 12 December, on urgent measures for the reform of the system of protection for unemployment).
(d) Health Protection duties: Article 43.2 orders that the law shall establish 'the rights and duties of all' with respect to public health. Various laws fulfil this mandate, such as the Organic Law 3/1986, on special measures for public health (widely used by regional health authorities to combat COVID-19); Law 14/1986, General Health; and Law 41/2002, the basic regulator of patient autonomy and of the rights and obligations concerning information and clinical documentation.
(e) The duty to preserve the environment: Article 45 not only proclaims the right to enjoy the environment but also establishes the 'duty to preserve it' and requires the law to lay down penal and administrative sanctions and the obligation on those who cause damage to repair it. Logically, outstanding amongst the considerable number of State and autonomous laws that regulate activities related to the environment (extraction of minerals, natural spaces, hunting and fishing, pollution prevention, etc.) is the Criminal Code, which has recognized the crime

of ecological damage since 1984. It is also worth highlighting the 'duty of caution and self-protection' to avoid the generation of risks required by Law 17/2015, 9 July, on the National Civil Protection System.

(f) The duty of appearing before investing Commissions: Article 76.2 lays down the duty of appearing before these Commissions, which is regulated by Organic Law 5/1984, making it applicable to both Spaniards and foreigners resident in Spain.

(g) The duty of collaborating with justice: Article 118 demands compliance with judicial resolutions as well as collaborating with the courts, which has been given legal form by several obligations, such as everyone's duty to appear as a witness in a trial (LOPJ) and that of being a member of a jury (LO 5/1995 on jury trial).

Chapter 7. Constitutional Protection of Foreigners

§1. THE LEGAL POSITION OF FOREIGNERS

444. We have already had occasion to see how the Constitution – or rather, the interpretation of it made by the Constitutional Court – does not remit to law the legal regime of aliens but that it establishes it itself, giving non-Spaniards three categories of rights: (a) those that they enjoy in equality with Spaniards (such as the right to life); (b) rights from which the Constitution excludes them (such as participation in State and autonomous spheres); and (c) rights that the Constitution gives them but with certain differences in their specific legal regulation as compared with Spaniards (freedom of movement, for example) (*see* paragraph 263). We have also seen how, within the group of aliens, the nationals of the other Member States of the EU have more rights, European citizenship, established in the Union Treaties (*see* paragraph 264). EU citizens are governed by the legislation of the EU, and the general regulation of Organic Law 4/2002 only applies to them 'in those aspects that could be more favourable' (Article 1.3).

We must now go into the peculiarities of the legal regime applicable to aliens a little deeper, dealt with in general in the Organic Law 4/2002, 11 January, on rights and freedoms of aliens in Spain, known more simply as the Aliens Act. It has been amended – with the aim of restricting a regime considered excessively generous to immigrants – by Organic Laws 8/2000, 22 December and 14/2003, 20 November. PSOE and seven Autonomous Communities lodged an appeal of unconstitutionality against Organic Law 8/2000. This gave rise to various decisions where the Court held as unconstitutional several restrictions imposed by the law on aliens for the exercise of their fundamental rights of assembly, association, belonging to a trade union, and to strike (SSTC 236/2007, 7 November; 259/2007, 19 December and 260/2007, 20 December). To clarify this case law correctly and, in passing, to include various directives of the EU on aliens, a new modification of LODEX was approved by Organic Laws 2/2009, 11 December and 8/2015, 22 July. Some of these modifications have not been without controversies, such as the hot returns at the borders of Ceuta and Melilla introduced in the LODEX in 2015 by the Organic Law on Citizen Security, approved by the absolute majority of the PP and appealed by fifty members of the PSOE before the Constitutional Court, which considered it to be per the Constitution (STC 172/2020, 19 November). Likewise, these returns of persons to Morocco immediately after having entered Spanish territory illegally, without granting them the possibility of challenging their return, have been endorsed by the ECtHR (JECtHR (Grand Chamber) 13 February 2020, case *N.T. and N.D. v. Spain*). To date, the new PSOE-UP majority has not repealed this legal amendment; indeed, it has used it as a punitive backing for its border control policy.

I. The Legal Situation of Aliens in Spain

445. The two main legal situations that, according to the law, aliens can enjoy in Spain are that of stay and that of residence. In the first group are those foreigners who stay in Spain for less than ninety days, while for a longer period, government authorization is required for residence, either temporarily (up to five years) or permanently (an indefinite period). The Aliens Act stipulates that those aliens who are not members of the EU[65] will need, to enter Spain, a visa as well as a passport and proof that they have sufficient means to support themselves for the time they intend to remain in Spain. Since the first Aliens Act in 1985, there has been a gradual toughening of entry requirements with the aim of avoiding a third situation for foreigners, not expressly referred to by the law: that of those who live in Spain but without authority to do so, either because they have entered illegally or because, although entering legally, they did not leave Spain at the time foreseen; the paradigmatic example is the 'tourist' who, after the expiry of the permitted time of stay, does not return to his country of origin and remains without authorization. Given that since the 1990s, it has been impossible to prevent a great number of foreigners described as 'illegal', 'undocumented', or 'without papers' from entering the country, at the beginning of the twenty-first century, various regularization procedures have been organized (in 2000, 2001, and in 2005, the last being the most important, with almost 700,000 applications) so that those foreigners who can show that they have lived in Spain for a determined time can obtain authorization to reside here legally.

II. The Rights and Liberties of Aliens

446. Following in the wake of constitutional jurisprudence, the Aliens Act declares that aliens shall enjoy the rights and liberties of the Constitution in the terms that the law itself shall establish, as well as in the treaties and laws specific to each right, adding the 'general interpretation criterion' of the exercise of these rights as being 'in conditions of equality with Spaniards'. Moreover, it not only repeats Article 10.2 of the Constitution to indicate that these norms of rights and liberties shall be interpreted in accordance with the UDHR and the Treaties but also prudently stipulates that religious and cultural beliefs cannot be put forward as justification to carry out acts against them. The law contains a series of anti-discriminatory measures and, logically, states that aliens shall have the same tax obligations as Spaniards. If the various provisions of the Aliens Act and some other laws that also affect foreigners are analysed from the point of view of the regime it establishes in comparison with Spaniards, we can classify the rights of foreigners in Spain into three main groups:

---

65. As we know, European citizens have a regime of freedom of movement and residence (Art. 45 TFEU). Exceptionally, a State may restrict the right of entry for reasons of public order or internal health, a decision subject to the control of the CJEU. In Spain these aspects have been regulated by Royal Decree 240/2007, 16 February, on the entry, free circulation and residence in Spain of citizens of the Member States of the European Union and of other States party to the Agreement on the European Economic Area, subsequently modified several times. Logically, during the COVID-19 pandemic, it became necessary to apply these restrictions, which the EU coordinated through the Council Recommendation (EU) 2020/1632 of 30 Oct. 2020 on a coordinated approach to the restriction of free movement in response to the COVID-19 pandemic in the Schengen area.

(1) Rights in which there is total equality between Spaniards and aliens, without distinguishing if the latter are residing in Spain legally or not:
   (a) All minors under the age of eighteen have the right to basic education, including grants.
   (b) All foreigners have 'the right to health protection and health care under the same conditions as persons with Spanish nationality' because this is established by Decree-Law 7/2018, 27 July, on universal access to the National Health System. Until then, foreigners residing illegally in Spain were only entitled to health care if they were minors, while adults who were not legal residents were only allowed emergency public health care (Royal Decree-Law 16/2012, 20 April, on urgent measures to guarantee the sustainability of the National Health System). Therefore, the current equality between Spaniards and all foreigners is legal but not required by the Constitution (STC 139/2016, 21 July).
   (c) Effective judicial protection is guaranteed 'under the same conditions as Spaniards' to all legally resident foreigners', and those "who are in Spain registered in the census of the municipality in which they habitually reside"' (Article 20 of the LODEX, which means admitting a category of residence that is not entirely legal). As for those who do not have either of these two residences, they have the right to free legal assistance and the right to an interpreter only in the expulsion process and in the right to asylum. They will also have these two rights if they have criminal proceedings.
   (d) Rights that LODEX (in the 2009 version) expressly declares that aliens enjoy, on the same terms as Spaniards, are freedom of association, assembly, and association, right to belong to trade unions, and to strike, basic social services and assistance.
   (e) Since they are rights inherent to all persons and because of the interpretation criterion of equality, here must be added rights that are not specifically included in the Aliens Act: the right to life and physical and moral integrity; freedom of ideology, religion, and worship; freedom and security; the rights to reputation, personal privacy, and image; freedom of expression and information; the right to be punished only in accordance with law; the right of petition; the right to marry and to have private property.
(2) Rights in which total equality with Spaniards applies only to aliens legally resident in the country, but not those here without authorization:
   (a) Right to work and to social security.
   (b) Right of access to post-compulsory education for those over 18 years of age.
   (c) Until the reform in 2009, all aliens resident in Spain had the right to receive public assistance to access housing in the same conditions as Spaniards. However, since 2009, this right only exists for long-term resident aliens.

(3) Rights that do not apply in the same terms to all foreigners and to Spaniards:
   (a) the right freely to select their residence, which can be restricted both when a State of emergency is proclaimed (*see* paragraph 452), as in individual cases by resolution of the Minister of the Interior.
   (b) The right to participate in public affairs, which can be exercised only in the local sphere and always reciprocally.
   (c) The right for housing for non-long-term residents.

§2. Extradition and the Right to Asylum

447. Extradition – from the Latin *extradere*, to return a person to his own country – is a legal institution known from ancient times as a form of collaboration amongst sovereign political entities. In the State of Law, its characteristic of arbitrariness in the return of a fugitive has been substituted by the creation of guarantees to make that international collaboration compatible with the defence of individual rights. Thus, the Spanish Constitution sets out in Article 13.3 that extradition will only be granted in compliance with a treaty or the law and according to the principle of reciprocity. Furthermore, it excludes political crimes 'not being considered as acts of terrorism'. Law 4/1985, on passive extradition, has developed this mandate in a guaranteed form, which is complemented by a good number of international conventions, outstanding amongst which is the European Convention on Extradition of 1957. But despite these guarantees, extradition has not lost its primary character: it is a political decision of the government (*see* paragraph 161).

In the sphere of the EU, the mandate of the Treaty of Amsterdam to create an area of liberty, security, and justice has resulted in the Council of Ministers of Justice adopting, in 2002, a Framework Decision relating to the European Arrest Warrant (amended by another Framework Decision in 2009) that in Spain has been incorporated in Law 23/2014, *de reconocimiento muto de decisiones penales en la Unión Europa*. The European arrest warrant (EAW) is a judicial resolution issued in a Member State of the EU with a view to the detention and handing over by a court of another Member State of a person sought in connection with criminal acts or for the execution of a punishment. It applies automatically to a large number of relevant offences (terrorism, trafficking in human beings, drug trafficking, corruption, racism, cybercrime, etc.), while for others – such as rebellion – the court receiving the EAW can check whether the acts charged against the accused are crimes in the country of destination, as happened in 2019 with the famous fleeing of the former president of the Generalitat Carles Puigdemont and the refusal of the High Court of Justice of Schleswig-Holstein to hand him over for that crime and embezzlement. It was, precisely, the Framework Decision of 2009 that caused the Constitutional Court to submit its first question before the CJEU: while this Decision requires the unconditional surrender of a person sought by a court of another State of the Union, the traditional doctrine of the Constitutional Court considered that this extradition could not be carried out if the defendant had been tried without being present at the trial; therefore, the Constitutional Court asked the CJEU if the decision was in accordance with the Charter of Fundamental Rights and, if it were, if the Spanish courts could grant greater protection by denying the delivery of the convicted person in absentia. However, the CJEU replied not only that the Decision was in accordance with the Charter but also that the surrender of a convicted person in absentia could not be conditional on the holding of a new trial in the State claiming it.[66]

448. As ancient as extradition is asylum,[67] the protection that a State offers to a person who is persecuted in another, which Article 13.4 of the Spanish Constitution recognizes as a legal right since it orders, in the vaguest terms, that the law shall establish the terms under which citizens of other countries and stateless persons may enjoy the right of asylum in Spain. The first law of asylum was passed in 1984, substituted by Law 12/2009, 30 October, regulating the right of asylum and subsidiary protection, which was slightly modified in 2014. The purpose of this law is to adapt the Spanish legislation to the European Council Directive 2004/83/EC, 29 April, in order to be able to establish a European Common System of Asylum. Logically, this new regulation maintains the essential core of the right of asylum that follows the 1951 Geneva Convention on the Status of Refugees and offers protection in Spain to foreigners persecuted in their own countries for political or ideological causes. This in no case includes terrorism offences – a term which under the aforementioned Directive – and must be understood in a broad sense: not only can asylum be denied to anyone who has personally committed acts of terrorism or has incited them but also to someone who simply belonged to a group qualified as terrorist (JCJEU (Grand Chamber) 31 January 2017, case *Mostafa Lounani*). Thus, the recognition of the condition of refugee means that one who obtains it cannot be returned to his country of origin and has leave to stay and work in Spain while the circumstances that give rise to his asylum application persist.

66. JCJEU (Grand Chamber) 26 Feb. 2013 and STC 26/2014, 13 February, case *Melloni*. The CJEU does not rule out that in some exceptional cases a State may refuse to execute a Euro arrest warrant. Thus, in its JCJEU (Grand Chamber) 5 Apr. 2016, it ruled that the court in Bremen (Germany) that had submitted the preliminary question for ruling did not have to execute a Euro arrest from Romania and another from Bulgaria, because there was a real risk of inhuman treatment for the two people claimed because of the unfortunate conditions of detention in the prisons of the states issuing the orders, demonstrated by the previous convictions of both States by the ECtHR. In similar terms, the CJEU (Grand Chamber) 25 Jul. 2018, in case C-216/18 PPU (Preliminary Urgency Proceeding).
67. The word asylum comes from the Greek '*asylao*', composed by an alpha privative and the verb 'sylo', to capture, so it means without capture and was applied to a religious place in which the criminals could not be arrested, as the Bible of the temples says. The most famous Greek to gain asylum – now leaving the mythical Oedipus asylum in Athens – was Themistocles, who some years after defeating the Persians in Salamis in 480 BC, ended his life paradoxically protected by Artaxerxes.

Part V. Specific Issues

Chapter 1. The Suspension of Rights

§1. The Collective Suspension of Rights: Emergency Laws

449. The constitutional movement in Spain, unlike those of the countries around it, was always aware that in situations of social crises, it might be necessary to suspend, temporarily, certain constitutional guarantees, much so in the manner of the Roman dictatorship limited by time, in order to re-establish constitutional order and to save the State of Law. For this reason, as long ago as the 1812 Constitution, parliament was permitted to decree, for a limited period only, the suspension of certain formalities for the arrest of criminals 'if in extraordinary circumstances the security of the state so demanded'. The 1978 Constitution is in this Spanish tradition of including norms to deal with states of emergency in the Magna Carta, although regulated in detail previously unknown, in line with the requirements of ICCPR and the ECHR for crisis situations. Thus, the Constitution distinguishes three possible exceptional situations and permits a permanent suspension of rights for those accused of terrorist crimes. Moreover, as a general precaution, Article 116 lays down that the declaration of any of these exceptional States does not modify the government's responsibility, nor can Congress be dissolved while any of them persist. In the event of the dissolution of Congress, its functions would be assumed by the Permanent Deputation. Article 169 prohibits the initiation of Constitutional reform when an exceptional state exists (*see* paragraph 52). Moreover, as an additional precaution, Article 4.1 of LORMR forbids the holding of referendums of any type in the territories subject to the emergency or siege as well as in the ninety days after its lifting. The constitutional mandate was developed by Organic Law 4/1981 on the States of alarm, exception and siege (LOEAES), which begins by detailing the constitutional precautions for the three states established by the Constitution. Thus, it requires the immediate publicity of its declaration, orders the maintenance of judicial control of all the activity of the administration and the patrimonial responsibility of the State, in addition to specifying that only those measures strictly indispensable for the re-establishment of normality will be adopted. For thirty years, no natural phenomenon or social crisis made it necessary to proclaim any of these states. However, in 2010 the government used the state of alarm to respond to an air traffic controllers' strike and in 2020 (three times) to combat COVID-19.

Before setting out these three states, it is worth noting that Law 36/2015 on National Security (*Seguridad Nacional*) provides that a situation of special risk to the freedom and security of citizens allows the government to coordinate, exceptionally, the resources of the police of the Communities and town halls without restricting any fundamental right and without altering the jurisdictional order between the State and the Communities.

I. State of Alarm

450. The government may declare a state of alarm for a maximum period of fifteen days by decree, informing the Congress of Deputies that it has done so. The Decree agreed upon by the Council of Ministers shall determine the territorial area to which the effects of the declaration shall extend (Article 116.2 SC). The Organic Law fixes the four serious situations that justify the declaration of a state of alarm: (a) catastrophes; (b) health crises; (c) paralyzing of public services essential for the Community; and (d) situations of scarcity of goods of prime necessity. The main consequence of the declaration of a state of alarm is that the civil authorities and the officials of the administrations concerned are put under the direct orders of the competent authority (who may be the President of an Autonomous Community) as far as necessary for the protection of persons, goods, and places, being able to impose extraordinary services for the duration or according to its nature. Moreover, the Decree may adopt certain restrictions on some fundamental rights, such as limiting the movement of persons or vehicles in specific places and at specified times, temporarily requisitioning all types of goods and imposing compulsory personal services, etc.

451. Royal Decree 1673/2010, 4 December, declared a state of alarm for fifteen days for the normalization of the essential public service of air transport, and it did so by including measures that were neither expressly envisaged in LOEAES nor that any academic had discussed: the militarization of air controllers, who were made subject to the Code of Military Justice, while the authority of the government was delegated to the Chief of the General Staff of the Air Force. This aroused an immediate legal debate in the press in which the majority of the participants considered that these measures were not permitted either by the law or the Constitution, which in Article 117.5 declared that military jurisdiction was to be exercised strictly in a military framework and in the event of a state of siege. On 15 December, the government decided to request Congress to extend it by one month, which Congress duly did, with the votes in favour of PSOE, CiU, PNV, and CC, the abstention of PP and the vote against IU, UPyD and other minority parties. The Supreme Court refused to judge the legality of this Decree because it considers that the proclamation of the state of alarm is a political act controlled only by Congress and not by the Judiciary, a thesis endorsed by the Constitutional Court, according to which 'although formalized by decree of the Council of Ministers, the decision to declare the state of alarm, given its normative content and legal effects, it should be understood that it is configured in our system as a decision or provision with the rank or value of law' (STC 83/2016, 28 April). For its part, Royal Decree 463/2020, 14 March, declaring a state of alarm for the management of the health crisis caused by

COVID-19, established such strict confinement that the Constitutional Court considered that the fundamental right to freedom of movement, the right to choose one's residence freely and the right of assembly, which can only be suspended in a state of emergency (STC 148/2021, 14 July), had been violated. Likewise, it declared unconstitutional the six-month extension of the second state of alarm throughout Spain established by Royal Decree 956/2020, 3 November, as this period deprived Congress of 'any possibility of periodically reconsidering the evolution of the state of alarm during the six months of its continuation' (STC 183/2021, 27 October).

II. State of Exception

452. The government can declare a state of exception with the prior authorization of Congress when 'the free exercise of the rights and liberties of citizens, the normal functioning of democratic institutions, of public services essential for the community or any other aspect of public order is so severely affected that the exercise of the ordinary powers is inadequate to establish and maintain it' (Article 2 LOEAES). The maximum period that this state can remain in force is thirty days and can be extended for a further thirty days. The authority responsible for implementing the measures established by the decree will always be the government, with no delegation provision, unlike in a state of alarm. The rights that can be suspended in a state of emergency are (Article 55 SC and Articles 20 et seq. LOEAES):

(a) The right to personal liberty and security (Article 17 SC). Once the state of emergency has been declared, any person may be detained for a maximum period of ten days, provided that well-founded suspicions exist that this person is going to disrupt public order, although the judicial authority must be informed within twenty-four hours. Habeas corpus is also not suspended.
(b) The right to the inviolability of the home (Article 18.2 SC), the governing authority being able – informing the competent judge immediately – to order house searches if considered necessary for the maintenance of public order and always in the presence of the owner or of two witnesses.
(c) The right to secrecy of communications, especially those of the postal, telegraphic, and telephone services (Article 18.3 SC), always informing the judicial authority immediately.
(d) Freedom of movement and residence (Article 19 SC): the movement of persons and vehicles, or more modestly, to demand that individuals communicate their movements.
(e) The suspension of all types of publications, radio and television broadcasts, cinematographic shows, and theatre performances, provided that the authorization of Congress includes the suspension of Article 20, Subsections 1(a) and (d), and 5 of the Constitution. Equally, the confiscation of publications can be ordered (Article 20.5 SC).

(f) The rights of assembly and demonstration (Article 21 SC), the governing authority being able to require previous authorization for meetings and demonstrations to forbid them from being held to proceed to their disbanding. Those organized by political parties, trade unions, or employers' associations are expressly exempted.
(g) The right to strike and to adopt measures in collective conflicts (Articles 28.2 and 37.2 SC).

III. State of Siege

453. Congress may declare a state of siege by absolute majority at the exclusive proposal of the government when 'an insurrection or act of force against the sovereignty or independence of Spain, its territorial integrity or constitutional system occurs or is threatened' (Article 32 LOEAES). As in the previous cases, the declaration must stipulate the territorial area and the time period of the measures needed to overcome the crisis situation. The rights that can be suspended are the same as those in a state of emergency, plus the legal guarantees for those detained (assistance of counsel, right to be informed of the accusation, etc.) set out in Article 17.3 of the Constitution. The major difference between the state of siege and that of emergency does not lie in the catalogue of rights that can be suspended but rather in the intervention of the army since the government must designate the military authority that, under its direction, has to execute the measures to be taken in the territory to which the state of siege refers; in the declaration of a state of siege, Congress may even determine the crimes that shall be subject to military jurisdiction while it remains in force.

§2. Individual Suspension of Rights: The Fight Against Terrorism

454. If it is true that a new phenomenon requires a new legal response, the classic law for emergencies, with its limited time, was not a good instrument for the fight against terrorism. For this reason, Article 55.2 of the Constitution included for the first time in a Spanish constitutional text the possibility that, without proclaiming states of emergency or siege, an organic law would regulate the form and the cases in which certain rights and liberties could be suspended (those recognized in Articles 17.2, 18.2 and 18.3) 'for certain persons in relation to investigations into the activities of armed bands or terrorist elements'. After some legislative changes, the development of this article was incorporated in 1988 into the Law of Criminal Procedure itself in such a way that it allows (with the endorsement of the STC 71/1994, 3 March, and the modification of Organic Law 13/2015) the following fundamental rights to be suspended for persons suspected of belonging to a terrorist organization:

(a) The guarantee of a maximum of seventy-two hours of preventative detention, which can be extended for a further three days with the authority of a judge. When the detained person is held incommunicado, the right to counsel is restricted to the duty lawyer. This legal limitation to the right to choose a lawyer is compatible with the Constitution and the ECHR, provided that the judge gives reasons individually for each detainee, without using generic formulas, as to why a duty lawyer should be assigned (JECtHR 18 January 2022, case *Atristaín*).

(b) The inviolability of the home since the police can enter the homes of the presumed authors of terrorist crimes without judicial warrant.

(c) Secrecy of communications, so that the Minister of the Interior can order interception of the communications of persons suspected of having committed terrorism, although that decision must be confirmed or revoked judicially within seventy-two hours.

455. That same Article 55 of the Constitution specifies that the unjustified or abusive use of the faculties recognized in the said organic law will result in criminal liability as a violation of the rights and freedoms recognized by the laws. This Constitutional mandate makes clear that the fight against terrorism must always be kept within the law, which, in practice, has meant that some trials have been held against members of the security forces accused of having exceeded this fight, with sentences as spectacular as the conviction of a former interior minister to the penalty of ten years in prison in 1998 for illegal detention (STS (3) 8421/1998, 29 July). We have already seen elsewhere in this monograph how the Constitutional Court and the ECtHR not only considered that neither the Constitution nor the ECHR allows the torture of detainees accused of terrorism and, moreover, that the State has an obligation to investigate allegations of ill-treatment of detainees (*see* paragraph 372).

456. The special rules against terrorism do not end with the Law of Criminal Procedure. In the first place, there is the aggravated character of many crimes when committed by terrorists; for example, while the maximum penalty for murder is thirty years when it is committed by a terrorist, the penalty is whole life imprisonment. Other rules specially designed to fight against terrorism and that we have had occasion to deal with in this monograph are:

(a) The suspension and dissolution of political parties that maintain an attitude contrary to democratic principles (*see* paragraph 98).

(b) The competence of the National High Court for all crimes of terrorism (*see* paragraph 418).

(c) The declaration of ineligibility for any public office of persons convicted of terrorism even if their sentence is not final (*see* paragraph 124).

457. Finally, in its concern to fight terrorism, Article 13.3 of the Constitution states that terrorist offences are not protected by the right to asylum, a mandate later developed in the Asylum Law (*see* paragraph 445).

Selected Bibliography

Spanish Constitutional History

Artola, Miguel (ed). *Las Constituciones históricas españolas.* Madrid, Iustel, 2007–2010.

Fernández Segado, Francisco. *Las Constituciones históricas españolas: Un análisis histórico jurídico.* 4th edn. Madrid: Civitas, 1986.

García Costa, Francisco Manuel. *Algunas originalidades y aportaciones del constitucionalismo español.* Barcelona: Atelier, 1995.

Jiménez Asensio, Rafael. *Introducción a una Historia del Constitucionalismo Español.* Valencia: Tirant lo Blanch, 1993.

Tomás Villarroya, Joaquín. *Breve historia del Constitucionalismo español*, 13th edn. Madrid: CEPC, 2012.

Torres Del Moral, Antonio. *Constitucionalismo histórico español.* 8th edn. Madrid: Universidad Complutense, 2015.

Varela Suanzes-Carpegna, Joaquín; Fernández Sarasola, Ignacio (ed. lit.). *Historia constitucional de España: normas, instituciones, doctrinas.* Madrid: Marcial Pons, 2020.

Vera Santos, José Manuel. *Las Constituciones de España. Constituciones y otras leyes y proyectos políticos de España.* Pamplona: Thomson, 2008.

The Constitution and Other Legal Texts

Albertí Rovira, Enoch & González Beilfuss, Markus. *Leyes políticas del Estado.* 39th edn. Madrid: Civitas, 2021.

Balaguer Callejón, Francisco, Cámara Villar, Gregorio & Montilla Martos, José Antonio. *Código de Derecho Constitucional.* 15th edn. Madrid: Tecnos, 2021.

Bou Franch, Valentín and Cervera Vallterra, María. *Normativa y Jurisprudencia Básica del Derecho de la Unión European*, 2nd edn., Valencia: Tirant lo Blanch, 2016.

Gómez Fernández, Itziar and Pérez Tremps, Pablo. *El Convenio European de Derechos Humanos*. Madrid: Tecnos, 2010.

Oliver Araujo, Joan & Calafell Ferrá, Vicente Juan. *Los estatutos de los partidos políticos españoles.* Madrid: CEPC, 2007.

Cases Books and Compilations of Case Books

Gómez Fernández, Itziar, Quéralt Jiménez, Argelia and Álvarez Rodríguez, Ignacio. *Prácticas de Derecho Constitucional,* Valencia: Tirant Lo Blanch, 2012.

Selected Bibliography

López Guerra, Luis. *Las sentencias básicas del Tribunal Constitucional*, 3rd edn., Madrid: CEPC-BOE, 2008.

Ripoll Carulla, Santiago (ed). *España en Estrasburgo. Tres décadas bajo la jurisdicción del Tribunal European de Derechos Humanos.* Pamplona: Aranzadi, 2010.

Terol Becerra, Manuel, Álvarez-Ossorio Micheo, Fernando & Barrero Ortega, Abraham. *Las grandes decisiones del Tribunal European de Derechos Humanos.* Valencia: Tirant lo Blanch, 2005.

Torres Del Moral, Antonio. *Prácticas y Esquemas de Derecho Constitucional I.* 2 vols, 3rd edn. Madrid: Universitas, 2016.

Bibliographical Books

Espín Templado, Eduardo & González-Trevijano Sánchez, Pedro José (ed). *Constitucion Española: 25 años de bibliografía.* Madrid: CEPC, 2003.

Doctrine

General Studies

Agudo Zamora, Miguel et al. *Manual de Derecho Constitucional.* 12th edn., Madrid: Tecnos, 2021.

Alonso De Antonio, Ángel Luis. *Derecho Constitucional español.* Madrid: Universitas, 2020.

Álvarez Conde, Enrique and Tur Alsina, Rosario. *Derecho Constitutional.* 2 vols, 10th edn. Madrid: Tecnos, 2021.

Alzaga Villaamil, Óscar, Gutiérrez, Ignacio & Rodríguez Zapata, Jorge. *Derecho político español según la Constitución de 1978.* 7th edn. Madrid: Centro de Estudios Ramón Areces, 2021.

Balaguer Callejón, Francisco et al. *Manual de Derecho Constitucional*, 2 vols, 16th edn. Madrid: Tecnos, 2021.

Blanco Valdés, Roberto L. Introducción a la Constitución *de 1978.* Madrid: Alianza, 2016.

Fernández Segado, Francisco (ed.). *The Spanish Constitution in the European Constitutional context*, Madrid: Dykinson, 2003.

Ferreres Comella, Victor. *The Constitution of Spain. A Contextual Analysis*, Oxford: Hart Publishing, 2013.

Garrorena Morales, Ángel. *Derecho Constitucional: teoría de la Constitución y sistema de fuentes.* Madrid: CEPC, 2014.

López Guerra, Luis et al. *Derecho Constitucional.* 2 vols, 11th edn. Valencia: Tirant lo Blanch, 2018.

Pérez Royo, Javier. *Curso de Derecho Constitucional.* 17th edn. Madrid: Marcial Pons, 2021.

Commentaries

Alzaga Villaamil, Óscar (ed).*Comentario sistemático a la Constitución española de 1978.* Madrid: Marcial Pons, 2017.

González Rivas, Juan José. *La interpretación de la Constitución por el Tribunal Constitucional: comentario sistemático de la Constitución.* Madrid: Civitas, 2011.

Palomar Olmeda, Alberto y Cazorla Prieto, Luis María. *Comentarios a la Constitución Española de 1978*. Pamplona: Aranzadi, 2018.

Pérez Tremps Pablo y Saiz Arnaiz, Alejandro. *Comentario a la Constitución Española. Libro-Homenaje a Luis López Guerra. 40 Aniversario 1978–2018*. Valencia: Tirant lo Blanch, 2 vols., 2018.

Rodríguez-Piñero y Bravo-Ferrer, Miguel y Casas Baamonde, María Emilia (dirs). *Comentarios a la Constitución española*. Madrid; BOE, 2 vols., 2018.

Sources of Law

Aguiló Regla, Josep. *Teoría general de las fuentes del derecho (y del orden jurídico)*. Barcelona: Ariel, 2000.

Balaguer Callejón, Francisco. *Fuentes del Derecho*. 2 vols. Madrid: Tecnos, 1991–1992.

Eneriz Olaechea, Francisco Javier. *El Sistema de Fuentes del Derecho. De la Constitución Española al nuevo Derecho de la Unión European*. Pamplona: Aranzadi, 2007.

García De Enterría, Eduardo. *La Constitución como norma y el Tribunal Constitucional*. 3rd edn. Madrid: Civitas, 1991.

Goig Martínez, Juan Manuel. *El Sistema de Fuentes del Derecho Constitucional en la Jurisprudencia del Tribunal Constitucional Español*. Madrid: Universitas, 2019.

Otto Pardo, Ignacio de. *Derecho Constitucional. Sistema de fuentes*, 2nd edn. Barcelona: Ariel, 1993.

Sánchez Ferriz, Remedio. *El estado Constitucional y su sistema de fuentes*. 3rd edn. Valencia: Tirant lo Blanch, 2005.

Institutions

Álvarez Conde, Enrique & Catalá Bas, Alexandre. *El derecho de partidos*. 2nd edn. Madrid: Colex, 2013.

Astarloa Huarte-Mendicoa, Ignacio. *El Parlamento moderno. Importancia, descrédito y cambio*. Madrid: Iustel, 2017.

Ballester Cardell, María. *El Consejo General del Poder Judicial. Su función Constitucional y legal*. Madrid: CGPJ, 2007.

Bustos Gisbert, Rafael. *La responsabilidad política del Gobierno: ¿realidad o ficción*. Madrid: Colex, 2001.

Fernández-Miranda Campoamor, Alfonso & Fernández-Miranda Campoamor, Carmen. *Sistema electoral, partidos políticos y Parlamento*. 2nd edn. Madrid: Colex, 2008.

Fernández Segado, Fernando. *La justicia Constitucional. Una visión de Derecho Comparado*. 3 vols. Madrid: Dykinson, 2009.

Garcés Sanagustín, Ángel. *La caracterización jurídico-pública de la Corona*. Madrid: Iustel, 2021.

García Fernández, Javier. *Estudios sobre el Gobierno*. Madrid: INAP, 2007.

Gómez Corona. Esperanza. *La autonomía parlamentaria en la práctica Constitucional española*. Valencia: Tirant lo Blanch, 2008.

Guillén López, Enrique. *El cese del Gobierno y el Gobierno en funciones en el ordenamiento Constitucional español*. Sevilla: IAAP, 2002.

López Aguilar, Juan Fernando. *La justicia y sus problemas en la Constitución: justicia, jueces y fiscales en el estado social y democrático de derecho.* Madrid: Tecnos, 1996.
Martínez Sospedra, Manuel, Marco, Joaquín J. & Uribe Otalora, Ainhoa. *Sistemas electorales. Un estudio comparado.* Valencia: Tirant lo Blanch, 2007.
Oliver Araujo, Joan. *Cuarenta años de monarquía en España*, 1975–2015. Valencia: Tirant lo Blanch, 2022.
Oubiña Barbolla, Sabela. *El Tribunal Constitucional. Pasado, presente y futuro*, Valencia: Tirant lo Blanch, 2012.
Pérez-Cruz Martín, Agustín-Jesús. *Constitución y Poder Judicial*, Barcelona: Atelier, 2015.
Pérez Tremps, Pablo. *Sistema de justicia Constitucional.* 2nd. Madrid: Civitas, 2016.
Porras Ramírez, José María. *Principio democrático y función regia en la Constitución normativa.* Madrid: Tecnos, 1995.
Rallo Lombarte, Artemi. *La Constitucionalidad de las administraciones independientes.* Madrid: Tecnos, 2002.
Rubio Llorente, Francisco & Jiménez Campo, Javier. *Estudios sobre jurisdicción Constitucional.* Madrid: McGraw-Hill, 1998.
Santaolalla López, Fernando. *Derecho Parlamentario español.* Madrid: Dykinson, 2013.
Torres del Moral, Antonio. *Estado de derecho y democracia de partidos.* Madrid: Universitas, 2022
The Autonomous State
Aja Fernández, Eliseo. *El Estado autonómico y reforma federal.* Madrid: Alianza, 2014.
Albertí Rovira, Enoch. *Autonomía política y unidad económica.* Madrid: Civitas, 1995.
Álvarez Conde, Enrique. *Reforma Constitucional y reformas estatutarias.* Madrid: Iustel, 2007.
Blanco Valdés, Ricardo. *El laberinto territorial español*, Madrid: Alianza, 2014.
Carrasco Durán, Manuel. *El reparto de competencias entre el Estado y las Comunidades Autónomas.* Valencia: Tirant lo Blanch, 2005.
Castellà Andreu, Josep Maria & Olivetti, Marco (eds). *Nuevos Estatutos y reforma del Estado. Las experiencias de España e Italia a debate.* Barcelona: Atelier, 2009.
Fossas Espadaler, Enric. *El principio dispositivo en el Estado autonómico.* Madrid: Marcial Pons, 2007.
García Aranda, Santiago. *La autonomía local en la Constitución de 1978*, Madrid: Dykinson, 2015.
Lago Montero, José Luis & Gil Rodríguez, Isabel. *El sistema de financiación de las Comunidades Autónomas. Comentario a la Ley 22/2009 de 28 de diciembre, tras la sentencia del Estatuto catalán.* Madrid: Dykinson, 2011.
Muñoz Machado, Santiago. *Derecho Público de las Comunidades Autónomas.* 2 vols, 2nd edn. Madrid: Iustel, 2007.
Ruipérez Alamillo, Javier. *División de competencias y forma territorial del Estado.* Madrid: Reus, 2012.

Ruiz Robledo, Agustín. *Sub-National Constitutional Law in Spain*. Alphen aan den Rijn: Kluwer Law International, 2018.

Solozábal Echavarría, Juan José (ed). *La reforma federal: España y sus siete espejos*. Madrid: Biblioteca Nueva, 2014.

Tajadura Tejada, Javier. *El principio de cooperación en el estado autonómico*, 3rd edn. Granada: Comares, 2010.

Tudela Aranda, José. *El fracasado éxito del Estado autonómico.* Madrid: Marcial Pons, 2016.

Tudela Aranda, José (ed.). *Estado autonómico y Covid-19: un ensayo de valoración general.* Zaragoza: Fundación Manuel Giménez Abad de Estudios Parlamentarios y del Estado Autonómico, 2021.

Fundamental Rights

Aguilera Vaqués, Mar & Serra Cristóbal, Rosario. *Rights and Freedoms in the Spanish Constitution.* Valencia: Tirant lo Blanch, 2015.

Bastida Frejeido, Francisco et al. *Teoría general de los derechos fundamentales en la Constitución Española de 1978.* Madrid: Tecnos, 2004.

Cruz Villalón, Pedro. *Estados excepcionales y suspensión de garantías.* Madrid: Tecnos, 1984.

Díez-Picazo Giménez, Luis María. *Sistema de derechos fundamentales.* 4th edn. Madrid: Civitas, 2012.

García Roca, Javier. *La transformación constitucional del Convenio Europeo de Derechos Humanos.* Pamplona: Civitas, 2019.

Gavara de Cara, Juan Carlos. *La dimensión objetiva de los derechos sociales.* Barcelona: Bosch, 2010.

Gimeno Sendra, Vicente et al. *Los derechos fundamentales y su protección jurisdiccional.* 2nd edn. Madrid: Edisofer, 2017.

Lasagabaster Herrarte, Iñaki (ed). *Convenio Europeo de Derechos Humanos. Comentario sistemático.* 3rd edn. Madrid: Civitas, 2015.

Lucas Murillo De La Cueva, Pablo & Carmona Cuenca, Encarnación (eds). *La tutela jurisdiccional de los derechos fundamentales por los tribunales ordinarios.* Valencia: Tirant lo Blanch, 2008.

Medina Guerrero, Manuel. *La vinculación negativa del legislador a los derechos fundamentales.* Madrid: McGraw-Hill, 1996.

Pacho Blanco, Xosé Manuel. *Lenguas y Constitución.* Pamplona: Aranzadi, 2018.

Pérez Luño, Antonio Enrique. *Los Derechos fundamentales.* 11th edn. Madrid: Tecnos, 2013.

Pérez Royo, Javier (ed) & Carrasco Durán, Manuel (coord.). *Terrorismo, democracia y seguridad, en perspectiva Constitucional.* Madrid: Marcial Pons, 2010.

Prieto Sanchís, Luis. *Justicia Constitucional y Derechos Fundamentales.* 2nd edn. Madrid: Trotta, 2009.

Rey Martínez, Fernando. *Derecho antidiscriminatorio.* Pamplona: Aranzadi, 2019.

Rodríguez Boente, Sonia Esperanza. *83 argumentos que convencen al Tribunal Europea derechos humanos. Jurisprudencia que afecta a España.* Pamplona: Aranzadi, 2016.

Rodríguez Ruiz, Blanca. *Los derechos fundamentales ante el Tribunal Constitucional. Un recorrido jurisprudencial.* Valencia: Tirant lo Blanch, 2016.

Selected Bibliography

Tajadura Tejada, Javier. *Los derechos fundamentales y sus garantías*. 2nd edn. Valencia: Tirant lo Blanch, 2021.

Web of Institutions

www.casareal.es. The King and the Royal Family.
www.congreso.es. The Congress of Deputies.
www.senado.es. The Senate.
www.la-moncloa.es. The Spanish Government.
www.poderjudicial.es. Judicial Power.
www.tribunalconstitutional.es. Constitutional Court.
www.defensordelpueblo.es. Ombudsman.
www.consejo-estado.es. The Council of State.
https://transparencia.gob.es. Transparency Council.

Index

The numbers here refer to paragraph numbers.

Index

Index

Index

Index

Index